IN THE DRIVING SEAT

The Story of a Disabled Person
Making His Way in an Able-bodied World

David Withnell

To Christine,

happy birthday,

D.A. Withnell

UPFRONT PUBLISHING
LEICESTERSHIRE

IN THE DRIVING SEAT
The Story of a Disabled Person
Making His Way in an Able-bodied World
Copyright © David Withnell 2002

ISBN 1 84426 113 1

First Published 2002 by
UPFRONT PUBLISHING
Leicestershire

IN THE DRIVING SEAT
The Story of a Disabled Person
Making His Way in an Able-bodied World

Chapter I

It was 1987, I think, when it first hit me. I was six years old and my brother Daniel or Danny was five. He'd just got his first bike without stabilisers. I watched him excitedly pedalling up and down the Grove, with a sort of perpetual motion, faster and faster, but as his joy and speed grew the tears began to well up in my eyes. I knew I would never get to do this thing that all children of that age should naturally be able to do. It was as easy as riding a bike, but I couldn't even do that. I went into the house, and my Mum knew there was something wrong immediately. It was an annoying trait of my Mum's character which would be there to help, wanted or not, from that moment until this and beyond (I hope). I'm nineteen years old now and she's still fussing about, but it's all part of life's rich tapestry.

Now where was I? Oh yeah, I went into the house and my Mum said, 'David, what's wrong?'

'Nothin',' I said, 'I'm fine.'

'What's really wrong?'

'Nothin'.'

This exchange repeated itself a few times before I burst into tears.

'Why can everyone else ride a bike? I want to do it. It's not fair.'

'I know it's not.'

'Why me? Why does it always have to be me?' I sobbed.

'I don't know, come here,' she said caringly, and she just hugged me. That always makes a kid feel better, a hug from Mum. Yeah they're embarrassing but mine was and is always there. A quick hug and I was ready to face the world again.

I soon got over that one, like most things in my life, and was back to being my normal happy self. But there were to be a few more of these moments to come.

The bike riding incident is my first real memory of being

5

upset – of anything really. Up until then it was a normal childhood, well as normal as it gets in our family! Teddy bears, bottles, nappies, all that baby stuff. Our Granddad-attacking Rottweiler, Rommel, was put down, we moved into Grandma's old house. We're still there now and the living room's where I'm scribbling down the beginning of this book. The house is the same as it ever was, slightly extended however.

I'm going off at a tangent again but I think I was three years old, or so I'm told, when my Mum's observant streak kicked in. She noticed that I didn't crawl before I could walk. I just held myself up by the walls. That's why we had to move house, because the walls were so dirty, our first house was uninhabitable! Anyway, I didn't learn to walk until quite late and when I did I kept falling over. My Mum, as committed to action as ever, panicked and took me straight to the doctor's and to the hospital, where a very caring nurse told her that there was nothing wrong with me and that she was a neurotic mother. But my Mum knew, she always knew, and I was sent for a muscle biopsy. Now that was the most painful experience ever! I said I had no memories before the bike, but that searing, excruciating pain has remained as a memory anyway. I'm in pain just thinking about it. Don't get me wrong, they tried anaesthetic twice, but what can I say? I'm thick-skinned in more ways than one!

When we finally got the results of the biopsy back, the nurse was made to eat her words, but that was a false victory for Mum, who at twenty-four would have to devote her life to helping me, for which I will be eternally grateful.

It was when I was four years old that we moved to a bigger house so it would be easier for me to get around in the future, and Ringley Grove was the base from which all the ups and downs on the emotional roller coaster that is my life have taken place, under the watchful gaze of our neighbours who have always been there when we've needed them. At about the same time as I moved into Ringley Grove, I also started school. Yes Sharples Primary was where I met Dexter, my best mate, who's been there for me through thick and thin, and who's also been the cause of many of my most frightening moments which you'll read about later.

One of the most difficult aspects of being a disabled kid is being accepted amongst able-bodied kids and adults alike, which is why Mum stuck her interfering oar in again to get me into a mainstream primary school, which wasn't as easy as it would seem. Many of the schools in Bolton didn't want to know, didn't feel they could accept the 'responsibility'. It's a natural human reaction to be wary of things that are different, but there's an exception to every rule and that arrived in the friendly shape of Mr Seymour, the headmaster of Sharples Primary who was certain he could accept the responsibility and I'm glad he did. He was the first of many who've tried to give me a normal life and I'll never forget that he started it all off.

It was nothing like as difficult to be accepted amongst children, but I suppose at primary school you're too young to worry about it, or you don't really understand disabilities enough to worry about it.

Right from the beginning, I've always had a few friends who are there to help me out, but the reason we're such good friends isn't because of that. The reason is that they treat me as a real friend; the disability isn't an issue. I mean they even invite me out rollerblading and ice skating for God's sake! Nobody ever says, 'Oh Dave can't come, he can't walk.' And that's it, to my friends I'm just Dave, and hopefully it'll stay that way.

They say that your school years are the best years of your life. Well that remains to be seen, but having just left year thirteen I can say mine have been both eventful and enjoyable. Sad isn't it?

Chapter II

Primary school was fun, no worries apart from that I might get knocked over in the corridor. Oh, and then there were the hospital appointments that never did me any good anyway.

I even had a love life back then. My love life is the main cause of my worries. Told you I was normal didn't I? Yes, young love, very young love. Great, isn't it?

I must have gone out with my first girlfriend Lydia for years on and off, when she wasn't dumping me for other people. Once she dumped me to go out with Dexter. The little sod said yes as well. Swine face! I'll never forgive him for that. Only joking! Back then though Dexter wasn't my best friend, he was just *a* friend. Anyway, Lydia always came back. It must be that Withnell charm or something. We had some great times though, us two. I had my first proper kiss with Lydia and I'll always remember that. I started early, but my lack of women since makes up for it. She was another one who was always there when I needed her, and to whom the disability didn't matter. I still see her around sometimes, struttin' her funky stuff in Atlantis (a nightclub in Bolton), but nightclubs are a story for later. When we finally split up for good I was gutted for a while. I loved her. Well you always do at that age, but there were plenty more fish in the sea. They've just been swimming too quickly for me since then!

I had everything though at primary school: friends, a girlfriend, great family, but it's the memories inside school that stick out. I had some great friends. Charmaine, Dexter, Heather, who are still with me now, and Jane, Nichola, Emma, Andy and Gaz. Great memories came from these people and this is what I mean about being accepted. We have these memories together and I hope they can remember them as well as I can.

As far back as I can remember, Dexter has always been the main cause of my memories, good and bad, but he's always been there, and that's what makes him the ultimate friend. Let me see, there was the bubbling blancmange incident. Well, Dexter and I were joking about talking rubbish as usual and I shouted, 'Bubbling blancmange!' as you do, but he thought I'd said, 'Bloody blancmange!' That's hardly a cardinal sin, I know, but enough for Dex to tell the teacher. To Mrs Entwistle the phrase 'cardinal sin' was an understatement. I'd sworn! I was six years old and I'd sworn! She lost all notion of perspective and went berserk, and me being the wimpy teacher's pet that I was, burst into tears. I mean to think, up until then I was her favourite. Anyway I'm David bloody Withnell, I bloody never bloody swear.

Mrs Entwistle turned against me after the blancmange debacle and proceeded to shout at me whenever she got chance, or whenever I was my stubborn self. One time our class was performing 'On the Ningnangnong', a poem by Spike Milligan. I stood there, in the rehearsal may I add, with my arms folded, looking extremely bored (which I was) and Mrs Entwistle took exception to this with a shout of, 'Me and you are going to have words!' Well at least her words made more sense than Spike Milligan's. I was just scared by all these monkeys going 'boo' and cows going 'bong'.

I ask you, monkeys going 'boo'? I was just protesting at the stupidity of it all. I'm a highly intelligent person, at school to learn, but she had me talking more rubbish than Harry Hill. So I went home and learned Einstein's theory of relativity to show my intelligence. Then I touched a red-hot iron just to show I'm human!

The thing about class two was that school didn't take too much out of me. I'm lucky in that I've been blessed with a good brain. The way I tend to look at it is that the brain makes up for what I lack physically.

Back in class two, schoolwork was easy. We did Peak Maths cards, and sadly enough I enjoyed doing them. There were no SATs back then, so learning was just fun. Really, testing and examining six-and eleven-year-olds doesn't make sense to me. The government can see how well people are doing without giving kids the pressure of exam conditions. For primary school kids, I believe social education is more important than academic education. Yeah everyone should be literate and able to do simple arithmetic, but from primary school it's memories of friends that stick. In fifty years' time, we'll all be non-thinking robots with no friends.

Well there's my cynical pessimistic streak showing again. My A level German teacher often says, '*Es macht mir Sorgen, dass ein Junge in deinem Alter so zynisch sein kann.*' Roughly translated it means, 'It worries me how someone so young can be so cynical.' I knew my German would come in handy one day. Confusing unsuspecting readers will do!

The thing about being young is that things change so quickly. Just when I'd got settled into nursery, I went to reception class. Just when I was settled there, class two came along. I'd got settled with Mrs Entwistle in class two and then Mrs Parker took over, and surprisingly enough once class two had begun to feel like home I was shipped into class three, to Mrs Ilinsky. All the teachers at Sharples Primary were great. I was just treated like one of the others, which I most definitely was.

Class three was all fun as well. The schoolwork was easy again, apart from art that is. I always blame my lack of artistic success on my arms being weak, but I think if my arms weren't so weak I'd hold my hands up and admit that I'm totally devoid of artistic talent anyway. Admitting I'm rubbish at something has taken away my will to live, but I think I'll finish this book first.

Really, in class three nothing exciting or really important happened. It was in class four where things really started to get going for me.

Class four was my first-year junior's class. A new teacher called Mrs Cooper, and finally we could now go to that haven of high-octane excitement, the bottom playground!

Sharples Primary had two playgrounds, called predictably enough the 'top' and 'bottom' playground. You spend all your time in the infants trying to get away from the top playground and all your time in the juniors trying to get back there. Me, Dexter, Andy, and Danny Walker tried so many times to escape the 'top' playground and each time we were thwarted by the same evil dinner lady/playground monitor. Our evil enforcer of the dinner time rules was Mrs Smith, and we could never defeat her.

It's amazing what's important to young schoolchildren.

Getting to the 'bottom' playground always seemed important but once we got there it was just the same as any other rectangular area of concrete, and exactly the same as the 'top' playground. At least now we could sit on the slope between the two playgrounds. It's one of those things though, I suppose. When we weren't allowed to go to the bottom playground, we wanted it so badly and tried everything to get there, but when we were finally allowed it took the fun away from it. Like if cannabis is legalised. People use it because of the buzz. It's illegal but easy to get hold of. Once it is legalised the buzz won't be there any more. And now I'm comparing the smoking of an illegal drug to going to a different playground!

My memory is beginning to become clear as I get further on in my life, and things started to get much more exciting in class four. We made clay pigs, papier mâché pigs, baked Christmas cakes and painted with oil paints in our arts and crafts lessons. All exciting stuff, but it was in class four where I began to realise I wasn't perfect. Up until then, maths was the most naturally easy thing for me to do, until it came to adding fractions that is. In everything I'd done before then, spelling tests, long division, anything, I always came back with full marks. I once even got nineteen out of twenty in a spelling test, once that is. Dexter had marked it and I was so sure I'd got twenty out of twenty that I accused him of changing one of my answers. I still maintain that today. He changed it, I know he did, he had to have changed it. He's always been jealous of my success!

But with this adding fractions, I'd met my match. It was strange though. I felt I had done exactly what Mrs Cooper said and although I found them difficult, I was convinced most of them were right. When I got my book back I had the shock of my life. Shock! One cross, horror another cross, terror a third, and no ticks! The worst nightmare of a school swot and it was happening to me! David Withnell. How did I react, .I hear you shouting? What else could I do? I used my disability to get sent home.

I sat in the corner crying and holding my foot while everybody went out for playtime.

'David? What's wrong?' said Mrs Cooper.

'It's my foot,' I said. 'It's really hurting.'

'Oh dear,' she replied, 'is there anything I can do? Should I call your Mum?'

'Yes please. She'll know what to do,' I sobbed.

Mrs Cooper was a very wise woman and she knew exactly what was going on. She gave me a knowing glance, as if to say, 'There's nothing wrong with your foot, you're lying.' She went and rang my Mum anyway in case my foot really was sore.

I've always been a very honest person, and because of this when I do actually lie I soon confess everything, which is exactly what happened when I got to the shop where my Mum worked. She was rubbing my foot in her usual caring manner when yet again I burst into tears and confessed.

'Mum,' I sobbed, 'there's nothing wrong with my foot.'

As soon as I'd said it, my Mum's face went from sympathetic and caring, to annoyed and disappointed, and I knew I was in for a telling off, which of course I deserved.

'What do you mean?' she said sternly.

'I got all my maths wrong, thirty-five sums, and I used my foot to get sent home. Don't tell Mrs Cooper,' I begged.

'I'll have to tell her, don't you ever do this again!'

I was humiliated. I'd lied, I'd found out I wasn't perfect, and just to add insult to injury, or more appropriately injury to insult, my foot started hurting! Sods' law, I suppose.

'Sorry Mum,' I mumbled, and that was the last we ever said about it. But that incident sticks out in my memory as one of those turning points, I suppose. Until then every piece of maths work I'd ever completed had been nigh on flawless and this page full of crosses was a bitter pill to swallow. It was the first time it had happened and at that time it seemed like the end of the world. Looking back though, I think it's how you deal with defeats in life, having the humility to accept defeats and admit you're not perfect. That's more important than how good you are at something. I think that incident helped to mould me into a more accepting person, knowing my weaknesses aren't all physical, and that that's nothing to be ashamed of. Anyway, it took me a while and some hard work but soon I'd perfected adding fractions and everything was fine again.

I also started to strangle cats in class four, so to speak. That was when I started playing the cello. It was a strange situation because my Mum was completely set against it. I presume it was because of my weakening physical situation and she thought that because it would only be a short musical career, there was too much fuss.

So our music teacher Mrs Porteous decided to ignore my Mum's worries and came to me at school.

'I heard you want to play the cello.'

'Yes,' I replied excitedly, 'but my Mum won't let me.'

She said she'd sort it out for me, and sure enough I was introduced to Mrs Jackson, the cello teacher, a week later. I really wanted to play the cello so I stubbornly went ahead, despite my Mum's hesitancy. Yes, admittedly my cello career only lasted three years but I got a great deal of pleasure out of my short musical career. To me, life's about enjoying things while they last. I can understand how Mum felt, but I believe that the enjoyment I got from it was worthwhile.

I did many things with that cello. I played in the school orchestra. I played at the Victoria Hall in Bolton, in front of hundreds of people, with the orchestra. I also took and passed two exams. The Initial Grade, and Grade One, and I played a solo in front of the whole school, parents, teachers and pupils, at my leaving assembly. Not bad for three years of playing. Especially for a disabled kid, whose arms were getting weaker all the time.

Class four was also when I joined the school choir. I don't know what happened to me after primary school but I could actually sing back then. We had to audition by singing 'Peace Perfect Peace' which of course I sang perfectly; well that's what I hoped anyway. The first year I tried and failed, but I was determined to get in, so I went back a year later and this time I did sing it perfectly. It was a case of 'singing perfect singing' and it just goes to show that, as with adding fractions, if you persevere nothing's impossible. In the words of 'Doc' in *Back to the Future*, if you put your mind to it, you can accomplish anything.

I succeeded in entering the choir. I even sang with them at the Victoria Hall, in between playing the cello and eyeing up women. Yep, Mrs Porteous caught me staring at a woman who went on stage before us. Of course I was only admiring the stitch work on her skirt, and I was accused of staring at her. How rude! So my short musical career was a huge success, even if I do say so myself. I even got my picture in the *Bolton Evening News* for that Victoria Hall concert. Is there no end to my fame? The songs we used to sing in that choir were... erm... interesting: 'Ain't Gonna Need This House No Longer', 'Gasoline Alley', '76 Trombones', and 'We Can Do the Hand Jive', only I couldn't without falling over!

But seriously, as I went through class four, the effects of muscular dystrophy began to rear their ugly head. (No, they're not that bad, honest.) I could now feel that I was becoming less stable. I also felt the floor quite often, which wasn't pleasant. Once I fell over when we had a supply teacher for a day. My feet just went from under me and I bashed my head on the floor. It didn't really hurt me, but I think it gave the teacher the fright of his life. He went as white as a sheet, and looked on the verge of tears. He even proceeded to teach me to hold out my hands so I didn't bash my head so readily. I didn't have the heart to tell him that that would only break my arms and then I'd still smack my head. I suppose he was only helping, though. I imagine he was very shaken up. I had a bloody lip and a bruised ego, but they soon healed up.

I once fell over, and quite embarrassingly landed in the middle of someone's chess game. Now that was funny though I'm a bit big to be a pawn! During class four I also began to realise that when I did frequently hit the floor or when I sat down in assembly, I was finding it increasingly more difficult to get up again. Sharples Primary was always very accommodating and the teachers always noticed when something was getting difficult for me. Even when they didn't notice, I felt confident that I could approach any one of the teachers and say I was struggling. With this particular difficulty, the teachers gave me a chair to sit on. No one even said anything about it. None of the other pupils said, 'Why can't we have a chair?'

That was another thing about the teachers. They always accommodated for everything I needed, but they didn't make an issue of it. They didn't act as if I was a special case or anything like that. The teachers were so caring that they would have done the same for anyone else, and I really appreciate that (in hindsight).

Even when Mr Seymour, the headmaster left, his replacement Mrs Wrigley was exactly the same. She was just as caring as he was, and she also did everything in her power to help me.

The walking thing was difficult enough as it was, without people erm... shall I say helping me to the floor? There were many times when I fell because of the intervention of others. One playtime I was pushed down the steps between the top and bottom playgrounds by a lad called Gareth. He deserved a beating for that and he got it, when my terminally aggressive cousin Andy decided to teach him a lesson. It wasn't the only time he helped me out either.

I was out on the grounds of Sharples High School with Danny my brother when a little boy, quite a lot younger than me, shouted: 'Ha, ha! You were born with a wheelchair stuck to your arse!'

Well, as usual I just laughed it off, but my ever-protective brother took exception to it and threatened to hit him with a branch he was carrying if our little friend didn't shut up. That was the last we heard from the youngster until Andy saw him at the cinema. He ran over, grabbed the boy by the collar, and bombarded him with expletives along the lines of, 'if you ever call my f***ing cousin again, I'll shove that lolly stick right up your arse!'

I think it worked because ever since then, every time I've seen the kid he's said, "Iyah David!' Poor little bugger!

Anyway, back to school, and being sent to the floor. Once I was sat on the sacred slope between playgrounds that I've mentioned earlier, when I decided I'd lie down using my arms to hold me up. I was just lying there, minding my own business when these two girls, both called Emma, jokingly picked my legs up. You can guess the rest. Needless to say, it was quite a painful experience. Another funny but painful incident happened at a junior disco where I was mistaken for my brother. I was just stood minding my own business again (notice how nothing's ever my fault) and a lad called Graham said, 'All right Danny?' and started having a play fight with me. Well Graham got a bit carried away and hit me, so I duly obliged, with my usual falling over show. I had a burst lip and bruised pride again and he was very apologetic as he stretched out a hand to help me up from the floor, on which he'd just put me.

'Sorry Dave,' he said, 'I thought you were your brother.'

I just said, 'It doesn't matter,' when what I really wanted to do was give him a taste of his own medicine. But the most embarrassing and humiliating part of the story was not that I ended up on the floor with a bloody lip whilst trying to impress a girl (I mean that had happened before), it was that my Mum was a member of the PTA (I'm sure she did that on purpose to keep an eye on me) and she was at the disco helping out. She came running over, probably even before I hit the deck, and shouted, 'David! Are you all right?'

I was thinking I was all right till she came running over, but I erred on the side of safety and said, 'I'm fine, just a bit shocked.' So she took me to the staff room and said (on the way out, with everyone watching and the music switched off), 'Let's get that lip bathed.'

As you'd expect, I was mortified and wanted the ground to open up and swallow me. For God's sake, why me? The funny thing is, though, that it's the little things that embarrass me. It wasn't falling over, getting punched and being mistaken for my brother in front of people which bothered me, but it was Mum rushing over. That's another thing that makes me normal: the things that embarrass able-bodied kids, embarrass me, and the obvious problem, the disability, fades into insignificance amongst everyday events, fun events, and when I was younger, childish or immature thoughts and worries.

If nobody else worries about your disability, then you don't have to worry. The problems and worries surrounding disability are usually caused by the ignorance and discrimination of others, and not the actual disabled people themselves who usually just deal with the problems one day at a time and as they come. When disabled people are integrated properly into society, which is very close to happening, then maybe nobody will worry about it and disabled people will be seen as an equal part of society who can help society as much as society can help them. If all disabled people got the chance to go to mainstream schools, then maybe understanding and acceptance of disability would come naturally.

The discos seem to be, looking back, the most dangerous place for a disabled person to be and it was when impressing, or trying to impress, girls that I seemed to be most unlucky. I was trying to impress Lydia when Graham poleaxed me, and when I was impressing another girl, Leanne, that Dexter took it upon himself along with Nichola to send me flying to my second home, the hall floor. They were childishly running around as usual. Nichola was probably trying to kiss Dexter again and they had to rain on my parade! Dancing was difficult enough for me without these two morons running past and knocking me to the floor. I looked ridiculous enough trying to impress Leanne with my dancing (my penguin dance as Dexter so eloquently puts it) and what must she have thought of me as I tumbled unceremoniously to the ground right in front of her?

At least... I began thinking, trying to find a silver lining to this huge black cloud, and then it happened. Yes you've guessed it, my Mum came rushing over to complete my embarrassment, helped me up, took me away to sort it out and I never saw Leanne for the rest of the night. Lovely! I should have realised then that my luck with women had deserted me after Lydia and given up, but you'll see later that I'm a glutton for punishment and I've got lots of it since primary school. You can probably guess that I never ended up going out with Leanne. Come to think about it, Dexter fancied her as well; he probably knocked me over on purpose. I'll kill him!

I got him back for that though, later. He'd plucked up the courage to ask her out and after we'd both watched her play netball we set off home, but little did I know that Dexter was going to wait at the top of the path down to Leanne's house to ask her out. I'd decided to go for a little ride on my trusty three-wheeled golf cart and conveniently decided to go past Leanne's myself for some unknown reason. I was probably going to talk netball with her.

Oh yes, I can just picture the moment now. Dexter stood at the top of the path, throat dry, heart in the top of his mouth as Leanne comes round the corner. He approaches her, opens his mouth to speak the words he's ready to speak and suddenly he's distracted by a noise from the other direction. 'Bzzzzzzz...' it comes, louder and louder, over the hill and 'Bang!' His worst nightmare, a Hell's Angel on a three-wheeled, motorised trike. The look of disgust and sheer anger on his contorted face sent me into fits of laughter as I cried, 'All right Dex! 'Iyah Leanne. Fancy seeing you here!' His bubble was burst and his moment of destiny had passed him by. I felt so sorry for him... not! As you can see, we're really good friends until a girl gets involved and then it's no holds barred all out warfare. Fantastic.

Class five, the final year of primary school, Mr Mclean's class, has also got many memories: the road safety quiz, the end of school, the nativity play. All very vivid memories. Class five was the last stop on easy street and the whole year saw the anticipation of secondary school build up into a crescendo. Secondary school would be a bigger, more dangerous road to negotiate but you don't worry about that, or I didn't. I loved school and the only feeling I had was one of excitement.

All this talk of roads brings me back to the road safety quiz. Five people from the top class of every primary school in England are chosen for this quiz, the hosts of which are two policemen or women from each regional police force who travel to every school in the area.

I was one of the 'chosen ones' and at the time it felt like a great honour to represent the school in a national quiz. Of course the team and a reserve spent hours learning rules about road safety, all of which I've forgotten apart from 'Wait for the green man before crossing the road'. I've still never met the elusive green man. Who is he? What is his purpose? The truth is out there I'm sure.

Don't get me wrong, I enjoyed working as a team and as usual I threw my all into learning everything I could to make sure there were no mistakes on the day. I don't know if it's a psychological thing, that because of my physical weaknesses I have to work hard to prove I'm as capable or more capable than everybody else, or if it's just a natural Withnell tendency to want to be the best (my Dad wanted me to call this book *Everybody's Different But My Dad's Perfect*) but I definitely never wanted to get anything wrong, especially in front of the whole school.

The road safety quiz however (now I've returned to cynical mode) seems pointless. Two traffic police are removed from their roadside posts to ask questions on road safety to five kids, who've only learned the rules to appear clever in front of the other pupils, most of whom aren't even listening, and this is supposed to improve road safety? The children would be safer if they were placed beside a road and told to cross it by trial and error.

When it came to the day of the quiz, our team degenerated into a blubbering mess. One member decided she couldn't take part because she hadn't learnt the information, so the success-obsessed maniac in the team, namely me, had a go at her and made her cry. The reserve stepped in. Another girl cried because she was worried about getting a question wrong. She calmed down before I had time to walk over and reproach her.

The girl in question got all her questions right. Then the third girl in the team got a question wrong and you've guessed it, she burst into tears! I took a different approach and tried to calm her down, probably because I'd have reacted in the same way if I'd got one wrong. I didn't of course because I'd been locked in my room all week with a glass of water and a box of Pro Plus to keep me awake, while I learnt every last word in the road safety book.

I kept my head while everyone else was losing theirs and in the end we got fifty-eight and a half out of sixty, and after all the crying we didn't even make the second round. (No that's not why I said it was pointless, at all.)

We soon recovered from that but it was my safety on my feet, more than road safety which was diminishing, and the nativity play or the evening thereof brought proof of that. I had a part to play in the nativity, I forget which one, but Dexter and I had other plans. Yes, my so-called friend caused another incident. He'd written a note saying I was having an affair with... (I won't mention her name because she'd be offended.) He then started chanting the same message over and over again. He wouldn't stop this infernal chanting and my rage grew and grew with each time he repeated himself. Suddenly something exploded and I jumped out of my seat, forgetting my lack of equilibrium, and chased Dex out of the room and into the toilets screaming, 'Give me the note!' in slightly less acceptable terms such as, 'Give me the f***ing note!' After my Linford Christieesque sprint from the classroom I mutated into Mike Tyson. I pulled my fist back and swung it towards Dexter's grinning little elf-like face. I'd soon remove that grin! Suddenly, as my head hit the toilet seat I remembered who I was. I was David Withnell and I just hit the deck. As I came round to the sound of Dexter screaming, 'Dave!' I was a bit dazed but okay. Then I saw the pool of blood I was lay in and the crowd of people around me and I wasn't okay any more. Then Mr Mclean, who hated the sight of blood, came in and he wasn't okay either. So we both missed the nativity play while I dabbed a piece of cotton wool over the pouring wound. What a night!

It was this weakness in my muscles, which were making walking and balance more difficult. I could no longer sit down in class; I had to kneel on chairs. I also couldn't or wouldn't go outside at playtime for fear of falling over or being knocked over by any overzealous friends. So, although I didn't show it, my weakening condition did have a subconscious effect and I was afraid to go out amongst the masses.

Despite all this weakness and fear, I was still determined in PE lessons. I'm a massive football fan, a Liverpool fan. (I can see all the Man United fans reaching for the matches to burn this book, but at least finish reading it first.) And when it was football in PE I always wanted to play. I was as useless as a cardboard cut-out but I always did my best. Every time the wind blew me over or I fell over the ball, I got up again and no one ever got frustrated when I fell over the ball three yards from goal (apart from me).

I know I was doing my best and that's all anybody can do. As long as you do your best with the ability you have, however small that ability may be then you can be happy with yourself. Being the best is not always the most important thing and that's something I've found very difficult to learn. It's one of the values my parents have taught me. The only pressure I've ever had is to do my best and I'm never criticised if I'm not brilliant at something. No seriously, the only pressure I feel is that which I put on myself, which as you'll see later is a lot of pressure.

Speaking of trying your best, the defining moment of my sporting career came during a rounders match in PE. I always stood in the far reaches of the back field and the ball never came anywhere near me, except for this one moment when a brilliant shot sent the ball flying towards me at warp speed. I thought, *This is it; I'm going to catch one.* I thought wrong. I ran backwards, anticipating where the ball would land, lifted my hands to catch it… and smack the ball hit me right in the teeth! Unlucky Dave! And with that moment I was condemned to sporting failure.

I still decided to take part in sports day. Just my luck that I always ended up racing the fastest runner. They always slowed down so as not to humiliate me too much, but I still lost by half a track. The thing is everyone I raced knew me very well and knew that I'd be annoyed if they let me win.

You may be wondering what the point of doing my best was, when the actual possibility of me winning was non-existent. The way I see it is that in my situation or other similar situations, you have two choices. One is to feel sorry for yourself and bemoan your weaknesses or inabilities. The other is to show determination and show that those weaknesses won't beat you. In my experience you gain much more respect by choosing the second choice. If you can replicate this determination in all aspects of life, then you have no reason to be disappointed in yourself.

For me, sports day was the best arena to show everyone that I was determined. All the parents and other pupils were there and they could see just how hard I was trying. It was easy for me to try hard with my schoolwork because I was good at it, but to try hard at sports day was another thing.

The work in class five was not really different to that in class four, so I had no problem there. It was the build-up to secondary school which was most important to me. I had to see the educational psychologist to make sure the disabled kid was mentally suitable for mainstream school, or that's how I saw it and I wasn't happy about it (to put it mildly). I passed that little test and all I had to do was wait for someone to offer me a place. Sharples was the most local and accessible school and they were very accommodating. Mr Kenyon, the headmaster, was another person who despite the possible pitfalls was willing to do his best for me. He had taught other children with Muscular Dystrophy (MD) and said he would rearrange my lessons to keep me downstairs for the majority of the time. He would put ramps in where needed and if I absolutely had to go upstairs he'd make sure someone was on hand to help. That's that sorted then.

So it was just a case of the series of visits to Sharples that were organised for prospective students. I felt all grown-up now and on the day of the first visit I was feeling a mixture of nerves and excitement.

Mr Brennan, the head of year Seven came down to Sharples Primary to accompany us on our 200-yard journey across the fields. I boarded my all terrain vehicle, well it was a golf cart, but I had some great fun on that machine, as you'll see later.

We arrived and as I entered the building, I was in awe of it. It was huge. *Thank God, I'll never have to walk around this building again*, I thought. It was the first time I'd ever been glad that I'd soon be in a wheelchair. It would certainly make things easier, or so I thought.

We went into the art room, which was full of older people, and I felt slightly intimidated. They were there to help though, and I soon calmed down. We were taught by the art teacher Mr Crook, to make clay pigs which was fun and then we went for lunch in the canteen. Later we departed back to Sharples Primary and once we'd arrived back, I parked my golf cart up and started to struggle back to the classroom whereupon I felt someone barge into me. I hit that familiar floor, hit my head and bent my glasses. Then I swung round to identify my assailant and shock horror it was Mr Brennan! Welcome to Sharples, Dave! I felt sorry for him really. He'd tried his best to accommodate me and help me out all day, and he was more upset than I was. I said I was okay but he was devastated. I was used to falling over and nobody was too worried when I did, but for a man who'd only just met me it was very worrying.

Overall, looking back the day had been a success and I was still looking forward to secondary school, despite my altercation with the floor.

We had other visits, maths lessons, to watch the school production and I really expected to fit in when I got there.

Meanwhile time was ticking away at primary school but I still had time to find another girl to turn my attention to. Leanne was the girl I mentioned before, who I ruined Dexter's chances with, and all the lads fancied her. So me, being my pathetic, wimpish self told someone, who told someone else and so on until the story reached Leanne at the other end of this particular grape vine. She said she'd think about it, and kept saying she'd think about till I became extremely pissed off, forgot about what a wimp I was and asked her out myself. A point blank 'no!' was her response. What a waste of time that was! My 'try your best' advice is wasted on myself when it comes to the opposite sex. It takes me forever to ask a girl out and I don't try often enough. Have you noticed how it's always the good-looking, confident people who say, 'The worst thing she can say is no?' Until sixth form, showing my feelings was never my strong point, but that's a story for later.

I spent the rest of my final year thinking about women, and being very sad while I stayed in at break. I decided I had to finish all the Peak Maths books before I left. I was just so into maths that I had to do it. I didn't quite make it, but I gave it my best shot. To be honest I haven't got a clue why I did it, it must have been boredom, or maybe it was something else. As you have probably worked out, I know exactly why I did it. It was childish jealousy. Lovely!

The situation was that at around Christmas time in class five a new lad arrived in our class. Paul was his name and from the first moment he sat at our table we knew he had a huge chip on his shoulder. I don't know where it came from but it looked ridiculous. Anyway, finding out his name was like getting blood out of a stone.

'What's your name mate?'

'Why should I f***ing tell you?'

Well he was destined to make friends quickly! He did. The first one was my girlfriend (I was going out with Lydia again) who soon wasn't my girlfriend any more. Then he said he was on Peak Maths book six. I was only on book five! That was it. I was no longer number one. I'd always been the best, but I wasn't any more. I couldn't handle that, I was very jealous and had to make sure I became the best again. It was now my goal, my obsession and I hated Paul at that moment. All the girls fancied him, and by the time I'd finished secondary school I was sick of hearing them mention his name. He also had this aura of someone who thought he was the big man on campus, and everyone agreed. At secondary school he was 'cock of the school' (the toughest guy in school, how cool) or so most people said, 'cock' being the operative word.

Surprisingly enough Dexter and I weren't fooled or intimidated. We knew that, as with a lot of so-called hard people, it was all just a front. He was as sensitive as any of us at heart, and Dexter proved it. Paul and I had something in common. He had a disabled brother, and I'm disabled, and that was his weakness. When he told us this, Dexter said something like, 'What, is he a cabbage or something?' and Paul actually burst into tears.

This was the real Paul, but being sensitive would not be the way to get the girls or to be cool at secondary school.

The incident with Dexter actually improved Paul's relationship with Dexter and me. He stayed in with me at break and even offered to help push me around at school. He meant it at the time but it was never really going to happen once we'd got there.

You'll find out more about Paul later, but suffice to say the fact that Dexter and I knew what he was really like meant there were no pretences when we were talking to him. When he was showing off, acting cocky, or just trying to show how macho he was, Dexter and I just gave each other a knowing look. To be honest, I think it's pathetic when people have to pretend they're something they're not in order to be popular.

The real Paul was also lazy. He didn't do any Peak Maths for the rest of the year and I was soon the best again. With that little problem solved I was free to enjoy the rest of the year which was approaching its finish.

I've either suddenly developed amnesia, or nothing much happened for the remainder of the year. It must have disappeared in a whirlwind of secondary school preparation and fun because I definitely enjoyed that last year.

The only part of the year I can vividly remember is the final week. The thing that's most memorable is the extreme nervousness I felt leading up to the midweek leavers' assembly. All the parents would be there, as would the teachers and the whole school and I'd volunteered, sorry been roped into playing a solo on my cello. I chose the theme tune to *Last of the Summer Wine* and as the hall went quiet my heart was beating at a dangerous speed. I picked up the cello and began to play. As I continued the nerves subsided and my heart returned to my chest cavity, and by the end of the song (which was perfectly played, even if I do say so myself) I was actually enjoying myself. I got a standing ovation for that show of my musical brilliance and I thought, *My work here is done!*

I find it very strange, even out of character in hindsight, realising I've done something that takes such confidence and that I actually enjoyed the adulation of the crowd. I'm not usually like that. I like to do well, very well at things, but I like to do so quietly with the minimum amount of fuss. Don't get me wrong, I'm confident within myself. I know my strengths but I try not to get carried away. There's being confident and then there's showing off and that's why I realise I have weaknesses. If a person feels that he is infallible then confidence can soon evolve into complacency and that's when things go wrong. I know, I know, that's very pessimistic and I sometimes want to be more confident. I can't understand why a person who played a cello alone in front of hundreds of people, can't talk French to his own friends (when they ask) even though he's got an A level in the subject, or why the same person hasn't got the courage to approach a girl in a nightclub. I don't think I'll ever work that out.

Anyway back to the last week of Sharples Primary and after coming out of my shell for three minutes of inspired cello playing, I went back in again for the last two days. When the final day came I went to school feeling very upset. What would happen to me when I got to Sharples High? My primary school years had been as perfect as anything could possibly be. Could the next era of my life possibly live up to it? Only time would tell.

At the time I don't think I quite understood the mixed emotions I was feeling. On the one hand I was upset about leaving one school and on the other I was extremely excited about joining the next one. I'm sure all my other classmates felt the same way, but I think for me, the feelings were stronger. I had to leave the security of Sharples Primary, where everyone had instinctively done what they could for me and cared deeply about me, and I had to go into the unknown. I would be in a wheelchair and would no longer be able to rely on myself to get around. Would the teachers be as caring and helpful? Would the new people (pupils) I was to meet be as accepting as my current friends? I didn't know and I was worried, but I'd enjoy myself finding out. The only consoling thought was that most of my friends would be there with me. Dexter and Paul would be in my form (we'd already discussed with Sharples who would be in my form, who would be most suitable to help out and so on) and Dexter had promised to push me around, so had Paul. The teachers I'd met from Sharples so far seemed friendly enough, so it wouldn't be too bad.

I had to get through the last day first without crying! I wanted to cry but I couldn't let myself. Northern men are 'ard, we don't cry, nor do we show our feelings. I bit my lip and went in.

My Mum had embarrassed me before, but she had one final, ingenious plan, more embarrassing than any before. Yes, she'd bought enough red roses for me to give one to each female teacher as a thank you. I couldn't have just said thank you. No, that wouldn't be embarrassing enough. Of course, I was very grateful to all these teachers, for everything, but roses? I mean, come on!

After this ordeal was over, I returned to the classroom where we had a little party, listened to music, etc. And soon the last day was over. I'd made it all day without crying, or so I thought! As the final bell tolled on the final day, I realised what it meant. It was all over and I felt this overwhelming urge to cry. I quickly made for the exit and as the door shut behind me I lent against the wall and cried. How sad is that?

Change is always a hard thing to take, and I was worried, but as one door closed for me, another one was soon to open.

Chapter III

The final bell had gone on my primary school career, but what had happened in between the other bells? In other words, after school and during the Christmas, Easter and summer holidays.

As a youngster much of my holiday time (during the daytime) was shared between both my Grandmas, my Granddad (my other Granddad, Granddad Frank unfortunately passed away when I was about seven), and my Auntie Joan, who'd take turns to look after us while my Mum was working at Asda or at the local corner shop.

My Grandma has frequently been a source of advice, is always there for anyone who needs her, and would do anything for anyone. She's been a great help to me and hopefully she will be for a long time to come. She's also, as I once told her, the most cheerful person I know. I remember once I had a pedal trike, before I got the electric version, the trike GTi if you like, and I struggled to pedal uphill. My Grandma decided to struggle to push the trike uphill, despite the painful bladder condition she suffers from, which must have been made worse by the effort of pushing me uphill. She carried on laughing and joking and I have the utmost respect for that. Even now, when she needs both hips replacing and is often in terrible pain she smiles and doesn't let it get her down. She won't let it stop her going on holiday, or even taking the 'old ladies' shopping, nor will she admit that perhaps she herself is becoming (God forbid) an old lady. She always says, 'You're only as old as you feel,' and mentally my Grandma's still twenty-five. Long may she remain so.

Imagine how frustrating it must be needing the toilet twenty times a day when you can hardly walk to get there. Very frustrating. It's very difficult for her but she won't let irritating or frustrating problems stop her from having a normal life. She says it's because of me that whenever she feels like giving up, she finds the determination to carry on. Even though that makes me feel extremely proud to have affected someone so deeply, I don't believe that for one minute. I believe that it's my Grandma's natural determination to carry on in the face of adversity, which has rubbed off on me, along with the same determination that my Mum possesses. Some people have it, others don't.

Every holiday time my brother, our two cousins Ben and Andy, and I would go to Grandma's and we'd pack a picnic, and off we'd go into the wide blue yonder to wherever the wind would take us, or wherever she had planned to take us. I was at that age, between five and eleven, where I was very inquisitive and I wanted to learn as much as possible. The others were at a similar age. There are only two years between Ben the oldest, and Daniel and Andy the youngest. I was sandwiched somewhere in the middle, and because of this small age gap we got on really well. We were more like four brothers than cousins, and we had some great times, we still do. We went all over the country on educational visits, to Martin Mere, Wigan Pier, Jodrell Bank Science Park, and to museums. We even went outside the country, to see friends of the family in Scotland, to Anglesey in Wales, even to Disneyland in America! I've been to Germany and to Northumberland, all great experiences, which have made my life richer. Education's not just about academic work, which can be mind-numbingly boring and repetitive, it's about where you've been, what you've seen and done. It's about a social education, how you interact with people, because as my Granddad says, 'People are the most important thing, not possessions or anything else.'

I'm the first to admit that an academic education is important. I mean, I've been obsessed with learning as much as possible for years, from books and with exam revision, and yes you can learn a lot from other people's experiences, discoveries, inventions. Indeed, I feel it's essential to know about other people's experiences and opinions, so that you can compare them to your own and establish your own viewpoints and beliefs, but there's only so much books can tell us. Books only give us a second-hand education and you can remember information from books but the most vivid memories and the biggest learning experiences have come from first-hand visits to places. Dexter is now doing a degree in nursing, which consists of around 50% lectures and 50% practical experiences in the hospital wards, and he tells me things he's learnt in the wards that he would never remember if he'd read them in a book.

My Grandma and I would always walk around at a sedate pace, taking in what we saw and trying to learn from the experience. Ben would usually walk with us and the two dots we could see in the distance would be Daniel and Andy. What did they learn from these visits? I don't know, but they always enjoyed themselves and came back laughing after their mischievous games. Grandma soon worked out that Daniel and Andy were bored on educational visits and I began to notice a pattern to our outings. Some days we'd go to an educational place and other days we'd go to Haigh Hall or to Tatton Park where there were fields for the others to play football, or swings and climbing frames to play on. We tried in vain to tire them out, especially one day when we were out walking in Anglesey. Daniel and Andy had played football and ran around for hours earlier that day, but after refuelling on sandwiches and crisps they had replenished their energy levels. We soon arrived at some steps leading down to a lighthouse and the annoying buggers were still frustratingly energetic. At the sight of these steps, of which there were around hundred, my Granddad thought he could tire the 'untireable' and he challenged them to run down to the lighthouse while we wandered slowly down the steps, taking in the beautiful sea views. Little did my Granddad know, because when we reached the halfway point down the steps, we saw two figures speed past us. We thought it was two professional runners training for the London Marathon.

'Was it a bird, was it a plane? No, it's Daniel and Andy!' we cried.

Granddad was dumfounded and just shook his head, as they carried on running and playing at the top of the steps. We made a U-turn and joined them at the top. We then handcuffed them to the car and left them to calm down... Only joking! We didn't have any handcuffs unfortunately.

We had a great time in Anglesey. We visited the Sealife Centre where there were all kinds of species of fish, lobster, sharks, everything. It was fascinating, even Dan and Andy were interested. Mealtimes were fun as well. Fish and chips by the sea, evening meals in restaurants. A good time was had by all. It's good fun being a kid. No pressure, no homework and you don't have to worry about anything. Well it was good for me anyway. In fact my life as a youngster couldn't have been any better if I wasn't disabled. Of course I wasn't in a wheelchair then, but ever since I've been in a wheelchair I haven't had anything to complain about, which is why I don't complain about my lot.

Eventually Dan and Andy were undone by their own enthusiasm on one of our trips to Rivington Pike. Basically it's a big park with a big hill in the middle called a pike. There's an old, castle type ruin on top, and a fence around it with only one entrance hole. They decided not to follow the marked path to the top, but to race to the summit as fast as they could. They, shall we say, omitted to look at the signs and ran towards the fence at the top like bulls at a gate, without realising that their way was blocked by this insurmountable obstacle. I watched this act of idiocy from my position on the path, alongside Ben and my Grandma, and I being smug said, 'Don't they know that they can't get past the fence if they don't follow the path?'

'No I don't think they do.'

They could have raced up the path, but no that would be too simple, and as they reached the fence they looked embarrassed and quite tired by their standards. They'd taken the steepest route to the top, their race had been pointless, and we'd beaten them to the Pike! It was like the story of the tortoise and the hare. No one gives the tortoise a chance to win the race but he does because of the stupidity of the hare. We weren't even racing them and we won. When they finally joined us they were shattered and just had to walk with us. Ha ha ha! Finally they'd tired themselves out and we didn't even have to do anything.

Another story that involved a race wasn't as amusing for me at the time. My Mum and Dad were going out for the night and we were shipped off to my Auntie Sharon's house (Ben and Andy's mum). We had our tea (Dan, Ben, Andy and I) and we went upstairs to watch TV. We soon became bored and I don't know which one of us it was, but one of us decided it would be a good idea to race downstairs for a bit of fun. Great idea that was! I had to join in didn't I? I could hardly even walk to the top of the stairs and I couldn't just watch. Obviously I lost the first few races and then I decided I needed a head start. 'Come on I'll beat you this time,' I shouted. Then I set off downstairs as fast as my little, unstable legs would carry me. At about the halfway point, my little, unstable legs did their usual caving act and I ended up in a heap at the bottom, crying in pain every time I moved my left arm. At least I won that one. Meanwhile, my Auntie Sharon had heard me hit the floor and came out of the living room with a rolled-up magazine. We all got smacked round the head with it, except Andy who ducked. He was chased into the living room by his angry mother and I think he got the magazine more than once, but I was in too much pain to care.

There was nothing we could do for my arm that night so I had to sleep in my Auntie's room away from the rabble. The next day I was still in a lot of pain and couldn't move my arm. Mum took me to accident and emergency to get my arm checked out. I was sent for an X-ray and it turned out I'd chipped a bone in my elbow. They didn't plaster it; I just had to wear a sling for a few weeks.

Why oh why do I always have to win? I could have just watched the other three pillocks run up and downstairs all night but I wasn't having that. The biggest pillock that night was definitely me.

I'm usually so sensible until someone mentions the word 'race' or 'competition'. I was always sensible when I was out with my Grandma. I'd walk slowly and take in everything around me, thinking about what I saw. I know I was forced to walk slowly by my physical condition and I think that's part of the reason I did take in more than my effervescent cousin and brother. I didn't feel I had to rush around all day, and even if I could run around I think I still would have wanted to walk slowly with Grandma, listening to her stories and learning from what she knew about life and its ups and downs. An example of me taking things in and thinking about what I saw was on a visit to Blackburn Cathedral with my Gran and the other three, when in the grounds of the cathedral we arrived at a sculpture. My Gran said, 'I wonder what that's a sculpture of?'

To which I replied, 'Grandma it's Jesus. Look you can see the nails through his hands and feet.'

Really it was just a number of twisted lengths of metal with four nails, two at the top and two at the bottom of this 'work of art'. Maybe it was my lack of artistic ability that meant I could spot what this 'artist' was attempting to recreate, but just taking a little time to look at and consider this sculpture meant I could work out what it was. I was very inquisitive and I was really determined to work out what was there. I wouldn't have moved away from that sculpture until I had worked out what it was. Whether that's determined or obsessive, you can decide for yourself. Determined sounds better but maybe the word 'sad' is more appropriate!

On one of the days when we went somewhere to keep Dan and Andy occupied, my determination showed itself again. We were at Leverhulme Park in Bolton which has its own athletics track, and Dan and Andy mithered non-stop to have a race around this 400-metre track.

'Can we go on the track? Can we go on the track? Can we go on the track?' Okay, so you get the picture.

'All right, all right, you can go on the track,' said my Gran frustratedly, and on to the track we went.

Of course I had to join in again. I wasn't going to watch while they had all the fun. We gathered on the track and crouched into the start position. Grandma was the starter. 'On your marks… Get set… Go!' she cried, and the race was on. It wasn't to be a normal race, to see who could get around the track the fastest, it was more an endurance race to see who could get around the most times before fatigue set in. She was always a sadist my Gran! She couldn't let us have a fun, one-lap race, we had to totally dehydrate and collapse before she got her money's worth. Anyway, it was a case of sports day revisited as I negotiated the first bend, knowing I couldn't win. I had to keep going despite this. I had to do my best and give it a go. I ate up the second straight and beat the second bend, and as the line approached I felt my legs begin to tire. As I crossed the line I had to do another lap. I wasn't tired enough to quit yet, and I imagined the bell ringing for the final lap and the crowd chanting my name. 'Withnell!

Withnell!' All right so my tiring state had sent me delirious but I had to go on. It had to be tunnel vision to the line, never give up. I took the first bend again. I was beginning to struggle now. Breathing was tough, my calves began to tighten, but I wouldn't stop. The tightness was spreading up my legs with every step and as I reached the second bend they threatened to capitulate. 'Come on, you can do it,' I told myself. 'Only 200 yards to go.'

The chanting of the crowd had reached a crescendo. 'Withnell! Withnell!' And I pushed myself to the limit. I came round the corner and the line was in my sights. The pain in my thighs and calves was shooting and piercing every time either foot hit the floor but the line was there. 'Keep going, keep going.' Five steps to go and I was running on empty now. 'Five, four, three, two, one, and I've done it!' The crowd went wild! Two laps and the work had paid off. The other three had done twice as many laps but that didn't matter. My Gran had been the only one to see it, but that didn't matter. I was proud of myself. I'd given myself an impossible target and achieved my goal.

Why would I totally tire myself out to run a race I knew I couldn't win? Don't people always want to push themselves as far as possible and beyond? It's like personal bests in athletics. The athletes whose personal bests show up on TV are proud of themselves. They've trained hard and improved themselves and although they're not the best at what they do, they've pushed their bodies to the limit and that's something to be proud of. That's why I always do my best, be it at school, college, university, or when I was younger sport, and despite my lack of ability even art. As I said earlier, as long as you're happy that you've done your best, then no one can criticise you and even if they do, as long as you're happy what other people say is unimportant.

Another sport I tried my hand at was swimming and it's down to my Grandma that I learned to swim. It was a tough baptism at first even with armbands on. The first time I entered the water I was terrified. After a while however I got used to the idea. I found I had a natural buoyancy – no that was the armbands sorry! After a few months of finding my feet in the water, I tentatively took the armbands off. I remember it well. Grandma had been taking all four of us to Horwich swimming pool. There were two pools: a small pool and a big pool. I started small and when I took the armbands off I was very worried. I don't know why because I couldn't possibly have drowned in that pool, it was only about two feet deep. For the first few armbandless trips to the baths I tried to swim on my front, across the pool. It was only five metres across but it felt like five miles because, as hard as I tried, I just couldn't remain afloat long enough to reach the finish line, as I had done on the racetrack, without letting my feet touch the floor.

I was also becoming very frustrated because the other three had graduated from the small pool and could hold their own in the big pool. I was used to doing everything with the others, but now I was alone in the small pool with no one but Gran for company. I was now determined to find a way to get myself across this pool, it was my new goal, and failure was not an option. It's terrible the pressure I put on myself. Swimming was supposed to be fun but it had become an obsession. I wouldn't be happy until I could reach the big pool. I was Indiana Jones and the big pool was the Holy Grail. I had to reach it.

I continued to attempt breaststroke, doggy paddle, front crawl, anything to propel myself to the other side, but after a few more visits I realised it was futile. I had to find a new way of swimming.

The next swimming excursion proved to be the turning point in my quest to become a swimmer. I was about to push myself off from the wall and explode into front crawl, when out of the corner of my eye I saw my inspiration. There was a young boy with armbands on, but he was swimming on his back. *Why didn't I think of that?* I thought, and I gave it a try. I found out I really did have a natural buoyancy and I could float for a long time. So keeping my head above water was no longer a problem, I just had to propel myself across.

For the first couple of tries, it was harder than it seemed but I eventually got the hang of it. It was a case of third time lucky as at the third attempt my head hit the wall at the other side. So my timing was a bit out but I'd made it. Yet again my determination had paid off and the Holy Grail was mine. I was ecstatic, I'd managed to swim five metres! I hugged my Gran and we ran to the big pool to tell my Granddad of the achievement. He was looking after the other three and on our arrival he was just dragging Ben out of the deep end, where he had nearly drowned. That put a dampener on my achievement and caused a rare argument between my two grandparents. In her best primary school teacher's voice she said, 'Why did you let that happen?'

To which my Granddad replied, 'How do you expect me to look after three kids at once Marg?'

She said, 'I've been doing it for years.' And with that the argument was over, as was the swimming session.

Oh yeah, my Granddad was very proud of me when I got round to telling him I'd swam five metres. It had been an eventful day and as I left the poolside for the changing rooms, I glanced back at the small pool. *Next time*, I thought, *I'll swim the length of the pool*. I wanted to swim as far as possible, to push my weakening body to the limit on water as I had done on land shortly before.

Even though my back swimming was improving, I still had that nagging feeling that I had to learn to swim on my front. The others were going for lessons at Turton swimming pool to improve their distance swimming and safety in the water. They had a beginner's group where everyone was about five years old, and I was about eight. However, I had to give it one last chance or I'd always wonder if I could have done it. I had already achieved my goal to swim, on my back, so if frontal swimming wasn't to be it wouldn't be a great loss.

So I joined the lessons for a while. One lesson, I was becoming very tired. That instructor was a slave driver. He came over to me (he'd obviously seen the look on my face) and asked what was wrong. I said, 'Nothing I'm just tired.'

I was convinced he was going to say, 'All right, I'll let you off,' and let me go, but I soon realised that that was the furthest thing from his mind. Obviously no one had told him about my disability because to my astonishment he snapped, 'We don't have tired ones here!'

Okay then, I thought and I carried on in vain for ten minutes. It was no use. I needed to plan my escape. When the evil instructor returned I told him my stomach was hurting and I felt sick. I think he knew what was going on but he let me go, grudgingly.

I was very annoyed, but at that age when I was annoyed I

didn't shout or swear, I just cried, and that's exactly what happened when I returned to the changing rooms. I told my Gran what happened and she was ready to call the manager down to complain. She did get the manager down and he was very apologetic. He hadn't explained the situation to the instructor. He said he'd let him know and that I could go back to the pool if I wanted, but I was too upset to go back. That turned out to be my last lesson, and I decided that swimming on my front wasn't destined to happen. Watching the others would suffice, but I was still determined to swim further.

Overall my swimming lessons were a total disaster. During another of my lessons my Grandma had to intervene because as I walked to the pool, the lifeguard and one of his friends started to mimic my slow, exaggerated walk. I couldn't see what they were doing, but she could and she wasn't going to stand for this insensitive act. The schoolteacher in her got the better of her and she approached the lifeguard.

'Little boy, come here,' she said, lulling him into a false sense of security with this neutral tone of voice. He joined my Gran and she said, 'How dare you make fun of my grandson. If you ever do that again, you'll have me to answer to. Now turn around and go back to the pool.'

I was just waiting for her to send him to stand in the corner as he returned humiliated to the pool, never glancing back. Of course he never made fun of me again.

With the swimming lessons behind me, I contented myself with swimming on my back. I wanted to push myself as far as I could, gaining as many swimming badges as I could, before my muscles became too weak. It was a race against time and like my cello playing exploits, I wanted something to show for learning to swim. I had a five-metre badge but as usual I wanted more. I returned to the scene of my former triumph and stood at the end of the small pool. Ten metres was the goal, and with my floating ability it was just a matter of whether I had the strength to clear the whole length of the pool. I got a great push off from the wall and from there it was easy. Ten metres at the first attempt and I now had the five and ten metre badges.

I was to wait until secondary school for a chance to improve on this distance, but having covered ten metres, I was now confident enough to join my brother and cousins in the big pool. I stayed in the shallow end because with all the boisterous children and powerful swimmers, the deep end seemed too dangerous, especially swimming on my back because seeing where I was going was a problem. If someone ran into me in the shallow end, I couldn't drown, but I couldn't touch the floor at the deep end, so drowning was a possibility. I didn't fancy that! I was no longer alone though, which was one of the reasons why I had been so determined to learn to swim in the first place. I was proud I'd achieved what I'd set out to achieve.

Although my swimming lessons had been an absolute waste of time, they had been very useful for the others. Ben became a very strong swimmer after his near drowning experience. He was never a fast swimmer but he could swim long distances and could look after himself in the water. Dan and Andy on the other hand swam with the same enthusiasm with which they had run up and down those lighthouse steps. They became very fast swimmers and took part in a swimming gala organised by Turton Leisure Centre.

Andy won the breaststroke race and won a trophy, but Dan wasn't as lucky in the front crawl. He did the best he could and swam faster than he'd ever swam before. It was a very tense and exciting fifty-metre race, and with ten metres to go, it was neck and neck between Dan and another lad. Their arms left and entered the water simultaneously, five metres, three, two, one metre, and it was over. It was so close that no one knew who'd won, except the starter. The tension built as he said, 'And the winner is…'

Dan was gutted as the other name was called. He'd lost by a fingertip. If his arms had been half an inch longer, he'd have won. My Gran was desperate for both grandsons to go home with a trophy but not so she could boast to her friends like many other parents, but because she knew one would be disappointed if he didn't get a trophy and the other one did. Her wish came true when Dan took part in the relay race. He was part of the winning relay team and that completed a pretty successful night. In hindsight, Dan coming second isn't a huge surprise. We often joke around, calling him 'the nearly man'. He does win sometimes but more often than not he comes second. He knows we're proud of him wherever he comes so the jokes don't bother him.

The primary school gala, where all the best swimmers from each school in Bolton gathered, wasn't so easy for Dan and Andy or any other Sharples Primary competitor. This time, neither Dan or Andy finished first, second or third, so one wasn't left disappointed when the medals and trophies were handed out. I am sure however that they were disappointed with their final positions. They had done their best and reaching the finals at all was an achievement. The whole family was very proud.

I remember watching Ben trying to qualify for the finals of the town athletics championships. He was throwing the shot put and the top six throws would progress. It was a tense affair as Ben came to take his final throw. I watched as he put his all into this throw. His build up was good, spinning faster and faster until, with an almighty thrust of his arm, he released the shot and it flew through the air. It looked long as it landed and we all willed it to be long enough. I have no idea how long it was, the place was what we were more worried about. The distance came first and then the place was announced. The 'S...' sound at the beginning of the place sounded promising but the '...eventh' after it broke the tension. We were all desperately disappointed, not in Ben, but seventh place was the worst place to finish, just outside the places. It's like finishing sixth in the Premiership when only the top five go into Europe! All the hard work, pushing yourself to the limit only to miss out by a whisker, must be soul destroying. I don't know how gutted Ben was, but we knew he'd done his best. Anyway, kids are resilient, they always bounce back and not being a shot put champion hasn't ruined his life. In fact being a young, promising champion at something, be it sport or anything else, can probably put more pressure on a child. My Dad told me about parents who were sat around him at the swimming gala with stopwatches at hand, timing their obviously well trained children as they won races by ridiculous distances. Did these parents cheer their children on their hard-earned success? No, they just accepted it and complained that the child was 'two hundredths of a second slower than in their heat', which they must have won by an even more demoralising margin for their 'rivals' to handle.

In my opinion children should by all means be encouraged and taught that doing your best is very important, but being perfect and winning shouldn't be the be-all and end-all of a child's sporting exploits. If a child has a talent then parents should nurture that talent and help the child to achieve what he or she is capable of achieving, but the enjoyment shouldn't be removed from that particular pastime or school subject. If a child does his best at everything, as a result of the encouragement of his parents, then if he is talented enough, winning will come naturally.

Enough about other people, this book's about me! What about my other sporting attempts? Remember how upset I was about my brother, when he first learned to ride a bike without stabilisers? Well eventually I did try to do it myself, ride a bike that is. I had been riding a bike with stabilisers all my life and was fed up. I don't know why this was so important to me, but hey I was a kid. All kids can ride a bike with two wheels, and I was going to.

I took the stabilisers off and I was ready. My brother and one of our friends, Murgy (Lee Murgatroyd), were there and they were going to teach me. I climbed on the bike and they gave me a push off. I tried to pedal but lost my balance and fell off. So I got on again, and fell off. So I got on again, and fell off. Then I got on again, and this time I er... fell off again! This wasn't going to work but the tunnel vision had set in again. If I didn't keep trying I'd have failed, I couldn't fail!

I kept trying, and falling off. I even made it to the bottom of the Grove once but I had a problem even pedalling, let alone keeping my balance. I had to face defeat; riding a bike had beaten me.

Although I had previously been really upset, I faced the fact that I'd never be able to ride a proper bike and started looking into alternatives so I could keep up with my friends. There were some disasters before I found my trusty golf cart.

First of all there was the Polo trike. It was a pedal trike and that negated the problem of balance encountered on the two-wheeled bike. The problem was that after a while my legs were too weak to pedal uphill, so I had to share my seat with another person to get me around, although I wasn't allowed to go too far anyway. My Mum didn't let me go further from the house than Outwood Grove, the next Grove up, about a hundred yards from my house and I was eight years old! I wasn't allowed past the lamp post in our Grove until I was six! My Mum was only trying to protect us from the dangers of 'Beyond Lamp Post Land' but it wasn't exactly the Bronx! It worked though, we've turned into very respectable and well-behaved young men (even if I do say so myself). I thought there were freedom of movement laws anyway!

However, this restriction on my movement didn't stop Gaz Lane trying to kill me. I'd managed to escape the confines of Outwood Grove without my Mum's knowledge, and Gaz had driven me to the top of the street on the Polo trike. We came down the street at warp speed, came off the pavement in Outwood Grove and went on to the opposite pavement without slowing down. We made for the bottom of the Grove and turned the corner, and crash! We came to sudden stop as the back wheel hit the wall, which jutted out on the corner of the Grove. When we moved the trike away from the wall and set off again, shaken but not stirred, towards Ringley Grove, we were deafened by an ear-piercing screech.

Shit! we thought. We knew there was something wrong. Dismounting to inspect the damage, we saw that the wheel rim was buckled, and that was the last time I rode that bike. It was an ugly machine anyway, huge red frame and hideous white mudguards. It had to go on the scrap heap.

When I think about it, I should never have let Gaz on that bike; he was always doing dangerous things.

There was a park near our house called Sandy Park. There was no sand there so I don't know why they called it that, but Gaz and his brother Danny came to the park on their bikes with my brother and me. I walked up there with them to watch them on their bikes. Now, on Sandy Park there was a steep grassy hill with bushes very close to the bottom, and Gaz, Danny and Dan would speed down the hill at breakneck speed and either brake or swerve quickly before reaching the awaiting foliage. So Gaz decided he'd go down the hill, faster than ever before and forget to brake. Not surprisingly he ended up face down in the bushes. Nice one Gaz, and I let this guy take my life into his hands and drive me around on a dangerous three-wheeled pushbike!

Gaz was one of those people who always liked to mess about and took great pleasure in winding me up, which didn't take much in the days before secondary school. Once when my brother and I slept over at Gaz and Danny's house, Gaz buried me under all the bedclothes and pillows he could find with only a small hole left. Of course I couldn't get out. I was stuck there for three days with only bread and water and unable to move until his mum came in to change the bedding! Actually it was probably about ten minutes and I thought it was quite funny really.

Another trick he had, along with my brother, was to play frisbee. Sounds innocent enough but not the way they played it. They would disconnect the wheels on my wheelchair and throw the frisbee to each other aiming slightly above my head, leaving me in fear of decapitation! That's an exaggeration really because every time they did hit my head, which wasn't too often, it hardly hurt at all. They knew, however, that I worried too much about things and that every time they threw it, it would be like torture for me. The little sods!

Gaz was also a pain in the neck when it came to computer games. He always used to beat me at them, but he didn't win gracefully and just cheer for himself. He'd make really annoying, repetitive noises, laugh at me very loudly, but the most irritating thing was the replay option on his 'EA Hockey' game. He'd replay every goal he scored over and over again, cheering along with the crowd every time. As you know I hated losing or not being perfect at the best of times, so you can imagine how annoyed and frustrated I got in the face of this infernal showing off. You know what used to happen when I got annoyed. Yes, one day I'd lost about ten games in a row on 'EA Hockey', and had just let the twelfth goal in, in the eleventh game. The red mist had descended by then and the pathetic tears were welling up in my eyes. Gaz knew what I was like so he replayed this goal more than ever before, making more stupid noises than ever before. On what must have been the thirteenth replay of the twelfth goal, in the eleventh game, I lost it completely, threw the controls down, burst into tears, and said, 'I'm not playing any more.'

How childish was I? I'd done the spoilt brat trick. 'I'm not playing any more,' is one of the sentences that when you hear a kid say it, you want to slap him and tell him to grow up, and I'd said it.

That little outburst made matters worse for me. You don't cry in front of a professional mickey taker like Gaz Lane and get away with it, especially after such a pathetic outburst. He laughed at me very loudly. I deserved it for being so sad, though.

So I let a guy who threw himself into bushes, buried me under his bed clothes, took the mickey out of me over and over again until I cried and threw frisbees at my head, drive me around on a bike over which I had no control. What a good idea! He probably drove my bike into that wall on purpose, to see how I'd react.

Seriously though, we had some great times with Gaz and Danny. Gaz used to make up strange but very amusing stories about people we knew. We spent a lot of time together over the holidays and outside school, passing the time of day doing what kids do. Playing football, tennis and whatever, or just playing on computers. We even made a tape of ourselves making a radio show. We made dens and all sorts. They were good times. We even had our own bobsleigh team. Well, we nailed a sledge to a skateboard anyway.

Danny was always the quieter one. He was brilliant with electrical or mechanical things. He helped us build go-carts and made his own speaker using a cardboard box. Even now he's still doing similar things, but on a bigger scale. He buys cars, always Volkswagens, and fixes them up.

It didn't matter what Gaz, Danny and Dan were doing, they always involved me. I played football with them and tried to join in as much as I could. No matter whether I slowed them down or not, they let me have a go. They, as many people have done, just accepted me as I am and never complained, even if I was terrible at something. No one ever got annoyed with me. That's what makes my friends such good friends.

I did have quite a good sense of what I could do and what I couldn't and if I felt I couldn't get involved without falling over or ruining the game, I'd just watch and experience the atmosphere of what was going on. Even then I felt as involved as I did when I was playing the games. I had just as much fun. It's similar to being a football fan. When I go to matches I enjoy listening to the atmosphere and the crowd cheering, and watching what happens on the pitch. I think most fans would agree that they enjoy watching as much as the players enjoy playing.

So the search was on for a new vehicle, a practical vehicle that could get me uphill without the help of my friends. It wasn't that I was ungrateful, but I'm very independent and wanted to get around myself so I could have 'the most normal life possible'. I know it's a bit of a cliché now from disabled people, but nevertheless it is exactly what most disabled people want. We don't want to be seen as different or be viewed with sympathy and I think society is coming round to that view, finally. Wheelchairs are becoming more and more advanced, as are facilities to help disabled children in mainstream schools, and my story is testimony to that. I'm the first person with my particular disability to follow the mainstream education process in Bolton, and I can only see that as a positive thing. I'll explain later how Sharples High was very accommodating towards people with various disabilities, as was Sharples Primary beforehand, but it's not just education where things are improving.

I remember one of my holidays in America, and people can say whatever they want about Americans having to do everything bigger and better than everybody else. But ten years ago when I was there, the facilities for and the attitude of the people towards disabled people was much better than in England, even now. However, things are improving. The wheelchair accessibility to buildings, football grounds, nightclubs and the like has much improved. Even the law has changed. All newly built buildings must by law be accessible for wheelchairs and that's due to a widespread change in attitude towards disabled people. I'm not the sort of person who complains about old buildings not being accessible, because disabled people weren't accepted when these buildings were built. It was a different world then. I do think it's great though when old buildings are renovated with disabled people in mind, but the fact that the law is there for future buildings and public transport is a promising thing.

The main problem with public transport is trains and buses. Again, in America all buses are accessible for the disabled but here we are a long way from a similar situation. Admittedly there has been an attempt to create such buses in big cities. However, in my first week at Manchester University I tried one of these 'wheelchair adapted buses'. It wasn't as easy as expected to get on and off this bus. The driver even had to get out of his seat and lift me on to the bus, with my six foot five inch mate, Alastair. The pneumatic mechanism to lower the bus to 'wheelchair level' didn't quite go low enough. Trains are slightly better in that they have ramps to allow wheelchairs to get on to them, but on many trains I end up sat in the luggage compartment acting as a fire hazard and feeling distinctly unsafe if the train were to crash. A bigger problem with trains is when I actually get on to them. I have to ask the driver to radio ahead to the next station to make sure there's a ramp at the final destination point, which they often forget to do.

It's just a bit of consideration that is needed. If people just think that someone in a wheelchair needs help, or another disabled person needs a thought, then things will be easier for everyone. Maybe we'll stop moaning then.

Hopefully the government's ten-year transport plan will address the problem but somehow I don't think it will.

I said that the mentality of people is changing and that's true, but sometimes the good intentions are there but the knowledge of what disabled people need, for example how big a disabled toilet needs to be, or how wide a ramp needs to be, is not there. There's no use in building the ramps or a disabled toilet if a wheelchair can't get into the toilet or on to a ramp! My opinion, for what it's worth, is that actual disabled people should be employed by building companies and architect's firms to offer advice on designs for ramps and the like, and also on measurements for such adaptations. The government is forever trying to cut benefits and get disabled people into the workplace. This could be a way of doing so. It's also a worthwhile job to do.

In a McDonald's carpet-burger bar, sorry McDonald's restaurant in Bolton town centre, the thought at least was there. The ramps on the ground floor are perfect. The whole floor is accessible. They also have a disabled toilet, disabled as in for the disabled, however also disabled as in unusable. The doorway is big enough but that's about it. There'd only just be enough room in there for me, if I could, to get out of my wheelchair and walk to the toilet! That's the most frustrating thing and the only time I've ever complained to the manager about anything. The manager was very helpful, honest. 'Just fill in a complaint form,' he said dismissively.

That's exactly what we did and when I returned, it must have been three years later, to my huge surprise the toilet hadn't grown one bit. I was really confident as well! My point is that half an hour with a disabled person would have sufficed to make that toilet bigger than an airing cupboard.

In Atlantis nightclub in Bolton, where they have admittedly brilliant facilities – ramps, a lift, disabled toilets on each floor – the job hasn't been finished. There are various raised seating areas, one of which has a ramp, the other three of which don't. If we go into the nightclub and there is no room on the ramped seating area, when my friends want to rest from their mad break dancing where do I go? My friends like to go upstairs, where there's no ramped seating area which makes things difficult, especially as the step up to this area is huge. Making a ramp up this step wouldn't have been more expensive than making the actual step, if cost were the problem. Again, half an hour with a disabled person and there would be a ramp there. There's no use in me going out if I can't be with my mates. It's a good job my mates are considerate and don't go too far away.

How the hell did I get from looking for a motorised vehicle to facilities for the disabled in a nightclub? I don't know, but just when I thought I'd rid myself of the horror that was the Polo trike, the creative imagination of the bikes for the disabled manufacturers went into overdrive, and out came the 'motorised Polo trike'. No, please no!

I thought, *Bloody hell, I might as well give it a go*. So I gave it a week-long trial, which nearly killed me or at least nearly threw me off a few times. The catch (there had to be one) was that the word 'motorised' didn't mean that in the strictest sense of the word. The trick was to pedal the bike for a while, then the motor would kick in to rest the strained muscles of the disabled person, and then stop when the brake was pressed. Sounds like an advertising campaign, but this was the general idea. So off I went on my first little out of Grove excursion on this, shall we say prototype, bike. It took a little getting used to at first and the motor didn't kick in until I tried pedalling a few times. The first time it actually worked was a liberating experience. I felt free and could actually move freely without becoming tired.

That feeling lasted the whole day, and that was my lot. The motor worked for that first day and then it went haywire. I was obviously the guinea pig for an untested, possessed bike.

I'd finally escaped the shackles of Outwood Grove and was allowed as far as Murgy's house at the top of the street, and that was my destination as my bike's possessed soul reared its ugly head. I reached Murgy's drive and eased the brake ready to dismount and knock on the door. Closer and closer I came to the door, then past it, then, 'Shi–i–i–t!' Closer and closer to the gate, then smack into the gate and on to the floor! Slightly bruised, I got up, dusted myself down and knocked on the door, with tears in my eyes. Thank God it was Murgy who answered the door, I didn't want to explain my emotional state to his mum. I was crying more from upset than in pain. The dream was broken as well as the brake. Would I ever be able to get around properly? I was becoming very upset and frustrated with the whole situation.

'What's happened to you, Dave?' he asked.

'That bloody bike wouldn't stop. I ran into your gate,' I replied.

His reaction was slightly insensitive, if that's what you can call bursting out laughing!

I told him I'd be back in three hours because that's how long it would have taken me to walk up that hill! As it happened Murgy came down soon after but the story isn't finished yet. Stupidly enough I got back on the demon bike and pedalled downhill, building up quite a high speed, much faster than the speed I'd hit the gate. If the brake didn't work this time the bike would either tip over coming round the corner into Ringley Grove, or I'd end up in a heap at the back of one of the Grove's many cars. I managed to negotiate the corner without a problem and applied the brake, which of course didn't work again. Luckily the bike began to slow down of its own accord. I thought too soon because I forgot that although the bike was slowing down the motor was still propelling the pedals. I think I'd mistaken the bike for the old Polo trike because, expecting it to stop, I put my foot on the pedal. I felt an excruciating pain as my pants twisted around the moving pedal, which continued to rotate, twisting and trapping my foot with every inch it moved. I was screaming in pain and was convinced that my ankle was about to snap. Then suddenly, and to this day I still don't know why or how, the bike stopped. My foot was still stuck in the pedal, and the group of kids in the Grove, including Dan, Andy, and Ben, saw me bent double over the handlebars, crying.

Andy was the first to run towards me. 'What's wrong Dave? Are you all right?'

'My foot, my foot. Move my foot!' was my pleading and pained cry. He saw my twisted foot and comforted me by bursting into tears himself. The rest of the group had reached us by then and they soon had my foot free. As I limped up the Grove on my sore foot I thought, *Someone up there is torturing me.*

The next day that evil bike was returned to whence it came, with a piece of advice attached: NEXT TIME, TEST THE THING BEFORE YOU INFLICT IT ON SOME POOR, UNSUSPECTING DISABLED CHILD. No I didn't write that but it was very tempting. With that, the search for a bike was resumed and this time we would do it without the help of the 'experts'.

The next offer of a bike was one of those trolleys that old men and women drive around on. A friend of Gaz and Danny's mum and dad could no longer use the trolley and so, when they told her about me, she said I could have it. It sounded like a good idea to me and later that week I visited this lady to try this vehicle out. Let's face it, it couldn't be worse than the last two. It was worse. I saw the lady, who was very kind and then I checked the bike. It looked good and I was very excited about the possibility of finally finding a vehicle. My excitement, however, was very short-lived. I got on to the seat, turned the trolley on and pressed the button to make it go forwards. That was the easy part. Turning round was not so easy because, as I went to turn the handlebars to the left, I

couldn't for the life of me muster the strength to do it. So bang
went that idea. I was beginning to think my vehicle search was ill
fated and that I was never going to succeed.

Then came my saviour in the shape of my Uncle Andrew who
was a member at Accrington Golf Club. During a golf round he
saw an old man on a three-wheeled golf cart and he was inspired.
He made some enquiries about the price and availability of these
golf carts and all that was left to do was for me to try one out.

When they told me about this, I pretended to sound excited.

'Well what are we waiting for,' I exclaimed, 'let's go.'

I was really thinking, *Here we go again, what's going to happen this
time? It'll probably blow up or something*. But out of politeness to my
Uncle who'd spent time finding the latest three-wheeled
possibility, I went along. It was worth a try, anyway.

My Mum, my Granddad, my Uncle Andrew and I piled into
his car, and went to try this golf cart.

Well when I saw it, it looked better than any other trike I'd
ever ridden. It almost looked cool. It was black with a yellow seat,
which had a black cushion on it. There was a black box on top of
the handlebars and a red lever to make it move. The further down
the lever was pressed, the faster it went, up to 8 mph! It even had
its own ignition with a little silver key, and its own name, 'The
Trio'. I'd look good if it worked. Hell's Angels eat your hearts
out!

I was just staring at it till my Mum woke me abruptly from my
daydream, with a shout of, 'Well, aren't you going to get on it?'

'Yes,' I replied. *Well*, I thought, *here goes nothing*, and I jumped
on.

I turned the key wondering if this was the one or if it'd just
drive without the lever being pressed! It didn't, so that was a good
start. However, starting had never been the problem with my
previous bikes, it was stopping that I was worried about. I took a
deep breath and pressed the lever slowly down. Off I went feeling
worried but at the same time I felt that amazing freedom that I'd
felt before the demon Polo went mad. I left the garage and set off
down the street, the sound of my Mum's voice ringing in my ear.
'Don't go too far, be careful.'

'I won't,' I shouted. After about a hundred yards, I decided to turn round, and pulled the handlebars to the left. It was surprisingly easy to turn and at that point a smile grew on my face. Was this it? Would it actually work? I reached the garage again and all that was left to do was stop. I let go, which was one of the most nerve-racking things I've ever had to do, and to my huge relief, I came to a smooth stop.

Things were looking good and I wanted to take it home immediately, but we'd have to get the money together first. My Uncle Andrew would pay the deposit, but the rest was up to us.

Anyway, my Grandma had organised a holiday in the Lake District for my Auntie Jen, cousins Rachel, John and Ruth, and Dan and me. I departed for the Lakes but my mind was still with 'The Trio'. I hoped upon hope that it would be waiting for me when I returned.

I did manage to banish it from my mind to enjoy my holiday. We visited Lake Windermere and went on many walks, taking in the beautiful scenery, the beautiful, inescapable scenery. I don't know why, but being surrounded by nature always makes me feel secure, like nothing can harm me or upset me. I feel totally relaxed, and that's how I felt throughout this holiday. There's no funny or defining moments from this particular holiday but my Grandma did it again. The holiday was very enjoyable.

As soon as the holiday was over and we piled into the car to return home, my mind switched back to my mean machine. I slipped into a daydream, thinking of driving this cart over fields, on the roads, on water (okay, so I had a very vivid imagination), always with my friends beside me. I wanted more than anything for that bike to be sat in the garage when I returned. I could visualise it right then. The silver key, the red lever and the jet-black frame. I couldn't wait.

I could hardly contain the excitement as the car turned up the Grove, but I managed to hide it as Mum hugged me and questioned me on the holiday. I tried not to look preoccupied, or to look at the garage door, but I think it was obvious to my ever-observant Mum. I can never hide anything from her. It's so damn irritating!

She soon said, 'I've got a surprise for you.'

'Have you? What is it?' I asked knowingly.

'Come to the garage and you'll find out.'

I didn't need asking twice as I ran excitedly to the garage door. I flung it open and my excitement turned to horror. The demon was back to haunt me. It was another, new and improved Polo trike!

Only joking! I had you going then, didn't I? Just as I had been daydreaming, it was there shining in the light, my passport to a new life, 'The Trio!'

I ran to my Mum and Gran, who I knew must have been in on the financing to make this possible, and hugged them. I didn't want to let go. I was extremely emotional.

This moment may seem melodramatic or exaggerated to you but to me this represented the difference between freedom and being confined to the house for long periods of time, the difference between independence and reliance on my friends. Life just wouldn't be the same without it. It was like a substitute for a pair of legs. Like a teenager's first car, although having never experienced that I can only speculate. This was what you could call a turning point. Life would be better from now on.

The first month or so with this golf cart was... eventful. My newfound freedom went to my head and I became a bit of a rebel – for about ten minutes. I was still about nine or ten years old and was only allowed to Murgy's house. Some freedom that was, and I soon became fed up with it. It wasn't just me who was limited to Murgy's house, my brother was as well, but one day, soon after my bike arrived, we wanted to sneak to the chip shop without my Mum knowing. Trust us to run into Rachel, our cousin, during our deceitful journey.

'Where you goin'?' she asked.

'We're going to the chippy. If you see my Mum, don't tell her,' I answered.

'All right then,' she assured us.

We continued on to the chippy, naively believing that Rachel would keep our secret. We quickly ate our chips on the way home. There was no way Rachel could have seen Mum, she'd gone picking my Nan up in Little Lever, five miles away. Our plan was foolproof!

I got home and my Mum, the all-seeing eye, looked stony-faced. I knew it. Rachel had got to her first. She said, 'Where've you been?'

I don't know why I bothered, because she wouldn't have asked the question if she didn't already know the answer, but I said, 'Oh we've just been at Murgy's for a while.' I hated lying and it always backfired, either through my inability to keep a straight face, or because someone grassed me up. It was hardly smoking on street corners, though. I mean I'd only ever seen three street corners before that day: Ringley Grove, Outwood Grove and Ivy Bank Road!

I'd failed the test my Mum was giving me. It was the old 'lull the child into a false sense of security, so he lies and then I can tell him off for two things trick', and it worked.

'I didn't know Murgy owned a chip shop,' was her sharp response.

'What do you mean?' I said. That was three things she could tell me off for, and the hole I was digging for myself was getting bigger.

'Rachel told us.' Right, that was my misery over with and then came the 'make him feel guilty trick'. I'd been sent to my room for the rest of the day and when Mum came in with my tea she said, 'It wasn't the fact that you went to the chippy that was the problem. It was that you lied about it and then pretended you knew nothing about it...'

That trick worked as well. I felt extremely guilty and vowed I would never lie to her again.

'Sorry Mum,' I said pleadingly.

'It's okay, just don't do it again,' she replied, with a look on her face that said, 'I'm really disappointed in you,' designed to make me feel even more guilty.

My Mum was a very fair person, she'd only banned me from travelling away from home so I didn't fall off my new bike and hurt myself. I knew that.

This act of rebellion did however have one positive effect, it set my Mum thinking, and two weeks later she said we could go further provided we weren't alone. The next week her earlier cautious attitude was proved correct. She's always right, why is she always right?

I don't know how, but my brother and I became friends with the paperboy who was quite a bit older than us, and one day he said we could go with him on his paper round, as long as my Mum let us. She said it was okay as long as we were sensible and didn't stray away from the paperboy. To be honest, it wasn't too far this paper round and not fraught with danger, so off we went. At least we were allowed to go somewhere for once.

We passed Murgy's house smiling and chatting away, and entered new territory. We went boldly where no children had gone before, into Ivy Bank Close! I felt very smug on my new cart and showed this smugness to a man who was out mowing his lawn on this sunny spring day.

'That's a nice vehicle,' he shouted.

I looked over to see who complemented me, and shouted back, 'It is isn't it!' I deserved what happened next for that act of smugness, for as I turned to face the road there was a parked van, which I'd failed to notice in my moment of glory. *Shit*, I thought, *I can't get out of the way. Shi–i–i–t!* Crash!

That brought me down to earth with a bump. I received a jolt to the ego as the man, the paperboy and my brother burst out laughing at the sight of me slumped over the handlebars, face slightly bloodied. It was like a scene out of *You've Been Framed* as they ran to help me up. They knew I was okay when I got up laughing, and we all had a good laugh as I wiped the tiny amount of blood from my lip. It was more bruised pride than bruised face and that incident has provided much laughter in the years since.

The only problem was how to explain this to my Mum, without forcing her to change her mind on how far we could travel. Would the paperboy get all the blame? Would my cart be returned? It didn't bear thinking about, so I didn't think about it. We finished the paper round first, before returning to face the wrath of mother.

We tried to keep straight faces as we relayed what had just happened, but she was more worried than annoyed. Once she knew I was all right she just said that these things happen, and we could all breathe a sigh of relief. The paperboy wasn't in trouble and the golf cart wasn't going back, as if my Mum would do that! I don't know why I was so worried.

That little incident taught me never to show off about anything. It was a case of 'pride comes before a fall' and there'd be a few more falls to come while I got used to it. I thought I could drive it perfectly the day I got on it and crashing into a stationary van was just a freak incident!

I used to go for little rides on my own, just because I could really. I still do sometimes. One day I decided I'd go for a ride on Sharples High School playing fields to see what the cart could do. I knew where Sharples was because I'd been there watching my brother having a kick about with Gaz and Danny Lane, and my Gran sometimes took us swimming at the Sharples pool, so I set off from home telling my Mum I wouldn't be long. I crossed the road using my memory of road safety rules. Yes, I waited for the green man and then rode the approximately 200 yards down Hillcot Road to the entrance to the fields. I entered the fields and drove full speed (8 mph) across the all-weather pitch, inhaling the sweet smell of freshly cut grass, the wind blowing in my face. I made for the relatively steep hill at the other end of the fields. *I'll see what this baby can do*, I thought and moved from all-weather pitch to grass, not thinking there might be ditches to avoid, and never looking at the floor to check. My mind was racing, 'I'm free, I'm fast… I'm falling sideways off the seat. Bloody 'ell that hurt!' I'd hit one of these bumps that I hadn't seen and hit the deck again. The bloody thing was supposed to stop that happening, but instead I'd fallen off twice in quick succession.

A family panicked and ran over to me. They dragged me to my feet and helped me on to my bike. I said my thank yous and drove home as quickly as possible. It was a stuttered drive home because the arm I used to press the lever down was sore and felt a bit weak. When I got home, I told my Mum what had happened while she surveyed the damage. I wasn't badly hurt, just a sore arm where I'd landed and a grazed knee, but I was emotionally shaken up. I burst into tears and sobbed, 'Why do I keep falling off? I thought it'd make things easier now.'

My Mum didn't have to say anything, she just gave me a hug and once again it comforted me. The dream had turned sour for a minute but that hug did wonders for me and I was soon ready to give the Trio another chance. After all, it was my careless driving and not the bike which had caused me to fall off.

It never ceases to amaze me how my Mum knows exactly what to do when I'm upset, angry or frustrated. She knows how I'm feeling, even when I try to hide it, and her hugs always make me feel better. Even recently, despite my being an adult now, when I need a hug or comforting she'll always oblige. Not that I cry or get upset very often. I'm a man now. I'm hard. I've made myself sound like a right mummy's boy but it's not true, she makes me hug her – honest!

There is only really one more incident where I nearly caused damage to myself that I can remember from these early stages of riding my bike and this one was on the grounds of Sharples High. There was, and still is a house attached to the school called Hillcot House. There were about twenty steps going down to the sports centre car park and at either side of the steps was a steep, almost vertical grass hill going down about halfway. At the bottom of each hill was the top layer of bricks on a wall, and beyond this was a drop of about ten feet to the ground. Me being the intelligent person that I am, decided to ride my bike around the garden at the top of one of these dangerous hills, getting as close as possible to the hill without going over the edge. This was not a sensible thing to do, because as humans do I pushed myself to the limit and then went too far, literally. I froze as the cart tottered on the edge of the hill before going over. I held on for dear life, approaching the layer of bricks faster and faster. I thought, *This is it*, and shut my eyes. I felt a sudden judder as I hit the brick, which slumped me to my usual position over the handlebars. I slowly opened my eyes and was terrified to see the ground ten feet below me. I was still alive and on my bike, just. Any faster and I'd have been dead. *What the hell am I going to do now*? was my first thought. There was no reverse gear.

There was no other way, I'd have to get off the bike and find an easy route to the car park. This would not be easy.

I lifted my head up from the handlebars and carefully leant back on the seat. Any sudden movement and I'd probably flip myself off the bike and over the wall.

Having hauled myself slowly off the Trio, I took each step at a time, holding my arms out like a tightrope walker as I went across. One slip could cause quite a bit of pain, especially as I'd be likely to fall over the wall. Another fine mess I'd got myself into. One step and I was okay. Two steps, and a little wobble, but I was fine, three, four, five, tentative steps and I'd reached the steps. Thank God for that! Now all I had to do was find someone to get my bike off that hill. I surveyed the fields for my saviour but he was on his way already, thankfully. I don't think I could have made it across the car park. I was knackered after five steps. A lad about my age must have seen my 'Evil Knievel' impression because he came running across the car park like 'a bat out of hell'.

'Do you need some help up there?' he asked.

I felt like saying, 'No, I'm just doing this for a laugh.' But what I really said was, 'Yes please, I got my cart stuck up there. Can you get it down for me?'

'Yep, just wait there,' he said. Well, I wasn't going anywhere. He brought my pride and joy back to me, all in one piece.

'There you go,' he said as I eagerly climbed back on.

'Cheers mate. I won't be doing that again. I'll see you later.'

He just laughed and I drove off into the sunset, never to tell my parents what had happened, until now that is.

Was the cart cursed? No. I just had no common sense. I'd soon get used to it though.

All my other memories with my cart, in this time before secondary school are safe ones where I didn't risk hurting myself. Driving to Lydia's house, her dad carrying me up the stairs. Driving to Gaz and Danny's house, their dad carrying me upstairs. Driving down to Sharples to watch my mates play football, golf or whatever. Going on bike rides with my brother, finding short cuts on the streets, and places I didn't know. Taking it up to my Grandma's and down the steep hill where she lived. Just being a part of things was the main advantage of my cart, and I thought it was the best thing since sliced bread.

Basically the bike riding rounds off my sporting attempts, no sorry, there's the one I really tried to forget. Horse riding. What a terrible and mentally traumatising experience that was!

I decided I quite liked the idea of horse riding after seeing a gymkhana on telly, so my Mum arranged for me to go to a disabled riding school. I thought that sounded safe enough and the next week she and my brother came to watch me during my first lesson.

When I arrived the instructor, who was very friendly took me by the hand and said, 'You must be David.'

'Yes,' was my nervous and articulate response, as she led me to a beautiful horse with silky black fur and gorgeous brown eyes. It was a lovely creature.

'This is Sparky,' she said, as I looked on nervously. 'Don't be scared. Here, stroke him.'

So I stroked him for a minute feeling comforted and relaxed by the instructor's quiet and reassuring voice. Now all I had to do was climb up on to Sparky. Beautiful he may have been but he was also tall, and I needed help to get up onto the saddle.

'Here,' said the instructor, 'put your right foot through the stirrup.'

She was pointing at something hanging down at the horse's side and I assumed that this must be the stirrup. 'Now with my help, push yourself up and put your other foot over the other side of the horse, and you're on.'

Once on Sparky, I looked down and was a bit shocked to see how far down the floor seemed to be.

'Don't worry,' came the friendly voice (not Sparky's), 'there's a thick layer of hay on the floor, and I'll be here. You won't fall.' She gave me two pieces of leather and explained that these were called reins.

'Pull on the left one to make him go left, and pull on the right one…'

'—to make him go right,' I interrupted. Why was she talking to me in a patronising tone?

'Sorry about that, it's just that most people here don't know their left from their right.'

So at least it was nothing personal.

'Are you ready?' she said. I was petrified but said, 'Yeah,' anyway. The friendly instructor signalled to the person who was obviously going to take the lesson. The new instructor told us to say, 'walk on,' to our horses, so I shouted, 'walk on Sparky!' and he did! It was an amazing feeling. I was riding a horse and I felt safe! Approaching the wall, I pulled the left-hand rein and Sparky turned left. *This is fun*, I thought. I was enjoying this.

I assumed I'd just be going at this pace for the first couple of lessons but I soon realised that someone hadn't told the main instructor that it was my first lesson. The next instruction I had to use was, 'Trot on Sparky.'

I thought it couldn't be too bad, not on my first lesson, so I shouted the command and was terrified! Sparky broke into jogging speed, shaking me like a rag doll in the process. He was hurtling towards the wall and I panicked. I didn't know how to make him stop and the instructor by my side wasn't a comfort any more. I thought I was going to fall to the ground and break my back. Being on the horse was like torture and then he stopped. I'd forgotten in my panic that a horse isn't just going to run blindly into a wall. What a relief! Then came an even greater relief, the lesson was over. I turned around looking extremely shocked and red faced, and was furious to see my Mum and brother laughing at me. I'd just been through one of the most traumatic experiences of my life and they were laughing!

I didn't admit that I hated it until the day of the next lesson. I was too stubborn to admit it, and the day of the lesson was a day of me changing my mind over and over again. Should I go or should I not go? I was torn between the two options. I told my Mum I was ready to go eventually and she took me to the riding school. In the car park, however, I changed my mind for the last time. I started to cry and said, 'Mum, I don't want to go.'

'Why didn't you tell me before?' she said sternly. 'We're here now, you might as well go in.'

'I can't Mum, please take me home, please,' I pleaded.

My Mum looked very annoyed but thankfully she didn't make me go to the lesson. It wasn't like me to give up after only one little setback but I thought I was just going to sit on a horse and walk sedately around a field or a barn. The horse trotting was a shock that I wasn't prepared for and it wasn't a pleasant one. It was for me a horrible stomach churning experience and I felt unsafe. You've probably guessed that I never went back to the riding school.

Anything stomach churning is not my idea of fun, especially

fairground rides. I don't know whether it's a fear of falling over or falling out, or whether I just don't like the idea, but from the first ride that I tried to the last, I know I've hated every single one. I just don't see how scaring yourself to death can be seen as enjoyable.

The first time I tried one of these rides was on a primary school trip to Camelot. It was only a little boat that swung from side to side but I was very nervous as I got on to the ride, and when it started to swing faster and faster, higher and higher I felt sick and absolutely petrified. I screamed and cried until the ride stopped. Afterwards I was in a state of shock and I didn't set foot on another ride for the rest of the day.

I managed to avoid every other ride for years, despite the fact that my brother loved fairs and theme parks and so did my Dad. Frequently I'd end up at the scene of my worst nightmare, stubbornly refusing to go on any rides. I'd go to the arcades and waste money on pointless games, but at least it was something to do while they let the adrenalin flow.

I only got on a ride for the second time on a holiday in Disney World, Florida, because I was tricked by my devious Dad and brother. We went past the tongue-twisting 'Rocky Mountain Rail Road Ride' and yet again I was mithered to go on. 'I'm not going on and that's it,' I moaned.

'But we'll go on the slow one,' my Dad said.

'What slow one?'

'Look there's the slow one going up the hill, and there's the fast one going down the hill,' he explained.

Being very naive and trusting I said, 'All right then but you'd better not be joking.'

'Trust me, I'm a doctor,' he said suspiciously, and with that I nervously joined the lengthy queue.

Halfway along this meandering queue was a window from which the train could be seen. I saw the train inching slowly up the hill. That must have been the slow train. Soon after, I saw a blur coming down the hill. That must have been the fast train. For a supposedly intelligent person, I was decidedly stupid that day. On any other day I wouldn't have believed my Dad in the first place. Then I would have wondered why I only ever saw the slow train going uphill, and why the fast train only ever went downhill. I also never saw both trains at the same time, which would usually lead me to believe that there was only one train. Oh well, I was on holiday. I must have just let my mind relax. (Well that's my excuse.)

We reached the top of the queue and clambered into the carriage. My Mum was there so I felt safe. She wouldn't let me fall off the seat. The carriage jerked slowly forward and approached the first ascent. As it reached the top I got slightly worried but I thought, *What am I worried about, this is the slow trai–i–i–i–n!* The g-force set in and I realised I'd been tricked. The swine! I looked across in terror at my Dad's grinning face and I wanted to dive over and rip his Freddie Mercury style moustache off!

When my stomach had returned to its natural position, I realised I was enjoying the fear. I never thought that would happen. I was too stubborn however to let my Dad see my enjoyment so I faked the look of fear, but not the screams.

When the ride ground to a halt my Dad said, 'Did you enjoy that son?'

'I can't believe I fell for that,' was my mumbled reply, 'but it wasn't too bad.'

I should have known it was a trick. He was always doing things like that! Like when he said he'd do a firework display for my brother and me, on bonfire night. We went outside, our excitement ready to burst. In the garden the first 'firework' was a banger and I thought the best was yet to come.

'Right, that's it,' he proudly announced.

One measly banger and that was it? I suppose he was just preparing us for any future disappointment we may suffer.

Anyway, I had the taste for these roller coasters now and on the same day we approached a much more terrifying proposition – Space Mountain. This was an indoor ride, which happened in a space-like environment in the dark!

How the hell there could be a mountain in the middle of space I don't know, but it took a lot of persuasion to get me on to this ride. Outside where I could see where the ride was going was fine, but inside, in the darkness was a different proposition.

I eventually took a deep breath and joined this queue. I didn't really want to go on, and then I saw it, my salvation! There was a final warning sign just before the final entrance to the ride which read something like, 'If you have a heart condition or any other disability then you should not go on this ride.'

That was enough for me to use the disability card again. 'Mum, Mum, I can't go on, I've got a disability.' But this time it didn't work as well as when I got my maths wrong.

'It doesn't mean your sort of disability, you'll be fine.' So with my stomach infested with butterflies I got into the shuttle shaped carriage.

We had to sit one behind the other so I didn't feel quite as safe as on the previous ride. My Dad held on to my shoulders, so I couldn't fall over and the stewardess who helped to strap us into the carriage must have seen the look of fear etched on my face. She reassured me by telling me her name and saying that if I got scared I could scream her name and she'd stop the ride. I knew she wouldn't hear me but nevertheless I felt much better. The ride sped off at what seemed like 100 mph. The g-force made me feel like I was going to fall. This was much more terrifying than the Rocky Mountain Ride. The darkness exemplified the fear, and going over the first hill my stomach threatened to explode. I tried to scream the name of the stewardess, but I opened my mouth and nothing came out. It was a silent scream!

When I got off this ride, skin tinted pale green, my healthy dislike for rides was restored. I don't think I've been on a ride since. You could say it was an experience, but not one I care to repeat.

That ordeal over, my Mum took us on some shall we say more sedate rides. No we'll tell the truth. Boring rides.

'It's a Small Small World' was the most embarrassing ride on the planet. You sit in a boat going extremely slowly around a little river, with little dolls dancing on the shores of this river. Fascinating, it was not. Many other such rides meant that the Magic Kingdom didn't live up to its name, for me anyway. For most people, for example my brother and my Mum, there was something to make the day amazing. The highlight of the day for me was getting Donald Duck's autograph!

To get an overall opinion of the Disney World complex you have to experience all parts of it, which I did.

The second part of three at the time I visited Disney World was Epcot Centre, yes the bit with the huge silver ball in the middle. Basically this place was teaching you about science, about space, about the body, about dinosaurs and about advances in technology, but it's only a long time after that I realised that that's what was happening, and that's the beauty of it. I never knew learning about science could be such great fun. It's an amazing place which keeps children occupied, whilst subtly educating them, and that's a difficult goal to achieve. Different characters teach you different things. For example, in the body zone one is taught how many calories you burn by running and cycling and so on by a computer, while the visitor is actually doing these exercises. This keeps the children and adults occupied whilst they are learning. I always learn more when I'm actually occupied whilst doing it.

In the giant silver ball there is a kind of ride which teaches you about space. You sit in a carriage which then tips back so you are lying down. You then feel the sensation of taking off in a rocket and the background turns to black, giving you the feeling of being in space. It's an exciting and original way to teach and inform people about space. The day at Epcot was more my scene than the Magic Kingdom. At least I didn't have to scare myself to death to enjoy myself!

The final part of the Disney complex was MGM Studios, which told us all about the movie industry, how films are made etc. There were themed rides that were being built. King Kong was one, but many things were still in the process of being built which was a shame because what was there was promising.

So overall Walt Disney can sleep peacefully in his grave, safe in the knowledge that he has provided many films and theme parks to keep every type of person happy. I recommend anyone with children of any age up to about thirteen to take their kids to Disney World if it's possible. I feel like the luckiest person alive to have been to America three times before I was twelve, and again I've got to thank my Gran who paid for at least two of these trips. I've done so many amazing things and been to so many different places and that's what I mean when I say I've done more in nineteen years than most people do in a lifetime. I've got some great memories from America, as you've already seen, but one of the best by far has to be Sea World in Orlando. I've always been fascinated by the sea and the creatures that live in and around it, and it's amazing to see a wide selection of creatures, and how they differ from land creatures. At Sea World I saw and was allowed to touch Stingrays. I saw many species of penguin. I saw dolphins and Shamu the killer whale doing some awe-inspiring tricks with their keepers on their backs. They're very intelligent creatures. The sea lion show was very amusing and the shark tank was the scene of one of my famous and pathetic scenes of panic. I've said it before and I'll say it again. For an intelligent person I can be extremely stupid.

We went into the building marked 'Sharks', and we listened to a talk on sharks and different species thereof. Then we were told to go through another door to be 'surrounded by sharks'. 'If you don't want to see the sharks then you can leave via this door,' she said, pointing to a door at the opposite end of the room.

'I don't want to see the sharks,' I insisted.

'Come on,' my Mum said, 'they can't get you.'

'We're going to be surrounded by sharks. I'm scared. What if they do get us?' I was almost crying by now but my Mum managed to persuade me by assuring me.

'I promise you they won't get you, and if they do I'll protect you.'

'Okay then,' I muttered reluctantly and we could all get on with our lives again.

I approached the door leading to the shark viewing area, and with fear etched on my face I went through it. All I could see were visions of *Jaws*. To me all sharks were vicious, man-eating killers and I was their next victim.

The reality of the experience was totally different. Granted, we were 'surrounded' by sharks, but we were in a thick glass tunnel on a moving platform, taking us to the other end of the tunnel. We could see many beautiful species of shark, which weren't bothered by us because we weren't bothered by them. There hammerhead sharks, tiger sharks, and many more, and I learnt more about the nature of sharks on that five-minute trip than I'd learnt in the previous ten years. All my preconceptions of sharks were put to bed and I learnt that they don't try to attack people unless they are provoked. I couldn't believe I'd been such a wimp. As if the organisers of a respected Sealife Park would put millions of innocent, unsuspecting tourists a year into a pool of man-eating sharks!

In the end I was glad I'd seen the sharks, but yet again it had taken my Mum to persuade me. If it wasn't for her reassuring tone I'd have missed out on so many things, which my irrational fear would have prevented me from doing. Sea World was another great day, but it wouldn't have been quite as great without seeing those 'deadly' sharks.

So that was another successful day in America. Of course we didn't spend every day on day trips, nor did we spend our whole holiday in Orlando. Some days, the weather was just too hot to be walking around theme parks all day, so we would spend our time by the pool or in the jacuzzi, or even in a mall where there was a good air conditioning system. The American shopping malls were bigger and better than anywhere else, with shops that catered for anyone's tastes. Only now are there such places in Britain, with the Trafford Centre in Manchester for example. These places had such a huge choice of merchandise that you couldn't help but spend money. The things you could find there were amazing.

As well as Orlando we've visited St Petersburg in Miami and Estero Island, also known as Fort Myers Beach, both of which have beautiful, silky beaches and clear blue seas. Fort Myers Beach has one of the most beautiful sunsets in the world, with deep purple, orange and red skies, an amazing sight. There's so much to do in Florida, but even if you just want to relax then Florida can't be beaten.

I could go on forever with this Florida advert because my holidays there were fantastic, but I won't because at this point I was only eleven years old. I've still got many memories to share with you.

The final school summer holiday I had before starting secondary school was spent on Sharples field, riding around on my cart, watching my brother's sporting exploits and so on. I also spent much time with Dexter who was to be my designated wheelchair pusher for the five years to come. Paul and Danny Walker had also offered their services but it turned out differently. They were always mates and if I needed them, they'd help but I've always had more in common with Dexter. We had the same mutual friends. No offence to the other two but if I had spent five years with some of their friends, I'd have gone insane!

Chapter IV

I've finally made it to secondary school, well almost.

The week before I was due to start was a very busy one. Firstly I had to visit the school to get my timetable early and to check the ramps that had been put around the school. Now I think about it, a week before I started was too late to change anything if the ramps weren't right, but the thought was there which I can't complain about.

I went into the building, up the newly inserted ramp at the back entrance. I met Mr Brennan again, staying at arm's length in case he knocked me over again, and the caretaker came with us to open any necessary doors. Dexter was away on holiday so my Mum had to come with me on this inspection. It turned out that I could get into every room on the ground floor with only a couple of ramps. There was a problem getting into the computer room where there was a step down and then three more steps up. The area where the steps were was too narrow to put a ramp there, which would cause a slight problem. At that time however I could still walk, or hobble. I could just about get up those three steps and even if eventually I couldn't manage that feat, there'd be someone on hand to help. The science desks would pose the biggest problem because they were so high, they'd be above my head when I was sat down in the wheelchair. A CDT teacher, Mr Smith, offered to cut the legs, or part of the legs, off a normal table so I could do experiments and such, whilst still in my wheelchair but I was very independent at that time and while I could still stand up I wanted to do as much as possible on my feet and on my own. So for as long as possible I declined this kind offer and stubbornly stood up in science lessons.

After the problems posed by the ground floor had been solved for the short and long term, we looked at the timetable which showed that I would only have lessons upstairs three times a week, but the way in which they'd organised it was so that I had a keyboard applications lesson followed by a music lesson and therefore I only had to go upstairs twice a week. Mr Brennan though insisted that I got two teachers to help me upstairs every time. This was his only rule really, and because I was a new first-year I wanted to follow this rule. I was a very quiet and respectful person and didn't want to get into trouble from the 'authority' figure. I was never destined to be a cocky little first-year who resented teachers and thought I knew better. I had the naive attitude that 'he's a teacher, I must do as he says'.

I said earlier that I always did my best and wanted to succeed and if you want to do that you have to have a good relationship with the teachers, which means being pleasant. You learn much more if there's a mutual respect between you and the people who are teaching you. The so-called 'hard' kids always go on about respect but really such people know nothing about that notion. They call hard-working people 'swots' and 'teacher's pets', but I believe that the 'swots' will have the last laugh in the end. The hard kids are always the ones who have regrets and wish they'd worked harder at school. Most of the time they wish they were back at school! I was never called a swot because I was friends with most of these people, and I don't mean any offence to them because I didn't have a problem with them. They didn't do me any harm.

It seemed that Sharples would be a perfect school for me because from this little inspection it seemed that everything that could possibly be done would be done to accommodate me. They'd spent money on ramps and I'd made the complicated task of making a timetable yet more complicated. It was organised around me and I knew then that I was really wanted there. I suppose I already knew that but this just confirmed it and that probably added to my respect for Mr Brennan and the other senior teachers at Sharples. They'd even organised a cupboard for me to keep my cart in during the day, and my wheelchair would stay there at night. That's if the weather was good enough to allow me to drive to school.

I was now very confident that the transition from primary to secondary school would be a smooth one. The only thing I had to organise now was my school uniform, and the day after my visit to school I went to the uniform shop. It was quite an exciting occasion for me. The uniform signified a change in my life, a change which I believed would be a good one. My life was moving on and I was no longer worried about it.

The Sharples uniform was like a funeral suit, very morbid. Black pants, black jumper, black tie and an optional black blazer. Thank God for the white shirt is all I can say. If it wasn't for that bit of relief from black, we'd all be on Prozac by now.

I took the uniform home and now all I could do was wait for the first day to arrive. It was only a few days but it seemed like an eternity and the closer it came the more nervous I began to feel. I was beginning to worry now and the previous week's visit seemed a long time ago.

The Monday of the first week arrived and the first-years, including me, were meeting each other, many for the first time. The other four years didn't have to go in until Tuesday, so we had the whole afternoon to ourselves on Monday. It was like a practice run for the real days that were to come.

I couldn't sleep the night before because of the excitement and anticipation of the day ahead, so I got up early and struggled to force my breakfast down. I just sat around, not really knowing what to do with myself until it was time to put my uniform on. I was determined to put it on myself despite the problems I had, and I struggled to do the buttons up. The tie defeated me and my Mum was on hand to tie it for me. Of course she'd bought me the optional blazer. Anything optional, my Mum thought must be necessary. I was unhappy about wearing it because I thought it looked silly and I knew nobody else would have thought it was necessary, but I humoured her anyway. I didn't realise it at that moment but it was quite an emotional day for her. Her first child was starting secondary school and she wanted everything to be perfect, that's probably why she bought me the hideous blazer. She was probably more worried about me on my first day than she was about my brother the following year. She always loved me more. No, she just had more to worry about when it came to my first day. Would I fall out of the wheelchair? Would someone bully me because I was disabled? Would I be left on my own somewhere, unable to move? All these worries and more probably would have plagued my Mum as I climbed on to my cart and turned the key, ready to set off.

I took a deep breath and set off on my five-year journey through school. *This is gonna be good*, I thought, but before I could reach the end of the Grove my Mum came running down the street shouting, 'Dave, Dave, stop!'

I stopped and she ran up to me and said, 'I almost forgot, your Nan bought you this pen.'

I didn't know why she'd stopped me really. She could have left it till later but she just wanted everything to be perfect, so I took the pen and placed it in my blazer pocket. Now I could finally go to school.

I drove to school feeling very grown-up in my uniform, and contemplating the day and years ahead. I definitely was nervous now.

When I arrived at school Dexter was waiting in the foyer like we had arranged. That was a good start anyway. We went to the cupboard which contained my wheelchair so I could change vehicles, and then I was ready for action. We were then all given our timetables, which I had already seen and Mr Brennan also told us what form we were in. I was in 7S.

Mr Brennan then told each form which form room they were to go to. My form room was M3, a maths room. We had all been to the school before, so we knew where M3 was. Dexter began to push me towards the room for the first time, and that was quite a nerve-racking experience. I must have been mad to let an untrained amateur take my life into his hands, especially the guy who caused me to bash my head on a toilet seat and knocked me over at the school disco, but eventually I was to be grateful for it. There's not many people who'd offer to push someone in a wheelchair for five years. That's quite a commitment, but I don't think Dexter ever saw it like that. I was his mate and I needed him, so he helped me out, and that made our friendship stronger. I'll be eternally grateful for all his help. I'm sure there were times when he didn't want to help me, when he just wanted to go to school and get on with his own life, but he never said that. The thing is though, I care about Dexter as much as he cares about me, and you'll see later that in different ways I've helped him as much as he's helped me.

Anyway back to that first day and M3. We got there, went in and sat down behind one of the blue desks. I looked round the room and surveyed the other faces, many of which I already knew. I think Mr Brennan had tried to get as many of my closest friends together as possible, well I know he had. Let's just say there'd been discussions between Mr Brennan and my former primary school teachers. He'd done his homework. In my form there were Dexter, Nichola, Emma, Heather, Leanne, Paul and me, which was reassuring to know. I'd have some help if I needed it. The faces I didn't know all looked as nervous as I felt, oh yes, and then there was the teacher. He was a young Scouser, with the typical Scouse sense of humour, and he was probably shorter than most of the lads in our form. He was called Mr Altdorf and he was to be very important in this first year, for me at least. We had something in common as well. We were both Liverpool fans. (While I'm talking about Liverpool, let me just get one thing clear. I've been asked why I'm a Liverpool fan when I come from Bolton, well I'll tell you why. When I was four years old Liverpool was the best team in England, so yes when I first started to support them I was a so-called 'glory chaser'. That doesn't mean I'm not loyal, because I've supported them ever since, even in recent years when Liverpool haven't been the best. Of course I also hate Man United!)

Mr Altdorf told us a bit about himself and then we had to say a bit about ourselves. I hate doing things like that, but at least everyone knew each other's names now. In addition to the Sharples Primary kids there was Phil, Chris, Sohail, David Cass, Isla, Louise, Ruwayda, Nasima, Bilkis, and Leanne or Leigh, as she liked to be called.

The introductions over, Mr Altdorf took us on a tour of the school which was a bit boring for me having already had the guided tour a week earlier. After the tour our first day was over. I got on my cart and made for home, feeling relieved that nothing had gone wrong, but thankfully not relieved that the day was over. I was quite optimistic about the future.

Surprisingly, my Mum was waiting at the door when I got home, eager to hear about my big day. I said it was really good and thought that would be enough. It wasn't.

'Go through everything from the first moment,' she insisted.

'Okay,' I muttered and I told her everything I've just told you.

Three hours later when all my Mum's questions were exhausted I was already bored of school! That was a shame really seeing as I had five years to go and I hadn't even had my first lesson yet.

That first lesson came the following day, and after seven weeks of rest, relaxation, and getting up as late as possible it was time to get up early again. At seven o'clock on the Tuesday morning, I was reluctant to go to school. The great adventure that lay ahead didn't seem quite as exciting when I could stay in bed instead. The problem was that I wasn't in a position to stop my Mum dragging me out of bed. Oh well, that's what I get for being disabled! I reluctantly made my way to the bathroom to have a wash. I then felt refreshed and ready to face the day ahead. On my arrival at school, Dexter, fresh from half a day's practice at pushing a wheelchair, decided he was now an expert and proceeded to my horror to 'try something different', namely to push me backwards down the maths corridor at breakneck speed, just to see my face. He obviously hadn't grown up over the summer, despite his new helpful streak.

Of course as we turned the corner he lost control, and on my second day I hit the floor, via a nearby wall. Luckily, I came out of it unscathed and could laugh it off. So much for me being safer in a wheelchair.

Having brushed myself down, Dexter pushed me into our form room where we told our new mates about what had just happened. It was definitely an ice breaker and if I was nervous in front of these new people before then I wasn't nervous any more. I think it also helped the others, because I know it's difficult for people to know how to react to people in wheelchairs and also how to treat them. When they saw me laughing about falling out of my wheelchair, I'm sure they realised I wasn't sensitive about my disability and that they could treat me as they treated each other. I was as 'normal' as they were, if you can call those kids normal. Come to think of it, are any of us normal? I just happened to flick through the TV channels recently and I also just happened to land on Granada, where the *Trisha* show was being aired. All right, so I'm really a closet Trisha fan. Anyway she said during the show, 'Normal is a cycle on a washing machine, nothing else.' I thought this was a ridiculous statement until I actually thought about it, and realised it does actually make a lot of sense. Nobody is normal; otherwise the world would be a very boring place.

For the first three months (until Christmas), we were told we would have our lessons as a form before being put into sets according to our ability in each subject. I looked down the timetable and found that my first lesson was maths, in M3, with Mr Twigg. Well, I'd heard many horror stories about Mr Twigg from some of his former pupils and from some of his current pupils. Apparently he was very strict and had psychotic tendencies, such as throwing blackboard dusters at people if they were cheeky or lazy. I was now scared. Also, now that the rest of the school had returned I had to worry about other stories I'd heard. Having your head shoved down the toilet just for being a first-year was the main one. I didn't really believe such stories because most of them came from my Dad. I didn't trust him after the Rocky Mountain Ride fiasco and so I wasn't too worried. They wouldn't do that to someone in a wheelchair anyway, would they?

At this moment in time, I thought familiarising myself with my newly acquired timetable was more important, so I put all thoughts of bullying and scary teachers to one side. Looking down the timetable I thought, *It's a good job I like blue because I'm going to see a lot of it according to this timetable.* Everywhere I looked I had lessons in M3, M4, M5 and all the rooms on the maths corridor had blue walls. I was upstairs on Wednesdays and Mondays. That was a relief. I don't think I could have coped with that on my first day of lessons, not while the nerves were still there anyway. At least with the timetable, I couldn't get lost. I didn't even have to move for the first lesson.

The bell went, Mr Altdorf left and we were left to wait with baited breath for Mr Twigg, the demon teacher. When he did finally arrive he was a peculiar looking guy. He was totally bald, apart from a strip of hair around the back of his head. He was around six feet tall and wore a pair of what I can only describe as semi-glasses, which perched on the end of his nose. He would look over the top of these glasses to see his latest 'victims', the latest group of unsuspecting kids who he could baffle with algebra and the like.

He had an air of authority, and the way he took the register by calling out our surnames seemed to have come from the style of the strict Victorian teachers. I expected him to wield a cane if we ever stepped out of line. The reputation that preceded him was however misleading. He wasn't quite as strict as the Victorian teachers, who would teach the rules to the children for ten minutes and then make them sit in silence and apply the rules to sums. If they spoke the cane would rap their backsides before they could apologise. Mr Twigg would teach us the rules, do an example on the board and then ask a person in the class to answer the next question on the board. If you got it wrong he'd shout, 'Bollocks!' and ask someone else. If someone ever spoke in his lessons he'd call them a 'brainless little fart' or embarrass them by asking who they'd like to play in the Wendy house with (we didn't really have a Wendy house). Innuendo and double entendre were an extensive part of his lessons and we would often hear stories about his children or stories about former pupils to punctuate the lessons. The lazy, insolent kids, who wouldn't do any work whatever anyone said, weren't tolerated by Mr Twigg. They'd either be kicked out as soon as they entered the room or if they spoke they'd be shot down quickly. The rest of the class could have a laugh and could take the mickey out of him. If you did the work you were allowed to have a joke, which I thought was fair enough. It was only the lazy ones who got the chalk thrown at them. I'm sure he was dangerous when he was allowed to use the cane, but the law had taken away his power to physically punish kids. I agree that teachers cannot be allowed to hit kids willy-nilly in this day and age but I can understand it when they snap, especially with some of the Sharples pupils. I'm making myself sound like a real teacher's pet now! I wasn't, honest, I just had a healthy relationship with the teachers based on a mutual respect. Okay so that's the same thing but at least it sounds better. Seriously though, I think my wheelchair-bound situation as well as my diligent personality made this relationship necessary. I needed to keep the teachers on side, because I needed their help, and in order for them to want to be of assistance to me I had to maintain a good relationship with them. The fact that all the teachers did what they could to help me from the first moment I arrived at Sharples added to my willingness to co-operate with them. They'd soon become tired of helping if I was cheeky or uncooperative. Don't misunderstand me, I did actually like most of the teachers, and I also wanted to succeed academically. There were then a number of reasons for my good relationship with the teachers.

Anyway the notion of teacher's 'petness' involves the idea that the 'pet' does everything the teacher says to the letter and doesn't express his own opinion. With me it was different, I was allowed to say what I thought because I did what was required to satisfy the teachers and to please myself. My relationship with the teachers was based on a mutual respect and I knew where the line was that I couldn't cross. The way I saw it was that only the lazy, cheeky kids complained that the teachers didn't give them any respect. What did they expect when they didn't do what was required to earn that respect?

I remember once when someone in my form, who shall remain nameless was having a 'discussion' with Mr Altdorf who had just given him a detention, probably for fighting although I can't be certain. I thought it was pretty fair but surprisingly enough, the kid in question thought it wasn't fair at all. His argument was that his 'opponent' hadn't got into trouble and he always got the blame for everything. He never thought why he always got the blame, but that's not the point. The point is he didn't express himself so calmly. He said something along the lines of, 'Nobody else ever gets bollocked and I'm getting done for jackshit!'

Mr Altdorf politely reminded the red-faced youth that he was digging a big hole for himself and wasn't helping his cause at all by talking in the way he was talking. That didn't shut him up and in an argument he was never going to win he just became more and more annoyed and abusive, and in the end he still ended up doing the detention. The point is that abusing and shouting at a person in a position of authority isn't going to get anyone anywhere, especially when the kid had so obviously done something wrong. If he had explained his dissatisfaction with the biased distribution of punishment in a calm and rational manner then, although knowing Mr Altdorf's stubborn streak he still would have had to do detention, he may also have made him think how else he could have handled it next time this situation occurred. For a kid like this though, the limited threat of detention is hardly going to curb his tendency to fight. He had the reputation of being the 'hardest' boy in school, a very dubious honour. As a result of his reputation he was always liable to get into fights, to prove himself 'worthy' of this honour and also because people wanted to knock him off his perch and take his 'title'. On a smaller scale it's a bit like the situation in a book I read, *Lenny McLean, the Guvnor*, an autobiography of one of London's hard nuts. He had a reputation for being hard, and he was, but he said he only ever fought to defend himself from people who wanted to become the new 'Guvnor'. Oh and he also fought bare-knuckle fights for money. Eventually Paul Ince decked him and that's why he's called the 'Guvnor', and if you believe that you'll believe anything!

So I think that the lad in question often had to fight to protect himself, and many times he was blamed for things that weren't his fault. He must have got this reputation somehow, so to that extent it was his own fault that he became a scapegoat, so I didn't feel too sorry for him.

Another incident showed how teachers could be provoked into a violent reaction. The story I got at first was that the teacher had taken the lad outside and hit him for nothing, a highly likely story. When I heard who it was that had been struck, that story sunk to the level of absolute stupidity. The real story was that five years of insolence, cheek, messing around and general cockiness had culminated in a very dedicated teacher losing control. All most teachers want is for their pupils to succeed, and this teacher was no exception. Eventually, realising that the teacher would very probably lose his job for this indiscretion, the lad apologised for his part in the incident and the teacher also apologised. I think it probably improved the relationship between the two. The only language that certain people listen to is a violent one and although violence is unacceptable, it is sometimes necessary.

These situations were never a problem for me but I felt very strongly at the time that it was not the teachers who were to blame.

Anyway, back to my first day of lessons, and having survived my first lesson with the not so scary Mr Twigg, I had an English lesson in the staff dining room. It wasn't actually used as a dining room any more but no one had bothered to change the name. My English teacher was Mr White but I hadn't heard any stories about his chalk throwing tendencies so I wasn't really worried. Come to think of it Mr Twigg was the only one I'd been worried about, and if he was the worst of the lot I wouldn't have much to worry about. Mr White wasn't scary at all and I was beginning to relax now.

My third lesson was French with Miss Heaton and I was back on the maths corridor, which was already beginning to bore me. French fascinated me from the first moment I started learning numbers from one to ten and how to say my name. There's just something about learning foreign languages that appeals to me. The way so many different races have learned to speak in so many different ways amazes me and French is such a beautiful and romantic language. Miss Heaton was a good teacher but I don't think it would have mattered who taught me languages because I was so interested by them that I would have worked hard, regardless of whether I liked the teacher or not.

I wasn't so cynical at the time, but the teachers were hardly likely to show their true colours on day one. This nicety, nicety approach was probably designed to lull us into a false sense of security before the years of slave driving that were to come.

The French lesson went by without a hitch and then it was already dinner time. The morning had gone well and I wolfed down my greasy, dangerously fattening school dinner of pizza and chips. I enjoyed my food in those days.

After eating, Dexter and I went outside for some fresh air and Dexter, unperturbed by the earlier accident, decided to push me around like a maniac with me feeling distinctly unsafe. There were hundreds of other kids in the school grounds but Dexter thought he was Michael Schumacher and that he had such control that he could avoid all the other kids. He proceeded to run round a blind corner without slowing down. Even Schumacher wouldn't do that and that was Dexter's mistake. Faster and faster he went and suddenly another innocent first-year appeared, running towards us and not particularly looking where he was going. The next two seconds before the inevitable seemed like two hours. Closer and closer we came, Dexter's eyes met the other lads eyes and smack! *Holy shit Batman*, I thought, as he fell in a crumpled heap on the floor, *not again*! At that point he was lying prostrate on the floor crying in pain and I was slumped forward, not feeling too crash hot myself. Unbelievable! Twice in one day and it was only dinner time. We found out later that we'd broken both of the other lad's legs. I felt a bit guilty at the time but now it's one of the stories Dexter and I laugh about when we reminisce about those secondary school days.

After I'd dusted myself down it was time for the fourth lesson, the penultimate lesson: science, on those amazingly over-elevated desks. In contrast to French I found that science was stiflingly boring from day one. It was the first lesson though, so I thought I'd give it a chance. Mr Dawber was the teacher and he was reasonable enough.

I don't mind telling you that Mr Lee the CDT teacher who taught me for the last lesson of the day *was* scary! I was a very timid and quiet first-year and Mr Lee was very strict. He took the opposite approach to the other teachers on the first day. He let us know through his actions that he wasn't going to tolerate any misbehaviour of any sort. Most of the class got into trouble and were shouted at during that first lesson. I'll give him one thing. At least he showed us his true personality straight away. There were no pretences and we knew what we could and couldn't do from the first moment we entered his classroom. The fear factor was definitely there and most of the class would fall silent when Mr Lee entered the room. There were however always some people who'd push him as far as they could, those who didn't worry about getting detentions. I was a good little boy and that's probably why I was scared.

As the bell went for the end of the final lesson I thought so far so good. My first day of lessons had gone okay and apart from nearly killing me and someone else, Dexter's pushing hadn't been too bad. The thing was though, that even when I was walking in an unstable way, I'd never fallen over twice in one day before. So much for the wheelchair being safer for me.

When I got home and was forced to go through the ritual of telling my Mum about every moment of my day, including the two dangerous driving incidents, I'm sure she was wondering if she'd made the right decision in campaigning to get me into a mainstream school. I could tell by the way her jaw dropped halfway through my stories that she was worried by what I had to say, but the fact that I was laughing probably assuaged her fears.

Two days gone and I felt very settled already. The only thing that remained to worry me was getting up and downstairs the next day.

The possibility of falling out of the wheelchair was always there for me, but it didn't play on my mind. It was only as likely that I'd fall out as it was that any other child would be pushed over in the corridor and trampled in the dinner time rush. I looked at it as if it was a replacement because I couldn't get trampled in the rush, but I could fall out of my wheelchair. It made me a more authentic pupil. Falling out of the wheelchair was probably preferable to being trampled anyway. When hundreds of kids want their dinner as quickly as possible you don't get in the way! It's like a herd of elephants coming at you. I was allowed to leave lessons five minutes early and was always the first to have my dinner, to the annoyance of some of the more eager kids.

The fear of falling out of the wheelchair whilst halfway up the stairs was a different proposition, which did play on my mind and the fear etched on my face on my first trip upstairs was testament to that fact.

It was like a military operation trying to get upstairs and Mr Brennan along with the Head of Special Needs, Miss Toole, was adamant that I had to get two teachers to help. Dexter wasn't allowed under any circumstances to help carry me upstairs. Of course we stuck to that order, for a while anyway, until we became more settled and rebellious.

Having survived the ordeal of my first ascent I had my first music lesson, followed by a keyboard applications lesson and then it was back downstairs for lunch. This second day went by uneventfully really. I managed to get through it without falling on the floor or nearly killing anyone, and that's how things went for about a month. I was having a whale of a time. The work was easy, I was getting on well with everyone in my form, Dexter was improving as a wheelchair pusher and the teachers were doing everything to help me. Perfect.

Then came the first setback. There was a trip to a place called Longsleddale organised for each form as a sort of 'get to know your form mates' exercise. Mr Altdorf and Dexter had offered to help if I had trouble getting dressed or with anything else. The accessibility was there and the fact that I could still stand up made it easier for me. I probably wouldn't need much help anyway. I was really excited about this trip but as being a Liverpool fan throughout the nineties has proved to me, if you get too excited about things you are liable to be disappointed. This situation followed that trend because around two days before we were due to go, as my Mum was doing my daily physio (this was before we realised that everything doctors have advised me to do has been an absolute waste of time and energy) I felt a snap and then the most excruciating pain I have ever experienced, apart from that muscle biopsy, consumed my Achilles tendon and I ended up in casualty. I was in a large amount of pain and unable to move my foot for about a week, which rendered my trip to Longsleddale an absolute impossibility. I never walked again after that day and I was very disappointed.

I think that incident knocked my confidence a great deal. Yes, I was in a wheelchair before I hurt myself but now I couldn't get out of it. At least before, I could console myself with the fact that I could still get out and help myself in certain ways, but now I felt trapped in a metal jail cell on wheels. I can now accept that being in a wheelchair isn't all that terrible but at that moment in time it felt like the end of the world. It's very rare these days that I look at the wheelchair and see it as a life sentence in a metal jail – I'm not that morbid!

So on their return from Longsleddale the whole form came

telling me what a great time they'd had and how one of the lads had jumped on a tractor and driven it around a field, without permission of course. I was thinking, *Great! I bet you had to be there. Shame I wasn't.*

When I'd recovered from that disappointment I had another month of the easy life. The only problem I had was with those annoying science desks. Being unable to stand up meant I had to sit at the huge desks, unable to see over the top of them and I also had to write with my hands above the top of my head. I'd already had a smaller desk made for cookery lessons so I could manipulate my arms better, but being stubborn I decided to carry on regardless in my science lessons. I wanted as little fuss as possible so I never mentioned the table to my science teacher Mr Dawber, who was always offering to bring a smaller table in. I know he was trying to help, as was every other person who offered assistance but I've always wanted to do things the normal, or in my case the difficult way, for as long as is humanly possible.

So I soldiered on like the little trooper that I am until there came an interruption in my routine. 1st November was the day I was due to go to America for the last time, for now anyway. I reacted in my usual way and panicked. I was very worried about missing two weeks work this early in my first year, so I went to see Mr Brennan to see if I could get some work to take on holiday with me. Now that's sad! I was convinced that I had to do well right from the start to get into the top sets and that if I fell behind now, I would never be able to catch up. Success was everything to me.

Mr Brennan didn't seem to think it was quite as cut and dried as that, in fact he looked slightly surprised at my request for homework. Looking back I can't believe I was so worried at such an early stage. I've definitely calmed down since.

I set off to America with thoughts of falling behind playing on my mind but once I arrived at Fort Myers Beach all thoughts of school were left on the plane. I would enjoy the holiday before returning to reality. Relaxing on the beach was now the priority. You've already had the low-down on my holidays so I'll just say it was a very relaxing couple of weeks, maybe too relaxing.

I'd only been away for two weeks but when I returned

everything seemed somehow different. I felt different and suddenly the reality of being in a wheelchair dawned on me. I was different to every other child in that school and that reality made me lose all perspective. I suddenly felt inadequate and worried that I'd always be looked upon as an outsider. Maybe I was realising the psychological effects of hurting my ankle and being permanently confined to a wheelchair, I don't know, but this feeling of inadequacy, added to my natural tendency to worry about my school work, equated to a total loss of emotional control. I'm reluctant to say it was a nervous breakdown but if I'm being honest, that's probably what it was.

Being in set one for everything was the only thing that would do in my quest for success, but having missed two weeks I felt I was behind in the race to achieve my goal. The thought that the teachers had probably already decided on the sets before I even went away, never even crossed my mind. They knew whether I was good enough or not and at this stage there was nothing I could do to change the sets I would be in. Hindsight's a great thing isn't it? If only I could have thought this clearly back then, I'd have been fine. The problem was that I'd totally lost confidence in my own abilities. The first time I really got upset about my work was during a history exam, just before we found out our sets. I was convinced that if I didn't do well in this exam I wouldn't get into set one and that, to me, would have been a disaster. We had to work out from sources who had committed a crime, and explain how we'd worked it out. The only thing that had to do with history was that the thought process used was similar to that used by historians to work out what happened in the past.

Unfortunately, it hadn't dawned on me that getting things exactly right in history isn't as important as the explanations of how you came to your opinion. I found that a difficult concept to get my head around because at that time I thought everything was black and white, right or wrong and that's why I enjoyed maths so much. Anyway, as the exam went on I became more and more flustered because I just couldn't work out the answer. I'd changed my mind several times, explaining my thoughts as I went along, and eventually I just guessed. There were tears in my eyes as I handed my paper in, and although I didn't know it at that particular time that exam was to be the starting point for one of my most difficult periods. Just the word 'exam' worried me. I'd begin to panic every time I was told I had an exam. 'Exam' just sounds bigger and more important than the tests I had at primary school. When a teacher said, 'test' I wasn't worried at all.

Nowadays, I can't understand why I did worry so much. The exams I did in the first year meant nothing in the greater scheme of things. They didn't count for anything when it came to my GCSEs or my A levels, and strangely enough I was much less worried about the important, maybe career deciding exams, than I was about the unimportant ones. Unfortunately in the first year I didn't have the benefit of such hindsight. I felt I had to be the best, as I had always been before, so each exam became a competition against everybody else and also against myself, and I was sure I wasn't good enough.

You'd think that when I found out that I was in set one for everything, I'd have realised that I was good enough. Not me. Like I said before, because I felt physically inadequate I also felt mentally inadequate. I couldn't cope with anything. Things began to bother me that hadn't bothered me for years, and I didn't want to go to school any more. I would also burst into tears at the slightest hint of an insult or disagreement. I just couldn't handle the everyday relationships with my friends. I was a mess.

I remember crying uncontrollably after taking a Geography exam, because I thought I'd failed. I begged the teacher to tell me my result early and when she did I'd got twenty-nine out of thirty. Why oh why was I worried? Then in a science lesson we did a practice for the science investigations, which wouldn't count for anything until the fourth year but of course I worried. I wouldn't find out the results of this mini investigation until the next Tuesday but the day after I handed it in I panicked and was crying in assembly. Mr Altdorf, who would prove to be one of the main reasons for my recovery from this difficult time, came to the rescue. He tried to calm me down by explaining that it wasn't the most important thing in the world. To me though, it *was* the most important thing. So having failed in his first attempt at psychology he went to see my science teacher, who explained – what I've just explained, that at this stage he didn't expect us to do well. He was just making sure that when we did come to do the real investigations, we would have some experience of how to structure them.

Yet again, then, I had no reason to worry, but that didn't stop it happening again and again.

When I say I was worried I think I should explain what it means, for those who may not have experienced it. I wasn't worried, as in nervous before an exam and nervous whilst waiting for the results, experiencing doubts as to my performance, I was worried sick literally. I'd throw up just to avoid going to school, and when I did go to school I'd cry uncontrollably, but it wasn't just about school work that I cried, it was about anything. I remember a number of my crying fits, one of which was at the end of a German lesson with Mr Griffiths. I just started crying and I genuinely didn't know why. Mr Griffiths asked me if it was because I'd seen people playing football at break, and I suppose it could have been that, but really it could have been anything that triggered it off. Changing school and going into a wheelchair had been a period of transition. I believed I was ready for it and could cope, but I couldn't. I was worried and depressed, and my crying fits didn't stop there.

One day on my way to school, having failed in an attempt to avoid school by throwing up again, I cried to my Mum and begged her not to make me go in. I couldn't stop crying but she pushed me to the door of the form room. I'm sure it broke her heart to see me in such a state, as I pleaded one last time, 'Please don't make me go in Mum, please.'

She went into the room and brought Mr Altdorf out to reason with me and make me feel better. I can't remember what he said but I do remember feeling better. I felt I could face the world again, for the rest of that day anyway. This must have been a difficult situation for both my Mum and Mr Altdorf. She must have wondered if she'd made a mistake by getting me into a normal school and he was a young man, with his first ever form and he had a basket case in a wheelchair on his hands! Unlucky sir! I'll be eternally grateful to both of them. I couldn't have got through that time without them, although I did hate my Mum on that day! When Mr Altdorf has a problem that he's struggling to deal with, he should remember that if he could cope with my nervous breakdown, he could cope with anything!

It seems like the only thing I can remember from Christmas onwards in the first year is being upset, but I did also have time to fancy another girl.

Isla was in my form and I fancied her like mad from the moment I met her. I thought she was lovely! Of course she fancied all the 'hard' lads and I had no chance, even though I was better looking, nicer and more intelligent than all of them, if a little fatter and in a wheelchair. What more could a girl want? Obviously more than that.

I didn't really want to tell anyone about it but I did tell Dexter. Big mistake. The devious little bugger told Isla and everybody else about my little crush and in my fragile state you can guess the rest. In case you can't guess, I'll tell you anyway. A couple of girls decided to take the mickey out of me in the usual secondary school way, by writing DAVID 4 ISLA on the blackboard and generally having a laugh. These days I'd take it all in good humour and laugh with them, but back then it wasn't advisable to laugh at me. I don't know whether it was what they wrote or said, or if it was just the fact that I couldn't get out of the wheelchair to stop them writing it, that upset me the most but I remember starting to cry again and not being able to stop. I explained what had happened to my RE teacher who was very sympathetic and told the girls off. I'm sure she thought I was being pathetic because I think I was being pathetic. No wonder Isla didn't fancy me!

I know the girls thought I was being pathetic because one of them brought up this incident in an argument three years later, and she said that it happened in the second year. It definitely happened in the first year, I know it did.

There were so many things that changed in the first year, not just at school either. At home, now I was in a wheelchair permanently, we had to have an extension built. We were having a bedroom and a bathroom built to take the strain off my Mum a bit, and of course it was going to be ready by the time we returned from America. Like that was going to happen! How did this add to my depression? Well, it was a further upheaval, a further change. Everything was changing too quickly, it was changing much quicker than I was growing up and I just couldn't handle it. I was in a daze. Everywhere I looked there was a change. It was like *The Wonder Years* in turbo and I couldn't keep up. On top of this I couldn't get to my cart and go for a ride, to escape from the hurricane of change which was sweeping my home, school and emotional life. I had no escape, and added to this my football team was crap and of course there were the two hospital visits which took place every six months and never failed to depress me. For years though, before I started secondary school, they didn't tell me anything bad. They would always have private discussions with my Mum about the next thing that would deteriorate on her doomed son. However, they would lie to me about what was going on.

'You're doing really well,' they'd say, but they'd be thinking, 'it's only a matter of time.'

I only found out recently that the questions the doctors and professors asked me with annoying regularity were a screen so they could find out if my symptoms were worsening without upsetting me. For example, 'How are you sleeping?' And, 'Have you had any headaches or dizzy spells?' were to find out if my breathing muscles were deteriorating, and to monitor whether I'd need a ventilator sooner rather than later.

Before the first year I went to the hospital happy, and came out slightly less happy. I just didn't want to go really. In the first year though I went into the hospital depressed and came out worse. I started to see a professor in the first year who knows who he is but shall remain nameless, who was probably very good at his job. I never questioned that but it was his tact and bedside manner that left a lot to be desired. I don't think he learnt that at university! The problem was that this professor, and this criticism by no means applies solely to him, saw each patient as a disease or a disability and not as a person or an individual. He wanted to dictate to parents and children alike what they needed and when they needed it, without explaining why. The language used was 'you need this and you must use it every day or you will have this problem', so the patient feels he or she has no option but to use it, and if you decide against it you do so at your peril. They really were doctor's orders.

The disadvantage to this approach in relation to a disability such as muscular dystrophy is that the disability effects each individual in a slightly different way. Approaching it in a uniform way across each separate case is dangerous and adds to the risk of mistakes occurring. When I say MD affects each individual slightly differently I should give you some examples: more than half of MD sufferers have learning difficulties, some are incontinent, others end up in a wheelchair much earlier than I did. Some people's spine and limbs become very twisted, and when that happens their breathing becomes difficult very quickly. I'm one of the lucky ones in all of the above respects and I've ignored everything that the doctors have told me. In many ways it's my Mum's ability to see that there are options beyond what the doctors say which has helped me very much. My whole family has always been tremendously supportive and has wanted what's best for me even if that means not being co-operative with the 'experts'. I want other families to know that there is always an option beyond the medical recommendations.

Dealing with disabilities should be a teamwork exercise, the parents working with the doctors to decide what is best for the child, not an exercise in dictatorship. The attitude of many doctors that they know better than their patients is outdated and not necessarily true. They know what the symptoms are and their medical implications, and they also know what treatments exist to delay the effects of these symptoms. What they don't know is how these treatments may affect each case, or how quickly a person will deteriorate, because with the best will in the world operations do go wrong and doctors certainly aren't psychic.

Doctors don't have the experience of actually having a disability, and only by listening to the opinions and the experiences of disabled people can doctors learn more. I believe that a doctor who doesn't listen to these experiences isn't a good doctor, and cannot do the best for his or her patients. Sometimes doctors just see the disability and offer these... 'aids' is the best word. They don't think that there's a life beyond disability and that maybe having a life is more important. I know I'm going to get weaker, I've always known that, but I want to have as enjoyable a life as possible without these aids or any unnecessary interference. Necessary help, such as to help breathing, where it's a matter of life and death is always welcome.

What I'm trying to say is the doctor's role in the treatment of a disability like MD should be descriptive rather than prescriptive i.e. the doctor should say what the symptoms are and what treatments are available, along with their possible benefits and side effects. If the patient has a problem which renders them incapable of making a rational decision about whether to use the treatment, then it should be up to the parents, considering medical advice to make that decision in the best interests of the child.

In the first year, I was bombarded with aids to 'help' me and the professor told me I needed them in his tactless way. 'If your spine bends to fifteen degrees, which it has, then you'll need this corset to keep you straight, because if it gets to thirty degrees then you'll need an operation.' You're right. I burst into tears again! The way he said it was so matter of fact, and at that time I couldn't handle hearing anything I didn't want to hear.

I already had night splints and was being offered day splints, to keep my ankles at ninety degrees all the time, because 'if my ankles became too twisted I'd need an operation', so that I could stand for two hours a day in my newly acquired standing frame. Oh yeah, the standing frame was essential because if I didn't stand in it 'my breathing would deteriorate more quickly and I'd need a ventilator sooner'.

Nowadays I'd say, 'Hang on a minute you insensitive pillock!' I mean really, if you're going to work with children then this way of explaining things is not acceptable, and anyone who thinks it is, is a fool. This professor allegedly said to one family in front of their severely twisted son, 'This child is a mess.' Bedside manner? What bedside manner?

You know what? I'd like to make the so-called experts stand in a standing frame for two hours a day and see how it disrupts their lives. Picture this, a day in the life of a person, with a similar lifestyle to my own but who naively follows doctor's orders and wears day splints, night splints and a corset, and who also stands in a standing frame for two hours a day.

7 a.m.	Get up, put your day splints on. Your ankles are now stuck at ninety degrees. You can't take them off yourself so you're trapped.
8 a.m.	After breakfast put your corset on. You are now in an upright position. You can't take it off yourself so your back is trapped all day. Go to school, which is a big enough ordeal anyway!
11 a.m.	You're preoccupied by discomfort. Your feet are sweating, tendons aching and you're feeling distinctly pissed off.
12 p.m.	Dinner time. You look miserable, your feet are aching even more and your back has joined in, adding to your discomfort. You've still got three hours of school to go.
1 p.m.	You're in your first lesson of the afternoon. Can you concentrate? Can you hell! You're too busy thinking about getting home and being able to move your back. Think how many times you move your feet and bend your back during the day. Now sit bolt upright with your ankles at ninety degrees, and don't move. Ten minutes will give you an idea of what it would be like.
3.15 p.m.	Finally the bell's gone, but you're not relieved because you're so frustrated by your sore back and aching ankles. It's like having an itch that you can't reach, but it goes down your whole back, all day.
3.30 p.m.	Arrive at home and have a cup of tea whilst deciding what to do first. It's a tough choice, homework or two hours in a standing frame. Well, whoopee!
4 p.m.	Having decided to do your homework first and begged your Mum to take your aids off you set to work. Now that's amazing! The only relief you get from discomfort is while doing your homework.

It's usually an inconvenience. The problem is you've not been concentrating at school because you were aching, so you can't do your homework anyway.

5 p.m.   It's teatime! Watch *Neighbours* and *Home and Away* whilst eating. For the love of God, *Neighbours* and *Home and Away* should never be taken off air! It's the only relief you get from reality!

6 p.m.   Now you've got something to look forward to. Two hours in a standing frame! It's like a medieval form of torture. Straps on your knees to keep your legs at one hundred and eighty degrees. A strap over your chest to hold you in a straight position and straps over your feet to keep them at ninety degrees. You look like a statue and you can't do anything, apart from go numb all over your body. You also can't do anything to alleviate this numbness. Your legs, which don't go straight, are forced into a straight position. Pretty uncomfortable, I can tell you that.

If you speak to the highly experienced experts, who of course have never stood in a standing frame, you can do things. You can play on your computer and you can even do your homework whilst standing. How exciting. It's great in theory but have you ever tried to write while standing bolt upright? It's not all that easy and I'm sure the experts have never tried it. Also, have you ever tried concentrating on homework or anything else for that matter while your legs are totally numb and consumed by pins and needles? I don't think that's easy either.

8 p.m.   Put your corset and day splints back on. Now you've got two hours left to see your friends, before you have to be in the house. I'll tell you what, it's a good thing disabled people don't have any friends or they wouldn't be able to spend

much time with them! (That's sarcasm if you can't tell.)

10 p.m.   You now get two minutes' relief while you take the corset off and swap day splints for night splints. Again your feet are at ninety degrees all night. The night splints have a sheepskin lining for 'added comfort'. Ha! That's a laugh! I had some of the worst nights' sleep I've ever had wearing those sweaty, ache inducing pieces of heavy plastic. I couldn't move my legs.

So there you go. Now, I was a naughty little boy, I wore the corset a few times and it was very uncomfortable and restrictive. I also couldn't ride my cart in it! I wore the night splints for years. Well, I wore them until my feet started to hurt (about ten minutes after I put them on) but luckily I had enough strength to flick one of the straps open and to release my ankle from its woolly prison. You can't imagine the relief when your foot is free!

I used the standing frame a number of times and didn't enjoy it. Eventually I threw a tantrum and refused to go in it ever again. Childish, I know, but I couldn't get my feelings across without crying. Why did I refuse all these 'aids'? Well, none of my friends had to wear them and I wanted to be as normal as possible, so I thought, *Why should I have to wear them*? I also couldn't see the benefit of having straight knees and ankles, when I knew I'd never use them. People also couldn't resist unclipping the frame from its base and flipping me forwards and backwards, just to worry the poor disabled boy. Evil sods! That's why I chose not to be inconvenienced by these things.

I'd never dream of criticising any parent who makes their child wear this 'uniform' because it's very easy to follow doctors' advice and to accept it as gospel. Not using them, however, hasn't made my back any more twisted than it would have been, and I'm sure my ankles would still be twisted if I had used the equipment.

My Mum mithering me to sit up has really helped as well, despite how much it used to annoy me. Cheers Mum, you've done it again. I've seen people with my disability, who are much more twisted than I am and they have used the equipment.

I was lucky because my family cared about me having a normal life as much as I did, and they didn't think I should have to wear what I didn't feel I should wear. The amount of annoyance I got from being constantly told to sit up was nothing compared to the discomfort I suffered when I did wear them, and in my case it was just as effective, if not more. So there is an alternative.

How was I expected to wear the things the doctors told me to wear, anyway, after some of the things that happened?

Firstly, the most incompetent splint maker in splint making history, the wooden spoon winning splint smith, whose name escapes me, was assigned to make my day and night splints plus my callipers. Making night splints was a simple case of fashioning a plaster cast of my ankles at ninety degrees and then cutting the dried plaster off my legs with a pair of industrial strength scissors. Well, the David James (a goalkeeper who makes a lot of mistakes) of splint making managed to make the plaster cast all right, I'll give him that, but when it came to cutting it off he struggled with the scissors. Then he decided he'd slice it off with a Stanley knife. The trouble is, he took two layers of my skin off with it, and hardly batted an eyelid, let alone apologised, when he left me bleeding and very annoyed. The splints came out all right in the end, admittedly.

The science of calliper making totally eluded 'Mr James', which I realised to my horror as he put two pieces of paper for each a leg on the table. He then placed me on top of the paper and proceeded to draw round my legs with a pencil. How can anyone possibly get accurate leg measurements from such primary school methods?

Obviously the callipers were as wobbly and inappropriate as his drawings. It took two years and three different sets of callipers, and still they didn't fit. By then it was too late for me to use callipers with any success. I couldn't walk for God's sake! Maybe it was a blessing in disguise because I don't think callipers are helpful in a progressively deteriorating disability. I suppose they keep your legs straight for slightly longer but once you can't walk, you can't use callipers if like me your muscles are too weak to hold you up. When you get to the stage as an MD sufferer where you need callipers, getting into a wheelchair is the most relieving thing in the world. I can say that in retrospect, although as you've already seen I didn't feel that way when I did actually go into the wheelchair.

If my faith in the equipment I was offered was dulled by those incidents, then the next thing that happened totally destroyed it. I went to see the aforementioned professor, the anti-Florence Nightingale, and after my back X-ray and a three-hour wait for a 9.25 appointment, with the overworked professor, I walked into his room, bleary-eyed. He watched my Mum put me on the bed and then carried out his usual limb-stretching routine. I was now prepared for his matter-of-fact manner and ready for anything he could throw at me. 'You need an urgent operation to lengthen the tendons in your knees, hips and ankles. You'll be in plaster for eight weeks, from the hips down.'

Okay, so I wasn't ready for anything he could throw at me but I was determined not to cry this time. I don't know why but I thought he got some kind of perverse pleasure out of seeing me cry. I now know that wasn't the case. He didn't want to make me cry, he just struggled to explain things in a sensitive manner. Anyway, this urgent operation never materialised. In fact I'm still waiting, six years later. I've never even had an appointment from the professor, since that day. Oh well, I'll cope.

I'd decided not to go ahead with it anyway, but you'd probably already worked that out. Again, I didn't think that the benefits of the operation would outweigh the discomfort I would suffer before and after it. Eight weeks of plaster, and not being able to move or sit up for that amount of time didn't really appeal to me. Why did I need this operation? Wait for it. It was so I could carry out my favourite pastime. Yes the joy of two hours in a standing frame! And so the circle is complete! One doctor's order helps you to carry out another and you're just the innocent, naive victim, the guinea pig to scientific progress. You may think I'm being ungrateful because people spend their lives making products to help me. I'm not. All I'm saying is the choice should be there for people to turn down the help, or to be a part of the design process so that these products are as comfortable as possible.

Patients and their families should not have to be rebellious or feel like a 'naughty little boy' as I put it earlier. Guilt shouldn't be a part of the doctor-patient relationship, but it's exactly what I've felt on many occasions, and that's why I have a strong resentment for Professor 'Nightingale'. 'Mr James' the splint maker shows how good intentions can be undermined at any stage from the doctor's room to the production line.

The first year disappeared in a whirlwind of upheaval and upset. I worried so many times, that if I only cried once in a day I felt like it was a good day. Mr Altdorf was always there to help me and make me feel better. There were days when Mum would come to the end of her tether and shout at me to snap me out of my depression, and other days when she'd be totally understanding and sympathetic. Science lessons continued to bore me, I was still terrible at art, and Dexter threw me out of the wheelchair a couple more times. All in all it was quite an eventful year.

Chapter V

I don't know what made me recover from my depression of the first year. It may have been my Mum's threat to send me to Woodside, a special school. No, don't get me wrong, I have nothing against special schools in the necessary cases i.e. where a child cannot in his or her best interests be part of a mainstream school. The time has passed however where everybody in a wheelchair automatically went to a special school and that's something from which I've benefited. For a person like me who academically and socially can at least hold his own amongst able-bodied people who are willing to help when necessary, then mainstream schools are a feasible option and indeed are the only acceptable option.

A disabled person doesn't have to be capable of getting A's in their exams to be allowed to go to a normal school, because let's face it, there's a broad spectrum of intelligence across able-bodied pupils. Many disabled children are as able, if not more able than normal pupils and even people with learning difficulties such as dyslexia amongst others can succeed if they are given the correct support. I started uni with a girl called Clare who was dyslexic, and she got three A's and two B's in her A levels, and there were dyslexic people at Sharples who would have missed out on a normal life had they not been given the opportunity to go to a normal school. There are also many deaf and blind people who go to normal schools, and that's how it should be. As long as there's the technology, the facilities, the personnel to help, and of course the inclination and willingness on the part of the disabled person, then normal schools should find places for disabled people.

I welcome the schemes brought in by the government which are designed to get disabled people into the workplace. It shows that integration is slowly happening. Ha ha ha! We're going to rule the world and there's nothing anyone can do about it!

I just hope that good intentions don't go too far and that

special schools aren't removed as an option, because not all disabled people can, or even want to be in a mainstream school. It's a common misperception that all disabled people want the same thing, and that's not always the case.

For me though, a special school would have been my worst nightmare. I would have gone mad. Thank God for the two Sharples schools, they saved my life!

Another factor in my depression recovery was probably my first-year report which read A, A, A, A, A... I think you get the picture. The grades aren't that important looking back, but the report provided proof that all my worrying had been pointless and totally unfounded. I was good enough! It's easy for me to say now, but even if I hadn't been good enough to get A's which were the only grades I'd accept, doing my best and proving my value as a disabled person in the able-bodied system should have been the objective. I was a crusader for disabled rights but really I just wanted to do well. The report was a welcome boost. I'd proven myself to the teachers and more importantly to myself. So now we could all get on with our lives, which was good.

The second year was never going to be as eventful or emotional as the first, but I don't think any year will be. I suppose that's a good thing really because the first year was only eventful because I was miserable most of the time. Let's see, the second year was when my brother started at Sharples, and in many ways that fact alone helped me stay in control of my emotions. It wasn't because of anything he actually said or did. It was more of a pride thing, in that I didn't want my brother to see me upset. If I ever felt like crying I'd say to myself, *Don't get upset, you don't want Dan to see you upset.* And it worked. I did still feel upset quite often but not every day like before. I learned to hide it by not being sick and by biting my lip when I wanted to cry. I began to enjoy school again, like I had at first. Of course when exams came around I still worried, but it wasn't the gut-wrenching, mind-blowing worry of the previous year. It was more the butterflies that I mentioned before and still suffer from now at exam time, even when I'm not taking any. I feel that that kind of nerves, rather than worry, is natural and almost healthy. It gets the adrenalin going when you get into the exam. At least this year I wasn't begging my teachers to give me my results early, and that was an indication that I wasn't quite as worried any more.

All the upheaval seemed to have died down. The extension was finished and I now had my own room for the first time ever. I didn't have to share with that freak any more! It wasn't that bad really. I wasn't given anything new by the mad professor and both Dexter and I were now used to the wheelchair. Our stair-climbing technique had evolved.

The stair climbing had to evolve when I couldn't get out of the wheelchair under my own steam. Once we were settled down at school, we began to feel more rebellious. No, I'll rephrase that. I was never rebellious, I left that up to Paul and company, but I began to feel less constrained by the orders of the teachers, especially the one about going upstairs. I know it was for my own safety that I was told to have a teacher supervising at all times but I think we felt it was an inconvenience, as if the teachers were watching our every move. We wanted to be left to our own devices and that's how our current technique, or Dexter's current technique came into being. When I couldn't get up the three steps to the computer room, Dexter had to think of a way to get up them. We tried going forwards which was never going to work, and then he realised that if we went backwards and lifted the front wheels up then he could get me up the steps without killing me! After we'd succeeded with that technique Dexter got a bit more ambitious and thought he could drag me up two flights of stairs. I mean from three steps to twenty was the obvious progression! It couldn't have been five, then seven, just to make me feel better. No it had to be twenty.

To be honest, he did get a teacher to stand at the front in case he dropped me, so I wasn't too worried, and it turned out that the dragging technique would work. In fact the only time I nearly fell downstairs after that was either when someone grabbed the wheelchair when we told them not to, or when Dexter wasn't in my lesson and someone else had to take me up or downstairs.

Once we got more confident going upstairs, we started to go up without supervision despite the teachers' adamance. I don't know what would have happened if I'd ended up at the bottom of the stairs with my head facing the wrong way, but thankfully it never happened.

The most adamant teacher had to be Mrs Fernside the keyboard applications teacher. She'd always catch us at the top of the stairs ready to go down, and she'd say, 'You'd better not be going downstairs on your own.' To which we'd reply, 'No, Miss. Would we do that?' As soon as she went round the corner we'd be on our way down. It's all part of the teacher-pupil relationship; it's got to be done!

I'll always be thankful to Dex for that, he put his back on the line for me and he didn't have to. He probably wanted me to be as independent as I wanted to be and I think he was forced to make sacrifices because of it. (When I said Dexter was used to the wheelchair I mean *only* Dexter was used to it.)

In the first year when I was totally self absorbed, I'd remained friends with Dexter, Nicola, Emma and Heather, who I'd been mates with at primary school but I hadn't given myself much of a chance to get to know anyone new. Jason, Matthew (Taylor), Chris (Laidlaw) and Steven (Pryce) were people I got to know. I became friends with other people in my classes, such as Suzannah, Pam, Amber, Brett, Paul Whitley and a number of others. I became close to Leigh and Isla and David Cass was also a good mate.

The problem with being in a wheelchair and having all these people who were willing to help is that some people get carried away or try to scare me, or just simply believe they can do it as well as Dexter without any practice. They'd seen Dex doing his stunts and wheelies and thought they could do it, usually with hilarious results.

Most people were part of the first two categories and Nichola was probably the worst culprit. She decided to play a game called crash dummies. I was the 'Dummy' and the object of the game was to push me from the back of the classroom as hard as she could, into the blackboard at the other end of the room. It was like torture as I flew across the room, unable to stop, and crashed into the board. The game ended with a large chalk mark on my head and a forehead-sized mark on the blackboard. I was a poor exploited wheelchair boy. I had no friends, so I had to let people ram me into a blackboard in a desperate attempt to gain popularity. Another time Nicola kindly offered to push me for a bit. There must have been a full moon out the night before or something, because she pushed me like a maniac and I ended up in the recovery position. So you can understand why I was reluctant to let anyone other than Dexter push me. Dexter's the only maniac I can't trust not to throw me out of the wheelchair, when he skids around a corner. I'm also helpless to stop him.

That school was a nightmare! I wonder how I ever survived it! Putting my coat on at break and dinner time was another ordeal. I remember Isla trying to put it on and almost breaking both my arms! I wouldn't complain though: Firstly, because it was Isla who was helping me and secondly, because if I didn't have people to put my coat on I'd have frozen. Also if I'd moaned all the time, maybe people wouldn't have wanted to help me at all. It would have been even harder to get through secondary school without their help. A sore forehead and aching arms was well worth it.

I was definitely happier in the second year and in fact I can only remember crying once, maybe twice. In PE lessons I used to do swimming because it was the only thing I could do, and I wanted to be part of it. I didn't mind watching football and the dance lessons were hilarious. I'm glad I couldn't take part in that. Anyway, the swimming lessons. Mr Altdorf had offered, yet again, to help me get changed so I could go swimming. That is, after I'd been convinced by the swimming instructor, Jan Eastham, that it would be a good idea. At the risk of sounding a bit teacher's pettish, good kids and disabled kids couldn't hope for a better form teacher than Mr Altdorf. He had his fair share of criticism, mainly from the uncooperative kids and their parents who didn't like the way he treated their children. They were parents of the 'my kids wouldn't do that' mentality. If they'd taken off their rose-coloured spectacles and took their head out of the sand, then they might have realised that their kids *would* do that.

For me though, and for anyone, even the cheeky kids, Mr Altdorf was always there. He'd do anything for any of his pupils. Anybody who offers to help me get changed for swimming must be either mad – or very helpful.

Anyway, why did I cry? Well I'd told Dexter to leave me in the changing rooms and then I waited for ten minutes. No one had arrived to swim, or to get me changed. Twenty minutes, and still no one came, and I realised that swimming had been cancelled. I panicked. How the hell was I going to get out of this one? I sat there worrying for another ten minutes. Someone had to come, surely. They didn't, and I thought I was going to be trapped there all night.

What if no one comes, I thought, *someone might lock the door. I've got to get out of here.*

And with that I pushed myself towards the door. 'Bloody hell, it's a pull door. I'll never get out of here.'

I then frantically reached for the door, trying to pull it open with all my strength. I couldn't do it the first time. But by now I'd lost my grip on reality. 'I can do this, I know I can,' I was telling myself while I dragged my arm up by my hair and flung it at the door handle. I missed again and I was really getting flustered. I must have thrown my arm at the door and missed ten times before I gave up, and there were still ten minutes of the lesson left. I was shattered, even more tired than swimming made me, and it had been much less fun. I sat there hoping that someone would arrive soon. Dexter would remember I was there if I wasn't in the form room when he got back, wouldn't he? No one else was going to come in the near future. So I had to sit back, red-faced and worried, until I was rescued.

Sure enough and almost on cue Dexter arrived with Mr Altdorf to free me from the changing room trap. When I came out, the relief was so great that I burst into tears. Thankfully, no one who didn't know I was a wimp came past. You've got to understand how it feels when you're in a room, on your lonesome for an hour and you're in no position to get out of there all night if no one comes. It's not a good feeling. All right, so I shouldn't have cried but that was just me.

There were some good memories, though from swimming. I managed to swim fifty metres (two lengths) on my back. Quite an achievement considering that I was now much weaker than when I got my twenty-five metres. It took all the strength I could muster but I made it. I could hardly walk when I got out!

I'd now pushed myself as far as I could go but I was very satisfied. Fifty metres was hardly a world record but it was the best I could possibly do. I'd pushed myself to the limit and beyond, and at that moment I felt proud of myself. I still feel proud of that achievement. I've never shirked a challenge and I think that day was one of my defining moments.

It was a great day and what I imagined was happening when I ran round the Leverhulme Park track actually happened. With every kick of my legs everyone was cheering me on and that spurred me on. I may not have managed it without them. Swimming fifty metres isn't exactly Michael Owen playing football in front of 45,000 fans every week but it's the nearest I'll get to it. I'm sure it felt the same though.

This just shows that I was getting back to normal. The determination, control over my own destiny and to some extent the confidence in myself that was lacking in the first year was returning. This was the real David Withnell and I quite liked it.

The other time I cried this year was because of Dexter's psychotic tendencies pushing my wheelchair. He was practising skidding at dinner time in the staff dining room and he got a bit carried away again. I hit the floor one more time. This time, unlike the previous, painless times I landed knee first and I don't mind telling you that landing on a tiled floor, knee first, after falling out of a wheelchair is quite painful. I got a shooting pain through my kneecap and I lay on the floor, crying from shock and pain. Dexter had to go and get a teacher to get the jibbering wreck (me) off the floor. Yet again it was Dexter who hurt me. Whose idea was it to let this maniac push me around?

It probably seems like Dexter throws me out of the wheelchair much more often than anybody else, but that's only because he pushed me around every day and nobody else had a chance to injure me. If you push a wheelchair around for that amount of time then mistakes are bound to happen. It's like even the best doctors, footballers and managers make mistakes. Nobody can be perfect even when it comes to things that come naturally, such as walking. People fall over and trip up every day, so even when pushing the wheelchair became second nature to Dexter, he was bound to make mistakes.

One day when we came rushing out of a cookery lesson, Dexter tripped over approaching a curb. He was sprawling on the floor and I was sent hurtling towards the curb with no one attending to the wheelchair. My face must have been a picture of fear as I screamed, 'Wheelie, wheelie, pull a wheelie!'

When no wheelie came I just shut my eyes and waited for that familiar feel of concrete to hit my face, but when I opened them again I'd stopped. Luckily I'd been travelling fast enough to defy the laws of physics, and Dexter had reached me before I hit the opposite curb and went flying to the floor. A close call!

These incidents all added to my integration and acceptance as equal and 'normal'. Everyone had bad, good and indifferent memories of school and the retelling of these stories when Dexter and I reminisce never fails to raise a laugh.

The actual work in the second year was much the same as the first year but I wasn't worried. I think I'd realised that all the little tests that we were given didn't really mean much. They weren't important and as long as I did my best, I had nothing to worry about, so I didn't worry, not until the end of the year anyway. I began to find out which subjects I was good at which, being modest, were most of them, and more importantly which ones I enjoyed. That may sound sad, but anyone who says they didn't enjoy any subjects at school is either liar or one of a very small group who actually didn't enjoy anything. The main subjects I enjoyed were maths, history, French and German. Science never improved after the first lesson of the first year. I hated geography. English never appealed to me even though I was good at it. There's too much reading involved! As for RE, don't get me started on RE. I'm the least religious person in the world, so learning about it was a complete turn off.

I'm not a complete atheist, I believe there is something more powerful than humans but I fail to understand His or Her methods. This scepticism is probably brought on by my situation. If some higher power puts humans on to the earth and says, 'Okay, get on with it,' the least he could do is create us all equal. There are so many diseases with which people are born and the question I ask is why? I only think about this subject when I'm having a depressed day, which isn't often, but it's an interesting thought. If 'God' does tell us to get on with it and gives us a free run of his planet, then diseases caused by humans along with disasters such as massacres are down to the imperfections in human nature and not down to God. Even if someone inherits a genetic disease brought on by nuclear radiation from power plants, or by a mistake made in the testing of a new drug, then as terrible as these diseases are, they are a product of advanced society. Pushing science further brings its risks and everyone accepts that. The problems resulting from progress cannot be blamed on a higher power. Having said that, I fail to understand how disabilities like mine and many others come into being, and why this higher power doesn't intervene to ensure that everyone has the same starting point.

My life, however, hasn't been ruined by my disability, it's just different to how it would have been if I could walk, and there's nothing to say I'd be happier if I wasn't disabled. I'm not in pain and my quality of life, although I can't play football or get out of bed myself, hasn't been greatly diminished. You may not believe that because it's difficult for most able-bodied people to grasp how people cope, being unable to do the most natural things that they themselves take for granted. The easiest way for me to explain it is using a quote from a court case where the judge said, 'Disabled people can find a quality of life unimaginable to able-bodied people.'

If you don't know what something is like, i.e. walking, then eventually you don't really miss it. I accept that if you're surrounded by people doing everything that you can't do, you're sometimes going to get upset or depressed by it. I just get on with doing what I can do, although whenever I weaken and realise there's something new that I can't do, as you've already seen, I do get upset and a bit miserable for a while. People are very understanding, even though they can't totally understand what it's like.

I think I'll go back to RE now and it wasn't just the actual idea of studying religion that bothered me, it was also the fact that the teacher, Miss Webster, and I never exactly saw eye to eye if you believe that. It was funny really, but I didn't really see it like that at the time. I did my work, never failed to get 80% in my exams, and still she didn't like me. I couldn't understand it. In the end it was just that we didn't understand each other. To be honest though, in the second year I just got the feeling that she didn't like me. I think it was my sense of humour she didn't appreciate and I certainly didn't appreciate hers. She was the only teacher who didn't like me, and she scared me. RE was never going to be one of my year nine options choices. Little did I know I'd never get rid of RE that easily.

The second year was when I first started to get to know Mukhtar, Matthew and Jason who were in all of my sets. Jason got what he didn't bargain for when he met me. I'm sure he didn't start school thinking he was going to end up pushing someone around in a wheelchair, but that's what happened. Matthew and Mukhtar were my main rivals when it came to schoolwork and I was determined to beat them. I think they felt the same way I did, and it was like a war, but a very friendly one. We always got very similar marks in everything but our best subjects were all different, mine being French. Mukhtar was a scientist, and Matthew was into history and maths. We spurred each other on to do as well as we could and maybe we wouldn't have done as well if we didn't have this friendly competition. It was good fun, once I'd stopped worrying because I could then take Mukhtar and Matthew laughing at me as easily as I could laugh at them – when I won one of our battles!

Jason wasn't part of this friendly rivalry. He was simply a mate, and a very good one. It was a weird situation because we never really said anything. We introduced ourselves outside an RE lesson and basically that was it. We ended up sitting together in most of our lessons because we were in the same sets, and he just started pushing me between lessons when Dexter had lessons in another room.

I had been very nervous about how I'd manage when I found out that Dexter would be in a different set for a few subjects. I also thought it was a bit unfair because he was good enough to be in the top sets according to his class work, it was just that he panicked in exams. Some of the dunces in set one, no offence, were much less set one material than Dexter. He ended up in set three for science purely on his exam result, something he was very upset about and which I didn't agree with. As a first-year though and a particularly nervous one, I was hardly going to go to the teachers and protest and nor was he. It wouldn't have done any good anyway so I was left to search for a new pusher. No, really I was just looking to meet new friends and if they were willing to help me out in any small way I would be very grateful. I know I still had some friends from primary school in my sets, but I didn't feel right asking them to help me all the time in case they felt they had to do it. I'm sure they wouldn't have felt like that and they would have been only too happy to help. I think they all liked me and enjoyed being my friends. I don't think helping me get a book out of my bag or pushing me into my classroom bothered them too much. Eventually, it just turned into a reflex action and I didn't even have to ask for their help.

Dexter and Jason soon got into a routine with the wheelchair pushing, Dexter still doing the lion's share. Unfortunately, they didn't get on with each other as well as they got on with me, but they managed to cope even though the urge to strangle each other grew stronger with every passing day. At first Dexter would take me to my first lesson and then Jason would leave me at the end of a corridor for Dexter to pick me up and take me to the next lesson. That continued for a while until I decided this was tedious, and that I might as well let Jason take me to my next lesson. If I were to go upstairs, I'd let Jason leave me at the bottom for Dexter to take me up. Dexter was the only one who I felt safe enough to allow to do this heart-stopping job at first.

When Dexter and I had one of our stupid rows about crisp flavours or whether I'd let him sit in my wheelchair or not, then Jason would take over for a bit, because Dexter and I were so stubborn we wouldn't talk for the rest of the day. You know that I hated to admit I was wrong. Well Dexter was just as bad. It's just that I had more problems than he did when we weren't talking.

I couldn't take losing an argument so I'd say things that I knew were wrong, and adamantly insist that they were right. Like when Dexter wanted to swap crisps at lunchtime. He got really annoyed when I said no over and over again, until I resorted to saying, 'All crisp flavours are the same anyway,' which caused a huge row consisting of 'No they're not!'

'Yes they are!'

'No they're f***ing not!'

'Yes they f★★★ing are!'

'F★★k off!'

'No you f★★k off!'

Then we ate our own crisps, looking at opposite walls, red-faced, and very annoyed. Dexter shoved me to my next room and stormed off and we didn't speak to each other until the end of the day.

What about that for a pathetic row? There were hundreds of more such rows, each one as pathetic as the last, but that is what made our friendship so great. All these rows could have ended up with us drifting apart but we never did. We don't even have them any more, well only once a week!

There were times when Dexter would threaten to leave me somewhere but he never did. He'd only threaten when there was someone else there to push me so I wouldn't be stuck, but there were times when I wanted him to leave me somewhere, mainly when he played badminton at Monday dinner times. I hated badminton but Dexter would always moan and mither if I said I didn't want to watch. It was a bit selfish of me really not wanting to watch, seeing as he put himself out every day to push me around.

When I did reluctantly go to badminton, it was quite entertaining, although it pains me to say so. Dexter would play against Mr Altdorf who wanted to win at all costs, just as Dexter did. I can't understand this idea that winning is everything. I also can't remember if Dexter ever won a match but he was very close on a number of occasions. Dexter was a very good player and always won his matches for the school team, but when it came Mr Altdorf he just couldn't manage.

I was always the umpire, which was one of the reasons why I didn't want to watch. If I decided against Dexter he'd look at me, as if to say, 'You swine, you always want me to lose!'

Why would I want my best mate to lose, apart from the fact that it was funny watching his face when he lost? I'm proud of the fact that I always remained impartial. Unfortunately, whenever I decided against Mr Altdorf the stubborn little man would play the seniority card and overrule my decision. Whenever there was a contentious point which caused an argument, I swore blind that I didn't see it (when I actually did), so as to avoid inflaming the situation. It was always an intelligent move.

On one of these occasions there was a huge row. It was one game all and something like 15–14 in the last game, and there was a shot by Mr Altdorf, which narrowly went out. I definitely saw it go out, but when questioned about it I suddenly remembered that I didn't see it at all. This sudden bout of amnesia saved me from being dragged into it. Dexter thought it was out, Mr Altdorf obviously thought it was in, although neither of them had seen it. An argument ensued with both refusing to budge. It ended with Mr Altdorf saying that he was the teacher and what he said goes. That was the end of Dexter's participation in the game. He stormed out of the room, only for Mr Altdorf to shout at him and tell him off for being cheeky. Poor, innocent Dexter, he couldn't possibly win, could he? Who'd play badminton against a teacher?

On the odd occasion when I did manage to avoid that hour of intense boredom that was badminton practice, Jason was always willing to push me at lunchtime – so I could talk to other people – when he turned up anyway. For a number of very valid reasons, Jason struggled to do a full week at school, and sometimes that meant me sitting on my own in some lessons. What a shame it was for me. When he wasn't there, there'd always be someone to help me. Matthew or Chris would push me into the room and get my books out of my bag. If all four of my 'buddies' were off school, which never happened, I'm sure some of my female friends would have helped me out. Speaking of 'buddies', I hate the buddy idea which originated in America where someone volunteers, or is volunteered to help out the local disabled person. My problem with it is that if someone is volunteered to do it, he or she feels an obligation to do it. They're not doing it out of a desire to be friends with or to get to know the disabled person as a person. If a person volunteers to do it then that could either be a good or a bad thing. It could be because of a desire to be friends with the person, which is good, or it could just be a self-gratification thing, a pat on the back for himself which is not a reason to do it.

You could say I'm paranoid or I think too much if you want, but if I was part of a 'buddy' system, I wouldn't be able to escape the thought that they were in it for the wrong reasons. I'd be constantly asking myself why they were doing it. Okay so I am paranoid, I'm a 'Paranoid Android'.

With my friends I knew they liked me for me, I was absolutely certain that they didn't just feel sorry for me, and I'm proud that I managed to fit in so well. By the end of the second year I was totally settled and adjusted to my situation. The wheelchair wasn't an issue to anyone, least of all me, which I know seems a strange thing to say. I had a routine and a number of friends who helped, without me having to ask. My life was as normal as anyone else's and I'd made friends naturally without the outside help of a buddy system, thanks to that higher power.

So the second year passed without any major incident, the exams came and went and I did well, without worrying too much. My maths exam showed my insatiable perfectionism. I got 98% and I searched frantically for the other 2%. I never found it, but the question is, why was I looking? This obsessiveness had to stop.

My report was really good again and everything was now going according to plan. The only disappointment was that I finally had to give in to my weakening arms. I had to end my cello career. I was sad to say goodbye to Mrs Jackson but that's the way things go. Anyway, I had more important things to think about. In ten years' time disabled people would rule the world, with me as their king and all able-bodied people as their minions! Mmm ha ha ha! I sense the men in white coats are approaching.

I felt that the first bell of the second year signified the beginning of a period of renewed optimism. I was enjoying myself and sadly enough I didn't want the holidays to come. Unfortunately, I couldn't control time and I had to cope with seven weeks off school.

During this time I got to know my brother's mates quite well. We'd always had mutual friends at primary school, probably because there were less people there so you got to know each other better. My brother knew Heather and Emma and other people who weren't in his year, and I knew people who weren't in mine. At one point, Dan was going out with Heather and his mate Keechy (John Keech) was going out with Emma, much to my annoyance. I as usual was the eternal gooseberry, but I also spent a lot of time with Keechy, Ian, Ben, Kenny and the others, which was quite an experience. I wasn't as outgoing as they were but it was interesting to say the least. My room was the venue for many sleepovers, where about ten people were crammed into my room. We were like sardines in there, but it was good fun.

I still spent most of my time with Dexter, doing the usual stuff we'd always done, just wandering around and things like that, playing computer games and arguing about them more often than not, and camping in a tent whilst eating several packets of crisps and about eight chocolate bars between us. We were fine figures of men back then! He used to drive my cart into the most awkward of places, just to annoy me. Once we went into one of his stupid dens that I hated, and never wanted to visit. It was at Sharples pond, in between the primary and secondary schools, and there was a gap in the fence. Hundreds of other kids probably had a den in exactly the same place, and I thought it was the most boring thing in the world to go and sit in a den. Anyway, after endless arguments I'd always give in and go reluctantly to this amazingly exciting place. No, more accurately I'd be dragged there complaining loudly on the way.

What turned out to be our final visit to the Sharples pond den was a terrifying experience. It took us about ten minutes to actually find a way into the den and once we had arrived there Dexter started to renovate it (he started hacking sticks down from the bushes and breaking others off with his hands). He felt a sudden squelching sensation under his hand and when he removed it from the branch it was totally red. The panicked look on his face made me think it was blood. When he lifted the branch to inspect what had caused the stain on his hand, it was worse than his own blood, it was beetle blood! Agghh! The branch was covered in bugs, a number of which Dexter had crushed to death. Poor defenceless bugs, they didn't stand a chance. With this thought flitting through my mind, I looked around the den and to my horror I started to see wasps! One, and then another, followed by another, until I saw about six, with more on the way. 'Another fine mess' he'd got me into, with his crazy ideas.

Dexter had obviously seen them as well for in the same movement our faces dropped, we said, 'Shit – wasps. We'd better get out.' He jumped on the cart and we drove towards the exit. If it took ten minutes to get in, it took us about ten seconds to get out! We flew out through the gap in the fence like wheeled bats out of hell! It's amazing what a swarm of angry wasps can do to an eight mile per hour golf cart. That's when he gave up on den building. It was just too dangerous!

My trusty cart had saved the day, but it was powerless to help when I let a lad called Gaz have a little drive on it. I said no about ten times before I finally gave in. It couldn't do me any harm could it? 'Course it could. He got on the bike in front of me and started to drive. I should have learned from my own experience and realised that everyone thinks it's easy to ride a golf cart first time. I mean how hard can it be? Well, we were on a field. To the left there was a large amount of clear green space and to the right was a slope leading down to a fence, which ran around a play-ground. Which way would you go? Yes, I'd turn left as well, but just to be safe I said, 'Whatever you do, don't turn right.'

'Okay then, I won't,' he said, and sure enough, two seconds later I ended up on the floor with my head in a fence and a sore shoulder. I never let anyone new ride it again.

We were stopped by the police once riding down a backstreet on Blackburn Road. He must have thought we'd done a drive-by or something so he came over and said, ''Ello, 'ello, 'ello, what's all this then?' Well no he didn't say that but it sounds good. He really said, 'All right lads, is this yours?'

I was too shocked to say anything, so Dexter intervened and said, 'It's his, he can't walk and this is his cart.'

'Okay then,' replied the officer. 'It's just that two lads on a golf cart isn't something you see everyday. I thought you'd stolen it.'

'No we wouldn't do that,' we assured him, and he let us go telling us to be careful as we drove off.

I can understand what it must have looked like, two lads driving a golf cart down a backstreet, but really if we were going to steal something like that, would we do it in broad daylight where anyone could see us? I don't think we would.

By the end of this particular summer I had to face two facts concerning this machine which had been my freedom for so long and had been my means of having so many good times. First of all, it was getting old. It was rickety in places and eventually we had to replace the screw that held the handlebars on the rest of the chassis, but not before the handlebars had fallen off at an inopportune moment. I think Dexter was driving me around Sharples fields and down a hill, when suddenly, halfway down the hill I heard an unhealthy cracking sound. I just held on for dear life and the handlebars dropped off. I lent back on the seat and hoped for the best. There was a thud which thrust me forward and threw Dexter off the front of the seat. Luckily, I remained precariously positioned on the edge of the seat and not impaled on a metal bar.

We tried and failed to put it back together and finally we had to call my Dad out to rescue me. That was just one of a long list of problems with the bike around this time. The batteries ran out, the spring on the speed lever broke, and it just wasn't running properly.

The second fact I had to face was that my arms were becoming weaker and turning the handlebars was now tiring me out very quickly. Dexter had to drive for me the majority of the time, which sort of defeated the object of why I got the Trio in the first place.

Needing a new vehicle though didn't pose as big a problem as it had when I was nine years old; in fact I already possessed a replacement. I'd been using an indoor/outdoor electric wheelchair in the house for about eighteen months but had been reluctant to drive it outside for fear of appearing more disabled than I felt I was. Nobody else was ever going to be bothered about this transition. What were they going to do, stop talking to me because I was in a wheelchair and not on a bike? I don't know why I was bothered, because being safe in a wheelchair was preferable to falling off a cart every five minutes. I wouldn't have looked disabled then, would I?

The main problem with the wheelchair was that it only went four miles per hour, half the speed of the cart. I had to work hard to contain the laughter, sorry excitement, when I got the wheelchair and the MD Society tried to exaggerate how fast it went. One of them said, 'And you'll speed round the corner at four miles an hour!'

Great, I thought, *but at least it'll get me around.*

Would it bring the same amount of good times as the cart? Well that remained to be seen, but I'd give it a go.

Chapter VI

I drove into the third year with the cart, a thing of the past, but at the same time I was looking to the future, with hope. I can now look back at it and smile.

This was, we were told, an important year. We had to choose our 'options' this year, the subjects we wanted to continue to study up to GCSE level. These choices could make or break our future. That sounded very final, but I'd learnt by then that sometimes things were exaggerated to motivate us. The first time I heard the 'this is very important' speech, I thought, *It can't be that important.* But by the end of the year I was programmed. I went into school every day thinking, *This is very important, this is very important.*

We'd also have to do our first externally assessed exams this year. The SATs had been boycotted the year before by most schools in Bolton and we had the honour, if you can call it that, of being the first year to do the exams, in maths, English and science, oh joy of joys! That was something to look forward to. The SATs though were treated opposite to how the options were treated. It was a case of 'they're not that important and if you don't do well it doesn't matter', so I wasn't worried.

This assessment of the SATs was very accurate because they meant absolutely nothing in the end. In the immediate aftermath of the SATs their results wouldn't change our sets, and in the future they wouldn't appear on our CVs. Colleges and universities would never look at the results. I felt it was a waste of time. The government wants to test how children are doing under exam conditions, but if they are exams without pressure then they're not exams in the spirit of exams. They're not a true reflection of how well you are going to do in the future. I did worse than certain people in my SATs, whose GCSE results weren't as good as mine, and the actual exam papers were totally different. What's the point in testing your ability with an exam, which resembles in no way the exams which are significant? I can't see one.

That's enough complaining for now, there was a whole year to go before either of these things happened, and suddenly I seemed to be upstairs much more often than before. People must have realised that Dexter could get me downstairs very quickly if there happened to be a fire, or more likely a fire drill, which usually happened on a rainy day or in the middle of winter. So I didn't feel like a special case any more. The rooms weren't rearranged for my benefit any more and it made me feel even more like a normal pupil.

I did feel like a special case however when I was assigned a carer to help me in CDT and cookery lessons. I also felt very annoyed about it. Everybody at Sharples knew I was independent and that I would detest this idea more than any idea anyone had ever had. Again they were only trying to help but this was one helper that I didn't appreciate, well not at the time. Dexter and I both resented the situation and in a very obvious way we made it clear to Miss Noden, who was only doing her job, that we didn't like it. We didn't particularly like her either but that's only because we felt she was interfering in a situation, which we felt we had under control. Whoever it had been who was plonked into my life in this way, I couldn't possibly have liked him because of what he represented – evil.

Don't get me wrong, I believe these helpers have their place when someone doesn't have a group of friends to help out, like I had, or when they have problems which need more than just friends to alleviate. The trouble was, I was happy with things the way they were, and so it seemed were my friends. Because Miss Noden was there to help, then that was what she wanted to do and I wasn't prepared to accept that at first.

I think we were at crossed purposes really. She saw her role as one where she was there to help, but I still had to treat her as I treated my teachers, and I thought she was there to do what I told her to. I thought she had delusions of grandeur, I now think differently. She just wanted to do her job and I made her life hell for the first few weeks. So did Dexter – I'm not going to take all the blame. We didn't co-operate at all and when she complained we either argued back or just dismissed what she was saying, sarcastically.

The trouble with me is I say what I think, sometimes without thinking it through first. When people first meet me now, I tone down the sarcasm and I have to work hard to do it, because I tend to offend people when I'm just joking. In the third year, it was a different story. I didn't know how to control myself and I didn't feel I had to. I didn't like Miss Noden and I showed it in a very immature way. But I was immature. I was only thirteen. Nowadays I'd just smile and be pleasant about the bad situation, but back then I did everything I could to show my negative feelings.

One day we'd gone upstairs without waiting for Miss Noden who was now designated observer. We couldn't escape them; there were eyes everywhere. Anyway, Miss Noden wasn't happy about us escaping and she told us off. We thought it was all just a laugh and became sarcastic again, making Miss Noden more and more annoyed until she erupted like Mount Etna and said, 'If you ever speak to me like that again, I'll report you to your head of year.'

That shut me up. Well, I didn't want anyone else to see my nasty side did I? We didn't stop speaking to her like that, and although we were only joking most of the time, things came to a head when Mr Lee, the CDT teacher I mentioned earlier, asked to see me and Dexter in his room at dinner time, and it was his turn to tell us off.

He seemed to have mellowed since that first lesson, either that or we were no longer scared of him, but apparently Miss Noden had been upset about the way we were treating her and had told Mr Lee about it.

To be honest, he didn't really tell us off, we discussed how we felt about what was going on. We told him we thought she was being unreasonable and that we were only joking and all that, which is what we believed was happening. Mr Lee advised us on how we should handle the problem. He also told us to see it from her point of view; after all she was only doing her job. Of course we already knew all that but we hadn't really been bothered by it, until we found out it was actually upsetting her. We weren't horrible lads and we felt really bad about our attitude. I didn't dislike her as a person; it was just the idea of her taking over and getting in the way.

That mature discussion with Mr Lee honestly helped our relationship with Miss Noden. It definitely got better after that. If I'd thought about it, I'd have realised that I'd only have to put up with the situation as it was for the rest of the year and then I'd choose the subjects which required the least amount of help. Then I'd be rid of the problem. However, when you're a young adolescent you're very impatient, and if you don't like something, you want it to change immediately. That's what I was like anyway. Little things seem massive, but as you get older you wonder why you were worried about petty things. I'm sure it's strange to hear a nineteen-year-old talking about maturity, but events since have made me grow up and realise that certain problems aren't problems at all.

The Miss Noden saga showed a change in my personality and proved I was completely over my depression of the first year. In the first year, a 'Miss Noden' situation would have reduced me to tears. In the first place I wouldn't have been confident enough to argue back, or even to take it when she told me off. I was like a balloon that had been blown up to its limit, and every time someone shouted at me, I'd pop. If you remember, when I got annoyed I used to cry, but once I'd become a sane person again and regained confidence in myself and in other people, I knew my own mind. So when I became annoyed, I'd shout, swear, become sarcastic or use a combination of the three. Fair enough, I'm probably more annoying when I'm happy and relaxed, but at least I'm true to myself. Miss Noden bore the brunt of my metamorphosis. Dexter suffered as well but we were both changing. I had to put up with him when he turned up to school like a bear with a sore head, and he had to cope with Jekyll and Hyde Withnell. This was about the time we stopped talking like Joe Pasquale and became Louis Armstrong. Or I did anyway, he still talks like a woman! Our rows also became more and more childish and frequent, the worst of which was when I threw Dexter out of my house for beating me on 'FIFA Soccer'. Apparently 'it's in the game' and whatever it was that was in the game brought out the worst in me. Just writing this embarrasses me. It was absolutely ridiculous. Every time I think about this incident, and of me shouting, 'Right, f**k off, get out of my house!' and of Dexter's shocked face when I said it, I cringe. It's all part of growing up, or not as the case may be.

This year must have been Mr Altdorf's worst nightmare, not because of the lads who counted one more after Liam joined from Smithills School. We were the most pleasant lads in the world. There was the odd outburst from Paul or David Cass when they got told off for being lazy sods, but that was bound to happen. We can't all be wimps like me. Anyway, those two were harmless enough, despite talking a good game. I had a good laugh with David and we took the mickey out of each other. They were good days.

It was the girls who were the problem as usual. Women! They were going through the female equivalent of what we were going through, and didn't we know it! It was that time of the month everyday, and Mr Altdorf struggled to control it. If he could cope with that, he could cope with anything that teaching could throw at him. No I'm being a tad unfair now. PMT gets the blame for too much, these girls were just a bunch of psychos. I'm only joking. I hope you can tell by now.

The way Mr Altdorf chose to deal with this harem of harlots was to keep them behind after school when they flipped out, and to let the lads go home amid accusations of sexism, favouritism, and absolute uproar. It was funny!

I'm sure it would have been easier just to put up with it but as usual he didn't want to lose an argument against a bunch of fourteen-year-old girls! I bet when he was a young Scouser, he was determined to steal more hubcaps than anybody else. That's not very PC is it? Can I say that? I just did. Oh no! I'm feeling an uncontrollable urge to complain again. It's like I'm possessed by the devil, I have to satisfy its evil spirit. Yes, political correctness, you'd think I'd love it being part of a disabled minority, but no I hate it. I believe discrimination shouldn't be tolerated, but when this intolerance goes too far, i.e. to the lengths of positive discrimination, then that's when problems occur. When employers decide to take on a proportion of disabled or ethnic people in every hundred employees before they've even carried out the interviews, then that's just crazy. What if this policy is to the detriment of the workforce? What if an employer takes on ten disabled people and only eight are good enough for the job. That's pointless and not really, in my experience, what people, especially disabled people, want. We may need help in certain areas in order for us to do the physical side of the job, but part of the idea of wanting to be treated equally is that we're given jobs on our merits and not simply because we're disabled. That's as bad as *not* giving someone a job simply because he or she is disabled. Speaking for myself, I wouldn't be happy in a job I'd got purely on the basis that I'm disabled. I'm very proud, and want to get a job because I've worked hard and impressed in my interview. I know a job's a job and it earns you money, but money isn't the most important thing.

Who decides what is politically correct anyway? Disabled people? Ethnic minorities? No. Politicians and people in authority. Apparently the word 'accident black spot' is racist, it shows the word 'black' in a bad light. It's 'accident danger zone' now, and if you write the words 'hard working' in a job ad, that's not PC. It discriminates against disabled people. We can't possibly work hard, can we? If we're being pedantic about things, then actually thinking that those words would upset disabled people is discrimination in itself. Next you'll be telling me that 'hard working' discriminates against lazy people! The point is that if these well-meaning people actually asked disabled people how they felt, they might change their ideas of what is discrimination which would make life much easier.

You can't even make a throwaway comment any more. Mukhtar used to call me a spaz and I used to call him a Paki. Of course we were joking. Does that mean I'm a racist or that he's anti-disabled? Does it hell! One of the ideas of being accepted is that you can joke about your relative differences to the run-of-the-mill white man. If I couldn't joke about being in a wheelchair, I wouldn't be able to cope with it on a day-to-day basis. Plus I'd be miserable, and have no friends. My friends are my friends because they can have a normal relationship with me, including the banter and jokes at each other's expense. They don't have to walk on eggshells or pussyfoot around my disability. They joke about it themselves, and I love that.

Mr Altdorf certainly didn't pussyfoot around the girls when they stressed out, and the amount of times the lads went home on time and the girls had to stay behind and put our chairs up for us was unbelievable. They knew how to make their feelings clear, staring daggers at Mr Altdorf with one eye and at us with the other. I don't know how they managed it but it was quite scary!

I shouldn't make the girls out to be too bad because most of them were great. I wouldn't change the people in my form for anything. I was good friends with nearly all of them.

If the girls knew how to show their feelings, then I had the opposite ability. I think it was the male thing to do. Young lads don't show their feelings, they don't cry, they don't wear pink and they have many other irrational preconceptions that make little sense. I still don't wear pink. (See what I mean?) There was only Dexter who knew exactly how I felt and I was the only one who knew how he felt, but it wasn't because we spoke about it often. It was because we knew each other so well that we didn't have to talk about our feelings. I think with me it was also a defence mechanism after the first year. From showing all my feelings very clearly, to totally hiding everything and being unable, even when I wanted to, to express how I felt (apart from to Miss Noden, and especially to girls).

For example, everyone knew I fancied Isla and it became a running joke, but could I tell her that? No. Everybody else did, but I couldn't. So eventually I got Dexter to ask her out for me. Now normally, if you get someone to ask a person out for you, it's because you're too shy to tell them to their face. So you tell them to ask her out when you're not there. (Do you get that Dex?) He didn't get that at the time and so he went and asked her out in the most embarrassing situation in history. In front of me and three of her friends. That's six people, six, who witnessed my latest point blank refusal. At least I didn't cry. I never would have lived that down. I knew she didn't fancy me anyway, but even this embarrassment didn't stop me fancying her and embarrassing myself on further occasions.

I explained earlier how tactless I was and how I didn't think about what I was saying until I'd actually said it. Well, one day Isla came in not looking very happy and told us that her dog had died. Before I could think about it, I'd said, 'Well you don't look very upset about it,' the response to which is unprintable. I can't understand why I said that. I didn't even think that, it was just that I'd got to the stage where I'd be upset if I didn't speak to her every day so I'd just say any coherent sentence, be it sensible, tactless or whatever. I hadn't learnt that it's sometimes better to say nothing. That hardly endeared me to the girl did it?

In a position like mine, saying something like that could be dangerous, let alone embarrassing. I can't really duck if a board duster comes flying in my direction.

I got over being turned down again quite quickly. I was quite used to it by now. I could take it. There were plenty more fish in the sea. Now that sentence rates number one on anyone's list of the most useless attempts at reassurance in the world, but it's absolutely true. Who wants to go out with a fish, though? Being serious now, there were a number of other girls I liked. I just couldn't see it at that moment.

When I say it didn't stop me fancying her, I did give up on the idea of asking her out and just concentrated on being mates. The problem I had was that nobody else got that message and they carried on asking her out for me, which she didn't appreciate and she told me that on one occasion, and it really upset me. I don't know why it did because I knew how she felt, but actually hearing it from her mouth shocked me. I didn't let it show, though. My face didn't even change as my heart broke in two. Bloody hell it wasn't that bad! I still remember that day though and the exact words. How embarrassing is that? She said, 'I'm sick of people asking me out for you. I don't even like you like that,' and I couldn't say anything in reply to it. I think that explained it quite clearly. Did that mean she didn't fancy me? I'm not sure.

On a more boring note the schoolwork was still depressingly easy. I was far too intelligent for that school! My genius IQ just wasn't tested by their tests! I had a bit of a reality check in art though. Miss March was my teacher and she gave me honest marks, not sympathetic ones like Mr Crook used to give me. I was now getting C's and D's instead of A's, but I knew I wasn't good enough to get A's, I wasn't that deluded.

Art was a subject in which I never got a better mark than Dexter, because obviously I wasn't as good as him at it. In fact there was only one homework of mine that got a better mark than his, until he complained that is. We'd been told to draw an eye so that's what I did. I drew the shape of an eye and all its features, and I coloured the iris in. That was about it. Ten minutes of a job, it was. Dexter, on the other hand had spent an hour on his, shading it in, and even going as far as to draw reflections of the furniture in his room, as if he was looking closely at the eye. It was very good.

When we got the marks, I couldn't believe it. I'd got a B and Dexter had got a C. I didn't say anything but I thought it was an absolute travesty. Not surprisingly Dexter was as mad as those wasps in his den and he explained his unhappiness to Miss March. He made her look at it again, and compared it to mine. I don't think she had the heart to lower my mark, so she just raised his until he got an A, and then he was satisfied. I wasn't bothered at all because I knew his drawing was much better than mine, and that mine wasn't worth a B at all.

To be honest I think even Mr Crook lowered his marks this year. They had to be honest because they knew that the options were important and we needed a truthful assessment if we were going to choose our best subjects. Art was by no means one of my best subjects but the lessons were good fun, when people weren't flicking paint at me or drawing on my face with felt tips. Dexter was bound to be involved and Nichola with her mischievous streak liked to join in more often than not. Most art lessons finished with me going mad at the annoying buggers and looking like an Indian chief. Once was funny, twice not so bad, even three times I could laugh through my teeth, but when it got to the stage where I might as well have put my face in a paint palate, I wanted to kill them.

I was always getting attacked with writing material. When I stayed in the form room at dinner time, Dexter used to 'board dust' my face. He couldn't use white chalk either. He had to use green. I looked like a refugee from Mars and everyone enjoyed laughing at my expense.

If art was a total doss, then I was more concentrated on the other subjects, but I still had a laugh whilst doing the work and after I'd done it. School was good fun and I was relaxed but still focused. I was just as successful with this new outlook as I was when I did worry. I was also much happier, so my mind was much clearer when it came to doing my homework and exams. Sadly enough, I actually enjoyed doing homework which is why I did it as soon as I got it. I also did that so I wouldn't worry about it. I was calm and was enjoying myself but it was controlled. I knew I was doing enough work, so I didn't have to worry.

We were introduced to Shakespeare for the first time when we read *Romeo and Juliet* in preparation for the exciting SATs. I hated reading but Shakespeare was interesting. I think it was the difference in language between Shakespearian and modern English that appealed to me, like learning French and German appealed to me. Or it could have been that the story was so timeless. Love stories like *Romeo and Juliet* never lose their impact. It was quite enjoyable as reading goes.

What weren't enjoyable were the more frequent trips upstairs. I was used to Dexter dragging me upstairs, watching the ground disappear further and further into the distance, but when I was upstairs for lessons without Dexter, I had to put my life into the hands of Jason, Matthew and Chris. That was worrying. Dexter would usually drop me off outside my lesson after taking me upstairs, and then I'd meet him at the stairs so he could take me down. That idea soon fell by the wayside. It was just too awkward. Dexter continued to take me upstairs but I got two of the three 'Musketeers' to take me down again. When Jason wasn't at school Matthew 'the most clumsy person in the world' helped Chris to get me down. Chris wasn't much less clumsy and it was like being on a white-knuckle ride. Space Mountain was a walk in the park compared to this! I should give them a bit more credit, though. I'm still here, although sometimes it was more like I was taking them downstairs than the other way around. There was only actually one occasion however where I seriously feared for my life. The other times there was a lot of wobbling, but I was like a Weeble. (I wobbled but I didn't fall down.)

On the one dangerous occasion we got halfway down safely.

My pulse rate was only twice its usual speed, but Chris decided to set off down the second flight too quickly for Matthew's liking. The back of the wheelchair was shaking and the front was bouncing off Matt's shins every time we went down a further step, until finally he could no longer hold on. It was another close your eyes and pray moment as Matthew landed at the bottom of the stairs, followed by me and Chris, who came flying down the stairs with Chris holding on with all his strength. It felt like an eternity as I bounced. One step and my heart wrenched, two and my heart rate was critical, three and cardiac arrest was imminent, four, five, *six* and I hit the bottom, hardly breathing but still firmly in the wheelchair. It took me a week to recover and I remind Matthew about once a month that it was six steps and not three, as he insists. He tried to kill me, and he's been trying to get rid of me ever since!

I can't believe I survived those stairs but I'm just glad someone offered to do it. Many people would have been too scared to do that job even for a mate. Cheers lads, I appreciate it.

Another time I feared for my life was on a class trip to Coalbrookdale to see the first ever iron bridge (we were studying the industrial revolution in history). This was a very worrying day from start to finish. Firstly, how would I go to the loo? Dexter didn't help me out back then. Then there was the problem of the coach. Would I be safe or would I flop like a character from *Rosie and Jim* every time the coach went round a corner? Thankfully, once we'd set off that worry was alleviated. I was quite safe unless we crashed, but then everyone would be in the same boat. We'd all be thrown from our seats.

Once in Coalbrookdale the next worry was who was going to push me around. We'd been separated into groups according to which teacher we had, so Dexter wasn't in my group. We were then split into smaller, more manageable groups so Matthew, Chris and Jason weren't in my group either. It was looking bad but luckily David Cass was on hand to help out. He'd helped me before so I wasn't too worried. I had to explain how to get me up and down curbs but he didn't have too much trouble. That is until we reached the most terrifying prospect for someone in a wheelchair. I'd been dragged up some hills before but this was the mother of all hills. It was almost vertical with a train track in the middle, which I think was used to transport material from about 200 feet below. There were no steps, just a very steep gravel path. Wheelchair friendly it was not. It was heart-in-throat time as the path through the woods joined this mountain about halfway up. This day was rapidly turning into my worst nightmare. Most people would have thought, *Great. A day off school, just what I need.* I'd rather have sat in a classroom doing algebra. At least I'd be safe there.

Anyway, when we set off up the hill I could see myself laying at the bottom in a pool of blood. It was a terrible vision. I had Mr Leggett dragging me up from the back and Cass at the front stopping me from falling, if Mr Leggett happened to drop me. I still would have broken my neck, but at least he'd have done his best. On a hill like that I could have had five people in front of me, but if Mr Leggett had dropped me, pain or more likely death would have been the consequence.

They inched slowly upwards with the scraping sound of gravel scaring me with every step. Then suddenly there was a slip, a thud and my head was flung backwards. Mr Leggett's legs had capitulated underneath him but luckily he'd kept hold of the handles and the only consequences were a view of the blue sky for me, and a change of underwear for all three of us! I don't know about me but Cass looked like he was about to collapse.

Having survived my latest battle with death we reached the top and the safety of flat ground, without a further problem. *I hope this is worth it*, but I somehow doubted that that would be the case. We walked over a bridge where there was a toll gate, from when there were tolls on the roads and there it was, the *coup de grâce*, our whole reason for being there, the iron bridge! This amazing feat of engineering technology was wasted on me, but that's probably because I was too worried that I'd begun to need the toilet and there were still a few hours to go. I'd have to hold it in.

Later we went to an old schoolroom, just to show us how lucky we are in these caneless years. I've noticed that everywhere I've been on a school trip, there is always a schoolroom with slates and charcoal for writing, and a very strict person acting as the teacher. Why is it that adults have to show us how 'difficult' they or their parents had it, and how 'easy' we have it? I'll tell you what, kids these days don't know they're born.

We stayed in the schoolroom for about ten minutes, then we moved on through a forest which would lead us to a mill of some sort. (I don't remember what sort of mill it was, so I won't lie.) We stopped off on the way for something to eat. This was our lunch 'hour' so we had to make the most of it, and then we were off back into the darkness to search out this mill. By this time Cass was knackered, so someone else had to take over pushing me. Just when I thought the ordeal that was this day couldn't get any worse, Barry took over. Now I haven't mentioned Barry before, but I went to nursery school with him, which I can remember nothing about. I hadn't seen him since, until we went to Sharples, but even then I didn't really know him very well. I do now, but I'll tell you about that later. At secondary school Baz was in the other half of our year and most of the time the two halves were kept separate. There was a set one in our half of the year and a set one in the other half, and it remained like that until the third year when there was a set 1A and a set 1B, and so on. This merging of the sets brought mine and Baz's paths back together, and we ended up in the same set for humanities. Therefore, he was in my group on this day. He started to push me, too fast for my liking, and as we went over the rough terrain made worse by twigs and rocks, I told him to lift the front wheels up, but he wasn't listening. As many times as I told him to lift the wheels up, he didn't do it and I felt really scared. Oh well, I'd been scared all day, another ten minutes wouldn't do me any harm. I longed for the day to be over, and strangely enough the day went quicker after I'd had that thought. We looked at the mill and everything else that Coalbrookdale had to offer, and soon enough we were back on the coach and returned to the safe haven of our homes. How I survived that trip I'll never know, but at least I had enough people to help me in the absence of Dexter and the other three.

If I were honest, I probably would have enjoyed the day much more if I hadn't felt like I was going to end up in pain, all day long. I still had it in me to worry, then.

When I returned to the safety of indoor lessons at school, I realised that there were only a few weeks of the year left. I was now further than halfway along this five-year journey and I thought there were still many more ups and downs to come. I was ready for them now though and believed I could anticipate them before they happened. That sounds complacent, like I felt I had made it, that I couldn't fail, but I never once thought that. My worrying side would never allow that to happen.

The year had come full circle now, and it was SATs and end of year exam time. Suitably prepared from my weeks of revision, I went into them ready to take up the battle for academic supremacy against Matthew and Mukhtar once again. There was just one problem though. Mukhtar wouldn't be here for the exams. He was on holiday. That just left me and Matthew to fight it out. Well that's what I thought anyway.

So I did the SATs and felt they'd gone okay. I just had to wait a few weeks for the results. One exam that I knew hadn't gone well was my German exam. When I say hadn't gone well, I mean I messed up at least one question, so I hadn't got my usual 94% or 96%. I wouldn't get the best mark in the year for once, which probably wasn't such a bad thing. It proved one thing once and for all; I wasn't such a wimp any more. A couple of years earlier I would have used the sore foot excuse or thrown up again to get sent home after such a poor exam, but I'd realised by then that I wasn't perfect. No one is. The exams wouldn't be important for two years yet. These were just to help me choose my options.

When all the exam results were in, it was time to make these choices. The SATs weren't back yet, but that didn't matter, considering we had to take maths, English and science, which was a shame because I would have dropped science like a hot potato. It bored me to tears.

The subjects I did actually choose were like this: French, German, history, IT, and for some totally inexplicable reason, art. I think my reason for choosing art was that I wanted a challenge. It would be harder for me to get a C in art than it would be for me to get an A in most of the other subjects I'd chosen. I'd narrowed it down to a choice of one from, art, psychology and RE. Although I always got over 80% in my RE exams, I hated the subject and I still didn't get on with Miss Webster, which was a major factor in my decision to choose something else. I know that's a really daft reason not to choose a subject I could have got an A in, especially as I quite liked her when I left, but that's what happened.

Psychology went out the window because it was a step into the unknown, and I didn't want to risk it in case I was terrible at it. That decision is the one I regret the most because I've since developed a healthy interest in psychology. I couldn't have been worse at psychology than I was at art.

French, history and German were the easiest choices I had to make because I enjoyed them so much. I had to do one technology subject, which is where IT came in. The technology decision had come down to a straight choice between IT and keyboard applications, and up until then I'd found IT more interesting than keyboard applications. I didn't even consider home ec' or CDT for a number of reasons. First of all my disability made these subjects difficult for me. Of course I could have worked around that with various helpers. Although I now actually quite liked Miss Noden, I was too independent to do a subject where I needed such help. I also didn't enjoy these subjects anyway.

That was it then. The 'really important, possibly life changing' decisions had been made. Were they the right choices? It didn't matter now. I had to stick to them.

By the way, I got 78% in that German exam, not quite the disaster I'd expected. I wasn't happy about it though. I did well in all the other exams and then the SATs results returned. I waited with baited breath as the results were read out and when it came to mine I was happy with the results. I'd got level six in all three (the exams we'd taken went up to level seven), but in English and maths I was two marks off level seven. I now knew how Ben felt when he came seventh in the shot-put! I was gutted about that but I knew I'd done my best. That feeling of being gutted was nothing compared to how gutted I was when I heard Matthew's results. He'd got level seven in maths and science, but luckily only level five in English. At least I wasn't totally thrashed.

Thinking about it now, I wonder why I was so bothered about competing. It didn't make any difference to anyone other than ourselves who got the best marks, but if I feel that someone is a threat to me, even if it is a friend, then I don't give up until I've beaten them or until I've got as close as possible to them. Even now I have to compete with my Dad on his little mobile phone snake game. I'm better than him, so there! Nevertheless, it was a fun competition. I didn't feel like a failure when I lost, as I would have in earlier years, and it spurred me on to do as well as I could. The important exams were yet to come and in two years time I wouldn't be beaten! Pathetic, wasn't I... Sorry, aren't I?

I'd made it to the end of the lower school and all the hard work was over for the rest of the year. All the exams and important decisions were over for the rest of the year, and in the final week fun was the order of the day. The 'mini-enterprise' week was an exercise in teamwork. Again we were organised into groups, this time of about ten people, and we had to think up a business, one which could reasonably be put together in a week and with a small budget. Our brief was to make a profit, however large or small it may be, and to prove that we could work as a team with people who we didn't necessarily know very well. The teachers had deliberately organised us into groups so that we wouldn't be with our usual friends. If we had worked with our friends it would have been about as businesslike as an 18 to 30 holiday in Ibiza, which wasn't really the idea. It wasn't supposed to be fun you know!

I'd actually been looking forward to the mini-enterprise ever since I was at primary school and the then third-years at Sharples came down to sell us their wears. Daylight robbery it was and I thought, *I can't wait to do that*. I was a bit disappointed when I heard the format had changed slightly and that I wouldn't be able to rob innocent primary schoolchildren of their pocket money. I've got a sadistic streak in me. I wonder where I got that from. Well it wouldn't be my fault, would it?

This year we had to set up our businesses in the same way as previous years, but we couldn't sell our produce until the school summer fair at the end of the week. The profits, if there were any, would go to the school, probably to keep the teachers in coffee and biscuits for the coming year. I'm being cynical again, sorry. It's a shame we couldn't redress the natural balance. We'd been robbed when we were young, so why shouldn't we be allowed to rob the next generation? It's like a food chain. One animal gets eaten and then its attacker is eaten by a bigger animal. If one stage is missed, then something goes wrong. Because of this mini-enterprise, younger people don't fear us, and that's why kids are more annoying now. When I was a lad… Right, that's enough now, I've finally lost it.

Mini-enterprise became even more exciting when my worry about how I'd manage, and who'd push me around was solved. I had a word with Miss March, my head of year, and she said it was okay for me to use my electric wheelchair for the week. I'd enjoy this week very much.

So on the first day of mini-enterprise, we got into our groups and after the initial quiet period, when we were nervous in front of people we didn't know very well, we got down to the business of choosing a business to set up. We rid ourselves of some stupid and useless ideas, and finally chose to make badges. They were low maintenance, very cheap to make, and there was a badge-making machine in school.

We were sworn to secrecy about our mission, 'should we choose to accept it'. No other group could find out our plans in case they copied it. God forbid that that should happen! Everyone knew what every other group was doing and no one cared. It was the worst kept secret in history. This week was a bit of fun, a week off lessons, none of us took that seriously.

Having decided to make badges, it was time to assign roles to each other. It was real authentic business this. The different roles were a manager, a treasurer, and designer-type people (people who cut pictures out of magazines for badge designs). I was chosen to be manager, whether that was an indication of my reputation for being bossy or whether it was because I couldn't go to the shop to buy magazines and badge materials I'm not sure, but I didn't mind telling people what to do for a week.

We started making these badges, which took much longer than expected, and it was a rush to get enough acceptable badges made by the end of the week. I was beginning to feel the pressure of my executive position and our quality controllers weren't doing much controlling by around Thursday. Some of the badges we let through were absolutely useless. Once we'd run out of money we

127

resorted to drawing simple designs ourselves. I only drew one, which with my artistic abilities was enough for me not to be allowed to draw another. It doesn't make good business sense to have a designer with the artistic talent of a fish! This meant I had to take on the role of observer which suited me very well.

Unfortunately the week flew by and before we knew it we were back in school on Saturday for the fair. Would we make any money? Probably not, but we'd give it a go. The way things worked during the fair was that each group had a rota and we took turns to man the stall. There were always two or three of us on the stall at any one time, which was helpful considering I wouldn't be able to man the stall alone. It got to lunchtime and although we'd sold a few badges they weren't exactly selling like hot cakes. In fact the cakes were distinctly lukewarm. By now everyone was looking weary. We'd been doing exactly the same thing for a week and even though it had been a good laugh, and a successful teamwork exercise, I was fed up of seeing badges. Indeed, gouging my eyes out with the badges would have been preferable to trying to sell them. I needed a break so I escaped from the hall. I'm glad I had the electric wheelchair otherwise I'd have had to sit behind that bloody table with my little badge friends all day.

The break was a relief and I managed to last the whole day, at the end of which we had made a small profit. It was a success. We'd made it!

And with that the year had come to an end. We'd done our bit for the school, done some pointless exams, chosen our options and I'd survived the infamous trip to Coalbrookdale. The holidays were a welcome distraction and a much-needed rest.

The first couple of weeks of the summer holidays passed by in their usual vein, apart from we'd quit the den idea. The wasps made us grow out of dens very quickly and not before time either. Cool people don't make dens. We did the usual thing, wandering around, listening to Dexter's dad's stereo and trying to build an extra seat for the wheelchair. With the cart gone, Dexter had to stand on the back of the wheelchair in order to drive me around. He didn't seem to grasp that I had an electric wheelchair so I could drive myself around but anyway, attempting to build the seat kept Dexter occupied for hours. It never worked but that's probably because his idea of a seat was a plastic chair, nailed to a metal bar, which he bent over the metal bar going across the back of the wheelchair. When he sat on it, the bar snapped. That didn't deter him. He was determined to make it work until, after about three hours I finally did what several metal bars had done in the previous three hours. No I didn't bend over the back of my wheelchair, I snapped, 'Just give up it's never going to work, you bloody pillock!' It took several other equally insulting but funny comments before he finally gave up. The lazy swine, too lazy to walk around, when I'd have given anything except my legs to be able to walk, poor wheelchair boy that I was!

It hadn't been to Dexter's liking, or to my brother's, when I finally sold my cart to an old man who needed it to continue to play his beloved game of golf. Of course I could have just given it away, but the offer of money meant I was blinded by the pound signs in my eyes. I just couldn't turn it down. These days I probably would have just given it away.

My brother had just taken up golf and wanted the cart to take him around the course, and also he said Granddad might need it when he got older. I knew that wasn't the case because my Granddad has always said if he ever needed a golf cart he'd stop playing golf. My Granddad wouldn't be needing the golf cart then. Dexter just wanted to have a golf cart to drive around on. Hmmm. It was a tough decision. Do I sell my cart to a man who needs it or do I give it to one of two people who can ride a pushbike perfectly well? The decision, it seemed, had already been made.

I didn't miss my cart as my wheelchair still gave me the same opportunity to get around, even if it did take longer. I was probably less ignorant when I could only travel at walking pace because I couldn't escape on my own and talk to myself any more.

The first few weeks driving the electric chair around were as eventful and calamitous as driving the cart had been, and I soon realised that it would bring just as many memories. My freedom hadn't been removed by the loss of my three-wheeled companion. I'd just added a wheel to my freedom. I didn't feel like a Hell's Angel any more but then I wasn't quite as excitable as

I used to be, in general.

One of the first times I went out in my new vehicle resulted in quite a predicament for little old me. I'd gone out with my wheelchair on relatively low power, and not knowing how far it could go, having hardly been out in it before, I ran out of power. Now that isn't a great problem when you're out with one or a group of your friends. The problem arises when you're on your own because when your batteries run out you can't get up to go for help. If no one comes along you could be spending a night under the stars. On this particular day I had another row with Dexter and stormed off. (I'm not sure what the row was about but it was probably something like I wanted to go home and Dexter didn't want me to, or he'd made me a cup of tea and it was too cold. Whatever it was, it was most likely something stupid.) Just after leaving Dexter's house I noticed that the last light on my wheelchair was flashing, meaning that very soon I'd come to a standstill. So what did I decide to do? I decided to drive across the fields. I don't know why I did that but sure enough, halfway across the fields I came to an abrupt halt. Oh dear! I didn't manage to remain this calm when it happened. In fact, I panicked and kept switching it on and off, hoping for a spurt of energy that was never going to come. When I finally settled down and began to think rationally, I knew I couldn't squeeze any more energy out of the batteries, and I was resigned to sitting in the middle of the field hoping that someone would walk past and rescue me. Just my luck that this was the only sunny day in history when the fields weren't chock-a-block full of people basking in the rare British sunlight. At least it wasn't raining.

I was just beginning to relax when my heroine came on to the field. I remember it well. It was quite an old woman with a big fluffy dog and she said, 'Are you all right there?'

I was going to say, 'Yeah I often sit in the middle of a field on my own,' but I thought she might not help if I did, so I said, 'No not really, my batteries have run out.'

'Oh really? What can I do to help?' she asked politely.

'Could you go to 138 Ashworth Lane? (Dexter's previous address) It's just down the road. And could you tell them Dave's stuck in the middle of the field in his wheelchair?'

'Will do. I'll just be a minute.'

I wish I'd said, 'Well I'm not going anywhere.' But I actually said, 'Okay, thanks a lot,' and off she went, returning with Dexter five minutes later. He unclipped the wheels and pushed me with great difficulty back to his house. 'Thanks again,' I shouted as I rolled off into the distance. I'd been saved. I've never seen that woman since but we had a laugh, and our row was soon forgotten. It was one of those 'swallow your pride' moments; otherwise we wouldn't have spoken for about three days.

Well the wheelchair had started off as badly as the cart riding, but at least I hadn't fallen out... yet. I soon did fall out, and it was probably funnier than when I drove my cart into the back of that van.

Dexter was putting my wheelchair through its paces. I drove it up a hill and Dexter would jump on the back halfway up the hill, like you do. It was certain that he'd go too far, he always did, and it was always me who ended up on the wrong end of his ambition. This time we went up a small but steep hill, on he jumped and, you've guessed it, there was too much weight on the back. It didn't just flop back and bash my head though, it flew back and I did a backward somersault! It was the first time I'd ever seen my own arse fly over my head as my wheelchair jolted and I was flung from the chair. It was a surreal vision and one which luckily I've never seen since. I just lay winded on my back, trying to squeeze the words, 'Dexter you pillock!' out of my mouth, but I couldn't speak for about a minute. Yet another potentially painful moment was saved for the woman who witnessed the whole incident. It must have been more harrowing for her than it was for me because she came running up the path I'd landed on very quickly. I could see her out of the corner of my eye and then bang! She hit the deck and it was now her who needed rescuing. She slumped in a pile on the floor and must have heard me burst into laughter, as I lay prostrate on the concrete, for she lifted herself up and hobbled off into the distance. She must have thought I was really ungrateful. She'd been really worried about me being hurt and I just laughed at her and my own misfortune. It was a classic moment though and I can still see her now.

Later on that summer I did another amazing flip and came out unscathed. Again it wasn't my fault. It was another person close to me that got carried away this time, my brother. My wheelchair had broken down again and my brother took me for a nice stroll. His idea of a stroll was jumping on the back of the wheelchair every time we went down a hill. On the way home from this 'stroll', we reached a hill. It wasn't a very steep hill but it was long enough to get up to a fair speed before we reached the bottom, and that was enough. There were no bumps that we could see but the road did go slightly uphill, very suddenly at the bottom. That was our downfall. Dan jumped on the back, let go of the wheels and we were off. The speed increased with every second and with each extra mile per hour, I became more and more worried.

'Dan slow down a bit,' I pleaded.

'It's all right you wimp, stop worrying.'

'No it's not all right, slow down. Pl–e–e–e–a–se.'

We hit the bump. Dan fell off and on hitting the bump the wheelchair flipped over several times in one direction. Amazingly I somersaulted the other way, defying the laws of gravity. Even more amazing was how I landed. From the middle of the road I'd somehow completely spun round, in the air, and landed with my back against the lamppost, sat bolt upright, without a mark on me or any pain whatsoever. It was a miracle fall, if a fall can ever be described in that way. I hadn't even touched the ground in about five metres of flying. I still can't work out what happened. What can I say, I'm immortal!

Maybe a change of country would do me good. Surely no psychotic people would throw me out on my trip to Germany that my Gran had organised. I went to Germany a couple of days after my latest escape from the Grim Reaper to visit a family friend, Frigga. I'd met her a few years earlier when she came to visit my Grandma and she struck me as a very wise woman, with a firm grasp of English. In fact, if it wasn't for the German accent I'd have thought she was English. We got to the airport and boarded the plane, which for someone in a wheelchair is not the easiest thing in the world. You can't get the wheelchair onto the actual plane because the aisles are too narrow. It's like hammering a twelve-inch nail into a nine-inch hole, impossible. So what has to happen is that the disabled person is lifted out of the wheelchair and on to a different chair with no armrests, and is then transported by two airport staff on to the plane. I felt like a circus tightrope walker and I didn't like it, but in the end the end justified the means. I had to brave the torture chair to go on holiday, and after the initial panic I felt relatively safe. When I finally got into my seat I could breathe a huge sigh of relief.

An hour later we were in Germany, ready to meet Frigga at the airport in Munich. When we met her she told us we'd be staying with her mother for a few days in a town called Augsburg before moving on to the small village, Kranzegg, where Frigga herself lived. Her mum, she told me, didn't speak any English and that was worrying considering that at that point my German limited itself to, *Ich heisse David, ich bin vierzehn Jahre alt.* And, *Ich mochte eine Tasse Kaffee.* That wouldn't get me far in the average German conversation, unless I wanted a cup of coffee or to tell someone my name. After that, I'd have to resort to *Ja* and *Nein* answers, that is, if I knew what Frigga's mum was talking about in the first place. However, in a room with a woman who could only speak German could only help my German. I thought I knew enough words, if she spoke slowly enough to get the general gist of what she was saying, and Frigga had told me how to say, 'Could you speak slower please?' *Konnten Sie bitte langsamer sprechen?* Surely that would be enough?

Blah blech konnden langed, was what I heard when Frigga's mum first spoke to me. What? No amount of saying, 'Could you speak slower please?' would make me understand what she had just said. I had a lot to learn.

The day after that sad indictment of my German knowledge, we went into the town centre in Augsburg because there was some kind of medieval type festival going on: music, demonstrations, etc. and I even tried some authentic German food. I think it was Sauerkraut but I can't be sure. It tasted quite good though. We were sat in a large square eating this cuisine and unluckily for me an ageing French woman took a shine to me. She must have been about eighty and she whispered something complementary in French, well Frigga said it was complementary anyway. Just my luck that anyone over fifty thinks I'm really cute or that, 'If he was twenty years older...' No one my own age wants to know. By the time I reach twenty-five or something I'll be the most fanciable man in the world. Now there's a thought!

Having had our fill of the seventeenth century and with that last thought ringing in my ears, we returned to Frigga's mum's, negotiated the ridiculously awkward, two-flighted semi-spiral staircase up to her flat and entered to the blissful smell of duck cooking in the kitchen. They had to be the best mash potatoes in the world, and the duck was cooked to perfection. The only problem with duck is the lack of meat. You might as well just eat chicken; it tastes the same. Nevertheless, I ate everything on the plate, and then I was ready for bed. I was full, enjoying myself and the travelling from the day before had tired me out. It all made for a good night's sleep.

The following morning I had a lie-in and was ready to face a new day. Today we went for a day out with Billa, Frigga's niece, who had also stayed at my Gran's several years earlier.

Afterwards she looked at my German schoolbooks that I'd brought and she told me that some of the words we'd been taught were a bit out of date. Good old British education, moving with the times! So I took what she told me on board, knowing full well that I wouldn't be able to use the information in an exam because I'd be using the 'wrong' words in the eyes of the examiner. I can still remember what she said though.

After another amazing meal à la Frigga's mum I was ready for bed again. I was now beginning to get a tan from the lovely weather I was experiencing and I felt totally relaxed, ready for the next day's two-hour car journey to Kranzegg.

We rose relatively early, said, *Auf Wiedersehen*! (I could just about manage that) to Frigga's mum and we were gone. Let's be honest, two hours in a car isn't the most exciting pastime in the world unless you're a boy racer or a car bore (which most of my male friends are), but this trip was different. Going from a built-up area to the countryside in Germany is slightly different to the same trip in England where you just see a few hills, fields and a couple of trees. In Germany you see some of the most amazing and beautiful scenery in the world (*schone landschaft*). The hills are the Bavarian Alps (mountains or big hills). The trees are forests and the fields are full of cows, but they're much more friendly looking than English cows. Yes that is a really strange thing to notice but it's just that everything about the German countryside is bigger and better, with quaint little villages scattered between mountains, miles away from the nearest large town. You wouldn't go there for a wild holiday, but for a relaxing couple of weeks it can't be beaten. I felt totally content without a care in the world for two weeks. I suppose you're not supposed to have a care in the world at fourteen but you know me, I was always worried about something. Sorry, I did have one care. It was the bloody steps. Just when I thought I escaped the semi-spiral staircase I found that Frigga had one as well. Those ruddy Germans, they just try to make things difficult for us.

It's not that good, living halfway up a mountain, especially in winter. If you get a snowstorm up there you'd better hope the fridge is stocked because you may be there for some time. I'd love to have a summer house in Bavaria to escape from the stress of life. It's like a different world, a paradise. You get up in the morning and open up the doors leading to the balcony and you feel instantly content. When you see a mountain, you see nature in its full glory and I can understand when people say they feel closer to God in such places, even though I don't believe in all that myself. The only annoying thing was the sound of screaming kids at 7 a.m. There was a Kindergarten on the ground floor of Frigga's apartment building and the kids would wake me up every day, but it was a small price to pay.

I think I've praised the German countryside enough now. What did I do for the rest of the holiday? Well, it was a case of exploring the beautiful countryside and experiencing the world of German cuisine. I tried Wiener Schnitzel (meat in breadcrumbs), the authentic German version, and a number of other foods. I also had the biggest sirloin steak I'd ever seen in a gorgeous restaurant. When I returned to this restaurant two years later, the waitress remembered me. What can I say, women never forget my gorgeous, sexy looks, or is it that they don't get many lads in wheelchairs in the mountains? You decide. I was and probably still am the only lad in a wheelchair to have visited that restaurant twice, but I still maintain that I'm gorgeous!

The highlight of my exploration of the countryside was

definitely my trip up a mountain in a cable car. Firstly because of the beautiful view, stretching miles in front of me from the top of the mountain. It's an awe-inspiring view, and it's very surreal seeing snow-capped peaks in the middle of summer when it's about ninety degrees at ground level. The second reason for my total enjoyment of this trip was seeing hang-gliders taking off from the summit. I had another one of my disturbing, Coalbrookdale-inspired visions, watching one man jump from the mountain top. I saw him skewered on a lower mountain peak after a sudden nosedive. It didn't actually happen, but I think I need psychiatric help for these morbid ideas. It must be fantastic flying or gliding above the mountain tops and looking down on nature. You may think I'm getting carried away with this description of nature but you only have to experience it to know where I'm coming from.

Anyway, the third and funniest reason why this was a great day was the way Frigga handled two Prussians. (I think of Prussia as the rest of Germany, i.e. not Bavaria. Bavarians and Prussians have a healthy dislike for one another.) When we entered the cable car Frigga wanted to get me to the front so I could see the scenery on the way up, but the two Prussians had other ideas. They looked at me and blatantly stood in front of me, so basically all I could see were the twin peaks of two German bottoms. Not quite the scenery Frigga had in mind! Frigga, on seeing this act of pure ignorance, went from easy going to mad psycho in about three seconds, and with a cry of, 'Those ignorant Prussians!' she sprung into action. You don't get on the wrong side of Frigga, she's stubborn and she won't back down when she knows she's right. That's probably why she gets on so well with our family. These Germans experienced the wrath of Frigga and sure enough they backed down, apologised to me and moved out of the way. The shadows cast by their bums dispersed and I could see the splendour of the mountains. What a day!

The holiday passed by much quicker than I wanted. Time flies when you're having fun.

So the day of our departure had arrived, we were all packed. I'd bought the cheapest presents in the world for my Mum and Dad – four 99 pfennig bowls and a 2 DM cowbell, respectively.

The cowbell has now disappeared and the ice cream bowls are used as ashtrays. (How ungrateful is that?) All we had to do was drive for three hours to Munich and leave.

The scenes in the airport were strangely emotional. Frigga wanted to come as far as possible in the airport but she and my Grandma had another one of their pointlessly stubborn rows over whether she'd spent enough of her time on us. I was beginning to wonder who was the kid there, me or them. She ended up going home after about ten minutes of hugging my Gran and crying. It was a sad moment but it wasn't as if we'd never see her again. No, I didn't cry, I told you I'm a man. Crying's for girls.

That holiday was very enjoyable, not just because of the days out and the food. Young people often think that going on holiday on their own with adults will be worse than sticking needles in their eyes. They think they know it all (especially at about fourteen or fifteen) and that there's nothing they can learn from their parents or grandparents. I, on the other hand, have always got on well with all my grandparents, and in that respect I've been lucky. I enjoy talking to my Gran and Frigga about things like religion and listening to their stories and conversations. It was the cultural differences between the English and the Germans that interested me. Maybe that sounds boring to most teenagers, but to me it's not. Obviously I love talking to my friends, otherwise they wouldn't be my friends, but at fourteen or fifteen years old what do people talk to their friends about? Basically it's football, girls, music, TV, girls and girls in that order, and most of the time I'm happy to talk about those things. Girls and football can't be beaten as topics of conversation, unless you're talking about girls' football. That's probably why I fancied Emma for a while. She's a girl who plays football – perfect! If girls were any good at football, it would be the most watched sport in the world. Football should be left to men, the women should just be there to wash the kits. (I'll just go and change my address and phone number.)

Sometimes I need a break from the mundane conversations. That thirst for knowledge that I had when I was little has never left me, and maybe that's why I enjoy serious conversations from time to time. Now I'm an adult myself, I can sometimes fit in a serious conversation with my friends but I still enjoy a good chat with my Gran. I learnt a lot from my Grandma and Frigga and from my Granddad's occasional witty comments in the middle. He's a man of few words but when he does say something, it's usually worth listening to.

When I went to Germany for the first time, Frigga was a friend of my grandparents. When I came home I classed her as one of my friends. If I ever needed her, I could count on her to be on the other end of the phone straight away. Frigga is another person who's expressed her admiration for the way I deal with my disability. She said that whenever she feels sorry for herself she thinks about me, and tells herself off for moaning. I'm glad I could be of service. I think, however, that people who say that about me underestimate themselves. Frigga's not had it easy herself, and she copes very well with everything that life throws at her, as do my Gran and my Mum. I'm proud to know that in some small way I'm helping people out, helping people not to moan about things. My Mum of course never says that I stop her from moaning. That's because she's always here when I'm in a moaning mood! My Gran and Frigga aren't here for that.

I went through the ordeal of getting back on to the plane and returned home to my Mummy. I'd had a great time. I was totally relaxed and happy when I got home, ready to get back to the immature reality that was my life. There were still a couple of weeks of the summer left. That was enough time to play a few computer games, wander around aimlessly and have sleepovers at Dexter's where we'd eat – again! Agghh, the photos from this time are haunting me. I was pretty fat at that time and I think that might be another reason why no one would go out with me. I was the fat lad in the wheelchair, with the sixties Beatles side parting. Very sexy! It was about this time that I made a conscious decision to lose weight and I also started to be more bothered about my appearance. I started using hair gel, trying to get rid of my retro-look, to bring myself into the nineties. I thought it might change my luck, but even if it didn't at least I'd look my best. Let's face it, my luck couldn't get any worse. It would take a lot of hard work, but I was determined to do it. There we go then, I had a new obsession, a new goal.

Obviously the only way for a person in a wheelchair to lose

weight is to eat less. Exercise was out of the question, so near starvation was the solution. Drastic yes, but it's been effective. I'd eat two rashers of bacon on their own for breakfast, one little sandwich and a sugarless Ribena for lunch, and a small evening meal. Sounds like an advert for a new fad diet, doesn't it? I also got a little help from our new canine, food-devouring machine. We'd been mithering my Mum for a dog for years and eventually she let us go to the Staffordshire bull terrier Rescue Centre 'just for a look'. She must have known that inevitably we'd get a dog. She'd given ground and all we had to do was chip away at her resistance and she'd let us have one. 'Staffordshires are one of the most gentle dogs in the world, with adults and children,' we were told, 'but they've been bred for fighting so they're a bit aggressive with other dogs.'

We were given this spiel and met the dog that the managers of the rescue centre owned. Danny it was called and it was huge for its breed, and full of energy. He pinned my brother to the floor and madly licked his face for about five minutes. He was lovely and I think that's what finally persuaded my Mum to let us have a dog.

When we went away she still wasn't completely sure, but she said she'd think about it. That was all my Dad needed to know and about a week later, when there was a call from the rescue centre to say that there was a dog in the kennels, he went to see it. My brother and I didn't know about it and we were shocked and excited when a couple of hours later my Dad came up the Grove, holding a lead which was attached a fat white beast with one black eye. This fat beast was wobbling up the Grove. When my Mum saw him she said, 'What the hell is that? He's brought us a pig.' As they came closer he looked cuter and cuter, the dog that is, but as the door opened we heard a loud grunting noise, and it wasn't my Dad. He had seriously brought us a pig-dog!

My brother, who always wears his heart on his sleeve, looked really excited. He said, 'Are we keeping him?' and automatically looked pleadingly at my Mum.

She must have seen the excitement on his face because she said, 'It looks like we'll have to now,' not wanting to disappoint him.

It would have disappointed me as well, but I was never quite as obvious with my feelings. I just smiled when I saw him, but I was inwardly excited. My Mum knew that, as usual. When she heard the story of how the dog had ended up in the kennels, she was only too pleased to keep him. He'd been abandoned and found locked in a garden shed. Then he'd ended up locked in a kennel for a week. Surely he didn't deserve that. No animal deserves that.

We think he'd been stolen to fight in illegal dogfights because that's what they're bred to do, and then he'd been abandoned because they realised he had very worn, almost non-existent teeth at the front, from chewing bricks. (He's a very intelligent animal you know.) I think teeth are a prerequisite for a fighting dog. So after this traumatic experience, he'd finished up with the Adams Family. Little did he know he'd be the most pampered pooch in the world, for the rest of his existence. He's got the life of Reilly here. He was on easy street now. All we had to do was name him. A few names were thrown around: Butch, Tyson, Killer, and then my brother came out with Ralph. We looked at him like he'd just come down from Mars, then we looked at the pig lying in front of the fire, and that was it. It had to be Ralph. Ralph's a cool name for a dog, and with that he was now part of the family. Every family needs a dog.

Later that night I seriously wanted to send Ralph back to the kennels. I was sat on the living room floor with him, so that he could get close to me and I could stroke him. It was also to stop him being scared of the wheelchair, to let him know I was a normal person without all this metal around me. I suppose that sounds silly but I've had little cousins who've been scared, so I thought maybe a dog would be scared too. I've never had to worry about that. Ralph just lies right next to the wheelchair all day. I'm always running him over.

At this particular moment I realised that Ralph was going to be frisky. I was just minding my own business stroking him, and he decided to take that the wrong way. I was just trying to be friendly and he thought I fancied him. It's an easy thing to do though, to mistake friendship for more than that. So he started to mate with my arm whilst nibbling on my neck, and basically just being a pervert. Thrusting his hips and scratching me with his nails. Very kinky! I then keeled over on to the floor and started crying in my panic. My Mum had to drag him off, and that's not easy to do with a fifty-pound bull terrier. I'd lost all notion of perspective again and I went a bit overboard. 'Get rid of him, I don't like him any more,' I sobbed.

That was a bit pathetic considering the dog had just been through a terrible ordeal, which he wouldn't have understood. He now had a new family and not surprisingly, he was a bit overexcited. All right, so he's been frisky like that ever since but that's not the point. I could have been a bit more understanding. That's my animal psychoanalysis for you.

I'm glad my Mum didn't listen to me and get rid of Ralph because since then he's brought joy into our meaningless existence. He's kept me warm by sleeping on my bed during the winter nights, even though my legs go numb under his rotund body. He eats like a grown man every day and that's stopped me eating too much. Ralph definitely helps with my diet.

He's a real character. You can tell what he's thinking. If you're ill he'll snuggle up to you in bed. When you're eating, he grunts louder so you know he's there. He cries when he wants something out of the fridge, and when my Mum's just put clean bedding on he'll go upstairs at the first opportunity and lie on the bed. He runs into my room whenever there's a row going on and he's terrified of fireworks.

What excites him most though is the word that sends every dog mad – 'Walkies!' He loves running around in the fields, around lakes and reservoirs, or even just in the park. As long as he's got a brick in his toothless head, he'll run all day.

Ralph's not really vicious with other dogs unless he's in a bad mood or if they attack him first. That's the only thing that makes him put his brick down, to teach them a lesson. Oh yeah, and to mate with other dogs. He's a randy beast and doesn't care whether the object of his lust is male or female. He puts the 'grrr' in swinger baby!

His fights are usually one-sided affairs. Even though he has no teeth he uses his strength to beat them in other ways. His flying headbutt is a killer and it works. When he got into a fight with a

Rottweiler three times his size, he put this move into practice. His charge started from about thirty feet away and as he reached his opponent he'd got up enough speed to put optimum power behind his rock hard titanium head. The Rottweiler was sent flying and that was the end of the fight. You don't mess with anyone or anything that can running headbutt you from fifty paces, and live to tell the tale!

If there's one thing he hates more than anything else, it's those little, fluffy white Scottie dogs. It's like when you have a little kid who just mithers you and mithers you until you snap and scream at him to shut up, only Ralph can't talk so he has to bite. Scottie dogs always seemed to follow him, sniff him, bite his legs, and do as many irritating things as possible. Ralph just walks along and tries to ignore this little rat-type creature nibbling at his legs, but with every irritating nibble and sniff the anger and frustration builds up, bit by bit, until he explodes in a rage, drops his brick, and attacks. They don't nibble any more once he's shown them who's boss. In that way he's very similar to me. I can put up with some people annoying me for hours on end and then I'll finally snap. I can take it for weeks, even months from some people, but eventually I'll let them know how irritating they are. I have a way with words and they know in no uncertain terms that I'm not going to take it any more. The trouble is people get upset because I take so long to let it build up, and then everything comes out at once like I'm firing a machine gun at them.

Ralph also hates sheep. Another classic moment came when Ralph chased a sheep into the Blue Lagoon (a lake near where we live). He looked over at this sheep, and it must have looked at him in a way that was unacceptable to him because he started to chase it as fast as he could. The sheep panicked, almost had a heart attack and ran off in any direction it could think of. It ran in a blind panic, and with Ralph snapping at its heels, it reached the water's edge.

Was this the end for Sheepman or would our hero escape the evil clutches of Doctor Ralphenhund? It was a scene reminiscent of Hollywood, where the hero reaches a cliff with water and rocks below, and it's a choice between certain death at the hands of a bad guy, or a large chance of death by jumping. He chose the second choice. Ralph didn't follow him in, the sheep didn't drown, and the risk had paid off. Tune in tomorrow for the next thrilling instalment of Sheepman!

Chapter VII

In amongst all this excitement, the summer had slipped away again and the upper school, the start of GCSEs beckoned. Would I cope? That was a good question, but I wasn't scared to find out the answer. I was ready and my latest obsession was about to begin. I must do as well as possible in these exams.

It's supposed to be two years of pressure, what with coursework in about seven of your ten subjects and pressure to get into college, but although I did feel it sometimes, it didn't bother me. I just carried on in the way I'd been working and basically just got on with it. It wasn't that bad.

This fourth year was also work experience year, and didn't we know it? Mr Roberts was the work experience co-ordinator and he came into every assembly every week and gave us a spiel about how important it was to apply as early as possible, otherwise you'd end up being a binman for two weeks. No offence to 'refuse collectors' but when you're fifteen years old you don't want to spend two weeks driving around in a truck full of household waste. Now finding a place to do work experience would be difficult, you'd expect, simply because there's a limited amount of jobs you can do when you're sat down and your arms don't do much. Basically it's an office job, or nothing. When you have a career there are ways round physical limitations, but for two weeks you have to do what you can. I wasn't going to take one of the helpers with me, was I?

There were a number of forms we had to fill in. There was WE (Work Experience) 1, WE 2, WE 3 and so on, and if you hadn't filled one of them in by the time Mr Roberts told you to, he'd come into assembly and read out your name to embarrass you. 'You won't be able to do your work experience if you don't fill in your WE 3 forms.'

It used to drive me absolutely mad, probably because I'd already filled mine in. I was extremely sad. I did everything the teachers said to me, but at least I did it. I was excited about work experience, if slightly apprehensive about how I'd manage, so I wanted to organise it as quickly as possible.

So where did I decide to go? I'd already decided I wanted to be a lawyer so the court seemed like as good a place as any. They could fit me in at the time I'd be doing the work experience but there was a slight problem. I couldn't get in the building. That put a little spanner in the works. Well, you know what they say about the best-laid plans of mice and men? No? Neither do I. Nobody ever gets as far as telling you that.

Now I had to find somewhere else to go. I was good at maths so I thought the bank would be a good place. We tried that. This time they could fit me in and I could fit into the building, but they could only take me for a week. I had to go back through the same old rigmarole and find a place to take me for the other week. Couldn't I just have had a week off? I thought it would be futile to suggest that, so I didn't bother. I just went off and Mr Roberts set to thinking about where else I could go. I was fresh out of ideas.

I got on with the important part of the year, my lessons, while he was considering the idea and soon found out that the other three years of Secondary School had been there simply to give us a grounding. Even if we hadn't listened for three years we'd probably be all right, because everything we needed to know for GCSEs would be taught to us over the next two years. That's what I mean by 'the exams in the first three years were completely meaningless in the greater scheme of things'. It's a shame I'd read so much into them that I ruined my first year, but anyway at least I'd got my worrying out of my system.

The lessons were similar to before. It was just that the homework sometimes took on a more important meaning when it was coursework. It counted for 40% of our marks, so the assignments came thick and fast. It was all good fun, though. For English literature we had to read *Macbeth* and *To Kill a Mocking Bird*. Ahh, those were the days! When I did actually have to read a book I enjoyed it. *To Kill a Mocking Bird* made me want even more to be a lawyer. I wanted to restore justice which seemed to be distinctly lacking in this story of racial equality where an innocent black man is jailed for rape, even though his white lawyer proves his innocence. I had a very idealistic view. I could restore justice by being a fair and honest lawyer. Yeah right! I also wanted to make lots of money.

Macbeth is a story of the thirst for power going to a man's head. As a thriller, with blood, guts, gore, witches, and apparitions (sounds painful) it can't be beaten, and it's an excellent illustration of the saying, 'Behind every man there's a strong woman.' I don't believe that saying for one minute, but it seems Shakespeare did.

The worst part was that we'd have to do a coursework piece on war poetry, lovely! That was the most boring piece of work I've ever done.

In history we studied the history of medicine, the Wild West (nothing to do with Will Smith) and we had to do coursework on both of these plus one on Northern Ireland and one about local history. I actually enjoyed history coursework and felt I was good at it.

English and history lessons were brilliant, not just because I liked the work but because Matthew, Dexter, Oliver and I used to have a laugh in history. I don't know about the other three but I was lucky. I could talk and work at the same time. Oliver was one of those unlucky people who got into trouble for everything, even when it wasn't his fault. Someone would call him and the teacher would hear it and move Oliver to a different desk. When all four of us were laughing and joking and being as loud as each other, it was Oliver who would get into trouble.

I think Mr Collins knew that Dexter, Matthew and I were working as much as we were talking. Oliver was doing maybe 75% talking and 25% work, and I think Mr Collins saw his potential and worried he wouldn't fulfil it. They weren't exactly intellectual conversations either. First of all we'd argue over who won at Sensible Soccer the night before. I always won but Dexter used to lie the next day. If he'd lost 4–1 he'd say he'd won and he did it just to wind me up. Of course it worked and it would end in a shouting match. How embarrassing. After that we'd just talk a load of rubbish and take the mickey out of each other. At one point Dexter started to sing the *Teenage Mutant Hero Turtles* theme tune to our absolute disgust. We looked at him like he was part of a freak show.

Yeah history was great fun, and so was English. I sat on a table with Emma, Heather and Nichola. I could take the mickey out of them and they wouldn't get offended. They knew I was joking and they could take it. They also knew that I was a nice lad and if they needed to talk seriously, I'd cheer them up in my own tactless and clumsy manner. They knew I cared. It was good for me as well. I love having female friends. They're more sensitive than lads. They're also better looking than lads and even though it gets a bit complicated when I decide I fancy one of them, it usually doesn't change anything.

I don't think I actually had a serious conversation with any of them in a lesson, unless it was about homework. Usually it was just calling the teacher Mr Gething (jokingly of course) or just being silly, but it made for a good couple of years.

Now we were fourth-years, part of the upper school, the teachers treated us more like adults and Mr Gething was more like a mate than a teacher. When on the rare occasion he actually told someone off it wasn't in an aggressive manner, it was more a kind of pep talk for anyone who was doing less than the required amount of work. It went something along the lines of: 'You've got great potential, everyone in set one has, but if you don't do the work you'll never amount to anything.' It'd work with many people but if you've got one terminally lazy person in your class, who thinks he can pass without working hard, then that person is too lazy to listen to the teacher's laments. That's what I think but I'm so cynical I can't be impartial.

I think most people in our set had a lot of respect for Mr Gething. He really cared and wanted everyone to do as well as possible. We weren't just a class, we were a group of individuals, whom he wanted to get to know. It's probably easier to teach a good group of kids, who know where they want to go with their lives and know how much work they have to do to get there. He knew we were on his wavelength so he could laugh and joke with us whilst teaching at the right pace. Most of our lessons were good fun.

He was probably more aggressive teaching lower sets, not necessarily because they were without intelligence but because they didn't feel they were cut out for school or because other things were more important to them. When someone feels like that, getting them to work is like getting blood out of a stone and it takes a very good teacher to inspire these people into working. That's where you separate good teachers from great ones.

Enough on the philosophy of teaching. I keep forgetting that this book's about me!

When I'd returned to school this year I'd realised that most of my lessons would be upstairs, in fact looking at my timetable I noticed that every lesson that could possibly be upstairs was upstairs. Now why would the teachers do this? Had they decided they just didn't care about me any more, or did I act in such a normal way that they'd forgotten I was in a wheelchair at all? The truth is it was neither of those answers. What had happened was that Miss Toole along with a number of senior teachers had had an ingenious idea. Yes, they'd rented a stair climber. My first thought at the unveiling of this blue monstrosity with tank-like caterpillar tracks was, 'There is no way I'm being taken upstairs on that! Someone must be punishing me for being a murderer in a past life, or for being an atheist.'

I didn't say that, what could I say? I just smiled politely and said, 'I'll give it a go. It looks okay.' My heart was in my throat at the time, so how I could manage to say anything escapes me, but I forced it out. Within a minute or two I'd been strapped to the 'tank' whilst still in the wheelchair, with Dexter and my mother observing. Dexter would soon have to learn how to use it. The person who'd loaned us the 'Jimson Stair Mate' (more like 'stair enemy') turned the key and pressed the start button while I started to sweat. I was very worried but was reassured that it worked, and with a shrill buzz the machine was trundling slowly up the stairs. Once it got going it felt surprisingly safe, almost therapeutic. As they brought it down I consoled myself with the thought that it was my Mum's turn next. I've got an evil streak and seeing my Mum's fear-filled expression brought a feeling of immense joy into my life. It's amazing what makes you feel better, isn't it?

With Dexter in control I could now do whatever I wanted, freely. It wasn't the same after that. I couldn't defy the teachers by going upstairs quickly, and alone. If we set off without supervision the teachers could catch us more easily, what a shame!

We still tried to defy the helpers and made them feel guilty whenever they appeared late to help us upstairs. It was usually Miss Noden, or a new helper called Miss Miller. We were told to wait for them if we got to the stairs before they did, which was invariably what happened, probably because we got out of our lessons early so we could beat the rush and so we wouldn't be late for the next lesson. If the helper arrived after the bell then it sort of defeated the object of leaving early in the first place. I'd be early out of one lesson and in late to the next. Admittedly it wasn't their fault but I wasn't willing to wait around. As soon as we got to the stairs Dexter, or later Chris, would hook me up to the tank, and we'd inch slowly down the stairs. It was much slower than the manual way that we knew and trusted, and often we got caught by the bell. Everyone else who came behind us was then late. No one else was bothered but I've always hated being late for anything. I also didn't want to miss what could have been an important piece of knowledge for the exams which were approaching rapidly. Why do I keep admitting to these sad quirks of my personality?

Dexter and I had a number of arguments with Miss Miller over this lateness. She objected to us leaving without her, and we objected to her expecting us to miss part of a lesson just so she could be seen to be doing her job. I had the key to the machine, Dexter and Chris knew how to use it, and really we didn't need any help. So why shouldn't I go downstairs at the most convenient time for me, regardless of whether there was any supervision on hand? It was too heavy for a woman to manipulate anyway!

It was maths that I missed once because Miss Miller wasn't there to help me get downstairs. Fed up with the way we always left without her, she'd taken the key with her and promised to be on time. Five minutes after the bell, she hadn't arrived. I was beginning to get annoyed. Ten minutes and she still wasn't there. I sent Chris to tell Mr Twigg I'd be late. Fifteen minutes after the bell, and just as I was plotting her untimely and very painful death (psychotic tendencies again), she arrived. I smiled and said, 'I promise I'll be on time,' mimicking her high-pitched feminine voice. She looked suitably guilty. I wasn't that worried but it was nice to get one up on her. She didn't run off with the key again in a hurry!

I'd be lying if I said I didn't use the machine to my advantage when on the very rare occasion, I did actually want to be late. Well it was the compulsory RE lesson that I didn't mind being late for. I mean you'll forgive me that, won't you?

Just when I thought it was all over, that I could rid myself of RE once and for all, I had to endure one mind numbingly boring hour of 'ridiculous education' per week. What was the point, was what I wanted to know? We spent an hour a week sat in a room, just waiting for the lesson to end and not listening to a word which left our teacher's mouth. Oh yeah, and joy of joys our teacher was... Yes you've guessed it – Miss Webster! I experienced the wrath of Webster on one occasion, when through no fault of my own we couldn't get to the machine till after the bell. I'd already got in trouble with Miss Noden for going to the staffroom and asking for the machine and not for her. What a terribly nasty thing to do. It's not as if I'd tried to blow up the Houses of Parliament. I bit my lip though, and didn't argue back and with blood dripping from my lip that I'd bitten too hard I attached myself to the machine, and off we went. We arrived in the room about eight minutes late. Don't get me wrong I never actually did anything active to make myself late, I just didn't mind when it happened, and I had an excuse when it did. Or so I thought. From Miss Webster's face I actually began to believe I had blown up the Houses of Parliament, for she looked at me like a Rottweiler whose steak had just been stolen! It might have been the bloody lip that did it. I don't mind admitting that the Rottweiler impression put the fear of God into me, so I apologised rapidly.

'Sorry we're late, the machine came late.'

'What do you mean the machine came late?'

'Well, the machine that takes me upstairs didn't arrive on time,' I said sarcastically.

'Sit down!'

Okay then, I thought, *that was a bad move.* I refrained from saying, 'I am sitting down,' although I wish I had said it. At least if I was going down, I'd go down fighting.

I had to be chewing gum at the same time, didn't I? Not a good idea because as I got annoyed my chewing action became more and more exaggerated, and of course she caught me. I was blowing up Buckingham Palace this time!

I was snapped out of my daydream about Cindy Crawford running towards me on a beach, by the piercing sound of, 'David, get rid of that chewing gum!' She brought the bin over and everyone watched me struggle to put the chewing gum in it. I was getting a bit pissed off by then but I should have known that bad luck comes in threes, because just a minute later Oliver asked me a question and stupidly I answered it.

I heard the voice again. 'David you're being downright rude today. I'll send you to Mr Mitten's office and you can explain to him why you're behaving like this.'

'He asked me a question,' I protested and that was as bold as I got.

'Shut up,' she shouted.

If at any point later in the lesson she'd told me off for any other little incident, I'd probably have snapped, I was that annoyed. I'd had enough.

Maybe I shouldn't have been chewing or talking but the original reason she was annoyed with me was not a reason to be annoyed with someone, considering it was out of my hands. Thinking about it now I wish I had been sent to Mr Mitten's office, it'd have been a welcome respite from this pointless interruption to school life.

Anyway, organised religion should be banned, let alone RE. Sounds a bit drastic but hear me out. First of all, it may unite people within a certain religion but it also marginalises each religion. It creates a tribalism in that each religion promotes itself as the best one, or even the 'right' one, and instead of creating love for God it creates hatred between the groups. The way I see it is that religion is based on one fundamental belief that there is a supreme being who is all powerful. It just has a different name in each religion, so why there has to be fighting between different religions whose ideals are (if people would only stop to think about it) basically similar, is beyond me.

Hindus and Muslims fight, and even different groups within

the same religion fight, e.g. Protestants and Catholics. Why?

People complain about football hooligans and of course football hooliganism is disgusting but is it really much different to the tribalism and war caused by conflicting religions? Liverpool fans hate Man. United fans for no valid or apparent reason other than being jealous and Protestants hate Catholics for equally invalid reasons. People may think I'm over trivialising religion by comparing it to twenty-two men chasing a piece of leather around a field, but at least the ball is real, and the trophies and glory at the end are plain to see. If your team wins, you feel you've done your bit to achieve it, by paying for the tickets or buying merchandise, and if your team doesn't win you are united in defeat.

With religion, the arguments are about a God who may or may not exist, the proof of whose existence is based on scriptures and stories, which may be fact or may be fiction. Nobody really knows, people just believe. Why are there wars about such an uncertain thing? I think it's because people believe that they are right. They think their religion is the best, just as people think their football team is the best, but at least there is a definite best team at the end of a football season and that usually is Man. United (oh how it pains me to say this).

Why people can't just believe in something and accept that it is different to what other people believe, I don't know. Life's never that simple.

Some of the life and death situations which people allow to be decided for them by a book or by a belief is just crazy! The Bible says, 'Thou shalt not give blood,' so Jehovah's witnesses won't give their own flesh and blood a blood transfusion. Hmmm that makes sense! The phrase 'cutting your nose off to spite your face', springs to mind.

So religions are based on a particular interpretation of a book, which may or may not have any reflection of reality and which explains to us what a God, which may or may not exist, wants us to do. The main reason I wanted religion to be banned, though, was because I hated RE and didn't like my teacher until I was about to leave.

I've gone off on one again, haven't I? Where was I? Oh yeah, that's it. Once I'd got past the RE lesson every week I could get on with my life. I didn't have a problem with any other teacher but about six months into the year, when we started our first piece of IT coursework, I began to wish I'd chosen keyboard applications. We had to design (what – design?) a leaflet advertising a fictional event taking place in our area. I chose a beetle drive knowing full well I couldn't do well at this task. So suddenly the subject had changed from learning how to create spreadsheets, into design technology. I'd chosen IT to avoid design technology. I did my best though.

I felt a bit like a special case with my stair walker. I looked like something out of *Star Wars* but at least they didn't have to reorganise the timetable for me. I could even have my lessons upstairs now. I was truly integrated!

Around this time, a few months into the year, Mr Roberts had a brainwave. He'd found a place where I could do my other work experience week. Bolton and Bury Tec. 'What's that?' I asked. I thought it meant Technical College but it was a business and I would be working in the marketing department. I was just happy it was all organised because I'd been worried I'd be stuck in school, getting on with coursework. I could even get into the building, albeit through the tradesman's entrance, but it was better than the courts. It was a weight off my shoulders and I could now get on with the fourth year and think about more pressing issues, i.e. girls.

This year saw my ability to make a fool of myself reach its full potential and I think it still rates as my most embarrassing moment. I became the lowest of the low, an obscene phone caller. Well they weren't really obscene they just showed how far my obsession with Isla had gone. It was also Dexter's fault. How could my making phone calls be Dexter's fault? Well, I'd heard Isla giving someone her phone number and sadly enough I memorised it. That's a bad enough start. Then I told Dexter what it was when he was at my house and he got an idea, which was more evil and mischievous than any that had come before. He dialled the number, with me at the other side of the room. I had to get to the phone before it started ringing and turn it off. What an ingenious plan! Every time he did it I raced across the room, having begged him over and over again not to do it, and each time the ring beat me by one ring, about one second. Eventually as you can imagine the people at the other end of the phone started to get a little annoyed, and guess what I'd done, or more appropriately, guess what I hadn't done? I hadn't pressed 141 to withhold my number, so Isla's dad rang up and asked my Mum why our number was on his phone and could whoever was doing it please pack it in.

'David! Have you been using the phone?' my Mum shouted.

Okay, so I'd been caught, it was time to own up and take it like a man.

'No,' I shouted back.

How could I blatantly lie about something I'd been caught red-handed for? How else would the number have got on to their phone? That's what my Mum was eager to find out.

'Well why's our number on their phone?'

Even Dexter was willing me to own up now, but I just couldn't do it. 'I don't know, Mum.'

The worst thing was that my Mum actually believed me. She was so adamant that I wouldn't have done it that she was about to ring BT to ask them why our number had appeared on their phone as if by magic. It must have been the telephone fairy, or something.

That was it. The time had come to tell the truth as embarrassing as it was. 'It was me Mum. Don't ring BT,' I said guiltily.

I couldn't believe I'd done it. My Mum rang Isla's dad and apologised for her horrible, perverted son and I had to face the music.

Dexter denied any part in the incident. I could believe it. He'd left me to suffer alone, so he didn't look bad. It's funny now but I wanted to kill him at the time. When I mentioned what he'd done to everyone else, he just looked at me like I should be committed to a mental asylum. How he managed to keep a straight face, I'll never know, but what I do know is that I definitely suffered that morning.

I really didn't want to go to school that morning but I didn't say so to Mum. She would have slapped me if I'd tried to get a day off. She probably knew how I felt anyway.

When I went into school I had a horrible feeling in my stomach. I thought it was a bad dream or something. I wouldn't do that, would I? And to think I'd always prided myself on being mature for my age! At that moment in time however it dawned on me like a slap round the face that I still had a long way to go. The fear that it was Isla coming through the door, and the relief every time that it was Liam or Nichola was agony. I knew she'd be here soon.

On her arrival I felt stupid and like a sad little boy, which I obviously was. I gave her a nervous smile and she walked past me so quickly, she created an icy blast of air. I got a funny feeling that she didn't like me very much at that moment.

Most of the day continued in this icy vein. It was torture. I hoped she'd just take the mickey and laugh at me. I'd have been able to take that. Mr Altdorf took pleasure in doing exactly that, the evil swine. I'd just been through the most embarrassing moment of my sad existence and he thought it was funny. I suppose I did get exactly what I deserved and of course, if it had been anybody else I'd have been the first with the sarcastic (and usually very witty) comment. It was funny though, once the friendship warmed up from the temperature of an Arctic glacier. I didn't like being called a pervert for the following eighteen months but it was one of those moments. If childish moments like that didn't happen, you'd never learn from them. You've also grown up too soon if you never do anything childish. Maybe I went slightly too far to prove this point, but it's one of my most vivid memories.

So to my list of adjectives, describing myself at secondary school you can now add 'childish' and 'pathetic'. I wasn't mature enough to have a girlfriend really.

I never rang Isla again until we'd left school, although I got as far as dialling five of the numbers once. (There are some things you shouldn't admit to. That's probably one of them.)

Despite these strange and embarrassing lapses into childism, I wouldn't change the way I was back then for anything. I was young, innocent and naive. I thought girls wanted to hear suggestive remarks. It just expressed my healthy interest in the female form. I know why I made these remarks. It was to show off. I was embarrassed talking to girls, even though I'd always had female friends, and to compensate for that I sometimes went too far in what I was saying. I wasn't the same person normally that I was when I was at school and maybe that's one regret I do have, that sometimes I wasn't myself. That's why I didn't get as close to certain people as I wanted to. It was mainly the people who I met when I got to secondary school. They never really got to see my sensitive side. The people who'd known me since I was little knew I was really a sensitive new age man. I thought I had to be the way I was to be cool, and I think I spent too much time trying to be cool and not enough time being myself. I was never cool, you can tell that from how I've always enjoyed school and talking to my Gran. Not quite cool, but I was happy. I should have just been myself.

Looking back, I put it down to growing up. Even though I was mature in the way I handled my disability, I was a normal fifteen-year-old boy which is how I wanted to be. I was perfectly normal. I just used wheels instead of legs.

I would learn more from how I acted with girls at Sharples, when I got to sixth form. Women, however, would have to take a back seat in my life this year. There was a more important issue to think about. In fact, thinking about women seemed somewhat superficial in light of a new, devastating blow. I can't remember when exactly it was when my Mum and Dad split up, but I can remember how it felt when Mum came into my room looking a bit flustered, and not very happy. I'd heard them row the night before, but had thought nothing of it. They were always arguing, but I never once believed that it was that serious. Not my parents, they wouldn't split up. I was sure of that.

Intuition wasn't one of my strong points, then. I was just lying in bed, contemplating the day ahead but, as she started speaking I knew this day wouldn't be as much fun as I'd thought.

'I've got something to tell you,' she started.

That sounded ominous. 'What's up Mum?' I asked. I was worried now.

'Now, don't get upset.'

'What's goin' on Mum?'

'Me and your Dad have split up, he's moved out.'

Do you ever wish you hadn't asked a question? Well, that was one of those moments.

'Why?' I questioned, holding back the tears. I felt like my heart had just been ripped from my chest.

'He's been having an affair for a long time.' I didn't really want that to be the answer but at least it wasn't her fault. I didn't think it could be anything else... 'He hasn't left you, it's not your fault,' she added quickly.

The time for being mature in the face of adversity had passed. I just couldn't stop the tears any more. I started crying and she joined me in being overcome by the moment. We hugged and just cried for a minute. I felt like a kid again, and needed a hug. Mum obliged, and although it couldn't take any of it away, I think it comforted her as much as it did me.

'We'll be all right,' she said.

That somehow didn't make me feel better. 'It won't be the same though,' I sobbed. 'How will we manage for money?'

I can't understand that reaction. My Mum was absolutely distraught and I was worried about money. Not very sensitive. I suppose it was only the natural reaction from someone who'd just got one of the biggest shocks of his short life. Kids hate it when things change and even at fifteen years of age, I was no different. How would we manage for money? Did my Dad hate me and Dan?

If I'd been able to think straight, I'd have known that there were a lot of people who would rally round and help. My grandparents for three. My Dad would have to pay until we were eighteen anyway. I don't think he'd have let us go short. That's the first question answered. As for the second, of course he didn't hate me and Dan. He wasn't seeing other children. He was seeing another woman.

A while later, having recovered from the shock, I was still upset but now I could think straight. I wanted to castrate my Dad and strangle whatever her name was. I wasn't a happy camper but at least I wasn't worried about money and other insensitive things. My brother and I would help out as much as possible.

Now I'd become a fat, pathetic, perverted and tactless wheelchair boy with half a family, what did I do? I said stuff it and pushed all thoughts of my parental situation into the same cavity of my mind that contains thoughts about my disability, and these thoughts left that cavity very rarely. It makes life easier. There you go, I used my disability to my advantage in order to cope with this situation. It's easy if you try.

When you work as hard as I do, it's very easy to forget about your problems and to immerse yourself in schoolwork. I just worked that little bit harder and got on with my life. Overall, I think I discussed it with two people other than my family and they were Dexter and Emma. I knew I could trust them. It wasn't because I wanted to protect my Dad, far from it. It was just that that was what my Mum wanted. I was only too glad to oblige. This is where Dexter comes into his own as a mate. He can, as you've seen, be the most mischievous and irritating person in the world, as I'm sure I am to him at times, but whenever I need him for anything serious he's there. If I'm ever upset I can talk to Dexter and he'll always say what he thinks. In a situation like this it's about cheering people up. He knows exactly how to handle me and knows when to make a joke about things, and when not to. It's a mutual thing though. As tactless as we both can be, each of us knows how much the other cares and we know exactly what makes the other feel better. Emma was also very helpful when I needed to talk. I love friends like that. When you're so close that you know exactly how they feel and vice versa.

My brother didn't cope with it quite as calmly as me, which I understand. He's much more emotional than I am, or at least he expresses his emotions. He can't lock it away and stop thinking about it. He certainly didn't throw himself into his work; in fact he was so upset he stopped working altogether for a while. It definitely affected his studies in a bad way.

Just as I'd managed to put it to the back of my mind, having discussed it with Dexter, I had to dredge it all up again when my Dad came round, ahem, to 'explain' what had happened. Hmmm this would be interesting…

I really didn't want to see him at this particular moment in time. As far as I was concerned I knew enough already. My Mum had let him come round though, so the least I could do was listen to the rubbish he was about to talk. An affair seems self-explanatory to a thirteen and fifteen-year-old and I didn't want to know anything else. The fact that it had happened was enough for me to know.

To be honest, I have to hand it to both my parents for doing the right thing by us, as difficult as it must have been for both of them, especially my Mum. It probably wasn't that hard for my Dad because I suppose anyone who can have an affair has no shame. At least he was showing how much he cared about Dan and me, which is exactly what we needed to know. My Mum handled the 'speech' very well; indeed I find it amazing how she managed to remain calm. It just showed how she always puts other people before herself. She probably thought that crying would have been selfish and insensitive to Dan and me. We wouldn't have thought that, she had every right to think about herself.

He arrived on the doorstep, came in and sat in the corner.

Basically all I heard was, 'Lie, lie, lie, lie, lie.' Then there were a few questions from my brother, such as, 'Are you still seeing her?' to which the answer was, 'Lie, lie, lie, lie.' It was like Prime Minister's question time.

I didn't want to know any of this so I just sat there, not really listening till my Dad said, 'What do you think?'

Disturbed from my daydream I just said, 'I'm not bothered.'

'Yeah you are,' he said.

No really I'm not, I thought. The whole thing just irritated me. At the end of the day he was my Dad, I still loved him and I still wanted to see him. I didn't agree with what he'd done, in fact I was very annoyed and lost much of my respect for him.

As stressful as it was for Dan and myself, we did actually see my Dad more often than before. It probably sounds daft but it's true. Before he left he was on shifts so that even though he was living here, he'd be up when we were at school and in bed when we weren't at school. Now he'd have to see us once a week, so we went on day trips to Knowsley Safari Park and other such places. We had some good days and after a couple of weeks, I wasn't worried any more. It may sound callous but Dad not being here didn't affect my life one little bit. I just hated seeing my Mum upset all the time. She'd always been there for me and everyone else, and of all the people in the world no one deserved this less than she did. Now it was my turn to be there for her.

They've split up a few times since and each time my Mum's let him come back. I don't agree with that. I don't think my Dad deserved that but I also know that love is a funny thing. It makes you do things that maybe you know aren't sensible but you can't help it. I even told my Mum not to let him come back the last time it happened, but when I thought about it, it wasn't up to me. It's easy when you're detached from a situation to give out 'good' advice, but how do I know what I'd do in the same situation? I've always said I'd only give someone one chance if they ever did that to me. It's easy to say that.

Meanwhile, back at school things were going along quite nicely. I was doing well in all my coursework, except IT and art, which were always going to be very average. The plan was falling into place. Of course it was falling into place because I was working hard. Fate doesn't play a part in things like that. How intelligent you are is all down to genetics. You're born with a certain amount of intelligence, and from that moment on you're in control of what you do with that intelligence. Anyone with any intelligence who says it was fate that they didn't do as well as they could in an exam is lying to himself. It's because they haven't done enough to harness their intelligence.

In the film *The Matrix* the main character says he doesn't believe in fate because he 'doesn't like the idea that he's not in control of his life'. That's how I feel. If everything was decided for us, there'd be no point to life, so that's why I don't believe in fate.

There weren't many major incidents that I can remember from this year. Let me see, there was the week when I fell out of my wheelchair twice, a record for me. The first one was a simple forgetting to lift the wheels up incident, so I just flopped gently and didn't cause any damage to myself. That's what I get for letting my brother's mates push me around.

The second amazing stunt came as a direct result of the first, at a presentation evening (where they give awards for effort and achievement in all areas of school life). Keechy, who had thrown me out earlier that week, had let's say deliberately neglected to tell his mum what had happened, and my Mum, without knowing, made a joke about it. His mum replied, 'What? Our John threw Dave out of his wheelchair?'

My Mum, seeing the shock on her face quickly added, 'Oh he didn't hurt him,' and then we quickly left the building, my Mum's foot firmly in her mouth. That made pushing the wheelchair a bit difficult so she let my brother do the honours, and of course I couldn't wait to tell him about Mum's inadvertent grassing of John. Big mistake! My brother went mad at our Mum, which doesn't seem dangerous for me at first. When you're being pushed by someone, however, his mood can affect his pushing technique. When you're upset or annoyed, it affects the way you move your body and how you concentrate. You don't think clearly and you move erratically. You're movements also become more aggressive and powerful. My brother stormed off ahead of Mum, taking me along for the ride. Now, the hill leading down to our car was relatively steep and the concrete path always looked very hard to me. A steep hill added to my brother's anger leads to suffering... for me. He turned the corner with a bit more aggression than usual and I braced myself for the inevitable... Slap!

I hit the ground and found out exactly how hard the concrete was. I was right; it was very hard. The wheelchair had tipped sideways so my cheek and my knee, which hung over the edge of the seat hit the full force of the concrete. The searing pain in both as I hit the ground remains with me to this day. I'm twinging at the thought! My 'luck' up to now, of having never hurt myself badly in a fall had run out. I lay there on the floor for a few seconds, blood pouring from the cut on my cheek. I had a headache from the impact, my knee was killing me and when I moved my tongue to speak there was something missing from my mouth. My tooth didn't feel quite as smooth as it did a minute earlier.

I wasn't crying despite the pain, it must have been shock. My brother was crying; that must have been the shock of having nearly killed his poor disabled brother!

'I'm all right Dan,' I muttered as my Mum lifted my battered body into an upright position. That was an obvious lie but I was worried about my bro'. I don't know why, the little git had just tried to assassinate me but what can I say? 'A brother's love is… er… a brother's love.' That was the quote that ruined the film *Gone in Sixty Seconds*. What a ridiculously obvious thing to say!

I had half a tooth missing, blood gushing from my face and when my Mum picked me up under the knees I got the most terrible pain I'd ever felt, and yes I did start crying then. The trouble my Mum has when I've hurt myself or when she can't tell how hard she's doing something is that she has no way of knowing how much it's hurting. When she's shaving me she often cuts my face because she can't feel how hard she's doing it. She has also developed techniques of lifting and manoeuvring me, which unavoidably mean that my weight falls in a certain way. For example, when she puts me in the wheelchair or moves me from the bed to the toilet, my arms have to be held in a certain way to avoid pulling my shoulders from their sockets. If I hurt my wrist then she still has to lift me in the same way. To change technique suddenly could lead to a back injury for my Mum, and damage for me.

The problem with hurting my knee comes when transferring me from wheelchair to bed, wheelchair to car and vice versa. The weight is distributed on to one leg to form a sort of pivot so I can be rotated onto the seat or bed. This is the only way my Mum can lift me. It just happened that my sore knee was the one on to which my weight falls, and boy does it hurt. Thank God I don't get injured too often.

On my return to my house I was carried through the pain barrier and on to the couch, whereupon my Mum decided that the best thing to give someone with a broken tooth is a boiling hot, blackcurrant flavour Lemsip. If you've got sensitive teeth, you know what it's like when you eat something either very hot or very cold. When your tooth is broken halfway down, then that same hot or cold item feels twice as bad. Needless to say, I didn't drink it.

Mum gently wiped the excess blood from my cheek and it wasn't as bad as it looked. There would be a cheek-sized bruise and some scabbing but no stitches, and I wouldn't be able to eat properly till the tooth was fixed. My knee would be very sore for a few days, but apart from that I was fine.

The next day my mother sent me back to school looking like I'd gone twelve rounds with Lennox Lewis. Dexter said I looked like Oliver Twist, like I'd been living on the streets! I thought I looked hard, until it got to dinner time and I saw my butties. They were cut into spirals like I had at my sixth birthday. How to ruin a mask of toughness in five seconds! I felt like an old man now and hoped that Mum had managed to organise an emergency dentist's appointment. The day had been a nightmare. Every time Dexter pushed a door open, I felt it right through my leg and by the end of the day I was fed up. Thankfully, Mum had got me a dentist's appointment and I now had that to look forward to.

I arrived at the dentist's, where he told me he was going to give me a temporary cap to stop my tooth from hurting while I waited for a proper appointment. He put a couple of pieces of foam in my mouth to move my lips away from the tooth. Have you ever wondered why those pieces of foam have to taste so disgusting? Couldn't they make them taste like strawberries or something? Now there's a thought for you. Anyway, with these foam pieces you slaver uncontrollably while he drills and sticks a load of white stuff to your tooth. It's not the most pleasurable half an hour I've ever had and I thought I had another, more painful appointment to come. Luckily for me, this 'temporary' cap is still holding strong after about five years. My dentist Mr O'Flynn is a miracle worker!

The next day, with my facial scars fading, I showed everyone my new tooth, but I was now yesterday's news. It always happens like that. There's so much going on at that age, so much rubbish going through your head that something different happens every day. The apathy I was greeted with, having just had my tooth rebuilt was typical. There was probably a fight or something going on somewhere.

Dexter used to be really frustrated when there was a fight. Everyone was running towards it but by the time he'd managed to drag me over to the far reaches of the fields, where the fight took place out of the view of the teachers, it was too late. It was over. When we did eventually make a fight, it was always 'ten paces, turn and draw your handbags' stuff. It was a terrible anticlimax. The only good fights that ever happened were in full view of the teachers, usually in the PE changing rooms. I don't know why that happened, maybe everyone was so excited about playing sport that they just got carried away. Silly really.

It used to really annoy me when teachers told people off for watching fights and for 'encouraging' people to fight. If no one 'encouraged' them, did they think that the fights would stop? If anything it was the other way around. The fights encouraged people to watch. If no one fought, no one would watch, simple. There was usually a reason for the fight, which meant it would happen whether anyone watched or not. 'You snogged my bird.' 'No you snogged mine first.' Or, 'Your mum's a fat bitch.' 'You f★★king what? I'll 'ave your 'ed off.' And that was it. 'I'm going to deck you because I want to be cock of the school,' was another one. It was a matter of honour.

The best fight was when the current dick, sorry cock of the school finally lost a fight. I'd been waiting for that for years and it had finally happened. I felt really sorry for him. He was the master of the school and now he'd become nothing. Oh well.

On a more important note, I was given the most important choice of my life in PE lessons. Picture the scenario. It's the middle of winter, it's freezing cold, raining, and the fields are muddy. The lads are playing football outside and the girls are doing trampolining inside. I was given a choice. 'Do you want to watch football or trampolining? David, stop drooling!'

Hmmm! Let me think. Would I like to see Dexter and Matthew running around a field with their legs out, whilst freezing my genitalia off, or would I like to watch the girls jumping up and down for an hour? I loved football but that's hardly what they were playing. It was Unibond Premier League stuff. No, that's an insult to the Unibond Premier League.

'No it's all right, I'll watch the girls. I don't want to get cold do I?'

Mr Altdorf gave me a look that said, 'If I was your age that's the choice I'd make.' Who says I was a pervert? It's what any other red-blooded male would do.

Getting cold was a genuine worry at that time. If I got cold at dinner time I'd be cold and unable to write for the whole afternoon. The teachers soon realised this and they let me stay in our form room at dinner time, where Dexter and I would be joined by Nichola, Isla, Leigh and David Cass who just wanted to talk to Nichola although he'd never admit it. It was real primary school stuff. They argued all the time. It was a case of, 'I hate you but I love you really.' I've got to hand it to them though, when they did get together it worked. Last I heard they were still going out, but that was two years ago.

We had some good laughs, conversations and arguments in that room; that is when they weren't board-dusting my head, or playing badminton with a board ruler, a shuttlecock and me as the net! The arguments were amazing, really childish and hurtful, and the one who could take the most hurtful comments for the longest usually won the argument. If we annoyed the girls too much they'd flip out. There'd be books and chalk flying, usually in Dexter's direction. We were too nice to hit them back; well Dexter was anyway. I couldn't hit them anyway. Pain was often the price we paid for winning an argument.

The fact that we started most of the arguments with our ill-timed and tactless comments meant we probably deserved it but they were very good comments, usually about Isla's boyfriends whom I hated, I can't remember why. One of them had a penchant for kleptomania. I never met him but would gladly have cut his heart out with a spoon, and Dexter and I enjoyed making below the belt comments.

I got a Coke can thrown at my head for making a comment when her nan had been robbed. 'Did your boyfriend do it?' I asked. Fair comment I thought. When he'd bought her a watch for Valentine's Day, Dexter said he'd probably nicked it. Childish? Yep, but very funny. We were just trying to be mates, showing her the error of her ways. Why girls want to go out with people like that when they could go out with me, is beyond me. You're not cool when you're like me. You have to be thick and ugly to be cool. No, I'm not jealous!

I should really remember that I can't walk or escape when I make my comments or shout at people. I'm so busy thinking I'm normal that I say things without thinking. One day I'll pick on the wrong person, a man who would hit someone with glasses who just happens to be in a wheelchair. Then I'll be sorry. As it is, it's usually the person I'm with who experiences the anger of the person I insult.

A prime example of this is when I was out with my brother and his mates in Egerton. We were just sat minding our own business on someone's wall, when the owner of the house came running out like a bull at a gate. He was obviously drunk and chased us round the front, calling us useless dossers or something equally untrue. So Andy, true to form got annoyed and called him a pisshead. His barely coherent response was, 'I'd rather be a pisshead than a f★★king dosser.' Instead of setting us an example this pillar, sorry pillock of the community, was picking on some innocent kids, who were doing nothing wrong. So I had to get involved with a shout of 'go away you silly bald person', or words to that effect and he hit my brother! I really should be more controlled. I hate it when I get annoyed. All my wit goes out of the window and I tell them where to go.

For about three years now I'd not been too worried, even in the face of getting weaker and the problems at home. I'd just learned to deal with it. I finished my end of year exams, feeling confident for the GCSE year ahead. I got A's and B's in most of them and I knew I was good enough to do well. If I kept working hard I could go to any sixth form I wanted, but that was next year's task. As for this year I still had to look forward to what I'd been looking forward to all year – work experience. I was worried about how I'd manage for two weeks without Dexter and all the other help I had, but I was very excited. I also took my maths GCSE in the fourth year. Mr Twigg had entered a few of us early because he thought it would be a valuable experience. He also thought some of us would do well, without having the pressure that the fifth year would bring. If we did well we could keep the grade, should we lower our standards a year later. Sounded like a good deal to me.

On the first day of work experience I woke up and it was like my first day at secondary school, all over again. Those familiar nerves resurfaced and as I struggled to force my toast down I thought about how it would be. Would the people like me? Would I like the boss? Would someone meet me for lunch? Would I be able to do what was asked of me? Did I think too much! They were worries I'd had before and things had always turned out okay before. That rational thought never seems to comfort you when you're actually worried. It's natural to be nervous, it gets the adrenalin going and I always seem to be able to perform better when I'm worried. If you're never worried I think it leads to complacency and that's dangerous.

Then disaster struck! It was the first time we'd ever booked a taxi and they said they could take an electric wheelchair. It arrived on time, I'll give them that but it was just one of your run of the mill Toyota cars. It wouldn't get my wheelchair in, in a month of Sundays. I panicked. 'What am I going to do now?' I cried. My mind was like a bomb had hit it (all over the place) but my Mum, ever the voice of reason, stepped in.

'You're going to ring Diane up (I've forgotten her last name) and tell her you're sorry but you'll be a bit late.'

'Right then,' I said thinking, *Oh shit, I've got to use the phone*! I hated phones and had a lack of confidence, speaking to people I didn't know, but I had to do it. The only time I can do it is when I have to, so I rang and she was very understanding. After my Mum had given the driver a rocket, she ordered a black cab and off I went. As it happened, I was only ten minutes late and the reason why was an ice-breaker. I entered the room where my fellow workers for the next week were waiting. After all the introductions, I was given my first task. I had to pull stamps off envelopes, for what reason I can't remember. What I can remember is this huge pile of envelopes with stamps that I had to rip off. This was going to be a long week.

Three hours later, when I'd ripped enough stamps off to last me a lifetime, and when my arms had begun to burn, it was lunchtime. I'd arranged to meet my Auntie Sharon who worked round the corner. We went to Pizza Hut after I'd decided to forget about my diet for a couple of weeks. I'd live to regret that decision.

Lunchtime was the highlight of the day because my task for the afternoon was to put cheques into alphabetical order. I received another almost mountainous pile and I already wanted to be back at school. That task took me till five o'clock and then I was free to go home. Working nine to five, that's no way to make a living, especially when you're doing jobs which are as painful as pulling teeth. A lot of people have to put up with boring, monotonous jobs, though. I could cope for a week (if I was lucky.)

Day two started off much better. The right taxi arrived and when I arrived at work, there were no piles of cheques or envelopes but there was Diane's laptop. I'd climbed up a rung on the ladder, thank the Lord. I don't think I could have coped with another pile of boredom. What I did have to do was type up a newsletter for the staff, which was much more interesting, if not exciting. At least I could put my own touches to it and think, if only a little. Again that took me all morning. I've always been a bit slow at typing. It was now time for another pizza. I didn't dare ask how fattening they were.

Although I was bored, I did feel really grown up. Out of the comfortable, cotton wool wrapping of school, I felt like I was independent, doing things for myself. It was quite exciting. For the remainder of the week I was being shown the ropes in the different departments of the bank. How they do the stamping when new money is handed in, how the money is put into the cash machines and what a military operation it is to lock up at night. All amazing stuff. When the week was all over, I was given a Lloyds Bank calculator and I escaped very quickly. Saying goodbye to everyone, I did actually feel that they liked me. There were some interesting people there but how they ended up working in that centre of boredom I will never know! The week did serve one purpose, which I suppose is the main purpose of work experience. I now knew for certain that working in a bank was not for me. In fact, the experience probably helped me choose not to do maths at A level. I wouldn't need it if I was going to be a lawyer or a linguist.

I left the bank thinking, *I will never go back there. If I do it will be too soon.* Surely the next week could only be an improvement? I was tired out by the end of the week and just wanted to relax. I had to fill in my daily work experience diary, which I'd forgotten to do all week. I invented half the stuff on it, like everybody else does. If someone says you've got to fill in a diary, you always do it at the latest possible moment. It's got to be done.

Starting at Bolton/Bury Tec was like going into the unknown. I didn't know what I'd have to do, but I just hoped it would be more fun than the previous week. I think that's where I was a bit naive. Work's not supposed to be fun. People who enjoy work are few and far between. I was just finding out whether I wanted to do these jobs or not. I hadn't even chosen to come to this place but I trusted Mr Roberts's judgement. As I entered through the cargo entrance however, I felt just as nervous as I had this time the previous week. The same worries returned and even though I tried to comfort myself in the same way, yet again it didn't work. That is, until I met the two people I'd be working with. There was a man and a woman, both middle-aged, and they immediately put my mind at ease by talking to me and making jokes. They had a similar sense of humour to me, not that I spoke much. They were new people, and as usual I was nervous. If I only ever meet a person once they probably go away with a different impression to the one I make after a few meetings, which is a shame because first impressions are the most important. Although I always give a polite first impression, it's never as impressive as it should be. That's the biggest reason why I sometimes get jealous of my brother. He never shows that he's uncomfortable and he always looks confident. I also hate him because all the women in the world fancy him. Well I'm cleverer than him so there! I'm also very mature.

I soon settled down at this new place after introducing myself, and being introduced to everyone else, and I was soon given my first job. I had to set up a spreadsheet and put all the information into it. When I saw the list of information, I thought it was going to take all week. Working with computers was something I enjoyed doing, though. Knowing how to set up a spreadsheet made me feel capable in these adult surroundings. I couldn't do it now, though. The problem was that the coursework for the IT GCSE bored me so much I just lost interest, and now when it comes to making spreadsheets and databases my mind goes blank.

Being able to talk while I was working made the time pass much quicker, and it was soon lunchtime. I'd arranged to meet Ben, my cousin, for lunch this week and luckily for him he arrived on time. Another week of amazingly fattening lunches, this time at McDonald's wouldn't do me any harm!

The afternoon was tour time. I was shown around all the different departments and introduced to other people that I might bump into around the place. It broke up the day and I was enjoying myself. It was a real workplace this, with coffee breaks every five minutes. When people say they've had a hard day at work, don't believe them. No one works as hard as they say, apart from me.

When I got home after the day had flown by, I actually wanted to talk about my day. The week before, my mind had been so numb from boredom that I couldn't speak. I was afraid to go through it again, in case I sent my family into the same state as me. I was also having nightmares about giant stamps trying to rip me in half.

I told my Mum what had happened and she was just glad I was doing something interesting. 'I'm setting up a spreadsheet, Mum... Mum, wake up!'

'Mmm, that's nice David.'

Anyway the week continued in a similar vein. Coffee breaks, trips to the photocopier and chats with the workers broke the day up into manageable chunks, and the lunch hour got me out of the building. It was enjoyable. On the last day, shock, horror, I didn't go to McDonald's, I went to the pub round the corner with some of the workers. It was their usual Friday escape. Of course they had to lift me up a couple of steps and I didn't have anything low fat to eat. It was a very large chip butty and I didn't feel guilty.

We had a good chat and went back to the office where we shared the chocolates that I'd given them that morning, because I'm such a charmer! Then my wheelchair burst open because I now weighed seventeen stone.

I finished the spreadsheet just in time for the end of the week and amongst emotional scenes I said goodbye. It seemed like they would miss me. They even told me to ring them when I got my GCSE results and although I did genuinely mean it when I said I would, I just didn't feel I could when I got them. I even remembered that I'd said it on results day but I'd talked myself out of doing it. I didn't have to use the phone, so I didn't.

Obviously I'd enjoyed my second week more than the first

and that's no reflection on the people at Lloyd's Bank, but I equally didn't want to work in a marketing department. I knew that when the week began but at least I'd got an idea about work, and I knew two jobs that I didn't want to do. Even that negative outcome was one which I wouldn't have known had work experience not existed. Who knows, I could be sat in a bank right now if I hadn't done work experience!

I filled my diary in at the end of the week again and returned to the safe haven of school for the final week of term. Yes, that final week of quizzes and not much else. They might as well have given us the week off. We had to go through the whole boring story of what we'd done on our two weeks. By the time I'd told Mr Altdorf about the first week, he was comatose, so luckily I didn't have to go through the second week.

Dexter had been working at a hospital for the disabled for one of his weeks. That must have been my influence, but he didn't get what he expected when he got there. I think he expected the people to be like me but from a family, which didn't have the help that my family has. Most of the people there though had severe deformities and an abundance of both physical and mental problems. It was a definite eye-opener for Dexter and he did do everything that was asked of him. He's a compassionate person and I'm sure that working there upset him. It wasn't for him. Graphic design was where he wanted to go. He did almost get sacked though for treating one of the patients, who couldn't tell him to sod off, like he treated me. He was a very skilful wheelchair pusher. He almost made an Olympic sport out of it, but spinning people around, skidding round corners and making them do wheelies is not the general idea of being a carer. When one of the nurses caught him running down a corridor with a guy who couldn't speak in his wheelchair, she was horrified. She sat Dexter down in a wheelchair and said, 'How would you like it if I sat you down and started running around pulling wheelies?' And that's exactly what she proceeded to do.

He apologised and explained to her why he was doing it. Poor Dexter, he was just trying to bring joy into a man's life which probably consisted of getting up, sitting in his wheelchair, eating his tea and going to bed. It must be terribly frustrating when you can't express how you feel properly. It makes me count my blessings. I've got a good mind, a great family, brilliant friends and a life as full as that of any able-bodied person. These people have none of that and it upsets me to think about it. The best way I can explain how it would feel to be unable to speak or control your body is by using an example of a very seriously disabled man, whose able-bodied brother takes him to Liverpool matches. He can't talk and his limbs are just constantly flying around all over the place. I have to dodge fists and elbows for ninety minutes when I sit next to him but this guy obviously knows what's going on around him. He throws his arms around more excitedly when Liverpool score and makes angry noises when they concede a goal. My Dad had a chat with the brother of this man, who told him that he's very intelligent. He goes to the pub and the people even raised money so he could have a computer, which talks for him, like the one Stephen Hawking uses. He types using his mouth and a pointer and then he 'talks'. He expressed his frustration and anger one day in a picture he drew, which showed himself inside a bubble in his wheelchair. Everyone else was seen dancing away outside this bubble, doing what they do and having a good time. He looked miserable inside the bubble. It showed how trapped he felt.

Writing this book is the way I can show the good points, and there are many of them, of being disabled and also the depressing points. The way he can do it is by drawing these pictures and I believe that only by reading and looking at what disabled people draw and write can able-bodied people even begin to understand it. This man seems very similar to me in the way he deals with his disability.

Work experience was an important experience for all of us, even if it put most of us off doing the jobs we tried out. Waiting for a year had been worth it despite the stamp ripping experience, but now the year had finished again. It was the final summer I'd have as a Sharples pupil. One more year, and this latest era of my life would be over. Things change so quickly it's frightening and I could still remember the first day, changing golf cart to wheelchair, that feeling of being grown up. I could still feel the butterflies when I thought about it.

The first night of the holidays, I lay there and thought about how it would be after I'd disappeared over the horizon towards Turton Sixth Form (if I got in). I was sure I'd keep in touch with all my mates because I'd miss them a great deal. 'Shut up!' I said to myself. I didn't want to depress myself too much. 'You've still got a year to go, enjoy it while it lasts.' Talking to yourself is the first sign of something, I can't remember what it is.

I think you know by now what happened over the summer. Wandering the streets, playing computer games, sleeping at Dexter's house (without the usual eating binge) and falling out of the wheelchair.

A classic wheelchair-exiting incident took place this summer. It was Dexter's fault again, surprisingly enough. He's always going too far. He convinces himself that nothing will go wrong if he does something that I think is dangerous. Well this time he was about as right as the guy who said the *Titanic* was unsinkable. He was driving the wheelchair around Sharples, up and down hills and around trees when we reached a tree on a slope. The slope ran between the tree and a fence and Dexter, obviously mistaking the wheelchair for a Chieftain tank or some other all-terrain vehicle, decided he could get between the fence and the tree without the wheelchair tipping over and sending me sprawling.

'Dex don't, you'll never make it through there. Stop!' I warned, but by now the blinkers had come down. He was determined to make it and adamant that he would.

'You wimp, course we'll make it,' and he went through at full speed. We must have hit a root or something because seconds later I saw the tree coming towards us.

'Oh shit!' Dexter screamed and then we hit the tree. Fortunately the wheelchair tipped slowly and I landed quite gently, trapped between the tree and wheelchair. He managed to pull the wheelchair away and sent it to the bottom of the hill. I was left looking at the sky and wondering how the hell I was going to get from this position into the wheelchair, and then I saw a man with a dog. *Nice one, I'm saved*, I thought, and then he spoke.

'Nice day isn't it? How's your batteries?' he said happily and he just walked off! The situation had now descended to Laurel and Hardy level. Didn't he think it was strange that a lad was laid out on the floor, motionless, with his wheelchair at the bottom of the hill? Obviously not.

I looked at Dexter and we both just shook our heads. We could have said something I suppose but we were speechless at this act of stupidity. Then a young kid ran across to us. Surely he couldn't be as stupid as the previous 'saviour'. He wasn't and we sent him across the fields to get Matthew and Owen who just happened to be playing football at the time. Dexter lifted my arms and Owen the legs. It was a simple task of putting me back into the chair. Obviously not that simple because they managed to put me in feet first. It was classic comedy!

Once I'd returned to my rightful position, I went to watch them play football which was dangerous in its own right. Some of their shots were a tad wayward so it was like facing a firing squad.

It seemed Dexter spent most of his time putting me in dangerous situations. Life with Dexter 'was like a box of chocolates' and at least it spiced up my life, although he didn't have to go as far as setting my hair alight. Yes, he decided it would be funny to spray me with hair spray and light a match, threatening to set me on fire. He was only joking but like I said, he always went too far.

'Dex, you'll set my bloody 'ed on fire if you do that!'

'Will I 'eck, I'm not even getting close enough to set your 'ed on fire,' he insisted whilst bringing the match closer and closer to my explosive-soaked head.

I just shut my eyes knowing what was going to happen. *Why me?* I thought.

Then suddenly whoosh! My hair went up in flames. I nearly had a heart attack and Dexter sprung into action. He frantically slapped my head till the flames subsided! When we realised that I wasn't hurt, just slightly singed we burst out laughing from shock. Only Dexter could accidentally set someone on fire!

There was only one question left. How was I going to explain the fact that a patch of my hair had suddenly changed colour to my Mum and Dad? I couldn't possibly tell them the truth, could I? Maybe they wouldn't see it.

'David, what the hell's happened to your hair?' Ah, that put paid to that idea.

'What do you mean, Mum?' I asked innocently.

'Someone's burnt your head, who was it?' She sounded annoyed now.

'Oh someone dropped a cigarette on me. I didn't see who it was.' That was believable.

My Dad, not believing for one minute that I was telling the truth chipped in with, 'So you're telling me someone just jumped out of the bushes and blow-torched your head?'

I'm a bad liar at the best of times and I couldn't keep it up after that. 'All right all right, Dexter set my head on fire,' I admitted. I think they'd already worked out that I knew exactly what had happened and that Dexter must have been involved, but I had to at least try to cover it up. My best mate had begged me to.

Remember the hill with the brick wall and big drop, near Hillcot House? Well, just when I thought I'd survived my only brush with death on that hill, lightning struck again. This time I wasn't on my own. I was with Dexter. Why did I go near that hill again after last time, you might be wondering. Well I didn't go there out of choice. My tyre had popped on the electric wheelchair so Dexter had decided to take me for a wander in the manual chair. We happened to arrive at Sharples Sports Centre car park, from where we could see the steps and the evil hill. Something must have inspired the demons in Dexter's mind. His voices were talking to him again and they were telling him to go to the hill. He had to tell me where we were going as well, just to panic me.

'We're going to that hill near Hillcot House, Dave.' He had a mischievous glint in his eye again.

'No we're not, you know I nearly killed myself last time I went up there.'

'You can't really stop me can you?'

'Please don't Dex, I really don't want to.' I was begging now but that just made him want to go even more.

'You're a bloody wimp; we're going. Nothing'll go wrong.'

Oh dear, he'd done it now. Famous last words. I was now even more worried that something would go wrong. As we approached, I could visualise my death again. I think I need counselling for these visions.

We got to the top and he had the most evil thought he'd ever had. To my horror he pushed me towards the edge of the hill, lifted the wheels up and hung them over the edge. The drop was about thirty metres to the car park and fear consumed my body. I started to sweat and on the verge of tears, I shouted, 'Dex you dick head, stop it please.'

'Shut up, I'm only messing, I've got you.'

Suddenly there was a jerk and the front wheels jolted downwards. My life flashed before my eyes. Dexter, panic-stricken pulled me back quickly and dragged me from the hill. Safely away from the hill we were both laughing but it was nervous laughter. I genuinely could have been seriously injured or worse and Dexter, despite the laughter knew that. 'I'm sorry Dave, I won't do it again.' He was soon forgiven but I've never forgotten it. My best mate needed psychiatric help!

I spent a couple of weeks this summer 'hanging around' with the people who did the drinking on street corners thing. I thought I'd been missing out by not doing it, so when Dexter and I had one of our stupid rows, about me wanting to do one thing and him wanting to do another, I decided to show him I had other mates and that I didn't particularly need him. Very childish I know, but that's what our rows were like.

So I was hanging around with Laidlaw and Prycey, who I did actually like, and a group of people who I didn't really like but it was something I had to do at the time. Every time Dexter and I saw each other we gave each other a dirty look. How old were we? I soon realised that I hadn't been missing out at all. They just did exactly what Dexter and I did, only there were a few girls and a bit of crappy cider floating around. They'd sit around on Sharples, play football in a drunken state, usually a couple of windows would get smashed but it was mostly the older ones who'd cause the problems because they thought they were 'hard'. There'd be a couple of fights but mostly they were just teenagers having a laugh. Then the police would come onto Sharples, take our names down and get rid of us which would just result in us wandering the streets again.

They were all used to being stopped by the police but when it happened to me I was a bit shocked. Well, it wasn't me that smashed the windows, was it? It could have caused a bit of embarrassment for my Dad, who was a policeman but it was harmless enough. They even asked me if I'd been dragged there or if I'd gone because I wanted to. I had to say I wanted to be there. I couldn't really make it look like I'd been kidnapped by a group of drink-fuelled maniacs.

Although I had a good laugh with them and most of them treated me as one of them, drove me around in the wheelchair, and helped me out, I just didn't feel like that was where I wanted to be. After a couple of weeks, I went home after being out with them and didn't go out with them again. It didn't ruin my life and didn't ruin theirs. It was about time Dexter and I made up, so I swallowed my pride and went round to his house. We were soon mates again and doing exactly what the people 'to be seen with' were doing. By this time I felt I was mates with Rick, who wandered around with us. At first it was like I was Dexter's mate and so was Rick and the conversations usually happened when one of us spoke to Dexter. If me and Rick were left on our own we didn't have much to say, and this went on for a long time until Dexter had a row with one of us and stormed off. Then we were forced to talk, and we began to be mates with each other. It was a good job really, because Dexter had a row with one of us at least once a week. Always his fault of course!

We wandered like the Three Musketeers all over the place and after years of searching we found the Holy Grail, a place where we could have hours of unbridled fun – Astley Bridge Park. It was a park of three swings, one roundabout and some strange, people-shaped climbing frames. Exciting it was not. This park was to become very familiar to us especially as we would go there every night for about a year, even in sub-zero temperatures, without any alcohol because we couldn't get served. I can count about two girls that we saw on that park for the duration of that year and I grew to detest that place with a passion. Nowadays I'd rather be thrown out of my wheelchair on to a pile of hot coals and be told to crawl across, than visit that park again.

And finally that summer Rick got his results, which meant he could go and do his graphic design course and I went and got my maths result. I got a B and I was still considering doing maths at A level. If I got an A the next year, then that was exactly what I would do. I was very happy with that result and I went back to school for the last time, knowing I could perform in exam conditions. I had the ability, but did I have the bottle?

Chapter VIII

I was upset about leaving but during the year I hardly thought about it. Boringly enough I was too busy thinking about my work to think too much about leaving. I'd miss my mates like hell and even some of the teachers, and in the odd moment before I went to sleep (my most productive thinking time) I'd consider the end of this particular era. It had become as much second nature as primary school had been four years earlier. I never thought it would be but it would be as much a wrench to leave as it had been before.

I resolved just to enjoy the last year. Doing well in the exams and getting into sixth form was the main goal. The cycle of looking at sixth form colleges had begun and I only had three in mind; Thornleigh, Turton and South College. I went to look at all three and all three were very accommodating. They'd all change things around and make sure I could get to all my lessons, but the only place I really wanted to go to was, Turton. Firstly, it was because you had to have about five B's to get in. Being surrounded by intelligent people would, I thought, help me to do as well as I possibly could. But it wasn't just that, it was the whole atmosphere of the place. It seemed more grown-up than the other two. The common room looked welcoming and everyone seemed to get on well. It didn't look quite as strict as I'd been led to believe either.

I knew five B's was easily within my grasp if I continued to work as hard as I had been doing. I already had one B. B's however were not what I wanted. I wanted more, much more and then I got my IT coursework back. 'Hmm, I got a D. That's not really in the script.' I'd never got a D before, so I didn't know what that was all about. It was a blow and I was a bit upset about it, but it didn't spark a self-doubt phase or a spontaneous sore foot, it was more like a bump in a road that had become all too smooth. It was a pointless exercise anyway, and I knew I didn't want to do an IT A level. The other nine subjects, apart from art of course, were still going very well.

It wasn't all schoolwork and sixth form searches though. I did all my homework as soon as I got it and really it only took a few hours out of the week. The rest of the time I had free to sit in Astley Bridge Park, still with no women or alcohol. It was this year that started with our 'there's got to be more to life than this' conversations. You know the ones: 'We just do the same bloody thing every day...' 'Why does no one fancy us?' These conversations were usually tongue in cheek, and then Rick disappeared. No not literally. He got a girlfriend and we wouldn't see him for days on end. Then suddenly he'd appear again for a day. One day when he and Dexter turned up at my house I'd forgotten who he was! We didn't have a problem with him not being there, not because we didn't want him there but because getting a girlfriend was on all our minds. It was sandwiched somewhere between my schoolwork and football in my list of priorities. Now that's the list of priorities of a normal person isn't it? The only difference was, I couldn't get to the match without help and I couldn't actually play football. I'm a normal person who just needs help with certain things. There were the odd moments of depression about my disability and my parental situation but I didn't really think about it. If you dwell on the unavoidable then your life becomes pretty empty, and that's why I put things to the back of my mind. Granted, there are daily reminders such as when you wake up and you can't get out of bed, but once you've acclimatised to a situation it becomes second nature to you. I don't lie in bed every morning moaning because I can't get up; I just shout for my Mum and wait for her to get me up. I live the life of a king really.

What was that about Rick? Oh yeah, we thought, good luck to him, after recovering from the overwhelming jealousy we were experiencing. He was lucky, he just got there first and Dexter and I were desperate to be next. I mean the ideal situation would have been if we'd all got girlfriends at exactly the same time, but the likelihood of that happening was pretty slim. Julia (Rick's girlfriend) was better looking than Dexter and me, anyway thankfully.

At that point the latest girl I fancied was Nichola. I'd known her for eleven years and I suddenly decided I fancied her. I got on with her really well and I just thought we'd make a good couple. Why couldn't I accept just being mates with a girl? I've always fancied a good proportion of my female mates, which is probably why I become friends with some of them in the first place. Most mixed sex friendships are based on the man fancying the woman. Usually girls like friends that are boys and boys like girlfriends, it's a fact of life. Well that's my excuse.

This time, I received the ultimate insult to my advances. When Dexter told her I fancied her she just didn't believe him (notice how again I couldn't tell her myself). Was going out with me that repulsive a thought? It must have been. Well I wasn't going to sit back and take that. I'd do anything I could to convince her that it was true. I admitted it to her myself but she still didn't believe me. I even sent her a love letter (pathetically enough) but she didn't believe that either, probably because Oliver gave it to her but that's not the point. Nichola and I even had a row about that letter. She went mad at me for being childish and laughing at her expense.

'Stop messing about now.'

'I'm not. It's true, I do fancy you.'

'No you don't.'

'Yes I do.'

That exchange repeated itself for a while with me stopping short of actually asking her out. I couldn't do that! The argument ended with me saying, 'Think what you want, I'm going.'

'Fine!'

Fine! Yes she was really going to go out with me now! The next week she was going out with David Cass again which I was very jealous about. Just my luck really.

All this fun and games was a welcome distraction from the schoolwork. It was mock exam time and I revised. If you believed everything you heard you'd think I was the only one who did. Mukhtar said, 'I never revise, I don't need to.' Lying sod! You don't get the grades he gets by not revising. Show me someone who does and I'll show you a liar!

I got six A's, two B's and two C's. That was enough to get me an interview at Turton. Of course, with a backhander to Mr Taylor (Matthew's dad), a Deputy Head at Turton, I could have got in anyway. Fifty quid's his usual price. (This is only a joke; don't sack Mr Taylor!) At the interview I told Mr Mills (the Head of Sixth Form) that I wanted to do English, maths, history and French at A level. He told me that three A level's was what universities usually wanted, four might be too much. He also told me that at Sharples I was a big fish in a small pond but at Turton I'd be a small fish in a big pond. I just nodded and smiled, thinking, *You cheeky sod. I'll show you*, which I suppose was the desired reaction. All the people from the Education Authority were there to explain what I'd need. It used to really annoy me, I felt I was being analysed and people were interfering. It was as if my Mum and I couldn't explain what I'd need without them there. They'd come in and say things that I needed, and even if I disagreed I'd find myself saying, 'I might need that, you're right,' when I knew full well that I didn't need it or want it. A feeling of resignation comes over you and you just agree. Then when you get the stuff, you look at it for a while and then you shove it in a cupboard till they ask for it back. I got this expensive laptop computer which had capabilities for typing in French and German, with all the accents. The thing was I could write quicker than I could type, so the computer was redundant. Well that's not strictly true, I did play a golf game on it which wasn't really the idea. I know they were trying to help me but if that's what they really wanted to do, they should have given me their number and I would have rung them when I needed something. Another problem is that you ask for things and only half of them arrive, which makes a mockery of the whole system. I'm sure that between the three of us, my Mum, myself and Mr Mills could have sorted the whole thing out. As it was, I just accepted the help graciously and got on with it. The trouble with Britain is that the government won't accept the Education Authority people and social workers just giving their clients their phone numbers and letting them get on with it, only calling on them when they need them. In order to justify the existence of their jobs the workers have to be seen to be actively doing their jobs, with regular checks on their clients, and being present at meetings and interviews. It's not enough for clients just to ring when they need help, which is a bit daft.

At the end of the interview I was told I was in, if I got the grades and then I was given the guided tour of the place. At least I could get to the languages corridor. It was just like any other school building but I wanted to go there. I applied to the other sixth forms, but I had already decided on Turton.

As a result of the interview I decided I'd only do three A levels. I didn't want to risk doing badly in four when I thought I could do well in three. I decided on French, German and English because after about eleven years I was totally fed up of maths. Doing the exam a year early had had an adverse effect on me. I lost interest and didn't feel I wanted to do it any more. There were just too many aspects of it that I didn't understand and anyway, languages are the future, man!

I went back to school knowing all I had to do was get the grades, and I was up for the challenge. I was determined not to let the pressure get to me. I wasn't stressed because I never left things till the last minute. I did my work early most of the time and I always had time to relax. The only extra lessons I went to were for science and art; science because I was never confident with it and art because I needed a miracle to pass. As for everything else, I was confident I could do well just by revising hard and working to the best of my ability. Very sickening, but it's just the way I was. I'm still exactly the same.

It's a shame that when I think about the fifth year, the only thing I vividly remember is revising religiously for two hours a day from March onwards. I was determined to know as much as I could before my exams, then only the actual wording of the questions could cause me a problem. I vaguely remember the feeling that I had to savour every minute with my mates because it wouldn't last much longer. I'm a very sentimental person under this tough, 'nothing bothers me' facade but I never admitted it. That wasn't the way lads should act. It's a big regret of mine that I never really showed people my whole personality. I cared, they knew that, and I liked a laugh but I very rarely laid the real me on the line. When I did it was by accident. We were having one of our dinner time 'sit ins' in our form room, which would be one thing that I'd miss more than anything else. Isla, David and Leigh had become good mates for me and Nichola and Dexter had become even better mates. I'd miss them when I'd gone. There was only Dexter out of this group who was considering Turton. Nichola wanted to be a nurse, Isla was going in the army and Cass didn't really care as long as he didn't have to go to school any more. I don't know what Leigh wanted to do.

Anyway we were having one of our chats when Isla, one of the slimmest people I knew, said she was fat. We all looked at her as if she'd said the moon was made of green cheese. It was the most ridiculous thing I'd ever heard so I said, 'Don't be stupid, you're gorgeous.' My mask had fallen off and smashed on the floor, never mind slipped, and I went bright red and shut up. She just laughed and took the mickey out of me for the rest of the day. I didn't do that again in a hurry. That was actually what I thought, but from the reaction I refrained from mentioning it again.

I was still being attacked by board dusters and things like that. You'd have thought they'd have grown up by then! It was all part of the fun of being mates, but they wouldn't have done it if I could chalk them back.

So the year drifted away in an endless rota of revision, exams, interviews and all the boring bits that take over, as you get older. I remember the first two exams very well, they were French and German orals, not my favourite part of languages but I usually did well in them. It's strange that someone who calls himself a linguist can have so much fear about talking in a foreign language, but I did. I was sat in the queue outside the room looking in fear of my life and barely able to talk without my voice going higher and higher, but I went through as much as I could in my head. Fortunately my turn for speaking was sandwiched between Emma's and Nichola's and they were more nervous than I was. That would make most people more nervous but if I can calm someone else down, I don't worry about myself, and by the time I get to the exam I'm much calmer. I knew enough words and phrases to do well but I was worried I would suddenly go blank or lose it if I didn't know a word. That's the trouble with GCSE French and German; there's so many gaps in your knowledge that you don't often know a way to get round a situation where you don't know the exact words that are asked of you. That was my main worry and my stomach felt ready to burst. Once I was given the role-play sheets, I calmed down because I knew almost all the words. It was like the butterflies in my stomach had been suddenly murdered and when I started to speak I just relaxed, and each exam was soon over. It happened in exactly the same way in both, although I felt my French had gone much better than my German. Two down, about twenty to go.

Next it was history, and I was given 25% extra time which I was determined not to use. I was totally capable of doing as well as anyone else in the same amount of time. All the exams went fine, except one science paper, my IT exam and my third maths paper. I thought I was on for an A in maths after the first two papers, and then the third one which I always found the most difficult was an absolute nightmare. I could only do about half the questions and I knew I would be getting my second B in maths. I didn't let it destroy my confidence because I had a number of exams to go and I was totally focused on getting the grades I needed. If I didn't get A's I could cope with B's, and C's would do in IT and art. I needed to get to sixth form. One bad maths paper wouldn't get in my way.

Then when it was all over, I just had to wait a couple of months for the results. I wasn't as worried as I thought I would be, I just did my usual 'put it to the back of my mind' thing and it worked most of the time. That part of my mind was becoming a bit full. I thought it was liable to spontaneously combust very soon!

I still had my leavers' do to go and it was the first time I'd ever had a drink. We were only supposed to have one drink, which wasn't quite what happened. We were given these little ticket things that gave us half a pint each. God, we were hardened drinkers! As it turned out, the teachers kept giving us drinks every five minutes and it was that night that I was introduced to the only drink that I've ever been able to drink without throwing up, Southern Comfort and Coke. I'd already realised that I hated the taste of beer and cider so Mr Altdorf gave me a drink, and I've been addicted to it since. It was about time I started to drink but by the end of the night I had more alcohol on my pants than I had in my system. That wasn't because I was drunk either; it was because I was surrounded by clumsy oafs. First this lad called Christian spilt a whole pint on me. Then I spilt half a drink on myself trying to reach the straw, which looked like it had been fashioned out of a biro. Later on when I was on the dance floor, Owen and Prycey decided it was their turn to attack me. It was a brand new shirt, pants and shoes bought specially for this night, which was my first proper night out, and I was covered in beer. To be honest I couldn't have cared less. Everyone was having a laugh, enjoying themselves and a bit of beer on my clothes wasn't a problem. It was all part of going out. You're supposed to get covered in beer, throw up, lose control of your faculties and end up sleeping in a bush; otherwise it's not a proper night out! It's set the tone for every other night out since, because every night I end up covered in beer or burnt with a cigarette, or even lying on the floor in a pool of someone else's urine. I'm a sitting duck for flailing arms and people falling over. A night out with me is great fun – for everyone else!

I'll tell you about these stories later, but for the rest of my leavers' do I danced (moved my head and shoulders to the beat) away, dodging flying beer as I did so. I said goodbye to all my mates and good luck and I'll keep in touch. Of course the do was in the most awkward place in the world for a wheelchair. Three flights of stairs, another one up to the toilets and two steps down to the dance floor. It was at Eagley Sports Centre and it probably wasn't designed for wheelchairs. It's the last place you'd expect a wheelchair to visit and it had been designed when wheelchair users were shipped off to nursing homes as soon as they were born. I'd hate to see what Hitler would have done to hideous people like me. I'm lucky to have been born in this age of equal rights and acceptance. Although it's not perfect, it's infinitely better than thirty years ago.

So, I'm in this archaic excuse for a building and suddenly I need the loo. Even at this age, I was bothered about Dexter seeing my genitalia and he didn't particularly want to see it, so that idea was out. I'd considered waiting all night like I did at school. I could drink several drinks when I was at school without needing the toilet so I thought I could manage all night. That just proves how little alcohol I'd drunk before, because after a couple of drinks I could no longer hold on. My Mum, having anticipated this problem, had gone to the pub across the road and told me she'd be waiting for my call. When she said this I rolled my eyes in that teenage way that says, 'I know everything. I know my bladder will be fine. Stop fussing.' Then two hours later I called and she came over. Dexter dragged me up the steps and stood outside, telling people not to go in, while my Mum helped me out. I could hear a queue forming outside and I could tell that there were a few people because every time a new person arrived the person at the back shouted, 'You can't go in, David Withnell's having a pee!' I'm sure that call conjured up a few horrible images for a few people. I heard it about four times before I'd finished.

Having my Mum there wasn't the best scenario for me, I felt embarrassed, but I would have been more embarrassed if I'd wet myself on the dance floor. When I think about having a pee at the leavers' do, which believe me I don't think about often, I think it summed up how well I'd been accepted and liked at Sharples. There was a queue of about five people outside the toilet, probably bursting to get inside, and not one of them moaned when they were told they'd have to wait because of me. It just seemed a normal thing to happen, as if it happened every day, and not one of them cared. Maybe it was because they were drunk or because my Mum was there that they didn't moan, but I see it as a reflection of how I was one of them. I'd never been an outsider and it made my worries of the first year seem yet more unfounded though I wish it had dawned on me at the time. All that from going to the toilet.

That was it then, Sharples was over? Not quite. Mr Altdorf had planned to take us out for the day and we decided to go to Alton Towers. Sorry, everyone else decided to go to Alton Towers. I didn't bother wasting my time by disagreeing. My brother came along in case I needed any help and a couple of other people who weren't in our form came along. It was a glorious day, boiling hot, 'Sun was shining, weather was sweet, makes you wanna move your dancing feet' and there was quite a good turnout. Dex, Liam, Tonguey, Cass, Nichola, Isla, Emma, Heather my brother and I, and that was about it. Obviously there was a certain number of people who wanted to get out of school and never come back, or see anyone again. Fair enough.

The minibus trip was good fun and then we arrived. I had hoped that by some miracle we'd have got lost and ended up somewhere less frightening than a theme park, but I wasn't that lucky. I was terrified that someone would ask me to go on some frightening ride. Most of the time I could plead disability because the rides would probably give me whiplash or something. Other times Dexter offered to hold my neck so I didn't get whiplash. When that happened I had to argue with him for about ten minutes while he tried to change my mind. Finally I did give in. I would go on two rides and that was it. The River Rapids and the Log Flume because I knew they wouldn't hurt me if someone held on to me and also because I actually liked rides like that. Sedate, slow and sa–a–a–afe! The Log Flume had gone over the first drop and I was absolutely in fear. *They never went that fast when I was younger*, I thought as I looked in the water to find my heart which had just escaped through my mouth.

We were all lined up in this log, Dexter, Liam, Mr Altdorf, Dan and I, and I was behind Mr Altdorf and in front of my brother who was holding on to me so I didn't fall out. That wouldn't have been very good publicity for Alton Towers. It was funny on that ride, Liam was screaming like a woman while Mr Altdorf slapped him over the back with a cap, and we were all wet through. It was a good day.

I went on the Log Flume twice and on the River Rapids twice, which wasn't like me but I didn't want to look soft when there were females around. I loved all the rides I could get on to, honest! The best bit though had to be watching everyone's faces on the rides I couldn't get on. It's unbelievable that anyone can actually say they like these terrifying things. The day went very quickly and then suddenly we were on our way home. It was an amazingly quiet return journey especially for those girls. I'd never known them all to be quiet at the same time. I think we'd all realised that we'd only see all these people together, once more, and that would be on results day. After that we'd probably only see a few people from Sharples ever again. I said 'see ya', and to most of them it was a final goodbye. It was a sad moment.

I hadn't even cried yet. I was a bit subdued for the rest of the day and I had an early night. I started thinking about all that had happened over the last five years. I'd made some great friends, had some great times, survived a few near-death experiences and I'd even miss most of the teachers. From the first year onwards, life had been almost perfect, even the bad times hadn't dampened anything. I was the only disabled kid there but for a long time I hadn't felt disabled, which is an odd thing to say seeing as I only had to look at myself to see I was disabled. It had been an amazing roller coaster and I'd felt every emotion possible. The same questions came back from five years earlier. Would things be better when I got to sixth form? Could they get better? One thing I did know was that I'd spend more time with my new mates, if I made any. I never took anything for granted. My only regret from Sharples was that I didn't spend enough time with my friends outside of school.

Every emotion possible was what I also felt on results day. It was the most nerve-racking experience of my life, more nerve-racking than work experience, starting secondary school and Space Mountain put together. My stomach was churning all morning, and this time I couldn't get any food down at all. Then I escaped from my Mum who was annoyingly mithering me to let her come with me. 'I'm fine,' I snapped. 'I got there myself last year, I'll get there myself this year.' Always independent I am, and I didn't want my Mum to witness my potential suicide! It was agony on the way down and the thing that bothered me most was that Dexter would see my results before me, because I couldn't get into Hillcot House. I was also petrified of going near that hill of death that had got me in trouble twice before!

I'd arranged to meet Matthew before I got the results but the overwhelming curiosity was just too powerful for me, well for Dexter anyway. He went for our results and brought them back looking like the cat that got the cream. 'Five B's and five C's!' he shouted. 'Well done Dex, now give me my results.' Seven A's, a B and two C's, no that isn't a maths equation. I was totally relieved, more than ecstatic and I'd done very well. I wanted an A in maths but I didn't get it. That was the only thing I was slightly disappointed about but the rest of the results were good enough for me. Matthew didn't appreciate the fact that I went without him, and Dexter just ran off in his excitement, screaming, 'Ten GCSEs!' as he barged through his front door.

As for me, I was just smiling. I'd got my A's in French, German and English, and barring a sudden death I'd got into sixth form. That made for a good day all round and then I bumped into Mukhtar, who revelled in the fact that he'd beaten me. The swine! Well he'd won the war then. The funny thing was that I was happy for him. I'd like to have beaten him and shut the smug bugger up but the main thing was that I'd achieved my goal. Five good years had finished and my school life could continue. I'd see Mukhtar again at Turton.

That afternoon I went to Turton to let them know my results. They said no problem and I was in. Nice one. I was very happy.

There were only a couple of weeks to go before I started but the most important thing was the celebrations. We managed to prise Rick away from Julia for a night and my Mum and Dad took the three of us to the pub. I still hadn't figured out that beer didn't agree with me and I didn't want to ask for a poof's drink like Southern Comfort and Coke. I forced a pint of beer down my throat, even though I screwed my face up like a bulldog chewing a wasp every time I swallowed. After that one pint I was drunk. I just couldn't handle it. I was drunk enough to ask for a Southern Comfort the next time we got a drink, and by the time we started to do the pub quiz, neither Dexter, Rick nor I could remember our names let alone answer the questions. Dexter and Rick just carried on playing pool making a large amount of noise, and I was singing, 'Do Ya Know What I Mean?' by Oasis. It's amazing what you remember from when you were drunk! We failed miserably at the quiz and on the way home we were all very loud. Dexter and Rick were play fighting in the middle of the road, hitting each other harder than usual and swearing very loudly, and I was only just sober enough to know that it was Dexter and Rick who were fighting. Hmm, alcohol was my new friend. It was good stuff.

Before we went to sixth form, where Dexter had decided to join me at the last minute (as usual), his mum and dad went away for the weekend and he decided to have a barbecue for me, him and Rick. The only drink on offer was my favourite, beer. *Not again*, I thought.

The food was Dexter's usual spicy choice. I'm sure he just got the spicy chicken out to annoy me. He knew I hated anything spicy. I'm English. I like good old plain food. Sunday roast, steak and chips, you can't beat it. I don't mind a bit of spaghetti bolognese or chicken Kiev but anything spicy like chilli, curry or spicy bloody chicken isn't my cup of tea! So I was drinking beer and eating something that I didn't like. Not surprising then that after about a pint and a half I threw up all over the floor and I was totally hammered. I know, one and a half pints is a very pathetic amount of beer to get someone hammered, but it was only my third time drinking and I do drink through a straw, I add hastily. Anyway, I've always maintained that it was Dexter's anaemic chicken that made me sick and not the beer... All right then, it was the beer!

My sick was soon cleared up and I felt suddenly much better. It was now time to go home but which one of the three joysticks on my wheelchair should I use! I was seeing triple, but my mind was clear enough to choose the middle one. I pressed the middle button and despite being a bit wobbly, I found it quite easy to drive. I was slightly giddy as I went on to the road and got up to four mph. I felt mad, bad and dangerous and when a bus came towards me I lost all common sense and decided to play chicken with it. I was usually such a calm and sensible young man.

I swerved out into the middle of the road and looked the bus up and down. 'Go on, make my day.' The question why I was doing this didn't come into my mind, and off I went. 'I'm not going to swerve, I'm not going to swerve, I'm going to beat this bus. Shit that bus is ten yards away!' and I was soon back on the left hand side and safe. I'd win next time.

When I got home, I experienced my mother's wrath again. She looked at me sternly, like when I went to the chippy that time and she wasn't happy that I was drunk. 'David, you shouldn't be driving when you're drunk. You'll kill yourself,' she shouted.

'I'm okay Mum, I wash shafe,' was my slurred response. It was a great feeling when my Mum's annoyance didn't bother me. It added a new meaning to 'Dutch courage'. I was a rebel!

After that unsupervised flirtation with the demon drink, my

summer relapsed into its repetitive vein of wandering around, listening to music, or both when Dexter decided to humiliate me by sellotaping a radio to my wheelchair and playing Jazz FM. I saw a number of people I knew who all thought it was extremely funny and I just had to grin and bear it. Dexter is pure evil. Oh how I've suffered! He had to do something to occupy himself and with nothing of great excitement to do he thought annoying me was good enough. He'd finally grown out of building dens and sitting on Astley Bridge Park had become, sorry always was, boring. We sat in the Asda café a few times until a couple of muppets (people who hang around on street corners acting hard but not being hard) came in because even they were as bored as we were.

Surely life would get better at sixth form. It surely couldn't get more boring. Dexter did actually buy a motorbike, which was about twenty years old, and he and his brother rode it around on a nearby field. They loved it but they only actually rode it a few times before it broke down. It was the most expensive motorbike in history to maintain, and Dexter got it into its head that spray painting it green would be a good idea. It would have been a good idea if he'd bought some proper paint. 'Yeah Dex it looks good. No... really... I'm not laughing. It does look good!' They soon sold it on to some dunce for almost the same price they'd bought it for. It wasn't that bad, I suppose. At least it took up some time and occupied a certain amount of days. *Roll on September*, I thought.

One of the best things about leaving Sharples was getting rid of that morbid black uniform. We wouldn't have to wear one at Turton and that was an excuse to buy some clothes. We had to look smart i.e. shirts and ties, and of course I adhered exactly to the rules again. It had gone full circle. I was at the beginning of sixth form and I was still as big a wimp as ever. I just wanted to make a good impression and then I could take liberties later on when people thought I was a nice lad. What am I talking about, I never took liberties but at least I could pretend I was a rebel. I'd played chicken with a bus; no one could stop me now.

Top: Before the big adventure. My first day of primary school. I don't know why I look so excited. Obviously nobody had told me what school was about!

Bottom: After my big adventure. The leaver's ball had just finished. School had driven me to alcohol!

Top: My brother on his bike, the day I realised I was disabled.
You'd think I'd have worked it out before then!
Bottom: Al, Sarah and I at my 18th. After they managed to find the place that is!

Top: My brother and I in our early high school days. No, that isn't a dead cat on my head!
Bottom: My brother and I six years later, after we had discovered hair gel.

Top: My mum, my nan and I enjoying the festivities.
Bottom: My friends and I, before the leaver's ball.

Top: Dan, Ben, Andy and I.
Bottom: In America.

Top: Me, as a vampire. Why did I let myself get roped into this?
Bottom: The lads and I, looking a little worse for wear before a
night out! *(From left to right)* Dex, Rick, Baz, Laney and Matt.

Top: "Suits you sir!" My brother and I looking like classical musicians before the Victoria Hall concert.
Bottom: Ralph, in a moment of relaxation in between chasing sheep and mating with male dogs!

Mum, Dad, Dan and I together.

Chapter IX

By the time I'd woken up from these ridiculous daydreams about being a rebel, which would never come true, it was time to go to sixth form.

The usual feelings of butterflies returned but I didn't have much breakfast to force down. I was still on my two rashers of bacon and nothing else. I'd be a sex machine by the end of the year. All these new women to become friends with and then fancy and then ring up and put the phone down on. No I'd definitely grown out of that. I did actually keep in touch with Isla over the summer and for my first year of sixth form. We got on better when I decided I just wanted to be mates with her. I even got the courage to ring her up and talk to her. Amazing! I'd need a friend who was detached from it all while I was settling in. She wasn't going into the army till the end of November so I had someone to talk to other than Dexter and the five or six other people who'd gone from Sharples to Turton. She even said to me once that me and Dexter were her best male friends at school, even if she didn't realise that at the time. I remembered her being mates with a lot of lads, so that was nice to know. Looking back though, it was a pointer to the future. The problem with nice lads is that they're too good as mates for girls to want to go out with them (most of the time). I didn't think about that back then. I wish I had. It would have saved a lot of heartache. It's all part of growing up though and I don't mind admitting that I was very innocent when I started at Turton.

Sitting in my electric wheelchair, I entered the taxi that had been organised (I was very independent now) and the driver introduced himself as Ralph. The first thing he did was make a joke about my disability. It was a risky thing to do because he didn't know how I'd react. Whether I'd laugh along, or get upset. When I laughed he said, 'You'll have to excuse me. I often take people in wheelchairs and I like to have a laugh with them.' I was in for some interesting trips to college.

I was dressed in my brand new shirt, pants and tie and I thought I was pretty damn smooth. As I pulled up to school I was in a daydream. Thinking whether I'd like the people, whether the work would be too hard and whether I'd be accepted like I always had been before. I wasn't worried about accessibility to the building or to my lessons because after meeting Mr Mills I knew he'd do his best for me. Anyway, I'd have a few people from Sharples to help me out if I had any problems. Dexter, Matt, Heather, Charmaine and Mukhtar from Sharples High, and Jane from Sharples Primary would help me out, and my cousin Andy was in the fifth year at Turton. He'd offered to help me out, so at least there'd be some people I liked even if I hated everybody else.

The taxi stopped and snapped me back to reality. Now where was it we had to meet? That's right, the common room. 'Right can you go back up there Ralph?' I called, and he did. The first person I'd met that day was all right then. He even opened the door to the common room for me. Now service like this I could get used to! This was a far cry from the previous day when I'd had quite a scare. The taxi had been organised, or so we thought, because my Mum had specifically asked for a black cab and the Education Authority had said no problem. Low and behold, the day before I started sixth form a big Education and Arts bus appeared and its driver, a woman you wouldn't want to come up against in a rugby scrum, stepped out knocked on my front door and to the horror of myself and my brother, she said, 'Is David there, I'm here to measure him up for the bus.'

Whoa hang on a minute, I thought as my brother said, 'I think there's been a mistake. They've ordered a black cab.'

'Well they told me to measure him up,' replied the 'chauffeur'.

By now the red mist had descended and steam was coming out of my ears. I couldn't go to college on that bus. I was trying to build up an image! She came into the room and I told her the situation, not mentioning the image thing. 'Sorry about this, but they have organised a taxi. I won't be coming on the bus,' I pleaded. She looked a little put out but I don't think she was blaming me.

'Fair enough,' she said, 'I wish they'd told me though.'

'Sorry,' I repeated and that was the last I saw of the bus.

It's not that I dislike the idea of a bus to get disabled people to school. It's a good idea. It shows that the government cares about getting us to school. I just don't feel that in my particular case the bus is an appropriate mode of transport. I've always been independent and being strapped into a bus when I can sit up by myself without falling over doesn't seem quite right or indeed necessary. As a method of merely saving money I don't think it's fair either. A bus like that should be used by and reserved for people who genuinely need it, who can't sit up on their own and who need supervision by a driver who is trained medically, or in any other necessary way. I don't need that and nor do I want it. That's the main reason I didn't want a bus, the image thing was only secondary but I do hate things that make me look more disabled than I am unless I need them. The wheelchair makes me look disabled enough!

I was glad that I did go in a taxi and as I joined my friends in the common room, under my own steam, I felt very independent and very proud. The only help I would need would be to open doors and to get my books out. I was almost as self-sufficient as everybody else. The story about the bus entertained the rest of the Sharples group and suddenly, when we knew we already had some friends our nerves became less and less. We looked more relaxed than the people who did come from Turton which was strange.

I say, 'the Sharples group' because although we'd left I think we all still felt like we were Sharples people. I definitely did. I think I still do. Mr Mills gave us the talk about what he expected from us. He expected us to work hard but also to enjoy ourselves. He wanted us to do more working than enjoying, though! We were at a different level now, he said, and we wouldn't succeed if we didn't put the work in. Then I switched off. I've never liked listening to people babbling on for an hour. I'd have to listen to a few more hours of babbling that morning. Mr Mills also told us that we were no longer Smithills or Sharples pupils, we were Turton Sixth Formers. I'd only been there an hour; I didn't want to be a Turton Sixth Former yet!

We then made our way to the Arts Theatre to continue our

induction day with a 'mind mapping' talk (more like mind numbing), for half an hour, giving us ideas for revision techniques. We hadn't learnt anything to revise yet! And because of that I didn't listen to any of this talk. What I did hear struck me as more complicated than the actual work we'd have to do. I immediately forgot about it. Next Mr Taylor (Matt's dad) gave us another little talk for another half an hour on essay writing. How would he ever follow on from such a fascinating talk! No one listened to him, not because he's boring but because the mind mapping talk had rendered us brain dead. We just wanted to get to know people.

After that we got a short break but everyone had lost the ability to move. There was no point moving anyway because we had to be back there ten minutes later to listen to a debate, which I thought would rival mind mapping for the title of the most boring thing in the world. *Myself and the rest of the lower sixth*, I thought, *would be too nervous to say anything in this debate.* Well I didn't know much then. A lad called Adam didn't hesitate in joining in and in his best politician's voice he said something very smug. I dislike smug people with a passion and it set the tone for the rest of the year, although I have to admit he was quite funny in that first debate. You have to hand it to him, he wasn't intimidated by standing in front of everyone or by the fact that the people he was debating with had been doing it much longer than he had. I don't like people who show off about how intelligent they are. You don't have to achieve anything to be intelligent, it's just luck, like how good-looking you are. It's what you do with the intelligence that you possess that's important. There are always some people who let it go to their heads.

We got through the debate and by then we weren't nervous any more, and it was dinner time. My starvation diet always made me hungry, obviously, and by dinner time I had to eat something. We decided to go to the shop and ten minutes later, by the time I'd got there, I decided I wouldn't bother doing that again. It wouldn't be a good idea in the middle of winter to travel for twenty minutes just to eat a pasty. I wouldn't be able to write, or eat the pasty, by the time I returned. A sandwich would satisfy the hunger.

I wondered what excitement was in store this afternoon and when I got back we were having a quiz. At least we wouldn't have to sit in silence again. A few lower sixth people were put in a group with the upper sixth so we could get to know them. I'm sure it was more of a chore for them than anything else but they did it. The team I was in didn't do very well, which was par for the course for me. I'm terrible at quizzes and as a 'getting to know you exercise' I don't think it worked. The people in our year who came from Turton already knew the upper sixth people and we were too nervous to even talk, so we didn't get to know anyone. The nerves that seemed to have gone came back quickly and suddenly the day was over. It hadn't been bad. I thought I could get used to it, but I hadn't started lessons yet. When Ralph dropped me off at my house my Mum was there again, mithering me about what had gone on, on my first day. I was a big boy now! I told her about the mind mapping talk just to make her wish she'd never asked the question. She didn't ask another question that night. I'd survived the first day unscathed and at least I wasn't scared to go back. I hadn't been put off.

The second day was still part of the induction and I feared what talks could take place today. Luckily the only talk we got was a short one from Mr Mills before we got our timetables. Four lessons of each subject every week and one of general studies, plus free periods. Now they sounded interesting! Apparently we were supposed to work hard during free periods and not just waste them chatting away about nothing. All these horror stories about the amount of work we'd have to do were just a ploy to make us work harder, I hoped. It couldn't be that intense. We were then told what forms we'd be in and all the Sharples lot plus about ten people from Turton were put into one form, which was fine by me. We'd be glad of each other's company while we settled in, although the rest of the form didn't seem too bad. It was interesting to see the different interpretations of the dress code, with the people from Turton tending to push the boundaries a bit further than the externals. Familiarity usually breeds contempt and that was what some of the Turton people treated the dress code with. I wish I hadn't been such a conformist.

I found myself judging people before I'd even spoken to them because of what they were wearing or how they looked. Long hair on lads, Nirvana T-shirts, earrings. I thought I'd been transported to Glastonbury. The people here definitely liked to express themselves, but you do judge people dressed like that as Grebs or Freaks, and it's only when you give them a chance that you realise they're not any different to you. They just like different music. At first though, I didn't want to give them a chance, I didn't want to be associated with them. They were weird. When I think about my attitude back then, I realise it was stupid. I've definitely become more tolerant of all sorts of things since joining Turton. Grebs? People can wear what they want; I even like their music. Gay people? They're not doing me any harm. The thing I didn't realise was that Turton people had the same attitude about us at first, just because we came from Sharples. Everyone from Sharples was a scroat, a scruff and a cocky moron weren't they? It was a case of breaking down the barriers so we could all coexist. That would take a while but what I do realise is that my attitude towards Grebs was just as bad as that of people who hate disabled people, just for being disabled and that's why I can ignore the discrimination of some teenagers. What I can't accept is when adults who should know better show the same attitudes, and I'm not talking about jokes or throwaway comments. I suppose the kids have to learn it from somewhere.

That second day, we didn't have any lessons. We were just getting to know our form mates, or not as the case was, and our form teacher Miss Kershaw who seemed nice enough. Basically it was a case of Miss Kershaw talking to the Turton kids and then to us and everyone was listening to each other's comments, e.g. what A levels we were doing and so on. The process that I went through at Sharples five years earlier of getting to know people had begun again. How fleeting life is! Things change so quickly but I was really determined to have a good time here. Today Baz arrived at Turton. He'd gone to North College the day before and decided that he wouldn't do any work whatsoever if he stayed there. It would be a waste of time for him. I thought that was quite a mature decision, although mature didn't really describe any of us accurately at that time.

I'd taken a sandwich and a drink for lunch, and after quite a pleasant morning of chat, mainly with my Sharples mates, I was relatively hungry. We sat in a group in the common room with Jane and the rest of the Cannon Slade group (another school in Bolton). I hadn't really seen Jane for five years but we instantly got on again. That's the thing about close friendships. It's a special thing when you can pick up where you left off without even a hint of a problem. She was a good mate and a really nice girl. She also introduced me to a couple of other people, Alastair who's become one of my closest friends, and Stephen or 'Pog' as they called him (I still don't know why). I didn't speak to him other than to say "Iyah' after that day, mainly because our free periods fell at different times. I was doing languages and he was doing science. Alastair had a familiar face; I could have sworn I knew him from somewhere. I didn't but I'd probably seen him around. To be honest I couldn't have missed him, he was about six foot five! We had a chat and I got on with him straight away, although I couldn't understand half of what he was saying. He tends to swallow his words and I found myself concentrating intently. It would be the first of many chats, so I'd get plenty of practice.

After that day, I thought Turton was going to be a good place to spend two years. I'd made a couple of friends and rekindled an old friendship, it had been quite a successful day all round. Now all I had to worry about were the lessons, which started the next day. The honeymoon was over. Now it was down to business. Would I be able to do the work? I'd give it a go.

Arriving at college, I noticed that the door that led to the outside of our form room was locked, surprisingly. Ralph had to put his ramps up the huge step at the other entrance to let me in. He was good like that. Then I had to negotiate my way along the narrow corridor to get into the room next door to our form room, which happened to be my cousin's form room. At least I wouldn't be lonely while I waited for everyone else to arrive. While I was travelling in style and comfort, they all had to walk in whatever the conditions were at that time. I used to enjoy laughing at them as I passed them in the pouring rain: Matthew, Alastair, Heather, Charmaine, Jane, Dex and Baz. I laughed at them all every day. I would have given them a lift but the Education Authority would have stopped Ralph from taking me if he let anyone else in. I never understood that rule. Obviously when there were so many of them, I couldn't have let them all in the taxi, so they all had to suffer.

Mukhtar would always be there before anyone else, waiting to be let in. He was just so eager to get to college, to beat me in my A levels. Actually he said I'd get better A levels than him because I was doing 'easier subjects'. How he could say things like that and keep a straight face, I don't know. If French was so easy, why did he only get a B at GCSE? 'It was because Yunus used to put me off,' he said, clutching at straws and still keeping a straight face. He was a funny guy.

Now where was I? Oh yeah, the first lesson. I had to miss the first lesson, French literature, because I was called to a meeting with the 'interference brigade'. They'd been sent to find out what had been done to help me out, and what I needed in lessons. Well, I didn't know did I, because I hadn't been to any lessons yet! When I saw Heather who was in my French group after the lesson she told me that they all had to introduce themselves in French and that there was a lad who spoke absolutely fluently. The rest of the group were girls, and they apparently were much better than Heather and I were. Great, I'd have to speak on my own at the next lesson. Oh well, I'd have to get used to it if I was going to do well in two language A levels. Why was I so scared? I think it was because I was scared of talking to people I didn't know in English, let alone in French, even though I knew I could say enough to introduce myself without even thinking.

I still had that to worry about but the first lesson I actually got to was German. We had one and a half lessons of German lit per week and two and a half lessons of language, whereas in French we had two lessons of each for some unknown reason. You'd think it would have been the same in each but I guess it's just one of those wonders of the world. So my first lesson was a half-lang. half-lit. lesson. Mrs Stephenson was the language teacher and Mr Willis the lit. They both seemed very nice, if a little unorthodox. Mrs Stephenson seemed a very good and experienced teacher. She was also very forgetful and right from the first lesson she'd drift into conversations and lectures on all sorts of weird and wonderful things. By the end of the first year I'd mastered the art of listening to everything she said about languages and every piece of vocab. she gave us, but just appearing to be listening when she went off on one. Every time she looked at me I'd nod as if to say I understood what she was saying.

Mr Willis liked a bit of a laugh but he was very worried about covering everything in time. He'd become very stressed if we didn't do as much as he wanted in a lesson.

They were both very different and the biggest difference that I noticed was how they reacted when someone didn't do their work. I think Mrs Stephenson thought that if you didn't do the homework it was your problem. She'd just carry on teaching and would mark it when you did it. Mr Willis didn't like people who didn't do the work. He went mad at anyone who didn't do it, and would only mark late work when he felt like it. Fair enough. If people didn't do the work and didn't co-operate with him, then he wouldn't co-operate with them. They wouldn't have any problems with me on that score. I knew what I wanted and would do my best to get there. If I didn't do the work I couldn't help myself to get into uni to do Law, which wouldn't be the easiest task in the world as it was. I had already checked on what I needed to get in. An A and two B's, and right from the beginning that was my new aim in life. I'd have to do some hard work to get there.

The other people in the group were mostly female. There was just me and one other lad called Mark. Then there was Sarah and Vicky from Darwen (near Blackburn) and Laura, Carrie and Anisa from Turton. It was like a merry go round with people leaving and others joining, and the group didn't stop changing until the end of the lower sixth. In fact only Laura, Vicky, Sarah and I were in the group from the first lesson right through to the last, and we became very close. I was closest to Laura and Sarah when I left but the first time I met Laura, I thought she was gorgeous. I had no intention of just being mates with her at first.

Within three days I was determined to do well and I had found someone I fancied. I'd also made a couple of friends and I was settling in quite nicely thank you very much. It would however take a while before I settled in properly. My first lesson had started nervously but everyone seemed really friendly. I thought I would enjoy myself with these people, as well as getting my work done. The lesson had finished with everyone being relaxed in each other's company and ready for the free period which came next.

My first free period and nobody I knew was there. That was strange but I saw a couple of girls from my form, Hilary and Nicola, with their mates so I ended up talking to them. I was getting to know quite a number of people, although if I'd asked or answered the question 'What A levels are you doing?' again I think I'd have screamed, which wouldn't have made the best impression.

After dinner, I had English with Mrs Baddeley. Alastair, Heather and Dexter were in my group, so I had people who could help me out. I was sat with Dexter and Al (Alastair), and Carrie from my German group was also sat nearby. Heather had already made a few mates. She was very talkative and never got nervous, which made me so damn mad. That would be the only thing I'd change about myself if I had a chance. I'd be more confident with people. Not arrogant, but more confident. I definitely find it easier to talk to girls who I've just met rather than lads, probably because they're more likely to start a conversation and keep it going when I'm out of things to say. If someone starts talking about a subject I join in but sometimes I struggle to start talking myself.

Adam was also in the group acting very smugly again. I don't know what annoyed me so much about him. Probably because he had to be the centre of attention all the time, showing how intelligent he was. I was totally opposite to him. I knew I was relatively intelligent and could hold my own with other intelligent people. I didn't have to go out of my way to prove it. If you show off too much about your talents you're liable to fall flat on your face.

In English we'd have three lessons with Mrs Baddeley and one with Mrs Proctor per week. Mrs Baddeley reminded me of a primary school teacher, not because she treated us like kids or anything like that but just because she was so nice to us all. She wanted to encourage us rather than force us to work hard. After all we didn't have to be there, we were there because we wanted to keep on studying. Her enthusiasm for the subject was very evident, almost infectious, and I think that made some people want to work. When people didn't do their work she became very frustrated. She wanted us all to do as well as possible. I think she also wondered why people weren't as enthusiastic as she was and she became flustered when trying to tell people off.

So far every teacher had a totally different style but I thought each one had the ability to push us on to the next level. By the end of the week having had at least one lesson with all six of my teachers, I knew that if they taught me what they knew, and I went home and learnt it, then I would do well. Although I knew I could do well, it took a while for me to convince myself that I could be good enough to be accepted for a Law degree.

My French teachers, Mr Steeple (language) and Mrs Walker (lit.), had different styles although both had a good sense of humour. We could have a laugh with them. Mr Steeple worried about us getting enough done in each lesson and he always had something extra for us to do so he could fill every minute of every lesson. I don't think he realised how frustrating that was, no on second thoughts I'm sure he did realise that. He just wanted to annoy us! His sense of humour was similar to mine in that he'd say things he didn't really mean to get a rise out of the girls. I love taking the mickey out of people, just to see how they react and I've never understood why people call sarcasm 'the lowest form of wit'. Only people who can't use it effectively say that.

At the end of the day Mr Steeple and I had to stick together, we were the only males in the classroom. Well, there was one other lad Andy, but he was only really there in body. His mind was somewhere else most of the time, I'm sure he was stoned when he came into college. He didn't last very long at Turton anyway, even though his French was very good. No wonder Heather said his speaking was brilliant – he was Belgian. He put the fear of God in me when I first heard him speak. I thought, *I'll never be able to speak French like that.* If French A level was just about speaking he'd have got an A right there and then but he wasn't prepared to do the work that reading a French novel and writing essays on it required. You had to be good at English literature in order to be good at French. Maybe some people would argue that that isn't what learning a language should be about but unless you have a deep knowledge of grammatical terms and an extensive vocab. in your own language, you can't hope to learn another one.

In my French group there were a number of girls. Laura and Vicky who I knew from German were there and another (Amy) who would soon be in my German group was there. The other girls were Heather and Katy from my form and Rachel, Lynn and Louise whom I met for the first time at my first French lesson. I did have to speak in that lesson as well. So in my best Bolton accent I said... well as little as possible. I told everyone my name, what school I was from and which A levels I was doing and then I quickly shut up. I had a lot to learn.

I noticed quite quickly that I didn't know as much as everybody else, well everyone from Turton anyway. After a couple of lessons we started talking about the 'imperfect tense'. 'What's that then?' I asked myself, and then I looked at Heather who looked as bemused as I did. For one moment I thought about escaping and driving straight home, never returning to that place and then I thought, *I'm not leaving, I can do this.*

When I say I didn't know as much as everyone else it sounds like a criticism of the Sharples teachers but it's not. It's just that when a school only goes up to the age of sixteen, they don't really prepare you for A levels, they just teach you enough to get you through the GCSE. They teach you phrases to learn and enough vocab. to get you through an exam. So when I got to Turton, the grammar which had been used to teach the others was an alien concept to Heather and I. The teachers from Sharples knew that and had offered to help, but I don't think the Turton teachers realised it at first. They expected us to know things we couldn't possibly have known. It was the same in German, but when I did go to ask for help, they were very helpful. They gave us some books which explained things in a way that even uneducated peasants like Heather and I could understand. Notice how I mentioned Heather first. She goes to uni in Sheffield, so I'm safe. I also went back to my teachers at Sharples to beg for some help, which they gladly gave me although they did tell me something I didn't want to hear. There was no easy way of learning verb tenses. Great! I'd just have to sit there and learn it. I'd have to sit there and learn how each verb changed in the present tense and...

well that's bored you enough. Let's just say there were a lot of verbs and I'd have to learn them in both French and German. Could I be bothered? For me it wasn't a question of that, it was more like I had to do it. It was my new obsession and I wouldn't be beaten. I loved languages and there was nothing else I wanted to do. So I was stuck with it.

For the first few weeks I spent hours learning and trying to understand verb tenses and how each different tense works differently in each language. We were given sheets that explained everything but as for everything else in life, you always find an exception to every rule. If there was a pattern to how a verb was formed the sentence ended with 'except in the following verbs'. Why were there these exceptions? Probably so that the people who invented grammar would always know it better than anyone who wanted to learn it.

The jump between GCSE and A level modern languages was absolutely huge in the amount of vocab. and grammar you had to learn, in the complexity of the whole language, and going from reading fifty word letters about what clothes people wear to reading *l'Alouette* (a book about Joan of Arc and her visions of angels) was the most frightening thing in the world. It was even worse in German. When we first started we couldn't understand any of the words in the books let alone begin to understand the story and to learn to comment on it. For 20% of the mark in the final exam we had to read three novels in each language, answering questions in the language on two of the books and questions in English, using foreign quotes on the other one. I didn't see the point in all that work for so little reward. The sense of achievement you get though when you can read a whole novel in a foreign language, hardly having to look up a word, is unbelievable. I felt like the king of the world! As you can see, I get a little carried away about languages. In all seriousness, I think languages are the most amazing things. When you've studied them more deeply it's brilliant how people have invented languages and learnt to communicate on a more involved level than animals can, although the fact that we can think and consider things on this deep level does cause one or two problems. It's much easier for an animal to find a mate. They don't need any of this 'Do you want to go for a drink sometime?' or the agony people as soft as me go through before being able to say that. Nope they just move in and before you know it you've got a few cubs on your hands. Oh how I long to be a lion in my next life!

On a more sane level, looking back at those books we had to read I can admit I was wrong to think of it as pointless. Reading a book is one of the fastest ways to find out vocab, when you're learning a language. There's always a large amount of new words and ways of understanding the language. Every page is a gold mine of knowledge, and that's the beauty of languages, you can never know every word there is to know. There's always something new to learn. Learning languages at Turton also broadened my English vocab. My French and German teachers knew the foreign word for English words that I didn't even know existed and I wrote down every new word I heard, saw or read and then went home and learnt it along with the grammar. I had this unquenchable thirst for knowledge that pushed me on to learn more and more words. I also had this determination to improve and to get A's by the end of the first year. I wouldn't fail. I couldn't fail and that was why I worked so hard to learn as much as possible. I'd get into a law school if it killed me!

All this learning seemed futile for a long time and it wasn't until after Christmas that I actually noticed an improvement, when my translations actually looked like something that resembled a coherent piece of literature and when I could form a full sentence without looking up a word. It felt brilliant. Up until that time I frequently considered doing history instead of German. At least I could understand what I was reading! I can honestly say I never thought about dropping French but I found French much easier than German. The grammar was much more English. Usually, if you could form a sentence in English and you knew the words in French you could put the sentence together in the same order. In German, if you knew the words it didn't necessarily mean you could form the sentence. You had to learn when the verbs go at the end of a sentence and all sorts of scary rules. The amount of red ink that was on my first few pieces of German homework was probably more than the amount of blue ink I'd used. All those mistakes were disheartening to say the least and I wasn't happy.

We also had to have a speaking lesson once a week with a student who'd come over from France or Germany (one from each). We were being forced to speak. No, anything but that! In the first year it was Fabien and Frauke and it was an eye-opening experience to see how good their English was compared to our French and German, which was disjointed to say the least. Those first few months were an ordeal. I went to Fabien with Rachel and Laura, who I was fast becoming obsessed with, and they were much more confident speaking than I was. I'd sit there and make the odd French comment and then listen a bit before making another comment, and then luckily for me Rachel and Laura would natter on like old women in a bingo hall. Then the bell would ring and I'd be saved. It worked in every lesson, until Fabien got fed up and at the beginning of one lesson he decided to make me speak, telling Laura and Rachel to *fermes la bouche* every time they spoke, until he'd made me speak enough. It was hell on earth. My problem was that I couldn't change my personality when I spoke in French. When I spoke English I employed the same tactics of listening and then making a comment at carefully chosen intervals, usually upsetting someone along the way with my tendency to call a spade a spade, whilst in the same sentence taking the mickey out of it for being a spade. Give me a pressure situation where I have to talk or a subject I'm interested in and I'll talk till the cows come home, but in these lessons I was happy not to bother. I felt, maybe naively, that if I learnt the vocab. and could write in a language I could speak it when I needed to. Before then, when I couldn't write it, I was happy to remain silent. In German my tactics were useless against Frauke's enthusiasm for making us speak. I also went to the lesson with Carrie and not Laura, and if it was possible she was quieter and more shy than I was. It was like a competition to see who could talk the least, with me usually giving in first. The pauses became embarrassing after about two minutes.

Carrie soon decided that German was not for her, as did Mark, and Amy from French decided it was for her, as did a lad called James. Before I got to know him, I would have described him as a Greb. Long hair, Pearl Jam T-shirts and a goatee beard.

He was a Greb all right! However I soon began to describe him as a nice guy who just listened to different music to me. My musical taste has begun to resemble Greb music now. I've been affected! I've still got short hair and no Pearl Jam T-shirts, but there's still time.

Andy and Heather soon decided to leave the French group although Heather took less drastic action than Andy. Heather went to do English lit and Andy left college completely. What he's doing now is anybody's guess. Now I think about it I don't know what is more drastic. English lit, or leaving college. It's a close call!

The people I did languages with were great girls, apart from James obviously. We were part of a dying breed of male linguists but it was good fun having a laugh at the female contingent. I soon became close to the girls. They were really easy to get on with and they had personality. There were a large number of A★'s at GCSE in that room (none of them being mine) but none of the girls were stuck up or arrogant, or even boring intellectuals. Because of that the French and German lessons were very relaxed, despite the hard work we had to put in. They were all good-looking as well which I wasn't complaining about. It wasn't all one-sided though. They had the benefit of being in the same room as the most witty, intelligent and good-looking lad in the college and I'm not talking about Mr Steeple. James was the second best looking lad in the college, despite his facial hair. (They all paid me £10 to get a good comment in this book, Mr Steeple and Adam refused.)

Just listening to the girls taught me more about what goes on in women's heads than anything else. It's horrible how women bitch about other girls. Very funny though! They were mad those girls, especially Rachel. She was Spanish so when she was speaking French she'd accidentally put a Spanish word in the middle of a sentence, very strange.

Sarah from my German group was a lovely girl. Totally down to earth, no arrogance about her. What you saw was what you got with Sarah and I liked that. It meant we could be totally honest with each other, knowing that the other one was being honest. She even told me when I was being a pillock, and I told her when she was being oversensitive. The best friendships are ones when you know neither of you is lying. The truth may hurt sometimes but it's always better to know what's going on. Something always goes wrong when you're being dishonest and someone always gets hurt. That's why I always try to be honest with people.

I got on really well with Laura right from the start and we became good mates. Yet again I mistook friendship for more than that but I couldn't bring myself to ask her out myself. That's where Charmaine came in useful. We'd become much closer than we had been in five years at Sharples and in just a few short weeks, sadly enough, I got her to ask Laura out for me. How primary school! Laura said no and surprisingly my luck hadn't changed. I was gutted for the rest of that day but to be honest I wasn't quite as bothered as I had been about previous girls. It wasn't because I liked her any less than any of the others, but I'd just started a new college. There were plenty of other girls around so I wasn't going to give up just yet.

Meanwhile, just as I thought I'd escaped Sharples forever, we had to return for Presentation Evening so we could get our GCSE certificates. As I said before, I hate Presentation Evenings at the best of times but this one was even more embarrassing than previous ones. The idea was that the lad who got the best results in the school and the girl who got the best results had their picture taken for the *Bolton Evening News*. That was Mukhtar and Charmaine respectively, and I was only too happy to let Mukhtar have the limelight. After all he'd beaten me fair and square. But no! Someone got it into their head that I should be on this picture and that I should get a 'special' award for 'achieving such great results in the face of all my problems'. Dexter and I were both mentioned in the head teacher's speech; Dexter for being my 'constant companion' and me for 'achieving such... blah blah blah'. Dexter looked like he was going to die and I wanted someone to wake me from this nightmare. Of course I understood what he meant, and so did Dexter. The good intentions were there but the thought was sadly lacking. That may sound ungrateful but I had never made a big deal of my problems, I didn't want them to be an issue and this speech showed that the head teacher didn't know me as well as he thought he did. First of all, saying that Dexter was my 'constant companion' made it sound like he pushed me around because he felt sorry for me, which was never the case, and putting me on the photo was not really appropriate. It made something special out of something that I didn't feel was special. I didn't get the best results, so I didn't deserve to be on the photo. I've talked about not wanting to be a special case, but this showed that the head teacher had always seen me as special, and for special I read 'different'. I was upset about this but I didn't make a big deal out of it.

This Presentation Evening was a distraction from the first few months of college which had been difficult for me. I had to catch up with the other language students, then learn new things, plus I was getting to know a whole new group of people. As difficult as all that was, the additional difficulties disabled people are supposed to have didn't seem to exist for me. A bit of careful planning before I started and the transition from Sharples wasn't difficult accessibility wise. The people who had been kind enough to accept me into their college (they could have just denied that they had any way of accommodating me) gave me a key to the door of my form room, so I didn't have to negotiate a huge step. All my lessons were already on the ground floor, except English which was moved to the ground floor. I had a group of friends from Sharples, who'd walk round to my lessons with me to open the doors. They took turns, although Matt did it most often because he usually had free periods when I had lessons. The new people I met treated me like one of them as soon as they experienced my personality which wouldn't let the wheelchair get in the way. They were only too glad to help me get my books out of my bag and to put headphones on when we were doing a listening test. They'd also walk back to the common room with me after lessons. I was a mate to them just like other mates. I simply needed help to get my books out. Mr Mills had said that if I needed any help, just to call on him and he'd sort it out. In return I raised the profile of his college as one which championed equal opportunities. It was a good deal all round, and I could go and talk to whoever I wanted, whenever I wanted, without Dexter having to take me there. As grateful as I was to Dexter (I wouldn't have been able to get through Sharples without him) and as happy as he was to have helped me out all those years, I think the electric wheelchair made life easier for both of us. In fact, at times I helped him more than he helped me, especially when it came to his own women problems.

He fancied this girl and it was pretty obvious that she fancied him, but neither of them could ask the other one out. This rubbish went on for about a week until Matt, Al and myself told him off and called him a soft git several hundred times. (If that sounds a bit hypocritical considering my soft centre when it comes to women, then it is!) Eventually he snapped with us and went to ask her out. She said yes and we all breathed a huge sigh of relief. That particular saga had gone on long enough. It was like *Saved by the Bell* or some other sad American programme, but it wasn't finished yet.

He'd asked her out on the Friday and by the time it got to Sunday he decided, having not seen her since, that he didn't want to go out with her any more. He fancied someone else in his art group. After all that time and courage it had taken to ask her out in the first place, he didn't want to go out with her any more! I wanted to break his neck!

If the fact that he wanted to dump her was annoying enough, you can imagine how annoying the next thing he said was, 'Will you ring her up and tell her for me Dave? I feel tight.'

'Do it yourself. Anyway, you are tight. You've only been going out with her two days,' I refused in no uncertain terms.

'Please Dave, I can't do it.'

'No I'm not doing it. You asked her out, you can dump her. What is it you want to say anyway.'

'That I don't think it's working. I don't know, do I?'

'That's bloody stupid! How can it not be working, you've not even been anywhere with her. No, no way.'

'Please.'

'No.'

'Please.'

'Dex no, Dex no, Dex no...'

'After all the things I've done for you, you can't even do this one thing for me? You ungrateful sod.'

Oh no not the guilt trip, I thought. I'm a sucker for the guilt trip, even if I know that it's being unfairly used. 'Right, give me the sodding number. I can't believe I'm doing this when you don't know what I can say to her.'

I felt terrible. What if she started crying on the phone? What would I say then? Let's face it; that was unlikely after two days but it was possible.

Now I'd felt nervous before, but this was one of the most horrible feelings of my life as I sat next to the phone. I wasn't even dumping her for myself. I couldn't believe I'd got roped into this.

I didn't know her very well but I didn't want her to have to suffer going out with the invisible boyfriend any longer, so I sat down to dial her number. It felt like everything was happening in slow motion as I pressed the loudspeaker button on my phone and pressed the buttons one by one. Every time I reached the fourth number of the six, I got this overwhelming nervous twitch in my stomach and I had to turn the phone off before I exploded! This situation repeated itself over and over again until I dialled two-thirds of the number about ten times.

'This is stupid,' I told myself. 'Just ring the bloody number. She's not going to go mad at you, *you're* not dumping her.' Told you I was terrified of using phones didn't I?

When I finally managed to dial the whole number and it started ringing, I could feel myself becoming hotter and hotter and sweat was building up on my forehead. Everything Dexter had done for me wasn't worth this one moment. If I'd known I'd have to do this, when Dexter first started pushing me around, I'd have gone to a special school – a bit drastic, I know.

She answered the phone and I said against my better judgement, 'I don't think I should be the one doing this but Dexter doesn't think it's working.' I knew I sounded stupid saying that but I didn't know what to say, I'd never dumped someone for someone else before. Come to think of it, I'd never dumped anyone for myself before!

'Thanks for telling me,' she said, 'I was beginning to think that myself.'

'See ya,' I said and that harrowing moment was over. Thank God for that.

The thought that our luck would change with a change of

scenery seemed a bit misplaced at that moment in time. I suppose you could say that Dexter's luck had changed but I don't think he saw it that way. There were plenty of other women around but whether they'd be interested was another question. How did we know there were plenty of others? Well, in one of the rare frees Matt and I had together we sat down and looked around the common room to see who was going out with who, who was single, and who wasn't. It was a shock to see how many attractive girls were going out with not so attractive Grebs. I don't know what gave us the right to judge someone we didn't know to be ugly, or what made us think we were better looking than they were, but we thought they were weirdoes and wondered why these girls would go out with them. Maybe it was the personality because I have to admit some of them were funny and had personality. It could have been because they were different, and not your ordinary nice lads like we were. We were just nice lads who liked a good time and had a laugh. We were also funny but didn't try to get people's attention and make a funny comment every sentence. It's important to have a serious conversation once in a while.

Although we didn't understand the choice of men of our female counterparts, there wasn't much we could do about it. *There must be enough single women to go round*, I thought. Obviously none of the upper sixth would be in my lessons, and I was too shy just to go and talk to them in a free period, so I either had to turn my attention to girls in my lessons or girls that were introduced to me by my friends who did different lessons. Jane and Charmaine did sciences, and maths and geography respectively, so they knew different people to the ones I knew. Alastair did theatre studies and business studies, plus he'd talk to anyone who was near to him at the time. I wish I could do that. I'd usually join in when he was talking to someone else and it went on from there.

The thing with me was that I wasn't the sort of person who could just go over to a girl and chat her up or anything like that, so I had to get to know them first in a situation where they'd speak to me frequently over a period of time, i.e. in lessons. It won't surprise you then that there wasn't only Laura that I fancied in my French group. I found them all attractive and got on with all of them, and at different stages at Turton I fancied about four of them.

Amy was going out with someone, and I wasn't the type to try and ruin that so I gave up on that idea pretty quickly. After I got over Laura, or when I thought I had, I fancied Katy for a while. Eventually I asked Charmaine to ask her out for me, again. I shiver with embarrassment thinking about how pathetic I was. It really was bad the way I asked people out. What would I have done if either of them had said yes – got Charmaine to ring them up every time I wanted to go out somewhere with them? Probably! You probably gathered that Katy didn't say yes either. My detailed research into the women of Turton had unfortunately not gone as far as the most obvious detail. Finding out whether the girl I fancied had a boyfriend or not. She did and Charmaine also knew that, and assumed that I knew as well. She didn't know me as well as she thought she did, if she thought I'd ask someone out, who already had a boyfriend. I'd never try to ruin another relationship like that.

This tactic of getting Charmaine to do my work for me had now failed twice, and I decided I was being pathetic. I decided never to use Charmaine like that again. The next time I asked someone out I'd do it myself. It was about this time that Matt told me Charmaine was getting fed up of doing it for me anyway. She just didn't want to tell me.

Now, I'm not surprised it didn't work. A girl's hardly going to want to go out with someone who can't even ask them out by himself. No one wants to go out with a pathetic git like that. Charmaine knew that, but it's hard to tell one of your best mates that they're behaving like a loser. I'm really grateful that she did it for me while I was too immature to do it myself, but the time had arrived for a more mature approach to women. I knew I could make female friends easily enough, I just had to learn to read the signals, if there were any, and to push myself to the next step of asking someone out. The worst thing they could say was '**** off you ugly *****!' That's not too humiliating is it?

College wasn't the only way to meet new girls, there were places called nightclubs for that. I'd never been to one before. I'd always looked too young but my fifteen-year-old brother, on the other hand had been before. He had a sixteen-year-old girlfriend when he was fourteen and he went to a college do with her.

So at Euan Blair age, I was initiated to the bar and nightclub experience. It's not done me any harm. I did feel quite embarrassed about being taken around the nightspots by a fifteen-year-old, town centre veteran but someone had to come with me. For hours before this night out I felt absolutely petrified. What if they asked me for ID, or if they didn't let me in? If they asked for a date of birth I'd probably freeze and tell them my real one. It was a nightmare.

As the taxi pulled up outside the first bar and I drove my wheelchair towards the bouncers, the fear on my face must have given away that I was under age but it didn't stop them letting me in. 'Just go round t' side and we'll let you in t' back door mate.' They must have thought my disability made me look that pale or they were too scared to turn me away in case by some fluke I was actually eighteen, and I complained of discrimination!

Getting in was like I'd made it. I was a normal person now! After all the times I'd heard people my own age say that they'd 'gone out and got pissed', I could now finally say it myself and not be lying when I said it. What a victory! I was very naive and believed it was the best thing in the world to have got in somewhere without being asked for ID. I was the man! When it's your first time out, it's like any other first experience. You go out wide-eyed and oblivious to what's going on around you. You're fantastic, you're grown up and you're untouchable. I felt like nothing could go wrong and the buzz of all these mixed emotions together at one time went to my head. Who needs alcohol when you feel like that?

I was in awe of this place. My first bar and I loved it right from the beginning. The blinding lights, the deafening music and the extremely expensive alcoholic beverages. All my senses were being destroyed, but it was great! After a couple of drinks the music was just at the right level and the lights seemed only as bright as a 60-watt light bulb. Oh yeah, I forgot about the women, the beautiful women, who became more and more beautiful with every mouthful I drank. I'd never seen so many good-looking women in one room before and their clothes were pretty sexy. I

215

definitely wanted more of this.

The trouble with young people, especially lads when they feel untouchable, is that they get carried away. Just because they are in the same building as older people they think they can act like them, drink like them, and because they become aggressive like older people they think they can fight them and win. That's when going out can become dangerous for youngsters and that's why the legal drinking age is eighteen. When you're fifteen or sixteen you hate the legal age. You think, 'I can handle drink well enough, it's not fair that it's eighteen.' By the time you get to nineteen, like I am now, you hate the fact that the clubs 'are full of little kids' when only three years earlier you were one of those little kids yourself, except you didn't think you were a little kid back then.

I found out that night that drink loosened my gob a little. I had a couple of Southern Comfort and Cokes (I should get a deal with Southern Comfort to advertise their drink – 'Southern Comfort, it's what kids prefer' – no, I'll stick to my day job) and this bald lad walked in. He looked like someone you wouldn't mess with and he was at least four years older than me. My brother said, 'That's the lad who threatened to deck me. You know the one that Dad came to see with me?'

I was overcome with the same sense of hatred that I would have had, had I been sober, but being drunk I'd either become brave or stupid. I decided I was going to have 'a word with that tosser'. I turned the wheelchair on and made for where he was standing, but I wasn't moving anywhere. I looked over my shoulder and my brother was holding me back.

'Dan what are you doing? Get off me!' I shouted.

'What are you doing, you bloody psycho? You'll get us killed.'

'He won't touch me in here. He won't hit someone in a wheelchair.'

'Dave, he's just got out of prison for battering someone with a home-made metal ball and chain. He'll kill us.'

'I don't care… What did you say?' My anger had been replaced by fear. Maybe he *would* hit someone in a wheelchair! We soon left that place. I think my brother decided it was time for a sharp exit before we left in an ambulance.

We went to the bar next door and this place was very similar, although it was much harder to get into. There was one step up to a small platform and then one step down to the actual bar area. I don't know why it couldn't have been flat, that platform was pointless, but who was I to say that?

You're probably wondering why one step up and one step down is so awkward. Well I have to go up steps forwards and down them backwards, so somehow I had to turn through 180 degrees on a platform which was six foot by six foot, whilst people pushed into the place behind me, and others tried to get out past me. How I managed this feat whilst relatively drunk I'll never know but I did it and I liked this place as much as the last place. I was enjoying the night but it was strange to see that there were more fifteen, sixteen and seventeen-year-olds than there were over eighteens. Most of them were my brother's mates so at least I knew someone.

There were no bald psychos in that place but we only stayed there for one drink before moving on to a nightclub where again we had no problems getting in past the bouncers. This was easy. I must have looked older than I thought. I hadn't even been ID'd yet. This club was one of the most dark and dingy places I'd ever seen. There was only a small area of the club that I could get to and everywhere I looked I could see old men eyeing up the girls, most of whom were my age or younger. I don't think I saw one person between the age of eighteen and thirty-five in that place. There was one man who was wearing a flat cap. He must have been about sixty and he was watching these young girls gyrating on the stage. No don't get me wrong, he was having a good time, dancing away and chatting to the girls. He was probably losing his eyesight in his old age so he couldn't see how old they were! If he'd known, he probably would have averted his eyes... Yeah right!

I wasn't eyeing the girls up though. I wouldn't do anything like that. You've got to hand it to the old geezer; he had the courage to chat people up. I spoke to a total of zero girls that I didn't know, although with that lighting I couldn't see what anyone looked like. My self-confidence level was pretty low when it came to the way I looked and talked to girls anyway. I hadn't had much luck up to then and basically I wondered why anyone would fancy a lad in a wheelchair. I knew I could say the right things. I was intelligent enough to think of something to say, to flirt and show off my sense of humour, all at the same time but I just didn't think it would work. The trouble with me is that I think too much about all this. If I could just talk without worrying about what they could say back, I'd be fine. I was that nervous at that time, that if a girl spoke to me I'd give one word answers, go red and then escape as quickly as possible without trying to see where the conversation went.

An hour of this den of iniquity was enough for my brother and too much for me, and we were soon on our way home. It had definitely been eye opening and I was excited about going out with my friends soon. Hopefully we wouldn't go to that club again but I wouldn't mind going to those bars again. They were good fun.

I returned to college the next Monday feeling like I had something to do, when I wasn't at college and I told everyone that we had to go out soon. I'd decided to take a break from asking people out for a while until I had the courage to ask for myself. Charmaine was now redundant as a matchmaker and I bet she was really upset about that! She'd been a complete failure anyway.

Turton now felt like the right place for me to be. After a few weeks of concerted effort I was now beginning to understand verbs and acquire a more complicated vocab. I knew that languages were something that had to be constantly revised and that there was always something new for me to learn. I was therefore determined to do two hours of college work, even if I didn't have two hours' worth of work to do. If I didn't have enough work to do, I'd revise my vocab. or grammar. The amount of times I'd heard how much work A levels entailed had made me believe I had to do more work than I did have to, but even if I hadn't had it drummed into me I'd have done the same amount of work. It's just part of my make-up. The less work I did, the more I panicked, so hard work kept me happy, even sane. Two hours a day was hardly too big a task anyway. I could work for two hours without needing a break so if I finished college at 3.15 p.m. and got home at 3.30, I'd finish work at 5.30, just in time for *Neighbours*! Some days I only had one lesson so I finished at 10.30 got home at 10.45 and I'd done my two hours by 1 p.m. That gave me all afternoon to do what I wanted. This A level lark was becoming quite easy. I was definitely getting the right balance of work and relaxation. I didn't even have to do a part-time job, so I could afford to go out. No, I was getting paid income support for being in a wheelchair. Who says it's tough being disabled? By the time the lads came round (which was most nights) at about half seven to eat and drink us out of house and home and generally make a lot of noise, my work had long been done. There's about seven of us altogether: Matt, Dex, Baz, Laney (Daniel Lane), Al, Rick and myself, although when we first started college Laney was more Dexter's brother's mate. Rick had split up with his girlfriend by then so we were all embarrassingly single.

It was good fun when we were all together, taking the mickey out of each other, and it still is. No one got offended and I felt like I really belonged at last. My plan of spending more time with my friends outside school than I had done at Sharples was going according to plan. Dexter and I had never got fed up of each other and if we had struggled to make friends we wouldn't have complained at just the two of us being mates. It's just that if two lads go out on their own, people think they're gay. That wouldn't do us any good! I soon realised that going out in a group was much more fun.

The first time we went out for a proper night out was at a North College do. We weren't even at North College but we knew some people who were and they got us some tickets. Quite a few of us went, probably because we didn't like the idea of the first Turton do, a 'Ho Down'. It sounded a bit like a theatre studies do. You all dress up and swing your partners, like in an all-American barn dance. You had to be a complete extrovert, which I can say none of the Sharples lads were. I thought, maybe stupidly, that because I didn't know anyone very well I'd wait till I did before going on one of these nights out. That was the excuse I gave for not going anyway. I think the idea of the night was that we should get to know people by going to it but it didn't feel right. That was the trouble with Turton nights out – you had to dress up like a tool to fit in. Fading into the background was not an option! I've definitely changed in that respect, Turton's made me into a different person. I've even been to a 'dress up and act like a tool' party since then. I dressed up as a vampire. What an achievement!

That North College do turned into an experiment into how much I could drink before my already weak muscles gave up the ghost completely. If you remember that on my first night out I was pretty drunk after two Southern Comforts then you can imagine my gradual deterioration into a comatose wreck as I drank six of the same. I was about as useful as a human body with no bones when it came to holding my head up at the end of the night, but boy did I enjoy myself! I experienced the phenomenon known as Dutch courage and I was totally amazed when I suddenly had the confidence to try my luck with girls. I did get slightly carried away though, asking about six girls (one for each drink). They all said no but that wasn't the point. I just couldn't believe I'd got the courage to do it. I loved this alcohol stuff. It turned me into a new and confident person and even the word 'no' didn't feel like an explosion in my heart. My chat up lines still left a bit to be desired and weren't very imaginative. In fact they went from 'Will you go with me?' to the almost Chinese 'Weeigoyme?' as I got more and more drunk. I seem to have forgotten most details of the night, apart from Baz being too puny to lift my front wheels up two steps and me almost ending up on the floor, the amount of girls I asked, saying to Dex, *Je suis pissed*, and sitting there by a table looking at the ceiling and laughing uncontrollably whilst being unable to put my tongue back in my mouth or to lift my head up. I was in a state!

Somehow I managed to drive my wheelchair out of that building at the end of the night and up the ramps into the taxi I'd ordered without crashing into walls or throwing myself on the floor. I'd only thrown up twice and luckily I was in the toilets at the time, unlike most other people who'd just thrown up on the floor. As drunk as I was, and as loud and aggressive as I became, it wasn't me who threw up in the taxi. That honour went to a friend of my brother and I had to mumble an apology to the driver, hoping he wouldn't make us pay for his seat-cleaning bill. It wasn't just me who couldn't hold his alcohol.

Even though my attempted chatting up of girls didn't have the desired effect, I felt good about myself despite the fact that my new-found confidence was alcohol induced. Everything was brand new. My first trip to a proper nightclub which wasn't a dirty cesspool, well it wasn't dirty anyway! The fact that there was an atmosphere meant I could even enjoy the worst music in the world, the annoying beat of dance music. It needed a combination of hundreds of people, a lot of alcohol and very powerful speakers to make it acceptable. The evil dance music should never be played outside a nightclub. It destroys your sanity!

Maybe I had got carried away with the amount of girls I'd asked, maybe not. How many girls are you supposed to chat up in one night? I still don't know, but it was all part of the learning experience. Maybe being able to try my luck after drinking meant I became more confident when I wasn't drunk. Whatever the reasons for it, I had a good night and I wanted more. I wanted to go every week but money wouldn't stretch that far for any of us.

One thing was for sure, I couldn't take my Mum into a nightclub with me to help me with the loo, my reputation, as a mega stud would never allow that! No, I needed a new helping hand. I didn't want my brother to have to come out with me every night. It wasn't that I didn't enjoy his company or that of his mates, but I had my mates and Dan had his. I just wanted to go out with my mates and have a good time. Personality wise, my brother and I are very different. He's much more outgoing than I am, especially with girls, and I tend to let them come to me without much success. I got intimidated when he was out with me, I didn't want him to see the way I was with girls. That's a really irrational way to feel and I can't explain why it was, but this personality difference means he's mates with a different sort of person, a more confident sort of person than I am. Lucky for me then that Dexter didn't seem quite as disgusted by the idea of helping me have a wee, as he had before. He'd only do it on one condition, that he didn't have to touch 'it'. If all he had to do was hold the bottle, then he'd do it. Luckily, I still had enough movement in my arms to fulfil my side of the bargain.

I don't think it was the most pleasant job he'd ever done for me but I'm sure he'd rather I didn't wet myself. He wanted me to enjoy myself as much as he wanted to enjoy himself and if that meant helping me out, then he was willing to do it. We must have been close mates because most people would draw the line at that little job. I felt close to Matt, Baz, Al and the others but I didn't know Al well enough to feel I could ask. I knew Matt well enough and we were getting closer but to be comfortable in a 'toilets situation' you have to be really close. I don't think Matt and I had that until maybe the upper sixth, when as you will see we had to put up with each other's moods quite often. Those moods were fun!

My nights out in the lower sixth were very eventful but they've all sort of merged into one big blob of memories. It wasn't just the lads who went out; Jane and I had become very good friends again and she was also close to Al and Matt. She and Charmaine were best friends and Charmaine was close to me, Matt and Dex. Sarah quickly became one of my best mates and she knew Dex, Al and Baz from business studies. I introduced her to Matt, Charmaine and Jane and she got on well with them. She soon started to come out with us, and sometimes her boyfriend Jamie came with us. They seemed to have an argument every day. I know that because Sarah is a very emotional person. It was very easy to tell when she was upset. I hate seeing girls upset, so I'd always let her talk to me about what had happened this time. I soon began not to like him. The first time Matt met Sarah was when she was telling me about their latest row, and Matt also hated seeing girls upset. I shouldn't say all this, you'll think me and Matt are soft. We're not soft or even nice, we're sex machines. (You'd better believe that, it's a convincing lie… Damn!)

There was quite a group developing now and we did all sorts of things. Bowling, where I had to use one of those tube structures, which made bowling into 'rolling' for disabled people. It's quite an invention and it made aiming easier. I even won a game once in a blue cheese moon. Sarah got into trouble with Jamie for flirting with us all. I don't know why he was so paranoid. None of us would have noticed that she was flirting anyway! We went to the pictures a few times because someone had finally brought Bolton's cinematic experience into the twentieth century. They'd built a cinema near Bolton's Reebok Stadium. The only film I can remember watching in the lower sixth is *Lost In Space*. Every copy of that film should be dumped into space! It was terrible and it was Matt's choice. He's a big sci-fi fan and I just think it's a load of rubbish, apart from *ET*! We also watched *A Life Less Ordinary* with Cameron Diaz and that Scottish guy from *Trainspotting*. I don't care about him and I can't remember what the film was about but Cameron Diaz was in it. Did I mention that Cameron Diaz was in it?

Life did seem a lot less ordinary now I was at sixth form. I was having a good time with my mates and there were no problems at school. The work was harder but the lessons were much more relaxed. I even had a getaway vehicle, should Dexter decide to play badminton at any time, and Astley Bridge Park was a thing of the past.

We had video nights and nights in the pub, and everything seemed much more mature, even though we weren't mature. It was when these video nights became *Friends* nights that we had problems, but I'll tell you about that later.

As great as bowling and going to the cinema were, the main thing I really looked forward to was the nightclubbing nights. They were an experience and because it was all very new to us, something different seemed to happen every time we were out. You could get totally lost in alcohol and having a good time and you could forget which girl had turned you down at college that week. The lads were a little quiet at first and it usually took the girls to get us dancing. Once we were up though there was no stopping us!

All the pubs were a new experience and each one was slightly different, with the only constant being the fear in the pit of your stomach that you wouldn't get in. Although the pubs were great, they were just a means of being drunk before we got into the club. I don't think I've ever done the same combination of pubs in the same order more than twice. There are so many different routes to get to the clubs that I've never got bored of it.

The only limit I have on which ones I can go to is that I can't get into places where there are steps. I've found though that most of the places I'd want to go to don't have steps and they're easy to access so there's no stopping me going out. I'm also getting very good at finding a way into any place that has steps at the front.

There's always a back door!

Once we were in the club things really started to happen and we were so eager to get there early (so everyone in the queue didn't look older than us), that one night (the first one I think) we arrived ten minutes before it opened. How embarrassing! We were the first people in the queue and we decided that we had to go around the block for we looked very sad. We walked around twice but by the time the doors opened, there was still no one there other than us.

Being the first group of people in a nightclub has to rate ten out of ten on the sadometre, and we were on our own for about fifteen minutes before anyone else came in. They were from our college as well, which tells you something about our college! I've never been the first person in a nightclub since that night. It wasn't our fault. We didn't know that our taxi would arrive early. Well, it's all part of the life of a saddo! I don't know why it was but girls my own age, who weren't my friends, didn't seem to pay me any attention when I first started going out. It was usually much older women, approaching thirty who took a shine to me. Well, thirty was the average, going up to about forty. It was a situation, which brought me intense ridicule for a very long time and as you can guess, I wanted a forty-year-old about as much as sixteen-year-old girls wanted a lad in a wheelchair. My Mum was only thirty-eight!

I'm not trying to make you get the violins out by saying girls don't want a lad in a wheelchair, I use it as a good reason for why I don't pull all the time. I mean I know I'm good-looking, sexy and a nice lad and all that obvious stuff, so it must be the wheelchair. I've also got less chance of being noticed, which seems a bit daft, considering I'm surrounded by metal and wheels, and I take up more room than anyone else, but if you think about it you're less vigilant when you're drunk. You wander around, usually not looking where you're going and you look straight ahead to see if there's anyone of the opposite sex that takes your fancy. If you look ahead and wander, not looking where you're going in the middle of a large, tightly packed crowd, then you're very unlikely to see a wheelchair. Even if you do, then the wheelchair is an obstacle. You think, 'Shit, wheelchair!' and dive out of the way. You don't think, 'Oh there's a wheelchair, I wonder what he/she looks like?' And you certainly don't go out thinking, 'I'm gonna pull a good-looking lad in a wheelchair tonight,' just as I don't go out to pull a girl in a wheelchair. It just doesn't come into your thoughts. Anyway, the mechanics of me going out with a girl in a wheelchair are mind-boggling.

If I don't pull, I feel better blaming it on the wheelchair than thinking I'm ugly. The way I look at it is that there are seven categories of girls.

1. The girl who just doesn't find me attractive.
2. The girl who does find me attractive but doesn't know how to approach someone in a wheelchair.
3. The girl who doesn't want to know just because I'm in a wheelchair.
4. The girl who just wants to be mates because one, I'm in a wheelchair, two, I'm too nice a lad or three, they don't find me attractive.
5. The girl who approaches me and just wants a snog and nothing else.
6. The girl who would like more but can't handle the idea of going out with someone in a wheelchair.
7. The as yet elusive girl, the coup de grace. The girl who does find me attractive, wants to go out with me and doesn't care that I'm in a wheelchair. This girl is why I go out. She is the pot of gold at the end of a rainbow of rejection and I have faith that this girl is out there, looking for someone like me. Where is this girl? Answers on a postcard to D Withnell (junior) 6 Ringley Grove, Bolton!

That is my detailed theory which keeps me from going insane. It is why I am not a pulling machine and it brings me eternal hope. Who needs religion?

The older women always came over and chatted to me. They danced with me for a bit, which I didn't mind at all. I was only sixteen though, I liked sixteen-year-old girls and I could probably stretch it to about twenty years old, but thirty or forty was a long way over the top. I had a run of about a year where every time I went out I would notice an older woman smiling at me or looking in my direction. I didn't know where to look, nor would I have known what to do if one of these women wanted her wicked way with me. They must have assumed I was older than I was, or they thought it was 'dead sweet' that a boy in a wheelchair was out having a good time. I prefer to think of it from the point of view that older women are more mature and find it easier to approach me. Whether they fancied me or not didn't matter. It made me feel confident about myself. It made me feel attractive. You can act cool about things when people don't want to go out with you, and say there's plenty more fish in the sea, but anyone who says that they don't care and that it doesn't hurt is either a liar or they didn't really fancy the person in the first place. I needed the female attention that these older women gave me to restore my faith in womankind, and I think it worked. Of course, when I first started going out I didn't go out with that thought in mind. I just wanted a good time and if the women didn't come over, or if they turned me down when I asked them, it wasn't too bad. I was too interested in people at college to worry about people in clubs, and I felt like that for over a year. I tried my luck quite frequently in the lower sixth, and I might have got a bit carried away, but the confidence gained from my drunkenness couldn't be ignored. I never asked six people in one night again. Two rejections were enough!

The club we went to was like a gathering of Turton Sixth Form. It was a college do, away from college do's, and it happened every Friday in a seventies time warp. All the big disco stars turned up to sing when the DJ needed a break. That just showed how far the careers of Boney M, Leo Sayer and the Supremes had plummeted since the beginning of the eighties. I'm sure they all hate Wham!

Those nights were great but one thing frustrated me. Everyone from college spent most of the time upstairs. There was no lift and I sometimes felt I was keeping my mates from everyone else. That's why I didn't moan when they went for a wander upstairs. I liked to be on my own at times, so I could work my magic with the girls. I was embarrassed to do it in front of my mates because I knew they'd laugh! I enjoyed laughing at them, not that they did much asking! Maybe I should have followed

226

their example. There was only really Al who pulled regularly but his choice in women wasn't the best! I'd think, 'Bloody hell, why does he always pull?' and then I'd look at the girl and think, 'Thank God I never do!' When he was drunk the beer goggles came on and he thought every girl was really good-looking. He got a lot of stick for the girls he pulled. We still remind him of some of them. His taste has improved a lot since then. He's become much more confident, but I don't think he regrets any of those girls, even the ones who looked like Rod Stewart after an oestrogen overdose. He says it gave him confidence to think that someone found him attractive, when he didn't think he was. Anyway, you know what they say, 'Beauty is in the eye of the beholder.'

I've always been more picky than Al and I don't seem to have beer goggles. I'm too busy throwing up on myself and in the loo! If you ask the lads what the worst thing they've ever done for me is, I think cleaning up my vomit probably rates as number one. Al always reminds me of the time I threw up on my leg, probably after mixing several different drinks. That must be a really pleasant memory for him, as it was he who had to clean it up. Sorry lads, I apologise! I'd do the same for them though. Dexter gets a lot of my good points but because he helps me with the toilet, it's usually him who gets the worst jobs like sick removal. The people who can do things like that for you and not complain too loudly are true friends. You don't get many true friends in life, but I can say I've got quite a few.

Other memorable nights from the lower sixth are when a few of us went out with Sarah and Jamie, and Sarah got into trouble for flirting again. I'm sure that if she'd wanted to go out with any of us she'd have dumped Jamie first. She wouldn't have been dishonest about it. He had nothing to worry about though. Dexter and I went to Isla's leaving do before she went into the army. Since leaving Sharples I'd become closer to her as a friend than I ever had been before. She'd offered me good advice about Laura and we'd had some really long and interesting phone conversations. I even had a joke with her when Laura turned me down, saying it was her fault. If she'd gone out with me, none of this would have happened! It was sad to say goodbye and I'm sad to say that we've since lost contact completely, although I hear she's married with a kid and still in the army. It's funny how things turn out. So much has happened since Sharples. It's strange thinking about what everyone's doing these days and I still see most of them around.

The one night out that stands out from that year has to be New Year's Eve 1997. I can remember it in all its details, even the build-up to it. My brother, myself, Ben and Andy had always spent New Year's Eve at my Grandma's house. We took turns to let the New Year in, and celebrating it with family was very important when I was younger. The temptation of a night out in town however was just too great to ignore. There'd be thousands of women looking for a New Year's kiss. I couldn't let them down! New Year's Eve was the biggest night out of the year and I had to be there for it. The problem was that the night was for over twenty-ones only.

We sat down in the common room about eight weeks before the big night and ignorant of the age limit, we decided we had to go to Ritzy. 'How will we get the tickets,' I asked Jane, 'because we're only sixteen.'

'It's all under control, Alison'll get them.' That was the joy of knowing someone older than yourself. Alison was our saviour!

That was it then, the tickets were sorted and the excitement could begin to build up. I set to thinking about the endless birds, booze and... er... bouncers! What if we didn't get in? We'd have wasted twelve quid. Twelve quid was extortion at the best of times, but if we didn't get in it was extortion for nothing. We'd have to go home in a taxi and that was double fare. What is it about Christmas and New Year? It becomes silly season. I suppose the New Year starts as it means to go on, i.e. the prices go up. How cynical of me!

My daydream was ended suddenly by the high-pitched ringing of the phone, and a shout of 'David? It's Jane.' I feared the worst and these fears were vindicated when Jane gave me this shocking piece of news.

'Dave, it's over twenty-ones on New Year's Eve.'

'You're joking, we'll never get in.'

'I'm still going to go. It's up to you if you want to or not.' It was all right for girls. If they wore something short enough, caked themselves in make-up and fluttered their eyelashes the bouncers would let them straight in. It's male nature. They can't resist a pretty girl in a short skirt.

Annoyed by this thought or taken by absolute stupidity I said, 'Sod it. I'm going. If I don't get in, I don't get in.' I spoke for everyone else even though they had no idea of the age limit. They'd kill me if we were turned away.

When I did tell them (just before I gave them their tickets) you could say they weren't very happy about it. I said, 'They're not going to turn us away if we've got tickets, are they?' And then I read the tickets. 'The management reserves the right to refuse admission.' Now I was worried and so was everyone else, but we put it out of our minds till the end of term.

I filled the time between then and the end of term working hard and improving in my different subjects. I felt as if I could express myself quite well in French and German although I still didn't understand why my mistakes in German were mistakes at all, which was a problem. I did well in my first French essay, and I thought if I continued in the same vein I'd be good enough to get a good grade at the end of two years. German would take a lot of hard work, and I was bored stiff of English. I didn't put as much work into it as in my other subjects, probably because I wasn't behind everyone else when I started. I was doing well though. I never got less than a B in anything I did in English so I understood what I was doing even if I didn't enjoy it, apart from when it came to stylistic analysis. Even the title sounds boring and it was. We analysed how language was used to create imagery, emotion and all sorts of things. We analysed and analysed till we couldn't enjoy the language used any more. Every word became a building block to build a whole piece of writing and in the end I just didn't care why different words were used in different places. I couldn't understand why anyone would care. It's difficult to work hard at something when you find it so damn pointless, and English soon became an afterthought. I'd do two hours work a day on French and German, then I'd spend Sunday on English just so I'd done my homework and wouldn't get kicked off the course. I was stuck with English now, and I needed a good grade.

That's the only reason I worked hard enough at it.

In between my hard work I began to realise I still fancied Laura and the feelings constantly built up until one day I rang Matt and told him that if I didn't ask her out myself he'd never hear the last of it. He thought it was a good idea, even though I knew what the answer would be. It's funny how that makes it easier and anyway, I might have been pleasantly surprised. We were getting closer all the time and I actually did think she fancied me.

I just needed to go down the Yellow Brick Road and ask for some courage. I considered going into college drunk, but it wouldn't make a good impression, not to mention that I would get chucked out. I had a huge speech planned out but I was that worried about something I hadn't done for a long time, that I went blank when I was just about to ask.

I'd asked her to walk back to the common room with me, so I could get her on her own and I knew it was now or never. With the speech scrapped I had to think of something quick and easy to say, so I just blurted out, 'I fancy you like mad, so will you go out with me?' Well at least I'd managed that bit, and then I waited for the inevitable answer. Well it wasn't as inevitable as I thought, it was worse than I thought.

'Sorry but I fancy Ian.' Ian was the most irritating person in the world. He thought he was funny, really good-looking and the smartest dressed person in Christendom. I disagreed and now I had another reason to hate him. It made life easier though because I hated him rather than hating Laura for turning me down. I'm glad it worked out that way because Laura and I have become as close as I am to Dexter and the rest of my close friends. We've always been there for each other when we've needed each other and I love her more like she's my sister than anything else. She's a good mate. I can only remember having one row with her in three years of being friends and that was because she said Matt was miserable and Baz was annoying. She said it quite a few times over the period of about a week and eventually I flipped out.

'Why don't you just slag all my ****** mates off, all the time?' I shouted.

She was that shocked that she couldn't say anything in return and when she left the room for something a bit later on, someone said to me, 'On her birthday as well.'

I felt really guilty, despite being annoyed. I know how to pick my moments! The thing is that at times Matt *can* be miserable and Baz can certainly be annoying. It just wound me up because she didn't know them. Anyway, we all went out for her birthday that night and soon it was all forgotten. That was the first and last time we had a row. You'd think it would become boring, having so few rows with people, but it didn't. When you're not bickering over little things you can just get on with enjoying each other's company. Friendships become a lot more mature when that happens. It's not even as if you're consciously trying to avoid rows it's just that despite all the jokes and having a laugh no one takes offence. Nothing ever arises to cause an argument.

As I grew up I began to think more about what I was saying before I said it. I got closer and closer to people and eventually I worked out how far I could go before I upset certain people. When I did say something tactless I usually apologised pretty quickly, unlike when I was younger and I thought everyone else was being unreasonable.

Laura was soon going out with Ian and I gave up, deciding to concentrate on just being mates with her, and everyone else for that matter. I'd got into the 'friend zone' with most of the girls I wanted to get to know. I was trapped and for a while I just wanted to enjoy being mates with them. They were nice girls and I didn't want to complicate things. It was just so upsetting to be rejected that I couldn't take it any more. Sniff! Anyway there were plenty of women on my nights out, and I didn't know them. It's tough you know. How do you know when you're too good friends with someone? Surely you have to be mates first, but then you get too close and the girls 'don't want to ruin the friendship'. If I had a pound for every time I've heard that statement, I'd have about £23! It all just confuses me too much.

The last couple of weeks before the Christmas holidays had disappeared, and I hadn't even thought about it. Christmas just doesn't generate as much excitement when you know the truth about Father Christmas. By the time you reach the age of sixteen or seventeen all you want is money or driving lessons. You don't trust anyone to buy your clothes for you and you've either got a Saturday job, or you're on income support like I am, so you already know what it's like to have money. Your Christmas present represents a boost to your wages, your wardrobe or your CD collection and it helps you to afford that twelve quid New Year's Eve ticket. Unless you're the child of a Jehovah's witness, which means you have to feel totally miserable and left out of the festivities. I always feel down around Christmas time. On one of my most miserable days, I came up with this theory. Christmas comes at the end of the year and New Year represents a new beginning. To me New Year is the beginning of another year of weakening muscles, and I ask myself about the point of everything. I do this for a couple of days and then I tell myself to shut up and put up with what I've been given. I may have much to contend with, with my disability but I also have great family, brilliant friends and despite the fact that there are many bigoted people who think disabled people are freaks, there are also many people who are willing to help and for that I'm very grateful. I tell myself during periods of frustration at my problems that there are so many good things in my life. I'm not ill even though I'm disabled. It's not a painful disability and on the positive side I get everything done for me. I have the perfect life really.

This particular Christmas had something different. I wasn't stressed about schoolwork, I had a number of new mates and I was actually going out. I was really enjoying life and I had my first New Year's Eve in town to look forward to, if I got in that was. Every time I thought about it, I started feeling really excited and finished with a dull nervous ache in my stomach. 'I'm never going to get in. This is going to be very embarrassing!' I tried to banish it from my mind. I mean what was the worst thing that could happen. I'd lose £12. It wouldn't be the end of the world. If I invented a date of birth, I'd be fine. They wouldn't turn a lad in a wheelchair away, especially one with glasses on.

With that thought in mind I celebrated Christmas with my family, bought some clothes and CDs and let my innocent excitement build up. It was gonna be great!

When the night finally arrived, the excitement had given way to that familiar dull ache. I was no longer confident of passing the bouncers, even with my ticket. Dexter didn't help either. He was more worried than I was. 'Oh, we're never going to get in Dave,' he moaned. 'There's no way we look eighteen let alone twenty-one.' I slipped back into my favourite mode, the one where I wasn't as nervous if I could calm someone else down.

"Course we'll get in, they're not going to turn us away with tickets. It's the season of goodwill. Anyway, all the police will be drunk. They won't look for underage people!'

Maybe the idea about the police was a bit over the top but it made me feel better. I don't think Dexter believed it for one minute, and Matt was just looking out of the window waiting for the taxi. He was all right, he looked almost old enough.

As the lights of the taxi fell on my front window there was no turning back. The butterflies had left my stomach and were fluttering about in my throat. I felt sick and no amount of reassuring Dexter would stop this feeling until the bouncers either said, 'All right lads.' Or, 'Have you got any ID lads?' We just had to work on our poker faces. Bouncers can smell fear!

We left the front door behind us and my Mum shouted, 'Have a good night.' I could hardly speak but managed to say, 'We'll be in Doctor Faux (a pub) with you lot in twenty minutes!' It raised a nervous laugh from Dex and Matt. They knew that was a distinct possibility but we'd bought our tickets. We had to give it a go! We closed the taxi door behind us and sat in silence during the one and a half mile trip. As we arrived outside Ritzy we saw people who looked much older than us being given short shrift by the bouncers before being turned away. By now, our nerves had reached fever pitch and this little scene did little for our already flagging confidence. The fear was all consuming and it was like a nightmare as we approached the bouncers. What were we doing here? We were mad! I handed over my ticket feeling like I was outside my body, watching my inevitable humiliation.

'If you go round the side I'll let you in lads,' said the bouncer to my immense surprise. That woke me from my nightmare.

'What?' I replied. It couldn't be that easy. Dexter and Matt had also got in and now the fun could really begin. We went through the doors and the bright lights hit our eyes. The pounding music was sweeter than ever. We'd made it! There was just one more thing for me to consider. Was there a disabled toilet in the club? On the list of highly unlikely occurrences this one was second behind us getting in in the first place, so it was possible. I sent Dex to have a look and sent Matt to the bar to get me a pint. I was still too hard to drink Southern Comfort and even when I asked for one, Matt was too 'cool' to order one. We're veterans now, and we just don't care what people think. I think Matt would rather order a Southern Comfort than have to clean my vomit up after I've mixed my drinks. He is a bit of a weirdo, though, he probably enjoys cleaning up after me. I think Dexter feels the same way!

I'd have to be prepared to throw up on this particular night because Matt bought me a pint. I wasn't going to complain though, because getting hammered was the order of the day. I didn't start drinking till Dexter came back with the news that there was no disabled toilet. What a surprise! 'Sod it,' I said, 'we'll go in the normal ones. I'm not letting that ruin my night.' We then just stood there for a while waiting for Charmaine and Jane. While we were waiting, a girl from our college came over. 'All right,' said Matt and I but I don't think she saw us. She only had eyes for Dexter! 'Are you gonna give me a Christmas kiss?' That was the end of Dexter's involvement in our night out. He was busy for the next three hours!

Twenty minutes, one and a half pints and no women later, I decided I couldn't be bothered waiting for women. 'Bugger this for a game of soldiers. I'm getting pissed.' Where were all the women? I didn't care any more.

Jane and Charmaine soon came in. They'd fluttered their eyelashes sufficiently and we all had a good laugh, dancing the night away, and before we knew it, the countdown to midnight had begun 'ten, nine, eight, seven, six...' Everyone was counting down. 'Five, four, three, two one!' and everyone went around kissing each other and singing that song that no one knows the words to. A few women kissed me, which wasn't much but it made a good night better. The atmosphere was great, everyone laughing and joking and for once no one was aggressive. It was just a great night. I didn't pull but by the time I'd given in to an almighty urge to throw up, I didn't care. I'd only had four drinks all night but they were all different. I remember it well. One pint of beer, one pint of cider, one Metz, and once they were all drunk, I sent either Matt or Dex to get me a Southern Comfort. All that through a straw and I defy anyone to still be sober and not feel sick. I think I threw up on the floor this time. It came over me too suddenly to reach the loo but I managed to avoid myself with it. It provided a good excuse for Dexter to escape his woman who had just asked him if he wanted to start the New Year with a girlfriend. He didn't have the heart to say, 'Yes, but it won't be you.' It was time for a quick Houdini act and even helping me clean sick off my chin was preferable to that awkward moment. It was a tough choice though!

It was getting on a bit now and going to the toilet was the last act of a great night. It still rates as one of the best, in fact Charmaine and I still talk about it. Shows how much our lives have moved on doesn't it! But the night wasn't over yet. When we were in the toilets, a guy who was totally out of it came over to us. He was drunk, looked drugged up and we thought we'd do better to stay away from him and get on with what we were doing. We didn't want to say anything in case he became aggressive, but when I'd finished my bodily function we had no choice but to talk to him. He was still there, looking like he didn't know where he was and he mumbled, 'A'right lads, 'avin a good night?'

'Yeah really good,' we said enthusiastically, feeling slightly uncomfortable.

'I'm pissed me. I've had an E and I've broken my arm, but I can't feel it. Here do you want a drink?'

'What is it?'

'I think it's just Coke, mates.'

Being the stupid, innocent people that we were, we just took his 'generous' offer and took a huge gulp from his Coke-filled glass. Halfway through my gulp I thought, *What the hell am I doing, there could be anything in this. This guy's been on drugs.* It was now time to leave. We said, 'See ya later mate,' went quickly through the door and dived into a taxi.

On the way home I thought about the night and what had happened. I'd got drunk, had a laugh, thrown up and drunk a drink given to me by a drug-crazed moron. What a night!

That was the best New Year's Eve I'd ever experienced, next

year we'd have to do the same again. Maybe this year my luck with the women would change. I always think positive on New Year's Eve.

I went back to college a week later and I wasn't worried about anything. Life was pretty much perfect, apart from the woman thing but I wasn't really that bothered about it. I continued to progress at a fair rate in my A levels and was still working hard. The nights out and in were still coming thick and fast, and I became closer to the people in my French and German groups. I got to know Lucy at some stage later in the year. I was introduced to her by Charmaine and I don't even know how Charmaine knew her. The only thing I did know was that Matt fancied her like mad, but that's another story!

The first thing I noticed about Lucy was her long ginger hair. She says its auburn, but it's definitely ginger. She was a really friendly girl and I got on with her straight away. I spent a lot of time with Lucy over the following couple of years and hopefully I'll still see her for years to come. She's definitely one of my best mates but for a while it was just an in-college friendship. I'd see her in the Temple when we were out but we'd usually just talk in our free periods. Nobody did any work during those frees, it was too relaxing an atmosphere for that. I always felt better working at home, so I used my free periods as a means of socialising and 'chilling out' which didn't do me any harm.

I enjoyed talking to Lucy as well as Sarah, Charmaine and Jane, and we soon exchanged phone numbers. This moment coincided with a sharp rise in my phone bill. We'd talk about anything and everything. I could spend over an hour on the phone to Lucy and Charmaine. It definitely made me more confident using the phone. I saw the lads too often to bother with long phone calls and anyway we could never think of anything to say. The girls on the other hand tended to talk about things first and then I'd talk to them about it, at first anyway. I like to think I can hold my side of the conversation now, but that's debatable. My problem was that I started to be sarcastic with Lucy right from the beginning and I don't think she could tell when I was joking, especially when I was on the phone and she couldn't see my face. She's got used to me now though. I think people learn to ignore my comments, or they just laugh at them because they're extremely funny. These people know I care about them, despite my tactless comments.

Chapter X

The year passed by very quickly and although there weren't too many major incidents, I think that's what made it such a good year. Things were different from before and everything I did seemed exciting. I'd be lying if I said every night out was fantastic because it wasn't. Some nights I felt left out because I knew everyone wanted to go upstairs, so I let them go for walks, while I listened to 'Love is in the Air' for the seventh time that night. This usually happened on those rare nights when I didn't feel like drinking. I became bored very quickly on those nights and while I sat there alone I would wonder why love wasn't in the air for me? (This feeling comes over me about once every four nights, because I usually enjoy myself.) Whilst trying to look away from the longing gaze of an older woman, if I got chatting to one of them, which often happened (I never ignore people) the inevitable questions came along. First, 'How old are you?' (Which I never lied about) and second, 'If you don't mind me asking, how did you end up in that (the wheelchair)?' I was never bothered about answering the latter. It was a conversation starter. I always say, 'Oh it was something I was born with,' whilst dreading having to answer the next question. 'What's it called?' Try saying, 'Muscular dystrophy', when you're drunk. My disability doesn't upset me at all, so I just answer their questions as if they've asked me what my name is.

There were many hazards in the Temple: the glass on the floor which often popped my tyres (until I got my new wheelchair with industrial strength rubber tyres) and the flying glass falling on your head from the upstairs balcony where some fool thinks it's funny to smash a glass over someone's head from ten yards above! But by far the biggest and most dangerous hazard has to be people. I often clipped people's ankles with my foot rests, and was lucky until one day, when I sent a woman sprawling on the floor. I didn't do it on purpose but luckily she was as drunk as I was. Strangely enough she apologised to me! The amount of dirty looks I get from people whose ankles I accidentally clip because they're not looking where they're going is ridiculous. It's like I deliberately go out to attack people.

It was in the Temple when I started to get 'well done mates' as Baz calls them. Remember the woman who said I was 'so brave'? Well she was the most annoying of a group of 'well-done-maters' who congratulate me on my being out and enjoying life. Most of the time I don't mind it because they don't know what to say to me, and they think saying something is better than saying nothing. When people shake my hand and ask me if I've had a good night, I just smile and say, 'Yeah, not bad.' On the good side, a lot more girls give me a kiss when they walk past but it's when people patronize me that it bothers me. 'Well done mate.' What's that all about? It's not that difficult to go out. It's not exactly a huge achievement. It's a shame that more disabled people don't go out, but I'm not doing anything special, just enjoying myself.

Sometimes I get people who come over to me and say they've got a brother, cousin or son who is disabled and they're really glad to see me out. It gives them hope and reassures them that disabled people can have as normal a life as possible. That's not my intention when I go out but if that's the effect it has, then I'm glad to be of service. I once got a woman who asked if she could dance with me. I thought I was in there but yet again I was wrong. She asked me what was wrong with me, so I gave her the usual answer.

'It's just something I was born with.'

'What's it called?'

Oh bloody hell, not again, I thought, as I smiled and said, 'Muscular dystrophy.' As if she'd know what it meant!

'My son's got muscular dystrophy.' All right, so she knew what it meant! 'I hope he turns out like you.'

That was one of the most touching things anyone's ever said to me, but I didn't let it show. I'm not fazed by anything, me. I just carried on having a good time.

Later on that night, I showed my lack of signal reading ability again, but this time it was in the opposite way. Another woman started dancing with me. She was flirting and dancing with me for an hour but I didn't realise she fancied me. Eventually, feeling knackered I told her I was going home. Matt went mad at me for being totally blind to what was going on.

'She looked really disappointed,' he said. 'You're bloody stupid.'

'Next time I'm being thick, give me a slap,' I said, feeling very annoyed with myself. It was a missed opportunity but I wouldn't make the same mistake twice!

The classic example of this signal reading problem came in the Temple, where Rick and I had the same problem. We couldn't tell which women were lesbians and which weren't. Rick fell foul of this first. He was stood eyeing up this woman whose female friend soon came over to him and said, 'Are you staring at my mate?'

To which he replied coolly, 'I might be.'

'Well she's my girlfriend.' I bet he didn't feel cool after that!

After laughing at Rick heartily, I went on to the dance floor whereupon this very good-looking woman started dancing with me. I was loving it but thankfully, or unluckily depending on how you look at it, just when I was about to make a move she started snogging another woman.

Well that answers my question for me, I thought, very relieved. That just sums up my luck at that time, which was pretty ropey as you can see.

The problem with people who come over and say whatever it is they want to say, comes when they approach my friends. One girl went over to Baz and said, 'You're amazing you.'

'What?' he said.

'Do you stay with that lad in the wheelchair all the time?' she asked.

'Yeah, he's my mate,' he said angrily.

'That's amazing.'

I'm sure it was quite an ego boost for him, being called amazing twice. That doubled the amount of times he'd been called amazing in his whole life. It really annoyed him however and everybody else, because what this girl didn't understand was that Baz and the rest of them like me. They stay with me because they get on with me and enjoy spending time with me, not because they feel sorry for me or because they're looking after me. I'm as good a mate to them as they are to me. They don't even have any pressure from me to stay with me. If they want to go for a walk, I don't argue and moan about it, I'm too laid back for that. Most of the time, they prefer to stay with me. It's like any other friendship. Nobody stays together every minute of every night out and sometimes I want to go for a wander on my own. No one moans about that either.

That's what I mean when I say that problems for disabled people aren't caused by disabled people. They're caused by able-bodied people not understanding that disabled people want to be normal.

Back in college, the year was quickly disappearing and the end of year exams were approaching. Already we were being told about applying for and looking round universities. We'd only been at sixth form for what seemed like five minutes. This was just too much.

There was a bit of light relief in between all the information being thrown at us, when our German teacher decided we should go and watch a performance of a play we were reading called *Biedermann und die Brandstifter* (Biedermann and the arsonists). The problem was getting there. We couldn't get a minibus from school and I wouldn't be able to take my electric wheelchair because the school in Blackburn where the play was being held wasn't accessible, surprisingly. The worst thing was I'd have to trust James and the girls to push me around between them. Scary!

Having recovered from that shock, Sarah and I went over to the train station opposite Turton to find out about getting my wheelchair onto the train. Of course I couldn't get across the lines to enquire, so Sarah went over for me. She asked quite politely but the station attendant, in keeping with almost every other train service employee I've ever encountered, wasn't quite so polite in return. 'We don't let wheelchairs on trains.'

'What do you mean?' she said, astonished.

'Wheelchairs aren't allowed on trains,' he insisted.

Now usually Sarah would say something to him about that, but I think she was so shocked by his attitude that she was dumbstruck. She just came over to me looking very annoyed. She told me what he said, and if I could have got over and plunged my footrests very hard into his Achilles tendons I would have. What he said was insensitive and surely, I thought, it must be wrong. I'd got on trains before. Maybe it was a bit more difficult at this tiny station which didn't have a wheelchair ramp, but it must be possible. When I got home, I told my Mum and she decided to ring up and find out for herself. Conveniently there was no number for Bromley Cross station. It was difficult enough to find a number for Bolton station. The whole system was not disabled friendly but when we finally got through to someone with a brain, they said if we rang up on the day they'd put a ramp on the train as it set off from Bolton station. Whether this would happen or not was a different question. I'd have to see what happened.

It was all a lot of fuss over nothing. I could have managed without going on this trip, but I had a point to prove now. I wanted to prove to the miserable git at Bromley Cross that wheelchairs are allowed on trains and that they've got ramps to prove it. I wasn't going to put up with people who couldn't be bothered putting themselves out to help people. It doesn't take much effort to pick up a phone and ask for a ramp.

When the day arrived, it was like I was back at Sharples again. I had to plonk myself into the rarely used manual wheelchair and prepare myself for a day of no toilet. At the train station I'd been let down by the ramp sender, but that wasn't going to stop me. I was determined to carry on in the face of this uncooperativeness. I always try to sidestep the problems and get on with things in my own way but when you are relying on just a little help to make life easier or to make normal life possible, it's hard to sidestep. It wasn't the first time it had happened and it certainly wouldn't be the last!

In Blackburn we left the train behind but we still had two or three hours till we had to be at the 'theatre'. Sarah and Vicky were the only people who knew anything about Blackburn, so they were our guides as we wandered around looking for a pub for dinner. Vicky could smell a pub from about a mile away so we were in safe hands. The Coalbrookdale fear factor had returned, with me having to rely on people other than Dexter to push me around, and it was Sarah who wanted to push me first. She had a bit of a problem getting me on and off curbs in that she couldn't lift the front wheels up. I panicked and thought I'd better let someone else take over before I ended up lay in the middle of the road in front of a bus. Sarah's only a little thing and even though I'm pretty small myself, I'm heavier than she is. Pushing more than your own body weight and then having to tip it back while still pushing, is very difficult. Vicky and Laura were a bit stronger, so they took turns to push me. I was still scared though. I should have learnt from the nightmare of Coalbrookdale and never gone on a trip again. Being in fear of your life doesn't make for a good time. No offence to any of the girls or James but I just don't feel safe when new people push me. My life is in their hands!

We went to the worst pub in the world (for a wheelchair) for lunch. I looked at the front door, saw three old looking steps and thought, *This is going to be fun.* Inside it was even worse. Steps to the left, steps to the right, steps in front, agghh! I wanted to cry! The fear of falling grew and grew as James picked up the front of the wheelchair and Laura grabbed the back, to lift me up the steps. I had another harrowing vision of Laura falling, the handles spearing her through the stomach and James falling on top of me! Isn't it weird that when you worry about something, you always imagine that it will be worse than it could possibly ever be? That was about as likely to happen as Leyton Orient winning the Premiership but I was worried about it.

Even the tables in this place were awkward. They had to move my footrests so I could get under the table to eat my chips and have a Coke. I shouldn't have even had that drink because it was only about one o'clock. I wouldn't get home till seven o'clock and if I needed the toilet I'd have to cross my legs. It would be very uncomfortable.

We left this horrible place but we still had some time before meeting Mr Willis at the bus station. The 'Blob' shop was the next on the agenda. 'What the hell is a Blob shop?' I asked, knowing I was showing my ignorance. A Blob is a warm alcoholic drink. It's got lemon in it and I think it's whisky as well. Shows how much attention I paid to it doesn't it? I'd never tasted one before so I tried a bit of one. If I'd drunk a whole one I probably would have wet myself before the end of the day. Alcohol makes me need the loo quicker.

Having satisfied their 'Blob' thirst, we were now in a rush. The time had disappeared on us and we had to get to the station as rapidly as possible or face the vitriol of Mr Willis, which admittedly wasn't that scary. We made for the door of the shop and James and Laura did their lifting job whereupon an old man shouted, 'It must be great having a group of beautiful girls to help you out.'

'I can't see any beautiful girls,' I replied. No not really, I was too scared of them for that! I really said, 'Some people have it, some people don't!'

Old people are great with me. I think it's because they know what it's like to be physically weak. They can empathise with me rather than sympathise because they know what it's like to need help and to struggle with things which they used to take for granted, and with that thought in my mind we made for the bus station. Panting, but just on time, we made it to our meeting place. Mr Willis looked very worried but it wasn't about us. It was about the upper sixth, who seemed to have disappeared. He was frantic but they were eighteen years old. Surely they had enough in them to find the place themselves but Mr Willis became annoyed. 'I'm not letting everyone else miss this just because they're too selfish to turn up.' And with that off we went.

First of all I had to find a taxi with a wide enough door to fit in. Fortunately the first one I found could get me in. We didn't even need ramps because it was a manual wheelchair. Things were looking up until we found out that the driver didn't know where the school was. It took him three attempts to find it, but luckily he did. We paid him, jumped out of his taxi and tried to make it to the school hall on time. We swung round to look for the school and saw a sign QUEEN ELIZABETH GRAMMAR SCHOOL THIS WAY, with an arrow pointing up... not steps this time, but a huge hill. 'You're taking the piss!' (Pardon my French) I thought as images of my near death at Coalbrookdale came flooding back. 'Not again.'

That dull, nervous ache returned but at least there was no train track or slippery gravel this time, just a nice steep road. Another few seconds of fear lay in front of me, and then if I made it in one piece I could enjoy the show.

'Do you reckon you can manage that?' I asked Laura.

The fear resounded in her voice as she replied, 'Yeah, it'll be all right.'

About halfway up, things started to go a little slower.

'Do you want someone else to take over?'

'No I'm fine, I'll make it.' It was a show of amazing strength from Laura. Many people would have given up halfway and on this hill I wouldn't blame them, but she was determined.

Finally, after five minutes that seemed like an eternity, we'd made it. Laura was a little breathless and my suffering showed on my face. In fact Laura was knackered, I think my amazing weight had almost killed her! It meant a lot to me that someone would tire themselves out so much just to help me. She was a true friend. I knew Dexter and the lads would have done the same and Sarah would have, if she wasn't such a weakling. Sarah's helped me in many other ways though. At this moment I knew my mates from Turton were as close as my mates from Sharples had been, and in one year I'd become as close to people as I had in five years at Sharples. It was then and only then that I didn't feel like a Sharples pupil any more. I'd moved on and now I felt like a Turton sixth former. I no longer wanted to be back at Sharples. I just had some great memories from my days there. All that from being pushed up a hill!

Just when I thought I'd made it safely to the theatre, I looked up to see two flights of stairs. Now I really wanted to cry! If I never saw another step in my life I'd have been very happy.

I saw Laura struggling for breath and decided to let James and Mr Willis do the honours. After all they were the men. Eventually and when the floor seemed a mere dot in the distance I could breathe a sigh of relief. I'd made it and the fear was over, for a couple of hours anyway.

I really enjoyed the play, and I think I understood it better, but whether it made up for the problems I had getting there was a good question. It was now about five o'clock and I was absolutely dying for the loo. I was fighting my bladder with all my strength but I didn't tell anyone. If I wet my pants I'd be devastated.

We made it down the steps without a problem and then came

the killer hill. Going down was probably more scary than going up had been. I could see the main road at the bottom this time, and it looked a long way down. If Laura had slipped I would have reached about 60 mph before I got to the bottom. If I managed to cross the road without being hit by a car, I'd hit the curb on the other side and be launched at high speed into a wall. My worrisome side wasn't exaggerating this one. The reality of it was worrying enough!

I think I dragged Laura down the hill rather than her pushing me down, but we arrived at the bottom. A nice safe taxi to the train station followed by a nice safe train home was all that lay ahead. Then I could feel safe again.

I think I learnt more about the people in my German group on that day than I had in the previous nine months of lessons. It was a good day.

On the way home Amy asked me why I wore gel. Hmm, why do men wear hair gel? She'd obviously never seen me with spiky hair, or with my sixties side parting. I wear gel because I look like Paul McCartney in his Beatles days without it. Why do women wear make-up? That's more like one of the wonders of the world!

Now after that strange and exciting day it was back to reality and the end of year exams, for which I'd been revising all year really. I thought I knew what I was doing in French and English. As for German, I wasn't sure.

I got through the exams and thought they went okay. There were no disasters or anything and I wasn't too worried about them. They were only there as a means of knowing how well we were progressing. With none of my exams being modular, the pressure was off. I had nothing to worry about and felt calm during all the exams, apart from speaking as usual. Would what I said make sense? What if they asked me a question I hadn't prepared? Improvisation was not my strong point in an exam situation. I could do general conversation because I'd learnt it thoroughly, but the role-plays would be the problem. Going into the unknown, where only crazy language students had gone before, made me feel uncomfortable. Any new word could put me totally off course and it was impossible to know every word. It was going to be a nightmare and I felt sick. You had to act in role-plays, something I found very difficult. I never put a huge amount of expression in my voice, whether I'm happy, annoyed or upset, and having a go at someone was not my forte. In the role-plays, there's a situation where you're at a train station for example, or something gets stolen from your house and you have to make a complaint. The examiner is told to argue with you as much as possible and at A level things can get very complicated. You're given prompts in English that tell you what to say and you have to express those sentiments in a good foreign way, using flowery language and complicated grammar, which I would never use in the same situation in England. As I explained earlier I had to change from introvert to extrovert for about twenty minutes. That was the most difficult thing for me to do, but if I didn't do it I couldn't prove how much I knew. The sooner it was over, the better.

In my French oral, I forgot what language I was speaking when I answered the first question. 'Ich, I, je...' I just laughed and that settled me down. At least after that I could build a sentence properly, unlike in my German oral where there were so many pauses it was untrue. I hadn't learnt yet that it was better to say a lot and make more mistakes, than to say less and speak perfect German. Sounds a bit silly but as long as you can be understood you pick up marks. I hated speaking exams.

We still had a few weeks of term left after the boring bit was over and we didn't have too much work to do. We were given our English language project though. 2,000–4,000 words on 'anything to do with the English language'. That narrowed it down! I chose to do mine on the difference between TV and radio football commentaries. With the World Cup France '98 on the way, I could easily get the information I needed. All the England matches were on both TV and radio, so that was lucky. How long did we have to do this project? Eight months. When did I start mine? The week after I got it. England v Tunisia was the first match, and as we all piled into the Volunteer pub after college, my Mum was at home recording it for me. I told her several times what to do and if she messed it up I'd be very upset. I couldn't have done it myself because the voices in my head were saying, 'Go to the pub, go to the pub...' I had to go to the pub.

Matt and I must have looked like war veterans walking to the pub. Me in the wheelchair and Matt on crutches after tearing his ligaments playing football. He did it falling over the ball! Matthew has to be the clumsiest person in the world and after the incident on the Sharples stairs nothing he ever did surprised me. This is the person who headbutted a wall when the fire alarm went off and who lost his shoe kicking a piece of chewing gum. That moment was the most amazing show of bad luck, clumsiness or whatever you like to call it, that I have ever heard of. He didn't just lose his shoe, he booted it on to a nearby house roof and had to walk to college in one shoe and one trainer. He got a ladder from college and went back to retrieve his shoe. Reaching for the shoe, the gutter he was leaning on collapsed, and he fell into a pile of dirt and leaves on the roof. He finally found his shoe and returned to college where he quickly became a laughing stock and had to wear one of his dad's jumpers. If that wasn't embarrassing enough, it was also the day we were having our photos taken for our ID badges!

Back at the pub there were what seemed like hundreds of people and not one of them was willing to leave their seats and let a lad with torn ankle ligaments sit down. I'd have offered to let him sit in my wheelchair but I was using it at the time and just couldn't force myself to get up.

Not one of our so-called friends would move for him either! He ended up sat on the floor, a couple of yards away from the pub door, suffering terrible pain every time someone walked in and tripped over his legs. It was very funny!

The atmosphere was great despite everyone's selfishness. Hundreds of people cheering England on. There's not many Tunisians in Bolton.

Nobody would get us a drink either. How tight is that! We were sweating away in a stuffy pub while everyone else was enjoying an ice-cold beer or a Coke! It was hard work getting a drink though. People had to go out of one door, walk round the other side of the pub and enter through another door, fighting their way through the masses, to reach the bar. They were like sardines in there but they were sardines with a cause. None of them wanted to lose their seat, which made it doubly difficult to get to the bar. Oh well, I was there to watch the match, never mind the drinks!

England won, if you didn't know, and everyone was singing and cheering in the pub. I had to make a quick exit because being stupid I'd told the taxi driver to go to college and I had five minutes to get back. No chance, but I was only a couple of minutes late.

After England had lost in that epic match against Argentina, when that lad Michael something or other scored the goal that he's been judged on ever since, there were a couple of weeks left of term. My house had been a jinx on the England team. Two matches watched at the pub, two matches won. Two matches watched at my house, two matches lost. I don't go in for all that superstitious crap. They'd have lost wherever I watched it but people, namely Al, have reminded me of that World Cup ever since! So much so that in Euro 2000, Al banned me from watching at home. That put paid to the idea that my house was a jinx. I was at Matt's house when we lost to Romania, so there!

We were all very close friends by now and that's when the idea of a *Friends* night was thrown into being. It seemed like a good idea at the time. We'd all go round to one of our houses, get some food in, have a chat and a drink and watch some of Matt's *Friends* videos. We even went as far as saying there'd be six of us, three lads and three girls (like there are in *Friends*). How amazingly sad that was didn't quite dawn on us. There turned out to be nine of us. A bit of a disjointed friends night. There was me, Matt, Sarah, Lucy, Al, Dex, Jane, Charmaine and Baz 'I've got a name for everyone in College' Gibbons. He did seriously have a nickname for everyone in our year, whether they liked it or not. They were more insulting than anything else but they were funny. There was 'Porcelain Doll' for a girl who looked very young and fragile, 'Meatloaf' for a girl who looked like well Meatloaf, and 'George Doors' for a lad who looked like the bald guy from *Shooting Stars*. That name actually stuck, everyone called him George. I even thought his real name was George for about six months. Lucy was 'Red Squirrel Beudy' because of her red hair. He put 'Beudy' on the end so it didn't sound like such an insult!

We ended up watching one episode of *Friends* and half of *The*

Usual Suspects before having a nice, intimate, if very one-sided chat about our almost non-existent sex lives. By one-sided I mean us lads, being the gullible, trusting fools we were, let the girls ask us the questions first. We answered their questions honestly in the innocent belief that they'd do the same for us. Little did we know, we were sat in a room with four female Bill Clintons, who 'did not have sexual relations'. It's amazing how many times four girls can need the toilet at exactly the same time in one night! We learnt more about the manipulative female mind in one night, than we had learned in the previous seventeen and a half years of our lives. Never trust a woman is what I say. Pure evil, that's what they are!

It was a very enjoyable night and I suppose it shows two things. One, we felt close enough to the girls to tell them our most intimate secrets. The most embarrassing thing was the lack of intimate moments we could remember between us. It was a pretty poor showing. Oh well, things could only get better! It also showed that however close girls are to members of the opposite sex, they only trust girls with their intimate experiences. Men are the enemy. Well you know what they say, 'That men are from Mars and women are from Venus!' It's strange that, because men are probably better at keeping secrets than women in my opinion. Women can be very bitchy and can use these details against each other. Men seem to do that less often, or never in my experience.

After this introduction to the female psyche, we returned for the final week. I gave in my plan for the English project and we got our exam results. I got three A's and I couldn't believe it! I got 81% in French and just to make my head swell, Mr Steeple said it was one of the best-written papers he'd ever seen. High praise indeed. It would have gone to many people's heads, but to me these results just proved I could get the grades I needed to get a place on a Law degree course. I was still worried though. Things could only get worse from then on and that worry in the back of my mind would prevent Mr Steeples's words from making me complacent. There was a long way to go and if my written papers were so good, my listening and speaking definitely needed some improvement. My English and German also needed more work. I wanted to be comfortably in the 'A' bracket when it came to my mocks early next year. I was determined to improve.

The week ended with me getting depressed again. Yes, I asked someone else out. I'd had a long enough break from asking college girls out and with the abject failure in the trying to ask nightclub women out stakes, I decided to change tack. I couldn't just have a complete rest from it all. No, I liked the suffering really.

Maybe this time it'd be third time lucky with the girls in my French group. I made a promise to myself that Lynn would be the last person from that group that I'd ask out. I was sure it was getting to the stage where they'd be wondering who was next. It wasn't my fault I fancied them, it was just the luck of the draw. I got on really well with Lynn, as I did with most of the other girls I'd got to know at Turton. They were lovely girls and I didn't ask them out unless I really believed they were interested. You'd think I'd have given up on trying to read the signals after all the failures I'd had before, but I was always so sure!

So I asked Lynn out and then lost confidence that she'd say yes. 'Where's that come from?' she said, looking surprised.

'Well I've liked you for a bit.' I was nervous enough as it was without her being surprised but she said she'd think about it. I knew from experience that if a girl says she'll think about it, it usually means she'll think about what the best way to say no is. Cynical mode again! The following day was the last day of term so I had to ask her if she'd decided or not.

'No I can't we're just too different.' I feel guilty to say I took that to mean 'we're too different' as in 'you're in a wheelchair and I'm not'. That's a terrible thing to think about one of your mates. The truth is we were totally different, in everything really. The sort of things we enjoyed doing were different. She's very religious and I'm an atheist which is a problem, especially when you're as tactless as I am. No, it wouldn't have worked and when I worked out that it wasn't because I was in a wheelchair, I was gutted that I'd been so quick to jump to conclusions. I didn't realise that being disabled had made me so bitter that I'd judge one of my friends like that.

I was in a mood for the rest of the day but it was the last day of term. At least I'd have all summer to get over it. Anyway by the end of the summer I'd have switched my attention to someone who I didn't do French with. It's funny how quickly you get over things when you're young. It always seemed like the end of the world when someone turned me down but it never put me off asking the next person out. I put it down to being disabled. I'm used to coping with that and being turned down by girls is nothing compared to that. On the other hand, most of the time I only get frustrated by my disability when I've been turned down by a girl. I feel inadequate and yet it makes me feel better to put it down to being disabled, rather than being ugly. Then I stop worrying about being disabled and I'm happy again, and ready to continue the search for that elusive and perfect girl. That thought process just shows what a completely mixed up person I am! The problem with looking for a perfect girl is that she always remains elusive. Nobody's perfect and that's what I've learned through my experiences. There were more experiences to come, which proved that nobody is perfect, least of all me. I'm not far off though!

I missed the end of term do, the first do I'd planned to go to. Just my luck! I'd been struck down by my first serious chest infection and I've found out, that to avoid a chest infection for seventeen years when you've got my disability is pretty good going! Part of the reason is that when you're sat down all the time, you don't get as much air into your lungs as you do when you're walking around. You're also not exercising, so when you get a cold you find it difficult to cough phlegm up and to move it around. Therefore, the chance of it settling on your chest and becoming a chest infection is much larger for a wheelchair-bound person than an able-bodied one. Once it becomes a chest infection, you still can't get the phlegm up, so you've got more chance of developing pneumonia which I can tell you isn't very nice. When it's your first chest infection you have no idea how early to get antibiotics. I wasn't even aware of how bad it could get, and up until then I'd always swallowed my phlegm. Disgusting isn't it? It was the first time I'd experienced not being able to breathe properly and the feeling of panic is something I'll never forget. It's also something I've experienced since in all its glory. Breathing's quite an important thing when you think about it and until you can't do it you take it for granted. I definitely think about it now.

I went to see our doctor, Bunn, and he gave me some antibiotics. He was a good doctor, who always spoke to me about what was going on. He knew I wasn't stupid, that I knew this chest infection was the first of many to come. I took the tablets and took to my bed. We got the physio out and she showed us some phlegm removing exercises, which basically involved pummelling my back while I was lying on my front until the phlegm rose into my mouth. Sounds lovely! My Mum enjoyed whacking my back for hours every day. The worst thing was the coughing, twenty-four hours of coughing would tire anyone out, but when your muscles are as weak as mine you just don't want to cough any more. It's exhausting and I just wanted to sleep rather than lie there while my Mum belted me. I felt so bunged up and ill, and coughing was taking it out of me. It was a hard slog but I knew it would get worse if I didn't carry on with the exercises.

The night of the end of term do arrived and I was laid up in my bed, phlegm rattling through my chest, while everyone else was out having a good time. Being stuck in the house was probably second on the list of bad things to do with chest infections. It was definitely the most frustrating thing. Matt, Dex, Al and Rick, who'd taken my ticket, came round beforehand, and had a few drinks. I just lay in my bed watching them becoming slowly drunk before my eyes. It was nice of them to come round but I'm sure they only did it to annoy me! It worked as well. I longed for the infection to be over and after a few days of tablets, I began to improve. I was soon back to my best. I'm a very healthy person apart from the obvious. I hardly ever get a cold, it's just a shame that when I do it becomes very serious very quickly. My Grandma says I'm unhealthily healthy! At least I hadn't missed more than a couple of days of college. I'd probably have had a relapse into my depression of the first year if I'd missed more than a week. No, I'd definitely gone beyond that. I had more control over myself and nothing academic seemed to bother me any more. With the amount of work I'd done, I probably could have missed three weeks.

Being ill for a while didn't depress me, even though I knew I could become very ill every time I had a cold. I didn't really think about it when I was well. It didn't happen very often so there was no problem. As soon as I'd recovered I was as happy as Larry again, whoever Larry is.

That was probably because I had a holiday to Germany to look forward to during the summer. I was going with my Gran and Dexter to stay with Frigga, so I was hoping I'd have an even better time this year with someone my own age to talk to. My Gran wasn't as strong as she used to be, so she'd offered to pay for Dexter to come over and help. She didn't mind paying because he'd be helping her out. I wouldn't have been able to go if it wasn't for Dexter, so he was also doing me a favour. The mountain views would help him with his art A level and I'd be able to practise my German because it had supposedly improved. My nervousness with speaking the language, however, hadn't diminished with age. I had to get over that barrier.

We left the dull, depressing weather of Bolton for the sun and warmth of the Bavarian Alps. I needed a rest after my hard work of the school year and the Alps provided the perfect backdrop. I think I could appreciate the scenery and the beauty of the country even more this time because I was older. I'd forgotten how amazing it was. Ours wasn't the mad clubbing holiday that many of our friends were going on, and two seventeen-year-old lads going on holiday with two much older women may seem like the most boring thing in the world to some people, but that wasn't the case at all. We were there for the weather and the sights, and relaxing without a care in the world for two weeks seemed like fun.

I didn't let my schoolwork disappear too far from my thoughts, being the work-obsessed bore that I was. I took my German vocab. books with me so Frigga could help me out with words I didn't know. The best place to be when you need help with a language is in the actual country, where, wherever you look, on signs, leaflets, in windows, even cereal boxes, you are surrounded by vocab. When you've also got a woman who can speak four languages and who won't let you get away without speaking the language, you can't help but learn from the experience. She had to speak to me slowly because of the Bavarian dialect, which is difficult to understand if you've only ever learnt a northern German dialect. As in English there are different words and accents in different parts of Germany and Bavaria almost has a language of its own. I didn't know what hit me the first time I went to Germany, but this time it surprised me how much of what I heard I could actually understand. When you know what order the words are coming in, and you know a few words, you're set. Easy really!

Again it was a case of going on long drives, visiting all the sights I'd enjoyed before. We also went to visit a number of lakes with huge mountains towering above. Knowing as little about art as I did, didn't stop me noticing that these scenes were great for an artist of Dexter's calibre. At one lake there were mountains in the distance with a castle which seemed to be built onto the side of one of the mountains. Dexter would take photos of the scenes and he'd draw and paint them when we got back to the flat.

The lakes were huge and seemed like a popular place for Germans and Austrians (one of them was on the Austrian border) to spend hot summer days. There were large grassy areas leading down to the lakes, which were used like beaches for sunbathing and the like. You don't find many beaches in Germany. The good thing about visiting lakes was that they weren't as packed as British beaches are on the one hot and sunny day we get every year. No, their summer was much longer than ours and people could pick and choose what days they wanted to go to the lake. You don't get everyone going on the same day because they know they're going to get at least a week of one sunny day after another. It makes me so mad! It probably gets a bit boring for German kids though because they never have to leave their own country to get a warm climate for their summer holidays, it's already there. In fact, the only way to escape the country is by resorting to doing languages at uni. You'd have to be crazy to do that, especially if you're studying English and end up in sunny Bolton! Not very exotic.

We swam in the lakes, one of which was like the Arctic Sea but I didn't moan, not much anyway. Really Dexter swam and I sat in my wheelchair, spending five minutes getting my feet used to the temperature, then edging further until my shins were submerged and spending five minutes getting used to it again. Three hours later I could leave the wheelchair and attempt to float. A bit pointless if you ask me but Dexter can be a mithering sod. Even if I don't want to do something like dumping girls for him, I end up doing it, whilst at the same time asking myself why I'm doing it. Why was I in that lake? I don't know, but the other lake we visited was a bit more enclosed. It was like one of those lakes in America which suddenly appears in the middle of a forest along with a wood cabin and several families of hungry grisly bears, only this place wasn't quite as dangerous. The creatures here were more of the flying variety, rather than the man-eating kind, more irritating than dangerous. Dexter's fear of dragonflies was exposed here, along with my fear of black and yellow flying insects, which look suspiciously like wasps but are totally harmless. The dragonflies would come about an inch from your face then fly off and the 'not wasps' would land on you, scaring me witless, but not scaring anyone who could tell the difference. I don't know what the Germans must have thought of us, with me screaming 'Agh aargh get it off!' every five minutes and Dexter diving away from these innocent dragonflies at the same time. We must have looked like we'd been let out of the asylum for a day!

At least the water in this lake was above two degrees Celsius. It was quite warm actually. The midges or mosquitoes, or whatever they were, were horrible little creatures. They'd land on your hand looking innocent, and lull you into a false sense of security before plunging a sting into your hand. It was potluck whether it hurt or not, but when it hurt it definitely hurt. It was like a tattooist at work, stabbing you over and over again, and me being unable to get it off had to suffer it while Dexter called me a wimp! It's just, sob, so unfair!

Most days we'd go out for the day, then have a meal on the way home, before retiring for a game of cards and a drink of the alcohol we'd bought from the supermarket. On the days when we didn't go out, we'd potter around the house, Dex would paint, I'd attempt and usually fail to draw, my Gran would have a rest, and Frigga would do whatever she had to do. These days were a well-earned rest for Dexter who'd pushed me around for days at a time in towns which weren't exactly wheelchair friendly. There were hills everywhere and pushing me around could cause quite a strain on the arms and legs.

One of these relaxing days didn't turn out to be quite as relaxing as planned. We weren't going to do anything strenuous or mentally tiring, but Frigga and my Gran had other ideas for Dexter and me. They told us about this 'Alm' (a little pub at the top of a mountain where tourists or walkers can rest and have a quiet drink, whilst looking down over the countryside spreading as far as the eye can see). It sounded very sedate. Frigga took us to a flat area, telling us that there was a slight slope, and the Alm was about '100 yards' up there. 'It'll take you five minutes to get there.' Living in the mountains must ruin people's notion of distance and time, and also steepness because once Frigga had left us we were faced with a mountain bike course of about one and a half miles, at a gradient of about thirty degrees. Our faces fell and we definitely weren't relaxed any more. Dexter was straining every sinew to fight against the hill, and my heart was beating at an incredible rate. If the hill was too much and Dexter slipped, I'd be dead and he'd have to live his life knowing he'd killed me. I don't know what's worse, I mean at least when you're dead you can't remember!

It was about eighty degrees and we were both sweating from our respective tortures, mine mental and his physical. This was not my idea of a nice stroll for a little drink.

'I think we should go back Dex!' I said, the panic resonating in my shaky voice.

'I've... pant... got halfway... pant... now. I'm not stopping now,' he replied determinedly. I knew I just had to grin and bear it now, because once he's decided he's got to do something, he's as stubborn as I am.

One hour, four stops and two burst arteries later, Dexter had managed to reach the summit. We made a flag with our names on it and hammered it into the ground so that everyone could see that we'd made it! No, we weren't that sad. A drink was enough to calm us down for a while and a rest prevented Dexter's imminent collapse. In my best German accent I asked for a drink with a straw. Frigga had given me the word for a straw but I don't think she'd ever asked for one before because when I used the word, the waitress looked at me like I was an alien! Dexter did the action for a straw and luckily she understood. I don't think his arms would have been able to lift the glass up if I couldn't find a straw. It had been a disaster from start to finish and my six years of learning German couldn't get me a straw!

'It's gonna be fun going down,' I said prophetically, watching the path weave below me. That didn't go down well. By now neither of us wanted to be on top of this mountain looking down on half of Germany. We wanted to be down there where it was flat and safe.

We didn't stay for more than one drink, the mood had left us, but at least it would be quicker going down. I looked down and thought, *That's a long way down*. It was no Hillcot House hill and it didn't bear thinking about how Dexter was going to stop once he set off. He started to walk, then jog and I was shouting, 'Slow down. Slow down.'

'I can't!' he said and I thought, *This is it. I'm dead*. Faster and faster we went. Whoosh… past a group of hikers. I could hear his flip-flops slapping against the floor. 'Slap, slap, slap, slap, slap…' We approached the edge of the path where a cliff to our death, or my death, was waiting. It was all right for him, he could let go and he'd be fine.

As I approached, my life flashed before me. I shut my eyes again, as if that was going to help! Suddenly there was a jolt to the left, his flip-flops skidded, and I came to a stop. I tentatively opened my eyes and saw that I was alive. What relief!

I was at the side of the path, the safe side, and we had to review our strategy of descent. Dexter swapped his flip-flops for my trainers and put the brakes on so I couldn't escape. He snaked his way down the path so I couldn't go too fast. There were some hairy moments before we reached the bottom and Dexter moaned of sore feet. When we reached the safety of flat land we sat on a bench while Dexter got his breath back. He was knackered and his foot was bleeding. I looked at his foot and then at mine, and noticed I was wearing socks. 'Eh Dex, I could have lent you my socks.' I don't think that was quite the right thing to say.

'I can't believe you had socks all the time my skin was being rubbed off!' He was not very happy. At least we were safe now, although I was scared of what Dexter might do to me after the sock discovery. We made for the apartment feeling a mite relieved, and the nightmare was over. One question remained. How was Dex going to get me up those steps after all his hard work? It was a wonder he could walk and we expressed our unhappiness to Frigga. As we explained the whole ordeal to her, our usual emotional release occurred. We just started laughing. Yet again I had avoided the Grim Reaper, although I don't think Frigga believed we'd found it that hard going until Dexter showed her his missing skin. It was all good fun really!

We were now very close to the end of the holiday and by now tempers had become a little frayed. Dexter and I had always spent a lot of time together but we could always go home and escape if we got fed up of each other's company. For these two weeks we'd been in a flat together constantly, with no means of escape. We were getting to the strangulation stage and, although we laughed about it, the mountain climbing was the final straw. We needed to get home. All four of us had really enjoyed the holiday, the meals and swimming in lakes, for about a week and a half, but two weeks in a one-pub village eventually takes its toll on two alcohol-thirsty and woman-hungry teenagers. I didn't see more than about three girls of my age for the whole two weeks, not that that mattered because if I can't talk to a girl in English, how was I going to do it in German?

The one pub problem hadn't been that big a problem until we got a bit bored because the bad influences that were, my Gran and Frigga had plied us with alcohol that they'd let us buy. One night we were just having a chat and drinking rum, Southern Comfort, lighter fluid, whatever we could get our hands on and Dexter 'I can hold my drink' Slater decided to drink as much as possible.

After about half a bottle of rum and a couple of Baileys he was beginning to flop over the table. 'I'm not drunk honest,' he insisted. I was drunk enough to start talking German to Frigga, which was a struggle. My Gran suddenly started speaking French for no apparent reason. For someone who'd only learned French till the age of sixteen, she seemed to remember a ridiculously large amount of it, much more than I knew when I was sixteen. My French was pretty fluent for a seventeen-year-old. I was inspired that night but nobody was there to witness it. If there was an examiner there he would have given me an A right there and then.

By the time it was bedtime, Dexter was absolutely paralytic! He fell over helping my Gran get me into bed and basically he could hardly stand up. He could definitely throw up though. He was being sick for hours and my Gran was convinced he was going to choke on his own vomit, which was a very pleasant thought to go to sleep on. I wasn't worried; he was just a bit more drunk than usual! It was actually the best night's sleep I'd had for two weeks because he wasn't in any state to talk for hours. Other nights we'd stayed up for hours talking complete rubbish about theme tunes to cartoons we used to watch. I mean what's that all about? On this night I just nodded off peacefully, ready to go home the next day.

It was a good couple of weeks, better than my first trip, only because I had someone to talk to of my own age. Dexter even got to experience my Gran and Frigga in their famous and very childish rows over who was going to pay for the meals, food, and even petrol. 'I'm paying.'

'No you're not, I'm paying.'

'Frigga, you can't pay for everything. Here take this money.'

'No I'm paying.' Then Frigga would conveniently disappear to the toilet and pay on the way back. These two were supposedly looking after us!

We went home amid the usual tearful Grandma and Frigga scene. Dexter and I said, 'See ya, thanks for the holiday.' And that was it, it was over.

I arrived home feeling very relaxed. The holiday had definitely done me good but I was looking forward to the next Temple night out. I needed women! The only thing I was bothered about on the way back was whether Liverpool had won their first match or not. My Mum had recorded it for me and ten minutes of explaining the events of my holiday was all I could manage before asking her to put the tape on. I was definitely back then.

I added all my new nuggets of German knowledge to my vocab. and thought they would eventually come in useful. It had been a useful experience but now it was back to the grindstone. I had eight months left to do my English project, only eight months! It was time to get started on transcribing 'exciting' parts of England v Tunisia. I'd have to use the same parts of the TV and radio commentaries to compare them properly, which I thought would be a very long and drawn out task. There were different symbols for every change of pitch, tone and volume of the commentator's voice, and I had to keep rewinding the same parts over and over again. If I ever heard John Motson's voice after this, I would scream. It seemed to take forever, weeks of the summer holidays even, to get these transcriptions done properly. These few weeks coincided with a sharp drop in my interest in football. It was killing my love for the beautiful game and I still had eight months to go. Unfortunately I'd started now and there was nothing I could do about it. I couldn't change my plans at this stage, I didn't have it in me, and anyway I hadn't had any other ideas that I was confident of succeeding with. It had to be football commentaries.

After my German trip the summer went by very quickly. I was seeing my friends, catching up on French and doing the project. I had no time to get bored, or to think too deeply about anything. Life was moving at a rapid pace and now my brother had got his GCSE results. I went with him to collect them and it felt good to arrive at Sharples for the third year running without any pressure on my shoulders. My brother, on the other hand, was feeling the pressure. He'd been fine all the way through summer but suddenly as we came upon Sharples his confidence had gone swiftly downhill. 'What if I fail? What if I can't get into college?'

'You'll be all right,' I assured him, but how did I know? It's one of those comments you really regret making if you're wrong and it doesn't make anyone feel better. I was more nervous than he was, if that's possible. What the hell was Mr Tactless going to say if he failed? He came down the steps and his face gave nothing away. I was really worried now. 'Well, what did you get?' I demanded.

'An A, a B and the rest C's,' he said smiling.

'Nice one Dan,' I said, thinking, *Thank God for that*!

He didn't really want to go to college anyway and he soon got a job at an architects' firm. I'm not quite sure what he was doing there but eventually they'd train him up to do a degree in architecture. He'd be getting qualified while he was doing the job.

He started the job in midsummer and about a week before I was due to go back to college, he started to mention sixth form more and more frequently. Although he said he was enjoying the job, he seemed to be trying to convince himself that he'd made the right decision. Like me he had no pressure from our parents over what he did with his life, as long as he was happy and he did his best.

I had a sneaking feeling he'd end up at Turton, with his big brother looking after him. As if he needed looking after!

Chapter XI

As Huey Lewis and the News once put it, 'The power of love is a curious thing. Make one man weep, make another man sing!' Well, in my second year of sixth form I did a lot of the former, and not so much of the latter. Yes I fell in love, again. Altogether now... ah, how sweet! But this time it wasn't the same as all the other girls I'd fancied and thought I was in love with, it was somehow different. When I'd fancied the other girls I thought about them a lot and tried to flirt with them, without much success, whilst taking six months to work up the courage to finally ask them out myself or making the agony last so long that eventually I had to get someone else, namely Charmaine, to do my dirty work for me. Thanks Charmers, for ending the agony on so many occasions. That tactic was a complete failure, along with all my other tactics.

This time all the above ingredients were there, but never before had my feelings made me feel totally miserable and obsessed. It was agony! It even made me stop concentrating on my work, for a while anyway. I wasn't so obsessed though that my determination to succeed would be affected for too long.

I'd never really noticed Michelle before I set my brother up with her best mate Lauren who was in my English group, something for which my brother has never forgiven me. Lauren and Michelle were totally inseparable, they spent more time together than Dexter and I did, and that's saying something. It was a strange state of affairs really, but a lot of the times Lauren came to see my brother, Michelle was with her and she'd end up spending a large amount of time with the sexier, better looking Withnell brother. No I haven't got another brother I haven't mentioned yet, I mean me of course.

My brother had been mithering me for weeks about Lauren, and eventually I just said, 'Right I'll set you up with her.' As soon as I said it, I regretted it. I felt totally embarrassed about setting my brother up with someone, and I've no idea why. It's not as if I was setting her up with myself. Luckily for my brother, Al was at our house when I gave in, and my brother said he'd prefer Al to ask her for him because I was such a tactless bugger. Oh ye of little faith! At least I'd have got an answer out of her, unlike Al. After about a week of Al dithering over this subject, I became completely fed up of Dan going on and on, and of Al's dithering. I just wanted this saga to end, then we could all get on with our lives, so when I saw Lauren at the beginning of the day I just blurted out, 'So are you gonna go with my brother then?'

What? That's not tactless, it's just getting to the point. She said yes anyway, so my brother couldn't complain. What does it matter how you ask? She didn't have to say yes anyway.

That's the background to a story which started after the lower sixth exams, and finished some time after the A levels, a year later. Lauren was very quiet and I hadn't a clue how my brother the extrovert would get on with her. He'd mithered, he'd got the answer he wanted, and what happened after that was his problem. I'd always got on well with her though, despite the fact that she could be very cold at times. I always think you should be wary of quiet people. They must be thinking of something while everyone else is chatting away. If you can get people like this talking, you can at least then be sure they're not planning your downfall.

Michelle was Lauren's total opposite but she knew absolutely everything about her. If you wanted to bypass Lauren's quiet, mysterious side, the best thing to do was to ask Michelle what she was thinking. She wasn't often wrong about that anyway. She was much more talkative and affectionate than Lauren. She was always hugging people, and although I didn't fancy her at first, I was intrigued by her. She seemed like a lovely girl when she first came round, and she even seemed to have a similar sense of humour to me (sarcastic). I thought she was funny but it did take a while before I started to feel more than friendly towards her. She'd come round and we'd spend hours together while Lauren and Dan spent time on their own. I thought it was a bit selfish of Lauren to make Michelle come round with her, and then totally ignore her, but Michelle seemed to enjoy my company. She didn't complain about being stuck with me anyway!

I think I was too busy being jealous of my brother seeing Lauren (they weren't going out, they were just seeing each other – a distinction which seemed important to Lauren). She's a good-looking girl, blonde, slim, sexy and a lot of the lads fancied her. It's just her personality that leaves a little to be desired. But who's bothered about that? Obviously I was because after about a month or so of spending nearly every night with her opposite Michelle, of her hugging me and of having a good laugh, I began to miss her when she wasn't there. I'd be doing my latest English homework, where I had to analyse the emotion used on a baked bean tin label and, unbelievably enough, I'd lose concentration! I'd find myself thinking of Michelle all the time, even in the middle of a French listening exercise where total concentration is needed. From having my life totally geared towards doing well in my exams, with girls as a frequently considered afterthought, I had now let my mind be taken over by something else, and that was why this girl was different.

When I was in a free period and Michelle wasn't, I'd sit there wishing she was there, and hoping that she and Lauren would come round that night. When they didn't, I was miserable. When they did, I'd sit and flirt with Michelle all the time, hugging her and linking arms all night. I thought it was great, and she seemed to have a good time as well. I'd always thought she was pretty, but one night I looked at her and thought, *You're beautiful*. Sounds really soppy, and writing it down makes me realise how soppy I was, but it was how I felt. You know how terrible I am at reading signals, but this time I was sure, absolutely certain that she felt exactly the same way as I did. There were so many occasions when I wanted to ask her out but the courage just didn't arrive. The feelings grew stronger every day, and I knew I couldn't accept being just friends any longer.

People are often scared to admit their feelings in case it ruins a good friendship. Well our friendship was great, but maybe naively, I was convinced that it wouldn't be destroyed. After all, my feelings had only served to make other friendships stronger. I had, however, never experienced feelings like those I was feeling for Michelle. Love's a powerful thing and although I was sure of it in my mind, how could I know if love was too powerful for my determination. It was a fight to the death between my determination and that 'crazy little thing called love'. Which one would win? Which do you think?

I spent days, weeks, even months agonising over what I would do about these all-consuming feelings, until Michelle and Lauren went on holiday and I went to Germany. It was in good old Deutschland when I worked out, after managing to shut Dexter up for a bit, that I would ask Michelle out if she didn't have a boyfriend when she returned from Shagaluf, sorry Magaluf. I did seriously consider that a declaration of my undying love may ruin a fantastic friendship, but I didn't go in for any of that 'rubbish'. Anyway, the feelings I had were too powerful to be ignored. I needed to know how she felt. The fact that I had such close friendships with Lucy, Laura, Sarah, Charmaine and Jane, amongst others, made me feel better about the possibility of a broken friendship. I didn't need another friendship. I needed a girlfriend. The other girls were my friends, Michelle was the person I was in love with, and I'd go insane if I didn't ask her out.

If anything my friendships with Sarah and Laura were to become stronger as a result of the Michelle situation, although I didn't know it at the time. Lucy and Charmaine were good friends with Michelle, so it would be interesting to see how those friendships coped with the situation. Nobody else had ever got involved in my attempted relationships before, so I didn't see that happening this time either, but like I said, I'd never felt so strongly about someone before. Fancying people had often made me do and say things that are completely out of character. Stronger feelings may make me say and do evil things! I have trouble being myself when my feelings are out in the open, but I never even consider what's happening until after the event. I act on impulse with girls I fancy, and admittedly on numerous occasions it has been me who has caused a row by saying something I didn't necessarily mean.

I had a week left before the start of the upper sixth, after we'd returned from our respective holidays. My brother and the lovely Lauren had finished because Dan wanted to go out with her, and she wanted to carry on with her no commitment policy. That can only last for a limited period of time before one or the other of the two people involved wants more. How long can someone enjoy a relationship where you're allowed to see other people? It doesn't quite ring true to me. Dan was not happy when it ended, in fact he was very annoyed. It even drove him to attempt to break his knuckles punching a wall. At least he didn't punch Lauren, although he probably wanted to! He's not a violent person, which is lucky really. The wall complained of some internal bleeding though.

Once my brother had calmed down he was fine, and ready to start sixth form. Told you he'd end up at Turton! I think he'd done about a month of his job before he decided it wasn't for him. I told him Turton was the best place to go, because I knew that if he went to any other college he'd do absolutely no work whatsoever, and then fail miserably. It's no offence to the other colleges that I say that, but nobody forces you to work like they do at Turton. If you fail at another college, then it's not the end of the world to the teachers. At Turton, you have to have higher grades to get in, which means there's a certain expectation on each student to do well. If you don't pull your weight, you are threatened with being booted out. If you fail your first-year exams, you're advised to leave, or to start again, and should you get through the first year and it looks like you're going to fail an exam, you are not entered for it. It's a tough place! I've not heard of anyone being kicked out of North College, however little work they do or however bad they are at a subject. North College isn't a bad place to be though if you're motivated. I know people who've done really well there, but my brother wouldn't have, and he was intelligent enough to know that.

My brother's decision to join Turton was all interesting enough, but my mind was preoccupied with other things: college work, looking around and applying for unis, and most of all Michelle who I didn't see for the last week of the holidays. I didn't have her phone number, so my idea of asking her out never came to fruition. When I know there's nothing I can do about something, I can put it out of my mind, so I had a week to decide which unis to apply to before I stopped thinking straight and decided to go to Bombay University or something like that! I decided to apply to unis a little closer to home and whilst looking through prospectuses I became inspired! French had always been a means to get on to a course. It was the subject I was best at, and the subject I was most likely to get an A in. But now I knew more, I loved it so much, I wanted to continue it. Losing or forgetting seven years of hard work would have been a waste, so I had a dilemma. However, when looking through the Manchester prospectus, I found the perfect course for a man like me – 'English Law and French Law'. I only needed two A's and a B. Talk about pushing yourself! I couldn't just choose something more simple. It had to be Law, but Law in French? I'd be lucky to understand it in English! I'd wanted to do Law for about four years so I couldn't give up on the idea now nor did I want to. If I did my best, I knew I had the ability to get the grades. So now I had a new course, it was a matter of deciding where to apply to. I looked around Manchester, Warwick and Leicester, and also applied to Leeds and Liverpool after ringing about fifteen different unis up to enquire about facilities for the disabled. There was no guarantee of getting an offer from any of these places, as Law was such a competitive course, but at least I'd been told that people were offered a place on their grades, regardless of disability or any other handicap. That's the way it should be, I'd just have to wait and see what happened after going through the boring task of blowing my own trumpet in my personal statement on my application form. 'I would be great for this course because I am an amazing person, who never fails in whatever he does. I have achieved more than anyone else could possibly achieve, in my short stay on earth.' Well that's probably what Adam said on his.

I filled my form in before most people had even thought about it, especially Dex, who for his whole school life had done everything at the last moment possible. He wasn't going to change his ways now, and why should he? As usual, I'd panicked before anyone else had had time to let the words 'you're going to have to start thinking about applying for uni' sink in. I suppose it was easier for me to fill the form in because I'd had a plan for years. I knew what I wanted to do, and I knew how to get there, it was just a matter of doing it. Many people don't know what they want to do until after the forms have to be in, let alone five years in advance. I was lucky in that respect, although I did put all my eggs in one basket, so to speak. I hadn't even thought about what I'd do if I didn't get an offer, or the grades I needed. *I'll probably do languages*, I thought.

All this pressure was coming at once, but I didn't feel like it was getting to me. My only pressure would come whilst revising at the end of the year, and during the exams. Up until then I'd be relaxed. The only thing I was stressed about was women!

I returned to college, thinking about nothing in particular really, and I was about to meet a new person in my taxi of all places! The Education Authority decided that, with two of us going to the same college, it would make sense to put us both in the same taxi. For 'make sense', read 'be cheaper', but I wasn't particularly bothered about sharing a taxi with someone else. As long as I got to college, I wasn't going to complain about someone sharing my space. How would he/she get there if I refused to let them in? I didn't want to be responsible for them being stranded at home! The thought of refusing never crossed my mind.

This extra passenger meant that the trip to college would take the opposite route. I needed a change anyway. The old route had become boring I was thinking, until Ralph interrupted me. 'Do you know Michael then?'

'No, definitely not,' I said, and then we pulled up his street and stopped outside his house (number 38, I think). I soon would know Michael however as he came wandering out of his house, pushing his walking frame in front of him. He came very slowly down his ramp and towards the taxi, until he reached the door where Ralph was standing to lend a hand if he needed it. He didn't need any help; he just improvised by climbing in on his knees. It didn't take too long. I resisted the temptation to say something sarcastic like, 'You made it then?' but Ralph didn't resist his temptation, making his customary joke at the expense of a poor disabled kid. Disability's about improvisation. If you can't do something one way, you try it another way, and if that doesn't work you try it another way, until when you're stuck you ask for help. I've always been too stubborn to ask for help, I'm too independent for my own good, and sometimes I've suffered because of it. I'm always falling over trying to prove I can do things myself, and from watching Michael reach the taxi (subtly of course), I got the feeling that he was as determined as I was. He seemed like a similar person to me. I could still remember what it was like when I had to struggle with walking, kneeling on chairs, and holding on to things to make it easier, or to make things possible. I could see that Michael was the same as I was a year previously, nervous to talk to someone new. It was a nervous first trip together, and after we said hello and exchanged names, an eerie silence fell over the taxi. I could tell we were both thinking of what to say next. The silence was soon broken by Ralph, who didn't like silence to last for too long in his taxi. He broke the ice with a loud but not very subtle, 'I hope you two aren't gonna be like this all year.' He was good at breaking the ice; I'll give him that. His jokes weren't funny though!

We did start talking after that, not wanting Ralph to think we were nervous. I haven't got a clue what we were talking about, it was probably about what schools we came from, and what GCSE results we got. Michael also mentioned that he had 'the meeting' to come later that day. I told him all about the dreaded meeting where they make decisions about what you need on your behalf. 'For the love of God, don't switch off during that meeting,' I said. 'They'll be giving you all sorts of rubbish.'

From the first meeting with Michael, we seemed to get on well, which was a good thing considering that we'd have to spend quite a lot of time together in a small cab. The disabilities remained unmentioned. He didn't ask me what was wrong, and I didn't ask him. That wasn't because we wouldn't have wanted to answer it, but because it didn't matter to either of us. It didn't matter that the disabilities were different, the goal was the same, and that's probably why we got on from that first day. I'd been through all the teething problems that he would encounter, and I knew how nervous he was feeling on his first day. Our sense of humour was similar; we were both sarcastic and liked to take the mickey. We really had a lot in common.

At college, it seemed Ralph was out of a door-opening job! We got to the door, and Michael opened it for himself and then held it open for me with the back wheel of his frame. See what I mean about improvisation?

That's where my mixing with the lower sixth ended, apart

from talking to my brother for a bit which I only did because I had to. No seriously, I'd got on well with a number of my brother's friends, especially Yak (Yakub) and Hulmey (Chris Hulme).

It was like home when I got back to college, except I had a different form room, and I could now see how many good-looking lower sixth girls were going out with Grebs! After registering, I went and took up my usual place in the common room and was surprised to see that there weren't many Grebs at all, not that it would have annoyed me if there were. I actually liked them now.

I was looking at the girls hypothetically, for when I'd ask Michelle out and she'd turn me down. I'd now gone past the confident stage, and was going through the 'What's the point in me asking her out?' stage. Then she came in and I realised that she looked as beautiful as she had the last time I saw her, three weeks earlier. The first thing she did was hug me and I was thinking, *Don't do this to me*! I loved it when she hugged me, and to think I thought I was getting over it. I got the urge to ask her out again, but every time I opened my mouth, I couldn't say it. That was the most frustrating thing in the world. How hard can it be to say a simple thing? Obviously too hard for me, so I let it go for the day.

I hadn't told anybody how I felt yet, and that was for one reason. The lads would take the mickey and laugh. They would make suggestive remarks when Michelle was around, and they would write embarrassing things on my wheelchair. I knew how childish they were, because I was exactly the same with them when they fancied someone. I could dish it out, but I couldn't take it on this occasion.

Dexter wasn't quite as cagey about who he fancied. He'd always fancied Lauren but never even considered doing anything about it. He always thought she was out of his league but it didn't stop him going on at me about it for weeks. *Oh dear*, I thought, *not Lauren again*. Dexter was also not stupid, and one day when Michelle had been sat with me, holding my hand, hugging me, and being her usual flirtatious self, he said, 'You fancy that Michelle don't you?' He said 'that' Michelle because he hadn't really spoken to her before.

You know about my lying techniques and how they always failed, well this time was no exception. My mouth said no but my grinning, stupid face said, 'Fancy her? That's an understatement.' Then I realised how primary school I sounded and said, 'Well yeah, I do.'

That admission got a roar of laughter from Dexter, so I told him not to tell anyone, knowing full well he probably would. Saying don't tell anyone to Dex about something like that, is like saying to a kid, 'Don't touch your plate, it's hot.' And within about half an hour, all the lads knew and took great pleasure in teasing me mercilessly. I couldn't argue because I'd been doing the same to Dexter about Lauren for weeks. Of course Dex doesn't tell people things that are really important. He never told anyone about my Mum and Dad splitting up years earlier, and there's a number of other things he knows about me that he's never told anyone about. I can trust him implicitly with every-thing that's really important, and although telling someone about who you fancy seems important at the time, it isn't important at all. That's why the secrets we have told people about each other haven't affected our friendship. When you say, 'I fancy... but don't tell anyone,' what you want is an easy way out of telling someone how you feel. I always begin to feel disappointed the longer it takes before Dexter's told someone, and set the Chinese whisper in process. He knows that, and I know he's the same. I wanted him to tell everyone so Michelle would find out without me having to embarrass myself. Easy. As well as being easy, it was pathetic, but that's me!

The first week of this year went by with me getting more and more frustrated at my ineptitude in the asking out stakes. My feelings were becoming increasingly intense, and by the end of the week when I went to the Temple, a building full of other girls, my feelings had overtaken my mind. Until then I'd always put thoughts of Turton girls behind me when I went out. I'd never let my feelings ruin a night out before, not even when I'd been turned down on the day of the night out. The feeling of warmth that I always got, when I fancied someone, had gone, and now all I had was frustration, and hatred of myself because I was so useless, when it came to confidence. I was sat there downstairs wanting to bash my head against a post, and knowing that Michelle was upstairs. I wasn't in the mood to drink, and being sober meant I started to think and depress myself about how girls never wanted to go out with me. I got so wound up that I wanted to go home. I didn't, because I was convinced Michelle would come downstairs and have a chat with me. I didn't want to miss that. 'As soon she comes down,' I told myself, 'I'm gonna ask her out,' and I really would have done, only she didn't come downstairs. She was busy calming down one of her mates who I think was going through the same depression that I was, but over a different girl. See what these women do to us! At about half twelve, I went home.

Now if I was turning into a depressive about Michelle, Matt had already become one about another of our friends, Charmaine. We'd found out that he fancied her at the infamous *Friends* night, and he was becoming increasingly confused by the mixed signals he was getting. I always thought it was girls who got more emotionally involved and fell in love more easily than men, but the next few months would prove the opposite, with us lot anyway. I don't know about anybody else.

The night ended with me lying in bed awake for hours, feeling immensely tired, the music ringing in my ears, and the frustration of the night swirling around like a cyclone in my mind. That's probably what caused my insomnia. It definitely made me dizzy! It's the most irritating thing in the world when you can't sleep, especially when you're shattered and when you're thinking the same thoughts you've been thinking for the past couple of months. *Why won't she go out with me? Because you haven't asked yet. What's the point in me asking her...* At which point my voices stopped talking, which didn't help. I'd think about Michelle all the time, but on this particular night I just wanted an end to it all. 'Will you go out with me?' 'No.' Done. It was as simple as that. I hate myself at times.

Once again I was thinking about taking the easy way out. It had to be done. The next day I awoke, baggy eyed from my zero hours of sleep, and decided to make my weekly phone call to Lucy. This time, there was a purpose to my phone call, other than to talk absolute rubbish whilst amassing a phone bill the size of the Third World debt. Lucy was really good friends with Michelle so I decided to employ her to make subtle inquiries about how Michelle felt about me. I didn't want her to do the asking out for me, I'd grown out of that. I just wanted to know if I had a wheelchair in the Sahara's chance of a change of luck.

'We asked, does Dave have a chance? Our survey said X.'

'She's not interested in going out with anyone at the moment,' Lucy informed me.

Hang on a minute, I thought, *a seventeen-year-old girl doesn't want to go out with anyone? That doesn't sound right.*

I looked at Lucy, trying not to make it obvious that I now had two half hearts rather than one full one. 'Right. Thanks for asking anyway Luce.'

'She says you can ring her if you want to talk about it.'

At the same time as I was thinking, *I don't want to talk about it. I want to forget it*, and saying, 'See ya later Luce,' I was getting an overwhelming urge to ring her. For some reason I had to ring her. Nobody had ever said that before, so I must have been intrigued because I wanted to hear what she had to say. When I saw Michelle at break I said, 'Can I give you a ring later?'

''Course you can,' she said with her usual contagious smile. I thought she was great. *Not many people would be considerate enough to explain why they won't go out with you*, I thought. That made me want her even more.

At home that night, the mood didn't take me to do any work. I was feeling so many mixed emotions: upset, relief that it was over, hatred towards the wheelchair, anticipation of what she'd say later. The combination of these sentiments didn't add up to the perfect mood to answer French questions about how much a brain-damaged, former mountain guide loved his sheep, interesting as that could have been! In my mood I could have come up with some interesting assumptions about this man but I don't think Mrs Walker would have appreciated it somehow.

I went to my room, having exited the taxi, and opened my French file. I told it to sod off for one day, and then pondered today's more pressing question, *To ring or not to ring? I might as well ring her… Oh sod it, she's not going to go out with me.*

My normally rational thought pattern made a sharp exit through the nearest window when it came to dealings with the heart. Love is one thing I don't understand, and I don't think I'll ever understand it. It'd be boring, anyway if I understood what was happening. The whole emotional turmoil caused by love would be ruined. The whole idea of love is that you have to take the rough with the smooth. The unrequited side of it stops you taking it for granted, when you do find someone who feels the same as you do. If you don't get turned down a few times, you begin to take love for granted. One thing's for sure, with my lack of luck up to now I know that when I do find love, I'll spend all my time trying to hold on to it. Which kind of sets me up for a fall really!

As it turned out, I didn't have to bother ringing Michelle because like many times before she and Lauren appeared on our doorstep without warning. For once I was hoping I wouldn't have to see her that night. Well, you can't have everything! I seem to remember there only being me in the house that evening. My brother was out with Charlotte who he'd just started seeing. My Mum had left the building, and my Dad was at the pub. So it was me and the two wandering minstrels. Lauren ended up sat on her own in her car while Michelle and I had an intense discussion about why she wanted to remain single when a lad who's better looking than Brad Pitt wanted to go out with her. Every time she came up with a reason, none of which were 'I don't fancy you', I had an answer for it. There were a lot of reasons such as 'I don't have time for a boyfriend. I've got college work, dancing, work.' She didn't have enough time to go out with me, but she had enough time to come round to my house nearly every night! Hmm. Interesting. I wished we hadn't had that conversation, it was emotionally exhausting. And I bet Lauren was bored to tears with only herself for company. I'd have been bored with just Lauren for company!

I eventually got fed up with this conversation, and after explaining that I always thought girls turned me down because of the wheelchair (she said it wasn't like that with her), I said, 'I'm not going to change your mind am I?'

'No, I don't think you are.' She could have made it a bit more definite. She wanted to go out with me, I was convinced of that. If you say something often enough, you begin to believe it in my experience. I'd definitely said that to myself a number of times.

Looking back now, that day had caused two things to happen, that I should have predicted at the time. First, Lucy was now involved in a saga which was to continue for a long time to come. And second, things between Michelle and I had changed forever. Until that day, our friendship had just been one about having a laugh and being able to flirt. A serious conversation like the one that had just ended had never come up before. An intensity had appeared that hadn't been there before. Even so, if the subject in question hadn't been mentioned again I'd have got over it soon enough. Things with Michelle were never that simple though and she decided to put that well-known woman's prerogative into practice. You know, the one where they are allowed to change their mind. She changed her mind to a certain extent, not completely of course. I told you it was never that simple. Even a change of mind wasn't a complete change of mind!

The next day was a typical day in the friendship of Michelle and I. The flirting resumed its usual path, and thinking I was still in with a chance, I went along with it and so it continued. That night the woman with no time appeared at my house with Lauren in tow. My brother was in this time, so Lauren didn't have to sit in the car. That was a debatable blessing, because Lauren had 'something to ask him', and Michelle had 'something to talk to me about'. I found that pretty hard to believe, considering she basically said nothing for two hours until Lauren made her tell me what she was here for. I sat there in anticipation, while she told me she'd been thinking about what I said and now she didn't know what to do any more. So thinking, *Bloody hell, make your mind up!* I said, 'Take as long as you want, I'm not going anywhere,' putting my patient act on. I wanted to go out with her so much that I was saying one thing and thinking something else. The trouble is, that if she'd taken all year to give me a straight answer I would have waited. I'd forgotten what 'I'll think about it' meant. I was so carried away, thinking I'd changed someone's mind that I let it happen. I was either a really nice lad, or I was extremely weak, because after a couple of days most people would have demanded an answer but not me. I wasn't in control of my feelings now, they were in control of me. That's where I went wrong. Every day that week I went into college with my mind totally taken up by a feeling that today might be the day I got an answer. At first the feeling was accompanied by excitement, but the longer it went on, the more I lost confidence that I might get a 'yes' this time.

Oh yeah, Lauren had come round that night because she'd decided she wanted to go out with my brother, just when he'd found someone new. So he was thinking about that, and Michelle was thinking about what to do about me. It was, needless to say, a stressful week. Michelle was ill that week as well, so I told her I wouldn't pressure her which I thought was the right thing to do, although by the end of the week I wanted to strangle her and myself. It was an agonising week, and I was on edge all the way through it. *At least...* I thought on Friday, still without an answer, *...I've got something to distract myself with, this weekend.*

Dexter's uncle had gone away, so Dex, Matt and I decided to have a barbecue. There was a wide range of bottles of spirits and other alcoholic beverages which of course I'd never have touched. All right, so I did touch them. His uncle had said we could drink what we wanted, it would have been rude not to. After eating Dexter's dangerously incinerated burgers and sausages, and surviving, Matt decided it was his turn to attempt to murder me. Murder by alcohol, now that's the way to go! He made me the most ridiculous cocktail ever made, a dangerous mixture of Bacardi, Southern Comfort, port, rum, Vimto, and Tabasco sauce just for good measure! Any normal person would have refused to drink such a concoction, apart from William Hague, no sorry I said any normal person! Being easily influenced by peer pressure and not wanting to look like I couldn't hold my drink, I drank the whole thing. Not the most sensible thing to do. I was hammered, I lost control of my neck again, and I was very wobbly. My gob was also loosened a bit as I went into abusive mode, but this time my target wasn't there to defend herself. We were having a 'sensible' discussion about Charmaine and I told Matt she was messing him about, and that she was a 'shit'. Maybe that was slightly over the top. I was frustrated with her because of the way she was treating him, and I had told her that several times. I never would have even thought she was a 'shit', let alone said it if I hadn't been on the verge of drunken collapse. At least I wasn't thinking about Michelle though, and soon after I fell into a deep sleep. I'd failed in my bid to look like a hardened drinker but then Matt and Dex already knew that I was a crap drinker. The swines tried everything to wake me up. They made Roscoe (Dexter's uncle's dog) stamp on me and lick my face. They slapped me several times and still I didn't wake up. What did they expect after forcing terrible and murderous drinks down my throat? I was probably unconscious.

The morning after the night before was painful. The mixture of barbecued food and several spirits made me feel more rough than I've ever felt before or since. How dry can a mouth possibly be? I think the French word for hangover just about sums it up. *Une gueule de bois* (a wooden gob) and that's exactly what I had. I'd totally forgotten everything I'd said that night, but Matt revelled in winding me up about what I said about Charmaine. He convinced me that he was going to tell her. God I was gullible. As if he would have told her that! I can tell when he's joking these days but I have a problem when it comes to upsetting my friends. I had to do something before Matt got to Charmaine, so as soon as I got home I made for the phone. Knowing what to say was the problem. How do you tell someone you called them a shit?

'Charmaine?' I said.

'Yeah.'

'Last night I was absolutely slaughtered and I called you a shit and Matt said he was going to tell you, so I thought I'd get in first and tell you, I didn't mean it… I was just really drunk. So sorry.' I was saying these things and feeling increasingly stupid. I was regretting telling her, even before I'd finished that clumsy sentence as she was probably wondering what the hell I was telling her for. She took it quite well, even though she reminds me of it every time I speak to her. 'Just remember I'm a shit, Dave.'

Woe is me! I've done some embarrassing things but that rates pretty highly, somewhere below my heavy breathing phone calls to Isla. Why did I tell her? It seemed like a good idea at the time, but finding out that Matt was never going to tell her in the first place, and watching him laugh very loudly, made me realise what a prat I was. It's one of those moments that makes you cringe every time you think about it, and it remains as plain as day in your memory for the rest of your life!

There was a silver lining to this incident: it put Matt in a good mood, or at least made him smile because the whole Charmaine thing was driving him to distraction. We'd go on nights out and he'd sit there with a face like Frank Butcher, and even if he pulled he'd talk to the girl about Charmaine! Scary. Until I experienced a similar level of being messed about, I had little sympathy with his moods, which was a little unfair. We were all the same with him though, especially Dex and Al who wanted to smack him on numerous occasions. The effect it had on us all was amazing, but it was sad to see him like that. He was so down, he couldn't do his homework, as much as he wanted to, and it was a waste. He's probably more naturally intelligent than I am, but he lets things happening to him and around him bring his mind to a standstill. He struggles to block things out, and that's not a criticism, it's an observation.

When he was going through his 'Frank Butcher' stage, I often wondered how he'd cope with a disability like mine, but it would probably make him stronger. I spend my whole life blocking out my biggest problem, so when it comes to smaller problems I can fight against them, even if I can't forget them. Nothing could have stopped me doing my work, but I do understand that love moves in mysterious ways. It can affect different people in so many different ways, and it was about to affect me in a similar way to the way it was affecting Matt.

The Matt and Charmaine saga put a strain on my friendship with Charmaine more than the one with Matt, as I played piggy in the middle. Or should I say sexy young man in the middle... no I'll say piggy. One minute Matt'd ring me up, telling me what Charmaine had done this time, but I couldn't tell Charmaine. Then five minutes later, Charmaine'd ring me and tell me how Matt had been nasty to her, but I couldn't tell Matt. Agghh! That infernal ringing tone! I was losing the will to live, while at the same time telling them both what I thought without upsetting them. I needed some time to do my English coursework. Didn't they realise that? I also had my own problems with the opposite sex to contend with.

Knowing the problem that was being stuck in the middle, I should have thought before getting Lucy involved in the Michelle situation, but hey it's easy to say that now.

The night he pulled and just talked about Charmaine, happened to be his eighteenth birthday. The week before, Lucy had introduced us to her friend Emma from work. When she came in, Matt and I looked at Emma, then at each other, then at Dexter, and our jaws hit the floor faster than the jaws of a snake eating a rabbit. We wiped the drool from our mouths and let Lucy do the introductions. This girl was seriously gorgeous, she looked like Elle MacPherson. *Bloody hell Lucy*, I thought. *Where've you been hiding her?*

We all got on with her really well, but I think Matt was more to her taste than I was. I wasn't impressed about that. Notice how I forgot about Michelle for a minute? Anyway, on Matt's birthday he got Lucy to invite Emma to his meal and to come out with us after. It was good work by the boy. So he pulled with his innovative chat-up line, 'I fancy Charmaine, you know?' How she fell for that one I'll never know, but it was a good night.

Lucy did that a few times. She'd appear with one of her mates, and they'd look amazing. Of course Lucy looked amazing as well.

Back to the day after the barbecue now, and it had been a whole week since Michelle told me she'd think about it. Surely it wasn't that big a decision. There must have been some really good reasons to go out with me and some really good reasons not to, but I never asked what they were. After clearing up the 'shit' problem, so to speak, I made a phone call to Michelle's nan's house, where she was staying while she moved into her new house. I pick my moments to ask people out, don't I? She was ill, moving into a new house and she had an annoying goon mithering her to death. When I asked her if we had a decision, she sounded rough, saying she hadn't had much time to think about it. I took it well on the surface, but I was really getting annoyed now, maybe unreasonably, but it was dragging on a bit. If she'd been ill in bed, all week, then she had had nothing else to do other than think!

Another week of college started and I still had no decision. My brother had decided what to do about Lauren, but he wasn't going to tell her till Michelle had told me. He wasn't quite as trusting as I was, and he thought it was slightly suspicious that Michelle was considering going out with me just as Lauren was asking him out. He had more experience with women than I did and I hadn't found anything odd about the situation. I just wanted an answer, one way or another, and I was about to get it.

That night the wandering minstrels appeared on my doorstep again. Surely she'd come up with an answer by now. There were only two options, unless you call 'seeing each other but not going out' a different option. Lauren disappeared for a minute and a deadly silence fell over my room. I braced myself for what I was convinced would be yet another rejection, and said, 'Go on then, what brings you here?'

'I've decided we're better off as we are.'

I was absolutely gutted. I was mentally exhausted from seven days of building myself up, only to have to do it again the next day, and it had all been for nothing. At least I had an answer, not that that was any consolation at that moment in time. It wasn't the end of the world, but it felt like it.

I must have looked upset because she said, 'Are you all right?' That was the most inappropriate and stupid question to ask in a situation like this, and I wanted to tell her where to go. Being the reasonable sort of chap that I am, I said, 'No not really.' I wish I could say exactly how I felt, like when I was younger, but I didn't want to upset her. It wasn't her fault she didn't want to go out with me, and if I carried on being nice to her I couldn't be accused of being nasty. So I let her go home.

You know how I said northern men are 'ard and they don't cry, well I went against that that night. I blubbed like a baby, and it's embarrassing for a man like me to admit that. I was distraught, but I could get on with my A levels now without any problems. Yeah right!

I went back to college the following day, feeling very unhappy, and not particularly wanting to be there. I had a chat with Sarah about why I was everybody's best friend, and nobody's boyfriend.

Was I ugly or something? Was it the wheelchair? What the hell was it? Whatever it was, I was getting fed up with it. So Sarah said, 'I'd probably say the same thing, if you asked me out.' Not really what I wanted to hear, but it made me laugh.

You'd think I'd have been getting used to being turned down by the time it came to Michelle saying no, but it still got to me and I had to talk myself out of being miserable. It's useful that I've got the ability to tell myself to shut up when I drift into depressed thoughts. Once my thoughts get to pathetic proportions, I stop myself thinking them. I find it pointless spending your whole life moping about something that you can do nothing about, although Michelle didn't make being happy easy for me. Knowing how upset I'd been the previous evening, most people would have toned down the flirting for a while, giving me time to get over it. That's what someone with any respect for a friend would do, but like many people she liked the attention and didn't feel that she should stop flirting with me. I was supposed to just get over it. When I went into a bad mood, I was being unreasonable in her eyes, but I couldn't help it. She was in control of the situation and I was a mindless zombie. She was wrong to exploit the situation.

If anything, the flirting got worse. The hugs became more frequent, the comments more suggestive. She'd sit with me at every opportunity and it was really pissing me off. I just couldn't understand why someone who said she didn't want to be more than friends was so visibly giving the opposite impression.

People started to notice what was going on, and when I mentioned it to Laura she said she'd noticed, and she thought Michelle was going too far which I did agree with. The trouble was, I wasn't in control at all. I was a slave to love! I could just about put up with it for four days a week, but my mood got worse every day. By Friday I was in a Matt mood, and there was nothing I could do about it. The result of this mood wasn't me having a go at Michelle for being an inconsiderate sod, it was me asking her out again, declaring that we were meant to be together, and generally acting like a simpering idiot. Even, shock horror, my work was beginning to suffer. Instead of getting A's, I was beginning to get B's. I was working as hard as ever, but the concentration wasn't there, especially in my Friday mood. I remember writing the most scathing review in history of a CD, for English, just because I was in a foul mood. It *was* a load of rubbish though, the CD that is!

This up and down mood went on for a few weeks, until suddenly Lauren started flirting with Dexter. Surprise surprise! They came round to see both of us, and we spent quite a lot of time together. To be honest we did have a good time for a while. I was sure something was going to happen, and that's why I didn't tell Michelle I was getting fed up of her flirting. I tried to make it look like I wasn't bothered, and it worked until Friday. I was completely confused by the whole situation.

It must have been once every Friday, at least once, that I asked her out and I remember each time exactly, and it goes a little something like this:

MICHELLE:	What's up?
ME:	Nothing. (Look away and then look back. Puppy dog eyes, for effect.)
MICHELLE:	Come on, there's something wrong.
ME:	No there isn't. (Smile pathetically, so she knows you're lying. Look away, look back.)
MICHELLE:	Tell me, I know you're upset.
ME:	You know what's up.
MICHELLE:	No I don't.
ME:	I still like you, go out with me.

Michelle silence.

Me silence.

(In background, on college radio 'I'm the one who wants to be with you' comes on.) I couldn't have scripted that better! She still said no, and then hugged me again!

The night of Matt's birthday was supposedly the first night of a new start for me, the night when I finally gave up on Michelle and began the search for new women. I did try, but when I tried my luck with someone, she had a boyfriend. That sort of thing matters to me. I would never pursue a girl, who had a boyfriend, so I had to face it, I had more chance with Michelle than I had with a girl who was taken, or at least as much chance! Having been turned down, my attempt at giving up on Michelle had failed, and my gaze unavoidably returned to the main object of my affection.

We were having a chat and a bit of a dance and we were getting on well. It's just a shame I started thinking again. *God, I love her*, I thought. I fell silent, and then I overstepped the mark again. 'Give us a kiss,' I said. It wasn't the cleverest chat up line in the world, I'm sure you'll agree, and she just said, 'I don't think it's a good idea.'

I thought it was a very good idea but I'd already asked her out once that day. It was obvious she wanted to kiss me but I let it go, and she soon left the building. I sat looking depressed for ten minutes and home was where I wanted to go.

When I got my wish and arrived home, I thought that maybe I was reading the signs all-wrong. There were a lot of them though. I made a decision that over half term I wouldn't get in contact with Michelle. That night would be the last time I asked her out. *She's probably getting annoyed with me now*, I thought. The amount of times we'd gone through the same tired exchange of words was ridiculous. How many more times would it take before I got the message? A break from her relentless flirting might help me get over her.

That night I'd also explained to Michelle that Dex fancied Lauren, which of course she knew, and that was what made my decision impossible to stick to. The lads and I had arranged to go to the cinema to watch *There's Something about Mary*, and Dexter had been mithering about Lauren again.

'Right,' I snapped, 'I'll ring Michelle, and get her and Lauren to come. You'd better do something about it.'

All I can say is hallelujah that Dexter's become more confident since then, because that day he was soft! We got to the cinema and Lauren sat down, so Matt moved subtly out of the way to let Dexter sit next to her. He didn't take the hint, but stood there looking thick for a minute and then told Matt to sit down. I'd got Michelle and Lauren to come for absolutely nothing. Dex just sat there looking like a prop all night, and to make matters worse, Michelle said, 'I'll sit next to Dave.' Marvellous. How badly can a plan go wrong? Instead of having a break from seeing her for a week, I ended up sat next to her for three hours, with her asking me if I was all right every five minutes!

'Yes I'm all right, yes I'm all right, yes I'm all right,' and so on, until I snapped. 'Stop asking me if I'm all right every five minutes.' I was finding it difficult enough to make it look like I was enjoying myself, without her making things harder for me. It's hard to force a smile out when your heart and stomach feel like they're tied in knots. Simply being in Michelle's vicinity did that to me. It's a horrible feeling wanting to be with someone so much, but hating the fact that they're always there, but there was nothing I could do about it. Not being in control of a situation is the most frustrating thing for a person like me. I hate not knowing what's around the corner. I'd always had a plan, you know, always known what I wanted and how to get it, but here, although I knew what I wanted, I'd tried everything and I just didn't know what more I could do.

I'm sure that asking if I was all right was her way of getting me to say, 'No, I'm not all right, I hate this,' and of making me ask her out for the umpteenth time. It flattered her to know that someone really loved her, but this time I'd just smile and pretend I was okay. I was determined not to give her the satisfaction of getting upset. No matter how I felt, I couldn't help but laugh at the film. I've seen it five or six times, and it still makes me laugh. It had me crying with laughter.

Even though to my mind I was being messed about, I was totally in love with Michelle and I'd got to the stage where I couldn't live 'with or without her'. That's when you know you're in love.

'I've got to get over this,' I told myself.

Apart from the film being good, the night was a total and unmitigated disaster, both for my plan, and for Dexter's love life. At home later on I had a chat with my brother, about how Michelle was asking me if I was all right all night, and about how I handled it, and he said that that was the best way to act. 'Don't give her the satisfaction of knowing you still like her,' he advised me, and I decided to take that advice on board.

I'd soon have a chance to try this new tactic, the next day in fact, because as soon as my plan got started again I got a call from Michelle saying that Lauren was interested in Dexter, and asking us if we'd like to go bowling with them. 'Yeah great, course we will!' I exclaimed. 'I mean, yeah if you think that'd get them together.' I don't think that was quite what my brother had in mind when he told me to play it cool.

Dex was pretty nervous about the whole thing, and I was resigned to spending more time with Michelle in the name of Dexter's love life. Now that was a depressing thought, although I didn't dwell on it. I was too busy calming Dex down to worry about how nightmarish this would be for me.

Dex and I arrived before they did, and proving that the art of chivalry wasn't quite dead we paid for them. Why I was paying for my 'friend' I didn't really know, so when she got there I made sure I said, 'I don't want you to get the wrong idea, it's just that we were here first so I thought it'd be easier if I paid.'

'What wrong idea?' she said. Talk about playing dumb. She knew exactly what wrong idea I was talking about.

So we got to the lane, and Michelle and I were talking away, giving them a chance 'to get better acquainted'. It was as if we'd put a Chinese person and a Brazilian together, the amount of communication that was going on. They were like two mutes sat there.

After the ball had rolled down the lane about five times, knocking a total of about five pins over in the process, it was a case of 'Right, this silence is awkward'. Michelle and I looked at each other, and we knew what we had to do.

'We're gonna go and get a drink, you two wait here,' we said in unison. We were about as subtle as an exploding landmine, but we had to get away, our sanity depended on it!

We'd been getting on like a house on fire all night, when suddenly as she queued for the drinks, her face fell in a similar way to the night she'd told me she'd think about it. So now it was my turn.

'Are you all right?' I asked.

'Are you over me yet?' Just like a woman to answer a question with another question.

'Yeah I am,' I insisted, seeing my brother's face in front of me. 'Why, are you changing your mind?'

'No, I'm not changing my mind,' she said, quickly followed by, 'Would it make a difference to our friendship if I kissed you?'

'I don't see why it should,' I replied, being stubbornly naive.

'Why do you like me then?'

'Because you're beautiful,' I answered, sickeningly.

'Can I give you a kiss?'

That was a difficult one! 'Yeah, if you want,' I uttered, trying to play it cool while there was a party trying to escape from my mouth. She didn't know how long I'd waited to hear her say that.

When she kissed me, it was the most amazing feeling I've ever experienced. (Yes I have led a sheltered life!) I shivered through my whole body, and that's no lie. Why couldn't she have done that earlier? She obviously wanted to, but that moment made up for all the messing about, all the agony. Well it made me feel better for that one night anyway. I've had some good moments in my life, but when I finally got somewhere with a girl, I felt like I'd made it. I was now totally normal! When you're disabled and you reach that moment where everything feels worthwhile, it's fantastic. I was 'the king of the world' and despite what had happened before, and what's happened since, I'll never forget Michelle, simply because she gave me that moment. *Nice one*, I thought. *My Gran was right. People in wheelchairs do have a chance with women!*

That moment over, Michelle went back to find Lauren, telling me she'd send Dexter over when she got there. I was feeling great, but when he came over looking less than happy, I told him what had happened and he told me what had happened between him and Lauren – precisely nothing.

I told him off for his lack of gumption. 'She likes you Dex. She wanted you to come here, remember? It's not as if you can be scared of what the answer'll be, you already know what it'll be.'

We went back to join the girls, and then Lauren and Dex went for a walk. This was the slowest game of bowling in history, but bowling wasn't really what we were there for. Michelle and I carried on kissing for a bit, and she was being really affectionate, then Lauren and Dex came back holding hands. *We have a breakthrough*, I thought. *Finally!* I don't know why Lauren was acting so innocent. She certainly had quite a lot of experience with lads. It must have been an act, but for whose benefit is the question. We all knew she wasn't as innocent as she'd been acting all night. She wasn't fooling anyone, except Dex.

I can't remember who won the bowling, we didn't even play the second game, but it was a really good night. Michelle did say some strange things, which would have really got to me if I wasn't so carried away by the moment. I couldn't argue with her just when I'd finally got somewhere, could I? She'd go all quiet for a minute, and then say, 'Is this a good idea?' Or, 'This wasn't supposed to happen.'

'Why the hell not?' was what I didn't say. The worst thing she said was, 'I don't want to upset you, because everyone's really protective of you. I'll get a lot of stick if anything goes wrong.'

I felt like saying, 'Well, you're more likely to get stick for messing me about the way you have been doing, rather than for this.' Anybody's friends would be protective of someone who was being messed about. Mine were no more likely to have a go at her for messing me about than hers would be if I upset her, she was just more likely to do it to me than I was to do it to her. It was just a means for her to say, 'I told you so,' if something did go wrong, which it inevitably would if what had happened up to then was anything to go by!

Despite Michelle's strange comments, Dexter and I went home thinking we were now part of the most perfect situation that had ever existed. Two best mates seeing two other best mates. Something had to go wrong. We weren't that lucky! I thought it'd be best to leave it a couple of days, even though I was desperate to ring her the next day. I didn't want to appear as eager as I was.

With all this Michelle stuff going on, you'd think that there were only four people in the world, but obviously there are other people and although I knew quite a lot of people from the lower sixth, I got to know a number of others in the upper sixth. I met Gemma through Sarah, who she did business studies with. Gemma was also mates with Lucy, and things basically came together from there. Lynn was good friends with both Gemma and Lucy, and I got to know all their friends: Helen Birtwistle, Helen Luxford, Lucy Golland, Fiona. I became close to all of them, as well as Alex, Alan, Graham, and I think that was about it. All our eighteenth birthdays punctuated the year, and with so many of us, it was an expensive year. We had a lot of great nights out, if you don't count all the little rows we had. With about sixteen of us, there were bound to be a few differences of opinion, especially with the stress that A levels caused. It was all fun and games, what with Matt's moods about Charmaine, my moods about Michelle, Dexter getting stressed about Lauren, and it was all their fault! Matthew and I weren't caught in a good mood at the same time for about six months, but my moods weren't as bad as his so there! Some of our birthdays were brilliant, especially mine, but I'll tell you about that later.

We also had some really good times, sitting in the common room, having a chat and joking about. Most of the time, these chats would involve the lads defending the rest of the male population, while the girls told us how awful men were in slightly more abusive words. It was great fun, but it was also more than just that. We were all as close as a group of friends could be, and we'd do anything for each other. I got on amazingly well with most of them all the time, apart from the odd disagreement. I can only remember having a row with Matt over something petty, with Dexter but then we always had rows, Lucy and Charmaine, oh and Michelle of course. I had three rows with Lucy, and two of those were about Michelle. That's because I always ended up looking like the bad guy for some unknown reason. Once I told her she was so far up Michelle's arse she couldn't see straight which didn't go down very well, but it was hard for Lucy trying to keep both me and Michelle happy. I'll say one thing for Lucy, she's a lovely girl and a very gentle person, but when she's having a row she gives as good as she gets! We didn't speak for about two days after one argument. Childish really, but she started it!

I had a few arguments with Baz, when he tucked my pants into my socks or generally acted like a little kid. However, I can't stay annoyed with Baz long enough to make him believe that I'm serious. He's like one of those little Scotty dogs that Ralph hates, but he really cares about me and would do anything for me. I shouted at Al once, just because Baz and Michelle were getting to me.

We were bound to have some disagreements. Life'd be too easy if we didn't, and with the amount of time I spent talking to Lucy, Charmaine and Michelle on the phone, something had to give. The good times with everybody, of course, far outweighed the bad times. I wouldn't change my time at Turton for anything. Even the bad times were all part of growing up. It just goes to show that if a disabled person acts normal, they are treated that way, and in turn they become normal. I was as much part of that sixth form, and all my schools for that matter, as anybody else, and that's my biggest achievement bar none.

Just one thing annoyed me about the girls; they didn't like Laura, in fact they disliked her intensely, and they made that very clear. If they'd got to know her like I did, I think they would have felt differently, but you know, everyone's entitled to their opinion. I didn't know why they didn't like her, and come to think of it I still don't. I never asked the question because I knew the answer would probably have really annoyed me, but it didn't get in the way, I just shared my time between Laura and the other girls. It was good to have someone detached from my circle of friends, and I think it worked out that way for Laura too. We could say things to each other, me about Michelle, and her about her boyfriends, and we knew there was no way it could cause any upset or conflict. That made us extremely close and whenever either of us was upset, we could count on one another. That friendship will never go away, however little time we spend together in the future. We'll always be there for each other, and I can now say that I'm glad she never went out with me.

Relationships usually come to an end, but friendships like I have never end. Even if I don't see them for a period of time that friendship starts again from where it left off. That's a special thing. I've only seen Emma Wright three times since I left Sharples, but each time we've got on as well as ever. Friends are something to be very grateful for.

Now, the two days in between seeing Michelle and ringing her up were like an eternity, and I realised then that I was too intense about her. It was taking over my life, and that wasn't healthy, but I also wanted it to be happening so much that I couldn't do anything about it. That sounds weak, and maybe I was, but I really couldn't help it.

So we were on the phone and I told her I'd had a really good time when we went out. She said we'd have to do it again, which I wasn't going to argue about. I think Wednesday was the day she could fit me in, but I knew she was busy. I was actually quite rational about it at that moment, so I didn't mind the idea of waiting a few days. *That's good then*, I thought, *I'm seeing Michelle*! It made me feel really good, but then I started thinking... again! 'Now that wasn't supposed to happen,' I told myself. I had a very deep hatred of the 'seeing each other' thing, it went against everything I'd ever believed about relationships, but I convinced myself it'd work. 'I've got the best of both worlds now. I can see other people as well as seeing Michelle.' But hang on a minute. It had taken me long enough to find one person who was remotely interested. Seeing other people was never going to happen, but I never wanted that anyway. Michelle was the one who wanted no commitment, and I'd let it happen.

When you feel as obsessed about someone as I felt, though, you grab on to any shred of hope you can. At least she was offering me something, which was more than anyone else had offered me in a long time. So I compromised. Maybe I should have expected what happened next then. I was new to this business, how was I supposed to know what she was going to say when Dex, Lauren and I went to her house on the Wednesday? I'm sure some kind of mind and personality transplant takes place every time I fancy someone because I wasn't behaving like myself that night. For some mindlessly obsessed reason, probably that I was mindlessly obsessed, I could no longer enjoy Michelle's company for the laugh that it had always been. Oh no, I wanted to spend every minute staring into her eyes, so much so that I made her stop watching the film we were watching so we could go away from Dexter and Lauren who were another constant part of our 'arrangement'. An interesting conversation ensued, the upshot of which was that Michelle said that she'd 'go with' (snog) someone else if we were both in the same building, i.e. the Temple, but not right in front of me. Well, that's all right then! I was struggling enough as it was with the whole seeing other people idea, without her adding another reason for me to be paranoid. And that was the problem, I could never have felt comfortable in a situation like that one. Many people could and good luck to them, but I couldn't do it. I should have said, 'Back up a minute and say that again.' And then, 'No way am I having that! You're taking the piss.' In a sane mood, I would have said that.

'So would you do the same, if we were in the same building?' she asked.

Now was my chance to stop things all being on her terms… 'Well yeah…' I failed on that score then. I only said it because I didn't want to say anything that would change her mind, for the three hundredth time. I was so desperate to hold on to what I had that I said the complete opposite to what I felt, and that was the wrong thing to do. I now had to be with her every minute so I could know exactly what she was up to, and I soon realised that I wasn't cut out for this business. You shouldn't feel like that if you're going to have an open relationship. There were two sides to it though. I shouldn't have let anything happen, after she said she'd never go out with me in the true sense of the word. She simply didn't feel the same way as I did, and I was wrong to expect her to. For her part, she shouldn't have let anything happen knowing how I felt. For the sake of what she saw as a snog, a very promising friendship would never be the same again. It wasn't for the want of trying, as you'll see later. I tried to keep our friendship going for the sake of our mutual friends Charmaine, Lucy, and Matt who'd recently got close to Michelle.

Our micro-relationship hadn't received its death knell yet, however. There was still one more 'date' to go. We went watching *The Exorcist* with Dexter and Lauren, which believe me wasn't mine or Dexter's idea. It would have been nice to spend some time without the other couple, but that obviously wasn't part of the deal. I was beginning to feel increasingly let down by the whole situation. I wanted out, but decided to see how the evening went. I'd told Al earlier that day that I wasn't exactly enjoying the whole thing and he told me that if I wasn't happy I should end it. Good advice indeed, but I wasn't quite ready to take it.

Evidently Michelle and Lauren had swapped roles as the 'Ice

Queen' and the infectiously 'happy bunny' because Michelle was about as cold as a penguin trapped under an Arctic glacier.

Mistakenly, I didn't think you went to the cinema with a girl so you could just watch the film. Dex and Lauren weren't watching much of it. I wouldn't have minded if the film was more interesting than me, most films are, but the so-called 'scariest movie ever made' wasn't scary, or even good. I could have done with an exorcist myself to remove the demon that had usurped my soul and turned me into someone else. She was in a bad mood, that was obvious, but I wasn't prepared for the bad moods. My interpretation of just seeing someone was that it was casual, a bit of fun designed to get you away from bad moods and stress. If you're going out with someone, then you discuss your bad moods. If you're seeing someone you ignore the bad moods. Michelle didn't want to discuss them or ignore them and come to think of it I'd never seen her in a mood before. She'd always been pleased to see me. She was also less affectionate when she was seeing me than she had been before. I thought I was getting more than friendship, but it felt like I was getting less.

So I sat there looking miserable, and she looked like she really didn't want to be there. It was pointless, and I felt helpless.

My Michelle-induced mood carried through most of the night and into the next day, when I was so miserable I just didn't feel like smiling and that wasn't me at all. I told myself that anything that made me feel like this wasn't healthy. Al knew I was thinking of stopping it, and I'd discussed it with Dexter the night before. I hadn't told Matt what was happening, in fact I hadn't told him anything. I didn't really feel that he was approachable; I didn't know how he'd react. I don't think he thought I was approachable either. Our respective obsessions had turned us into strangers, and I was about to resent his friendship with Michelle as my relationship with her turned sour.

I had one more person to talk it through with, and that was Laura. I respected her and trusted her, and besides I was on my own with her walking round to my French-speaking lesson and she asked me what was wrong. I was paranoid that if I spoke to one of the girls in my group of friends, it'd get back to Michelle and Laura's advice was usually good anyway.

'If it's really making you unhappy you need to finish it, no matter how much you like her,' she said, and she was right although it was my French-speaking teacher, Fabienne, who made me realise how miserable I looked. She asked if I was ill and gave me an expressive French look to mimic what I looked like. I can see that face now as she lowered her jaw, and sucked in her cheeks.

'If that's what I look like, I'd better get out of Michelle's life,' I told myself. I was shocked that people had noticed how upset I was. I thought I was hiding it quite well. I took the advice of Laura, Dex and Al, and had a word with Michelle, telling her how disillusioned I was with the whole situation; especially that she wasn't showing me any affection. I just felt that things couldn't go on this way. She told me that I was very demanding (which was true) and that maybe she just wasn't as affectionate as me.

You could have fooled me, I thought. *You were the most affectionate person in the world before you started seeing me.* And that was it, the shortest relationship in history. When Michelle left the room that I'd taken her to, I was all alone, and an 'emotional release' occurred. All right, I cried again!

I'd forgive you for thinking, *Is that it? A week? Why the hell has he told me all this, and why was he so pathetically upset about it?* All these are good questions, but it was much longer than a week. The whole thing had been happening for months. All the messing about, all the mind changes. I was in love, and if it had lasted two weeks, a month, a year, I would still have been as upset. At least if it had lasted a year, I'd have had a clean break. We'd have left sixth form, and I wouldn't have had to worry about staying friends with her. She didn't deserve me as a friend.

I was now really annoyed about how much she'd messed me about, and with my way with words it wouldn't be long before I expressed my unhappiness. I really should have thought more carefully about who I rang up to confide in, the way I was feeling. Someone who wasn't close to Michelle would have been the best idea. So whom did I ring? Lucy. She was quite reasonable, while I told her exactly what I thought. She told me she wasn't going to slag Michelle off, which I didn't expect her to do, but I did expect her not to tell Michelle what I'd said.

Michelle didn't make that very easy for her, because she turned on the waterworks about how she was 'so upset' that she'd upset me. So Lucy told her some of what I said, to stop her crying so uncontrollably and to convince her that she shouldn't feel too sorry for me. And suddenly I was the bad guy! I thought I was supposed to be the one who was upset. I was the one that was in love, who'd been messed about, and who'd agonised over a decision to end a relationship that only meant something to me in the first place. Confusing or what?

It was about to get more confusing and upsetting for me when I saw her the next Monday. I'd managed to keep myself under control over the weekend, without seeing Michelle, but come Monday I was miserable again. By dinner time, I had to get out of the building. I wasn't concentrating on anything all day. I might as well have put a dummy in all my classrooms and stayed at home.

I ate my sandwich in silence, although I didn't feel hungry, and then I said, 'Al, I'm going for a wander.'

'Are you all right? Do you want me to come with you?' he said. He was always worried about me and I appreciated the offer. The idea of me going for a wander, though, was so I could get away from people. Just my luck then that as I was escaping via the sixth form car park, a car containing Michelle, Lauren and my brother entered between the gateposts that I was escaping through. *Shit*, I thought, and that was exactly what my face said. It was pretty obvious what I was doing, and why I was doing it. Very melodramatic it was.

I didn't think anyone would follow me, my face showed very clearly that I wanted to be alone. Of course I wasn't that lucky. Michelle couldn't resist her urge to follow me and 'find out' what was wrong, as if she didn't know.

'Wait Dave, where you goin'?' was what I heard, and I had to turn round. I could have kept going but she was faster than I was. Escape would have been impossible and anyway I wanted to hear what she had to say.

'I'm going for a wander,' I snapped. I really didn't want to talk to her, but she wouldn't let me get away that easily.

'Why, what's wrong?' she inquired, and I just lost it.

I was awful to her that day, telling her exactly what I thought and how I felt, the high point of which was when I said, 'Your mouth says one thing, and your face says something else.' That was supposed to mean that her mouth said that she didn't want to go out with me, but her face and all her signals, said she did. I was confused, but I think she took it to mean she was a liar in general. However she took it, it expressed how I felt. I was overcome with guilt, because I knew I'd upset her, but I was in no mood to apologise. After all, it was how I felt.

The row ended with the Niagara Falls on Michelle's part, and a volcano ready to explode on my part. I went into the common room alone and looked around. My anger turned to upset as I saw Matt and everybody else for that matter, hugging Michelle, and trying to make her feel better. I'd never felt more betrayed in my life, as Matt told Michelle it wasn't her fault. I felt like I was going insane, it was a crazy scene. *What the hell is going on here? Everyone's gone mad*, I thought. She was only upset because I told her the truth about herself.

One of my best mates, who knew how I felt about Michelle, was on her side and that was a scenario I'd brought on myself by not telling Matt what was going on. The only side of the story he'd heard was Michelle's, but because of this moment of 'betrayal' it'd be a long time before I told him the whole story. There was definitely a strain put on mine and Matt's friendship for a few months after this moment. Some of it was his fault, some of it was down to me, but we were so obsessed with women that our friendship was the last thing on our minds. That was wrong but we were both very down, and I don't think we were thinking straight. We should've been making the most of our friendship but we were too pig-headed. We had it under control. (Ahem!) When we did talk, we were giving each other the same advice, and even though we knew it was right we were too proud to accept it. 'I'm not listening to him.' Stupid really!

Over the next couple of months, to say I was unhappy would be an understatement. My mind was completely taken up with Michelle. It seemed I had blinkers on, not only on my eyes but on my mind. All I could see or think of was her, and I couldn't get over it, as much as I tried. Dexter convinced me to apologise about how I'd spoken to Michelle, when I didn't think I'd done anything to apologise for. Listening to that boy was a big mistake. It was an admission that I'd done something unreasonable and as soon as I'd admitted it, I wasn't an innocent victim any more. With the two words 'I'm sorry' people's perceptions of Michelle and I had gone from 'she's really messed him about', to 'they've both done things wrong, Michelle's not the only one to blame'. I hated that, because I'd apologised for telling the truth. I should've stuck to my guns, but I was worried about what people thought. Twice I'd compromised myself now.

We were now friends again, albeit very tenuously. Anything could tip us over the edge. The first thing she did at college was hug me, and with that we were back on the merry-go-round again. The weekly cycle began where it left off. The flirting all week and the gradual decline in my happiness until I reached Friday. I was in a foul mood and had a crap night out, the worst of which was Lauren's birthday. Dexter was still seeing her, so we all went out. Oh joy of joys! Matt was in a rare good mood and I was in the worst mood I'd ever been in. I sat in each bar we went into, looking like the weight of the world was on my shoulders and I don't think I smiled once all night. That was something I'd promised never to do. I think about the person in my wheelchair that night, and I can't believe it was me. I was horrible.

In the temple, I spent the night panicking every time Michelle was out of my field of vision. 'What if she goes with someone else?' I kept telling myself, and I became sure that she would. Then she made the mistake of going for a walk with Matt! Not normally a mistake, but on this occasion, I was convinced she'd 'go with' him. Being paranoid's one thing, but then accusing someone of doing what your paranoid mind's dreamed up is an entirely different thing. Yes I said it. 'Have you just been with Matt?' Agghh, no! I felt physically sick. I didn't want to say it, but it was just too powerful an urge. She just walked away and told Matt who, according to all sources, had to be held back from killing me. Matt would never have done that, just as I'd never do the same to him. Our friendship took time to recover from that, and I'm not surprised. That night I did the wrong thing by Michelle and Matt, but I knew it was wrong and thus I apologised profusely for days after the event. I hated myself for that.

The rest of the year up until Christmas remains a blur. I remember skipping speaking lessons and being largely miserable, except when Michelle wasn't there. Sarah's eighteenth was a great night, and that's when she got together with Noel. Michelle wasn't there.

My work got done, despite a lapse in concentration, and a distinct what's the point feeling. My heart just wasn't in it and my usually infectious optimism disappeared. On the last day of term I sat in the pub and I can still hear myself say, 'This Christmas is gonna be shit!' And with an attitude like that of course it was shit!

I felt almost as low as I did in the first year at Sharples, but I wouldn't let myself get that bad. No woman is worth getting like that about. After speaking to Michelle on Christmas Day, and going to the pictures for Matt's Boxing Day ritual with Michelle and Al, I gave myself a pep talk. 'Don't let this feeling stop you from working hard. You've come too far to let it slip now. There are other women, and when you've left sixth form you never have to see her again if you don't want to.'

Michelle was busy that Christmas working, so I wasn't forced to see her, other than on Boxing Day. I had a good New Year's Eve in the pub, although I froze my testicles off walking Lucy about a mile and a half back home, with Dex, Al and Charmaine in tow. Lucy was in the same boat as me in the love stakes. She was madly in love with someone who didn't want to know. We spent hours on the phone, discussing what was wrong with us, whether we were ugly, or whether we were just pathetically sad human beings. She always said the right thing and managed to cheer me up. I hope I managed to do the same for her, and for everyone else.

The Dex and Lauren 'relationship' had lasted about three or four weeks longer than mine and Michelle's, and then it ended, somewhat acrimoniously. I don't think they ever spent any time together alone, i.e. without either Michelle, myself or both of us, something I wasn't enjoying. It was really nagging away in the back of Dexter's mind as well. His vision of a romantic relationship was never more than a pipe dream and this frustration, along with his discomfort at the 'we can see other people' policy, added up to him losing the plot the way I'd done weeks earlier. The Temple was the beginning of the end for them. It was an amazing place, where we'd experienced the whole gamut of emotions. It was where we grew up!

Lauren on this particular night, it seemed, wanted to spend all her time with Michelle. No change there then. She just neglected to tell Dexter this.

'Do you want a drink Lauren?' he asked.

'No, Michelle'll get me one.'

'Do you want to dance?'

'No, I'll dance with Michelle.'

He was beginning to feel slightly redundant, and increasingly angry and upset. She disappeared for hours at a time, and I was left to deal with a nutcase. I'm not much use when someone's that stressed. 'You've got to stop seeing her Dex, she doesn't give a shit,' I repeatedly told him, but I could have been speaking Chinese because he'd worked himself into such a state, he wasn't listening. He'd also drank a lot, which didn't help, and the only therapy he got was kicking a chair across the dance floor. What is it about Lauren that makes people want to attack inanimate objects? This act of violence almost got him thrown out of the place because when told by the bouncer, he refused to pick the chair up. Eventually he must have realised that the bouncer was much bigger than him, because he picked up the chair and told the bouncer that it was a woman problem. I think he understood! I then sat Dex down and said, 'Who are you, and what have you done with Dexter?' No I didn't, but it would have summed up the situation. I told him we should go home, and lo and behold, on our way out we bumped into Michelle and Lauren. Marvellous.

So we all ended up back at my house: Dexter, Lauren, Michelle, my brother, Hulmey, Yak and I. Dex and Lauren went for a chat in my room, while he tried to get some honesty out of her. She lied blatantly and said she still wanted to see him, just as Michelle was sat in the other room telling us that Lauren didn't want to see him any more! Dexter's an honest lad and when he fancies someone, he fancies them like mad. All he wanted was a bit of honesty in return, but Lauren couldn't give him that. He still wouldn't end it though. He really liked her, however she was treating him, and he just couldn't bring himself to say it was over.

In the end, they still sat next to each other in English lessons, without speaking for weeks, and without ever saying they'd stopped seeing each other. Very odd!

Quite a saga, and within weeks our 'perfect scenario' had disappeared into oblivion. Dexter did what I should have done and spent as little time as was humanly possible with Lauren. He felt really hurt for a long time, and then he got over it, only mentioning it when he was in a mood about being single. That was two people very close to me who she'd messed about, and although I bit my lip and never said anything, I hated her for a long time after. I only got on with her because misguidedly I still thought I had a chance with Michelle. When will I learn?

That was a long story, but it just goes to prove one thing: I'm seriously 'normal'. When was the last time I mentioned the wheelchair?

Chapter XII

Christmas depresses me at the best of times, and this particular year was no exception. Every Christmas, I have a 'meaning of life' phase, but this year it was a 'meaning of love' phase, which in my limited experience is much worse.

Resigned to not enjoying myself, I channelled all my effort into revising for my mocks, which came just after the holidays. After Boxing Day, I tried not to ring Michelle for a while. I got a lot of good revision done, swot that I am, but at least I had control over my revision timetable unlike my so-called love life. I felt that I was in control of my own destiny. If I worked hard enough, I'd get the grades I needed, and I wasn't worried. Three hours a day, one on each subject would do, I guessed. Revision was something I'd never had a problem with; I found it a challenge, one that I was determined to rise to.

One way of not rising to a challenge is to forget when your exams are. Luckily this happened to me during the mocks, and not at the important time. I was in the common room, looking over my French notes for the speaking exams, the next Monday. They were definitely the next Monday.

'So how did your French exam go?' Katy from my French group asked me.

'Oh, it's not till Monday,' I insisted.

She looked confused. 'They're all supposed to be on the same day, so no one tells anyone else what the questions are.'

Then it dawned on me. 'Oh shit! You're right. I can't believe I forgot that!'

What I really didn't believe was how calm I was about it. It was an honest mistake, and the thing about mocks is you can always take them later if you miss them. If I'd become complacent, or too relaxed, then that mistake put me right. It wouldn't happen again.

Eventually, I went through my mocks without a problem, and waited for the results whilst putting the finishing touches to my now tedious English project. I can't listen to Trevor Brooking or John Motson any more without wanting to slowly and painfully removed their vocal chords with a rusty Stanley knife. I'd analysed their language so deeply, for so long, that football commentaries have never been the same. That season I was fed up of football, what with the commentaries, and the fact that Liverpool weren't playing good football. It was a year of transition, with the ill-fated Roy Evans and Gerard Houllier joint managership, but like many football fans I'm very fickle. You have a certain expectation of how your team should play, depending on their history and spending power, regardless of what's happening behind the scenes. I expect Liverpool to be in the top three or four every season. In my A level year, we finished seventh!

Anyway, my project got about 50 out of 60, so it was all worth it in the end.

With the mocks and the project over with, I decided to have a month off revision during February, until after my birthday on the twenty-seventh of the month. I had a big party planned at Dunscar Golf Club, where three generations of the Withnell family play, sadly enough.

'It was gonna be... what's the word... Big!'

I invited all three of my mates, and Dan had to invite his to make-up the numbers but I couldn't really help that – it was a big room! It took me weeks to organise the do. Well actually it took me about two hours of invitation writing, and half an hour of handing them out. It took the rest of my family weeks to organise it. I just had to turn up.

The biggest problem was that no one in their right mind plays golf, so they didn't know where the hell it was. If I'd had to draw one more map, I'd have screamed. It's a terrible road up to that club.

You organise a party on the assumption that for one reason or another some people won't be able to come, but when I gave out my invitations only two or three people said they couldn't come. 'Find out how many people are coming. We need to know, so we can organise the catering properly,' my Mum kept saying over and over again, as she fussed annoyingly over every last detail. There wasn't gonna be any pie and peas at my do, not that that mattered to me. I don't eat when I'm drinking alcohol. It defeats the object of drinking!

The room was free, but we had to use the Golf Club caterers, meaning it wasn't 'free' at all. Who cares, my Gran and Granddad were paying and they said no expense spared. Unfortunately, they had always used this policy of treating everyone of their grandchildren equally, so they'd have to spend the same on Dan and Andy as they did on me. Unlucky, but very generous. They just wanted to make my eighteenth special, and with all the people that were coming, it couldn't be anything but. Most of the family was coming as well.

February was a good month for me, and I had to savour it. The next three months I decided would be taken up by three hours of revision per day. We had just started our third book in French and German, *Le Colonel Chabert* and *Frühlings Erwachen* respectively, and in their own way they were both great. *Frühlings Erwachen* dealt with murder, suicide, masturbation, S and M, puberty. Bizarre and very sordid, but what an amazing story. Not one for the protective parents but it kept our attention most of the time, when we could understand it that was. Most of it was written in whimsical poetry that even a German would struggle to understand, and we had to remember German quotes. I was worried!

The night of my party then crept up on me, while I was concentrating on masturbation and S and M. My fantasies are coming out now! I got Ralph to take me up to the Golf Club so I could use the electric chair, and I hoped everyone would remember it was tonight. Right up until people started to arrive, I was paranoid no one would. I should have had more faith in my popularity than that though as a regular stream of people came through the door.

I was excited, I fell like a little kid again, but I was hopeful that my Mum hadn't anticipated that feeling and booked a clown or a magician. Then Matt, Dex and Al arrived, and I realised it was me who'd invited the clowns!

For a person who hates being the centre of attention, as I do, you'd think a party like this would be an ordeal rather than any sort of fun, but once everyone had arrived, including the very uncool DJ, I really began to enjoy myself. I danced with the girls for a bit, having my arms ripped off by Michelle and Lauren in the process. The lads eventually got drunk enough to dance, with Al's dangerously long and flailing arms soon clearing the floor, and everybody else having a laugh, mainly at Al's dancing! Gemma's boyfriend 'Perfect' Phil, as we like to call him (it's purely a jealousy thing as he's so much better looking than every lad, except me) was dancing away with us. I had a fantastic night, getting drunk at other people's expense and basically doing a tour of the place, dancing with several different groups of people. It was great fun. Everyone came, including Mr Altdorf and Miss Turner from Sharples, and Emma Wright who I hadn't seen for ages. We had a good chat and did some catching up.

Matt was there in body, if not in spirit. Baz was with his girlfriend, whom he hardly spoke to all night, and who soon became his ex-girlfriend. I was determined not to be miserable about Michelle and I almost managed it. I only went into a mood for about ten minutes and told myself I was pathetic, before cheering up again. It was my eighteenth, and I had much to be happy about. Great friends, the best I've ever had, a loving family, and everyone was here for me. When I got a moment to myself, I looked around the room and thought, *Once we've left, nights like this will hardly ever happen. I'd better enjoy however many we have left.* Eighteen months earlier, I had started sixth form and hoped it would be the best two years of my life. It certainly had been up to now but the hard work was on its way.

I danced the rest of the night away, even stopping to dance with my Gran and my Auntie Marg, who sadly is no longer with us. My speech was... er... brief, and then it was over.

Everyone left extremely inebriated and then there was me, a few other members of my family, and a room which looked like bombsite. I was all danced out, my muscles were aching and that's how I knew it was a good night. I was certainly ready for my bed!

Having asked Michelle out every week up until Christmas, I had a choice to make now I didn't have mocks on my mind. Do I carry on with this friendship the way it is and continue to be miserable, or do I tell her the truth, that even though I know she's not interested the continual flirting gives me the wrong idea as do her comments? For a while, I didn't mind forcing myself to look happy all-day and then being upset at night, because I really didn't want my prediction to be proved wrong. I knew in my own mind that things had changed between us, and I eventually had to admit defeat. I couldn't get away from her, like Dexter had done with Lauren, as we had so many mutual friends. Every time I went out, Michelle would be there, but there was nothing I could do about that. The flirting, however, had to stop. So I put it to her.

'The only way I'm gonna get over you, is if you stop hugging me all the time.'

She sounded a bit put out, and I can understand why. I'd asked her to change the way she was to please me, and that wasn't fair. The flirting was unfair on me, though, but I'd now created a problem for myself. Where do you draw the line? What is 'too much' flirting? What could she say, and what couldn't she say? So I gave her a list. No, that would have been too ridiculous! The truth was I'd run out of ideas. Michelle's presence in a room made me feel uncomfortable and depressed, and no cooling down of the flirting process would have helped. The choice was really whether to cut my losses and end the friendship, or to put up with it. I should have ended it, but instead I carried on and a series of disagreements about anything and everything ensued. At one point I was really upset about a row I'd had with Lucy, so after turning into Hitler to dictate our friendship, I suddenly changed my approach. 'Michelle, I really need a hug.' I wish I hadn't said that. I must have been driving her mad, and this had to stop. Why had I suddenly started to need a hug every time I was upset? I'd become a softie!

The disagreements began to build up. For example, there was Valentine's Day, another day which depresses me annually. I was sat with Michelle in the common room and some of us, not me of course, decided to make some Valentine's cards. How I got involved with these sad people I'll never know! Anyway Michelle, having a laugh, decided to make one for me which really wound me up. I felt like my head was being messed with. To be honest, looking back it all seems so pathetic, especially considering all the things I've been through since. As annoying as they were, and they were annoying, I used them as an excuse because I needed to get away from Michelle for a while. I needed a reason to do it, and these little things seemed the most appropriate.

Michelle didn't think things needed to change; we had a bit of fun, and that was it to her. It was me who had the problem, but that was because I'd been messed about. I could never trust her after that.

As I've said many times, there were more people involved than just Michelle and me, and if we weren't mates any more then things could become awkward within our group of friends. I felt like it was an impossible situation, and then one week I thought, *Sod it, I need to do this for myself. I'm not bothered what anyone else thinks.* When I looked at it sensibly, I realised that only two of my other friendships were being risked, and they were the ones with Lucy and Charmaine. The rest of the girls wouldn't act differently with me, neither would any of the lads, including Matt, to whom I'd explained the story by then. Laura couldn't be less affected by it, and Sarah wasn't bothered either. They'd both been saying for a long time that I'd be better off without Michelle. I didn't want to risk losing Lucy or Charmaine, but if it meant me being happy I'd do it. I hoped that if they didn't agree with me, they'd say so, but wouldn't let it affect things.

After all, I didn't agree with the way Charmaine was treating Matt, but I didn't act differently with Charmaine. I was there for Matt when he needed me, but that didn't stop me being there for Charmaine when she needed me. The way I saw it, we were in a group, but each of my friendships was separate. You shouldn't be seen to be taking sides when a row between two of your friends erupts. It makes life much easier!

So I set about avoiding Michelle which was very immature on the surface, but below, my heart was being torn apart. It pained me to accept that things had come to this, but I couldn't handle it any more, and I had no other ideas to make it less upsetting for her. I just stayed away from her, and when I was forced to sit round the same table with her, I avoided eye contact and didn't speak to her. I should have spoken to her when I had to, and at least been civil for however long we had left at college. But I was new to this malarkey. No friendships of mine had ever come to this before, to a place where I wanted it to end. It was a sad time.

That week proved that no one can be nice to everyone all of the time. I'd tried very hard to prove the opposite, and with most of my friends I'd succeeded. When emotions are running high, as mine were, it's sometimes impossible to be nice to someone.

I handled it badly that week, and I'm the first to admit it. I wasn't mature about it at all. Near the end of the week, we were all sat round a table, and every time Michelle said something I'd say shut up or something like that, under my breath. I only said it very quietly, assuming only I could hear it. No such luck. All the girls could hear it, and I made myself look like a complete arsehole (of course I was being one). I didn't know they could hear me until later on, when I got a backlash from Lucy. I walked right into that one as well, by ringing her up.

As I feared, things had been a bit awkward with Charmaine, but with Lucy, things were much worse than that. She took it upon herself to ignore me because I was ignoring Michelle, thus taking Michelle's side. So I rang her up, firstly to have a go at her for taking sides in an argument that had nothing to do with her, and secondly to tell her I didn't want to lose her over this. It was Michelle I had the problem with, not her. We had a huge shouting match over the phone, which makes me laugh every time I think about it. Neither of us was ever like that, but that day we were like two tidal waves coming together, a dangerous combination! *A Perfect Storm* even!

I told her it was none of her business, that she was pathetic for ignoring me, and that she was so far up Michelle's arse she couldn't see straight. She told me that Michelle had made it her business because she'd being crying on the phone to her, that giving her rules about hugging me and then changing them wasn't fair, and that the way I'd acted earlier that day was disgusting.

Oh my God, I thought, *they weren't supposed to hear that.*

After twelve rounds of verbal boxing, we calmed down and grew up a bit in order to discuss things like the close friends that we were. Lucy said that maybe she was wrong to ignore me, but asked me to see the problem that she had. I said I knew it was hard for her and that I was sorry to have put her in that situation. We were both sorry, and things improved slowly after that. I don't think either of us wanted to lose what we had. We're very close.

Being a naturally nice lad, even if I say so myself, I couldn't handle the fact that Michelle had been crying about me not wanting to be mates any more. Every time I was true to myself, or told Michelle the truth about herself, she cried. I hate it when girls cry! Why I then decided to write her a letter about exactly why I was doing this, is a mystery. Obviously that'd make her cry as well. I wanted her to understand why I had to stay away from her, so I wrote her a letter telling her all the things I've told you, embellishing it a little. It told her that I loved her, but that I didn't particularly like her. In fact I went a bit too far, saying I couldn't stomach being around her! It was an emotional thing, in which I thought I was being honest. She, however, thought I was being deliberately hurtful.

That letter backfired in the most backfirey way, in the history of backfires, and it was because I wrote at the end of it: 'If you want to talk about this, give me a ring.' And also because I showed it to Laura before I gave it to Michelle. I accidentally told Michelle that, and that got an eerie silence between all the shouting when she rang up to 'discuss' the letter.

We were on the phone for about two hours, going around in circles and arguing over what my sentences actually meant, and then I said something that made her cry. My tough stance melted like the Wicked Witch of the West in a swimming pool, and my vocal chords and mouth started to apologise. I couldn't stop myself apologising for what I'd written and how I'd acted. That wasn't in the script. Ee, I was a soft touch, and we were mates again!

I'd reneged now, so I thought I'd give friendship with Michelle another go, until the end of sixth form. I wasn't going to ask her out again but the old jealousies remained, except the one about her friendship with Matt which barely existed any more. The main reason I wasn't jealous of Matt was because we'd found out he'd been seeing Charmaine for weeks. We knew they spent hours every day together, but I'd asked Matt a week earlier if he was getting over her. 'Yep, just about,' he replied, lying sod! Charmaine had told him she fancied him right from the start of Turton but that for some reason, she tried to resist it, proving that she was just being a tease. She was messing with the boy's head but at least now his persistence was being rewarded, unlike mine, which is why I stopped asking Michelle out.

The Matt and Charmaine 'revelation', predictable as it was, proved to be the point where our paths reconvened. We soon got close again, and our friendship has never faltered since. It was a shame that my friendship with Michelle couldn't be as easily resolved. I wanted to prove to her that I could be just friends with her, and maybe I tried too hard. The best way to prove my 'just friends' capabilities, I thought, was to start talking to her about other lads. When she went out and I wasn't there, I'd ask her if she pulled to which the answer was always 'no' whether she had or not. When she asked me the same question, I was always honest. If I'd pulled, which did happen a few times before I left Turton, I'd say I had.

Why then did I ask a question that I knew the answer to, and one which if answered with a 'yes' would really upset me? Well, I wanted to prove I could be just friends, after all friends can discuss anything honestly. Also, if I heard that she'd snogged another lad I'd get over her, despite the initial upset. Thirdly it was a test. I wanted to see if she could be as honest with me, as I could be with her. That was devious, and I even challenged her about this a couple of times.

'You wouldn't tell me if you had, would you?'

'No probably not.'

Now you decide to be honest, I thought.

I'd have handled her saying she'd pulled better than I handled dishonesty. The daft thing was, I always found out she was lying a couple of days later. I'd hear her talking about it right in front of me, which was infinitely more upsetting than if she'd told me when I'd asked. It was stupid. At least by then I could control my moods until I was where Michelle wasn't. I'd talk to Laura about my moods, and she'd always cheer me up, when I wasn't cheering her up about her boyfriend troubles. She was going out with a lad called Darren between her mocks and final exams, and everyone hated him, especially Laura's closest mates of whom I was now one. He was horrible to her, insanely jealous, and treated her like rubbish. Once he told her to weigh herself, and then called her a fat bitch all night! I thought it was disgusting, and if I could walk

I'd probably have smacked him one. Never mind intelligence, violence is the way to go! It's the only language he'd have listened to. I'm probably lucky I'm in this wheelchair. Otherwise I'd be known for my prolific fighting, rather than my exam results.

Laura was really unhappy with this lad but wouldn't dump him straight away. I think it was during this relationship that she realised what a good friend I was. I'd have done anything for her, and she'd have done the same for me. So one good thing came out of the Darren situation!

There were more pressing concerns for Laura and me though, because our speaking exams had arrived. Again my most powerful feelings at speaking test time were worry, fear and apprehension. There were less gaps in my knowledge now, but of course at A level there were many more words to know, and the topics I could talk about were much more complicated. We also had an outside examiner to contend with. The exam board insisted on making the torture as extensive as possible. Despite my fluctuating moods, I'd done enough revision and I was thinking in French the night before. I was ready and confident, but there was that lingering possibility that I'd freeze. That was a frightening possibility, and if it happened all would be lost.

I didn't get time to ponder on that for more than a few seconds, as the door creaked and swung open. A large South African man walked in and must have felt our eyes staring at him. We were like startled animals. Then he spoke, in French, so we could acclimatise ourselves to his voice. He told us not to worry and that he hoped we'd enjoy the experience. That was highly unlikely but at least he wasn't an ogre!

My most frustrating problem was having a name that begins with a stupid letter like W, meaning I was to go last. I had to sit in a room for about two and a half hours with a bunch of panicking girls. The difference between lads and girls is that girls panic loudly! That meant I could calm them down, while those familiar butterflies had a field day. I was used to that feeling by now and managed to harness it and use it to my advantage.

One by one the girls went and came back, saying it had gone okay, and then it was my turn. I took a deep breath and went outside, towards the language block and to my doom! I had fifteen minutes to prepare, and when I saw my role-plays, I was pleasantly surprised. I knew all the words. It was just wording things properly and staying within the time limit. I made some brief notes and ran the gauntlet, into the room where my interrogator was waiting. He was a daunting man to behold. Before turning on the tape he put me at ease and then it began. General conversation came first and we started with simple questions, until I relaxed. I seemed to answer everything quite articulately and the conversation flowed naturally. Surprisingly I did enjoy it by the end. I was a little red-faced and very relieved when I left the room about fifteen minutes later.

Things had gone well. 'One down, ten to go,' I told myself and optimism filled my mind. French had always been my best subject, but it was German speaking next. I was really worried about that and it was next week.

Speaking exams came about a month earlier than written ones, so we hadn't left college just yet and I still had a few bad moods left!

Everybody was fed up of college by now. The curriculum had been completed and everyone was understandably a little touchy, with revision well underway. For most of us it was well underway. Dex and Baz had only just started and Matt and Charmaine had spent so much time with each other and upsetting each other that motivation was running on empty. Okay, so only about half of us were revising, but we were all stressed. We only really went out for people's birthdays but there were enough of them to keep us going. The duration of my misery on nights out gradually diminished until it almost didn't happen any more – almost.

Al disappeared for a couple of weeks while he frantically prepared for his theatre studies oral and stressed considerably about it. Once it was over, he returned to the planet as he returned to the common room. As for me, I hadn't been stressed whilst revising. I knew if things went well, I was good enough. As usual I was quietly confident. That was the upside of all the problems I'd had with Michelle. I thought about her too much to worry about exams! Of course subconsciously there was an inevitable effect on me and I was admittedly touchy. I wouldn't let myself panic because that's when you're in danger of failing. If you're too worried about failing you're likely to do just that. That wouldn't happen to me, would it?

People make A levels the be all and end all of life, but they're not. They're important but there's always a different route, and even if there isn't you can always do something else. It's hard to see that at the time, but what makes people so sure that uni or their particular degree will suit them? I think being disabled has helped me put things into perspective. If something goes wrong you improvise. If one avenue is closed to you, you do the same thing in a different way or you do something else, and it's the same with education. There's always something else you can do. Told you, disability's a good thing. You have to be weak all the time, and wait for someone to help you go to the toilet but at least you can look at exams with a little perspective!

The trouble with well worked out theories is that they tend to get lost in the heat of the moment, especially when you've got a German-speaking exam and German speaking puts the fear of God up you. I tried to think in German the night before, but it just didn't seem to flow, despite the fact that I knew as much German as I did French. It's the grammar you see, the evil, muddled German grammar that only makes sense to Germans. You spend so much time trying to remember where the words go in a sentence that you forget your train of thought. I was determined that this time my German would flow and I'd prove my ability.

It was the same set-up as the French. We met the examiner, a woman this time, who again put us at our ease with her very clear voice. That was the least of our problems. We had to fight against the force of fear and low self-confidence. Sarah was the most worried. She hated speaking more than I did, which is some achievement. I'm sure I failed miserably at making her feel better, but I tried!

By some freaky occurrence, I wasn't going last this time, even though my name was last alphabetically. Mrs Stephenson was trying to make sure I had someone to walk round with me when my fate deciding moment arrived. That was fine by me. When my turn did arrive, I did the usual preparation, which came up with some ridiculous and obscure words that I had never heard of. I could improvise by using different words with a similar meaning, but I had to invent one or two words which isn't the best thing to do. However, two problem words wouldn't ruin the whole exam. It was a test of what you did know, and not what you didn't know, if you know what I mean. They only penalised you once for getting a word wrong. Being consistent in your mistakes may not sound like a good tactic to use but if you use a different made-up word every time the problem word arises, you get penalised for each one. If you use the same word every time, even if you've made it up, you'll only be penalised once. You never know, you could be lucky and find out that it's the right word! It's all about tactics.

Inside the scene of previous interrogations I faced the 'German Inquisition' which I don't think was as intimidating as the Spanish one. My conversation was more awkward this time, even contrived. It didn't flow like the French had and some awkwardly long pauses took place. Nevertheless, I came up with some gems and felt it was my best German-speaking performance ever. My mock, months earlier, had been an absolute *alpentraum* (nightmare) but this I was happy with.

The examiner told me I was doing well and to keep it up. I think she liked me, but who wouldn't?

I only had nine exams to go and my next three were in English. The only one that required revision in the true sense of the word was the last one, four weeks later. It was a long wait.

Over the next two weeks, which is all I had left at College, I felt like there was no point being there. Everyone felt the same. Lessons were just a distraction, going over stuff we'd gone over several hundred times before and I was sure I'd get more productive work done at home with no distractions. I only wanted extra help with the French and German lit questions that would have to be answered in English. We'd practised everything else beyond the required amount but we couldn't practise this particular task in our mocks because we hadn't finished reading the books. It was going to be hit and miss, a veritable shot in the dark, and I was nervous.

Knowing me as you do now, you'll know I wasn't rebellious

enough to stop going in when I thought it was pointless. I did what the authority said and went into college, but I didn't listen. I was a frustrated rebel!

It wasn't only going to lessons that began to annoy everyone. We started to really get on each other's nerves. We'd become so close and had spent so much time together that every time one of us spoke, at least five other people wanted to tell them to shut it! It wasn't a healthy state of affairs, especially considering that before revision began we were happy to listen to what each other said. A level life had taken it out of us and we didn't even notice. We needed a break from each other and exam leave couldn't come quickly enough.

The first English exam was basically a creative writing exercise with a word limit. There wasn't much revision that could be done for this and looking at past papers didn't really help because no two questions were ever the same. This sort of exam wasn't amazingly difficult. You just had to have your creative head on and be in the right frame of mind. Luckily, I was in a good mood as Ralph dropped me off, my Mum's good luck wish still echoing in my ear. I was ready.

Exams, as anyone who's taken them except the most smug of people will admit, are a nerve-racking experience. Each one brings its own set of worries to each candidate and you know that the grades on your result slip are all the universities look at. The pressure is immense and it takes a certain kind of person to thrive on that pressure.

As we all gathered outside the arts theatre, I looked around to see how everyone else was handling the situation. There were the giddy ones who spoke too much; the ones who panicked loudly; the ones who just looked like they were panicking; the focused ones and the annoyingly overconfident ones, who say, 'It's easy this paper. I'll do well.' They're the ones who I'd normally want to viciously assault but tunnel vision had set in. I was focused on what I'd do in the exam and it was just reassuring to look at the others' faces.

Fortunately, I found a question that I could do because if I couldn't do any of them, all my positive thinking would have gone walkies. I would probably have cried! It's easy to be in control when you know what you're doing.

Two hours of absolute boredom later, I escaped my prison, having finished my piece without using my allotted extra time. I stubbornly refused to use it again. I'll do anything to make my life difficult! I even had time to check what I'd written and I was happy with it. Three exams gone, and no disasters so far. I was on target.

The next paper was the case study and because we had to prepare for it, the English students were allowed to leave three days earlier than everybody else, the following Tuesday. The messages had been written into our leavers' books and this time they were much longer and more sincere than the ones from Sharples. We all had a great deal of respect for each other and hoped to keep in touch. I'd definitely try but whether it would happen when we all went to uni was debatable.

Leaving would be really difficult. I'd made my best friends ever, I'd had great fun and I'd been accepted again, despite the disability. Sixth form had been all that I'd hoped for: the nights out; talking on the phone together; and just being part of the lives of such a great bunch of people was an honour. It's something that we should all be grateful for because I don't think we'll ever find friends like the ones we had at Turton.

The upset, which I knew I'd eventually experience, didn't materialise immediately upon leaving. I was too focused on the most important exams of my life. The leavers' ball after the exams would probably mark the release of my feelings. I'd seriously miss these people.

We finished on the Tuesday but even then we couldn't escape. We had to go back on the Friday to get our photos taken and to pick up the case studies. The photos now have pride of place on my bedroom wall, with one notable absentee. It was Matt of course, who disappeared just before the camera flashed to the annoyance of most of the girls. I didn't see what all the fuss was about. So what if he wasn't on the photo? People would remember him just as well for not being on it as they would for him being on it. If you spend two years with someone, you don't forget that person simply because he wasn't on a photo. It was a quirk of his personality. He never did things the conventional way!

Although that Friday was the last day, I knew I'd have to go in on Monday for an exam, so I didn't feel upset. I couldn't go to the pub to 'celebrate' leaving. By all accounts it resembled a funeral, with everyone blubbing like the babies that they were. I couldn't go because I actually was at a funeral. My Granddad's sister, Auntie Marg (Margaret) who I mentioned earlier, had passed away in her sleep. I'll always remember her as one of the nicest and happiest people I've ever known. She also baked the most amazing Mars Bar cakes in the world.

Funerals are events that no one wants to go to. The trouble is everyone has to have one. This one was poignant and emotional. She had lots of people who loved her, and I think we gave her a good send off.

I was a little reluctant to go out that night, but when I thought about it, Auntie Marg wouldn't have wanted us to mope and stay in. It was my last day of sixth form; I had to show my face. Everyone was going out.

The weekend was a busy one, what with a funeral, Friday night, Gemma's party on the Saturday and case studies to prepare somewhere in between all that. It wasn't ideal preparation for an exam, having to read through thirty pages of sources on two out of three mind-numbing subjects, whilst suffering from a hangover. It had to be done though. We couldn't let Gemma down on her eighteenth.

Most of the people at that party, including Gemma, had an English exam on the Monday and the pressure told on our faces. Hardly anyone was drinking, none of the lads wanted to dance, and on top of that I was sat in my manual wheelchair and couldn't move. I hate that wheelchair!

Guess where the party was. Eagley Sports Centre, the home of a thousand steps and the venue for the Sharples leavers' do, two years earlier. Dexter hated those steps and it was like déjà vu as he dragged me up one by one. It's horrible when you're not in control. At least when I fell out of my electric chair it was my fault, but in the manual one I lived in fear of drunks trying to kill me. Those steps are a nightmare!

It wasn't that Gemma's party was boring or anything like that, it was your typical eighteenth do. You know us eighteen-year-olds: dance floor, a group of mates, music and alcohol, and we're happy. We're easily pleased! Gemma's party had all that but in the middle of the exams, the inhabitants of a morgue would have had more life in them. That night was when I realised I was stressed. It hadn't hit me until then. The stress of the exams, the exhausting effort of trying to look happy in the same room as Michelle and the frustration of being in the restrictive chair combined to thwart the urge to party.

For the first time in a long time, I waited outside the exam room on the Monday feeling extremely worried. Two nights out the weekend before an exam hadn't seemed like a bad thing at the time, and I didn't get drunk. I'd been a sensible boy, but the guilt and worry I felt were overwhelming. I knew my case studies were prepared as they always had been before, and that I didn't have to worry about cutting things out. Mrs Baddeley would do that for me at the end of the exam. Somehow, despite all this, something just didn't feel right. The adrenalin wasn't flowing and the focus wasn't there. Even listening to people and looking at their faces didn't have its usual calming effect. Everyone was irritating me and I just wanted to get the exam over with and go home. I wasn't in the right frame of mind. My body had been decapitated of its creative head. Today would be a struggle.

Looking at the paper, I saw that the questions were difficult, the easiest one being linked to the one case study that I hadn't prepared. Everything it seemed was conspiring against me. The question I did choose was about calligraphy – yawn – and from reading the case study I knew that it was really boring. I had a tactic though: this was the hardest question and also the one that the lowest number of people would be stupid enough to do. That usually meant the results would be higher on that question. What I hadn't anticipated was that if my mind had been numbed beyond all recognition I wouldn't be able to write! As I was writing, I could tell it was disjointed and I kept losing concentration. It definitely wasn't the best piece of writing I'd ever done, but luckily I finished.

At home, I thought about my performance, feeling a little disappointed. It wasn't a total disaster but it also wasn't A-grade standard. Oh well, I wouldn't let it put me off. I was still confident.

The rest of the exams went pretty much according to plan. The French lit. questions fell perfectly, and the other papers were fine except my third English paper. It was a nightmare and I was a little worried about getting less than a B, God forbid. That would have been a disaster!

I was optimistic about French and German but it was time to put all thought about exams out of my mind. I had a really exciting summer planned, after the leavers' ball that is. I'd been looking forward to that for quite a while, in between exams, and now with the exams finished the night was almost upon us. All I had to do was find myself a monkey suit because it was a 'formal'. That was enough to put Baz off, who still suffered from Rockport-wearing-Muppet-syndrome and wouldn't be seen dead in a suit. He's grown out of that now! Dexter wasn't coming either, for some reason. It was a shame that two of my best mates wouldn't be there to celebrate the end of two really good years but it wouldn't stop me enjoying myself. After all, everyone else would be there. It would be a good night.

I went into town to find a suit and came back with a black jacket, black pants, white shirt and burgundy bow tie, just to be really different. It looked very sexy, despite its lack of imagination, but that's only because I was in it! I was ready for the night ahead.

We all decided to meet up at one of our houses, which turned out to be mine. That was the easiest way to do it because it meant I wouldn't have to mess about changing wheelchairs. It was the best way to get us all together. My Mum was delighted to have us all at our house, basically because she's embarrassingly sentimental. She always wanted a daughter! I have to be honest though, the lads looked smart and the girls all looked gorgeous. We were going out with a bunch of supermodels, and that was just Al and Matt!

My biggest worry, my only worry really, was going to the toilet in the absence of Dexter and any of my usual helpers. Al offered, which I was grateful for, but the first time anyone does anything for you involving pulling you to the edge of a wheelchair is a worrying moment. You have to put your trust totally in that person and have faith that they won't drop you on the floor. Strangely enough, the only person who's ever dropped me on the floor whilst helping me with the loo is Dexter, but that's a different story. Suffice to say I was terrified of Al dropping me. I had to live in fear till he'd successfully helped me the first time, which would be as late in the night as I could possibly last! My worries were irrational. Even if I did end up lay on the floor, Al was big and strong enough to pick me up.

My toilet problems however weren't the most important thing about this night. I'd spent too much money to spend all night worrying.

After we'd all gathered in my living room and three million photos had been taken, with about sixteen different cameras, my Mum decided we had to go outside and line up in the street, so we could take some big group photos of us 'all dressed up'. The taxi driver had to wait while the same photo was taken twice with each of the sixteen cameras. Eventually we managed to get in the taxi and go to the do. About time!

The outside of the building didn't look very 'formal', unless you can call fat men sunbathing with no tops on formal! However, you should never judge a book by its cover and I was surprised by how welcoming the function room was. It scrubbed up quite well.

We all gathered away from the dining area while the meal was being prepared so we could tell everyone how nice they looked, lying to most of them! No, even the Grebs looked smart in their suits rather than their usual uniform of Nirvana T-shirts. James from my German group had even shorn off his sacred Hanson haircut, and sported the haircut of a normal person, or at least one who owns a pair of scissors. I got the shock of my life when I saw that, it was one of the highlights of the night.

The meal was elaborate and looked expensive. Now I knew why the ticket had cost me £16. The first course was fish, the second was some sort of chicken dish and the dessert was profiteroles. Shame I couldn't enjoy it because being stupid I decided to have Southern Comfort to drink, making me unable to eat most of it. It looked like a lot of work had gone into the meal but give me pie and peas any day. Listen to me! I belonged outside with the shirtless commoners. I'm common as muck at heart and long may it continue! All the hard men are brought up on pie and peas. Only southern softies eat fish and chicken as part of the same meal!

The meal was good though, everyone looked amazing and by the time we'd finished eating, everyone was a little tipsy. I had to give into my need for the loo. It was just too powerful. Alastair's maiden experience with this most pleasant of tasks passed without me falling on the floor or peeing on Al's shirt. That could have been more than my life was worth! Now I knew I was safe, I could get down to the real business of enjoying cheap booze, the company of my mates and the cheesy pop music you don't normally hear at a 'formal'. It was all a lie. We just had to look formal. We did have the school orchestra playing while we were eating, which was nice, and Charmaine and a couple of others did some singing. She didn't miss a note from what I can remember. That girl has the voice of an angel. Matt was told to stand as far away as possible because he'd put her off and he obeyed her order!

The leavers' ball had to be the only night in two years when everyone made an effort to mix with everyone else, apart from the people they hated with a passion. There was a lot of passionate hatred in our year but it was the last time we'd have to see certain people. It was worth making the effort to make this night as enjoyable as possible.

I had a dance, a laugh and a drink. The atmosphere was merry and I found myself having a really good time. I said goodbye and good luck to everyone I knew I wouldn't see again, and to some people I knew I would. My miserable Michelle mood only lasted for about five minutes and then I thought, *This is my last night with most of these people. I'm not going to be miserable*! and made myself cheer up. Everyone was dancing, laughing and drinking and suddenly it was over. The music stopped and with it the curtain came down on the best two years of my life. I kissed everyone goodbye and Matt kissed me good night! He's still in denial about that moment, says it was me who kissed him, but the Lord and I both know the truth. It's about time he admitted his bisexuality!

It's a shame Baz and Dex couldn't be there to enjoy a rare

night, when everyone was in a good mood. It was a great night.

Back at home my Mum was waiting to mither me about what had gone on. I was drunk so I don't know whether what I said was understandable. I tried to explain to her how sad I was to be leaving and how brilliant it had been getting to know people, and continuing to be mates with Matt, Dex and all the other ex-Sharples people. I couldn't express the feeling of belonging when I was sober, so how I managed it at that moment I guess I'll never know.

In bed, the place where I'm alone with my thoughts ('alone' being the operative word) and therefore where I think my most productive and profound thoughts, I let my mind wander over the two years of memories I had.

Sixth form had been the place where I'd done the most growing up. I'd become a man over those two years, but it wasn't just that. That happens to everyone. Who you shared those two emotional and stressful years with, and how you helped those people through the same experiences you went through, are very important. I'd experienced every emotion possible, with some of the most caring, loving and influential friends possible. I'd been happy, miserable, upset, excited, annoyed, angry, jealous, all in two years, but most importantly I'd been accepted again. I'd also had people who cared deeply about me to help me through everything good, bad and ugly. I cared just as deeply about them and I'd even learned to show that, and to accept that there's nothing wrong with a man showing how he feels, quietly anyway! It had been two years of first experiences: my first night in a nightclub; the first time I'd been seriously in love; the first time I'd pulled in a long time; and even my first taste of being messed around by a girl, and of friendship going sour.

When I left Sharples, I'd had a great time with a different group of friends, but I was determined that sixth form would be better. It exceeded my expectations, both inside and outside college, and as I lay in bed I was overcome by a deep melancholia. The bad, depressing times and the rows had passed and they were regrettable, but they were also part of what made sixth form life so eventful. I wouldn't have swapped one moment of it or changed anyone who I got to know, and leaving was hard.

Things would never be the same once uni started, and that was the most depressing thing about the whole two years. As that thought travelled through my racing mind, a lone tear (there was only one) rolled down my cheek. It was a sad night.

Whenever I'd left somewhere previously, I'd wondered if the people at the next place would accept me, or if it could possibly be as enjoyable as the last place. How could the friends possibly be as good at the next place? That was the question I asked myself on the night I left primary school, secondary school, and I now found myself asking it again. This time it was a rhetorical question. The answer was clear and it was no. My friends at Turton were special and I'm sure there'll never be another two years when I'm so close to so many people.

While I was thinking about the past and what had gone on for the past two years, I also felt a strong excitement about the next chapter. I, David Withnell, was going to uni! I had this perfect vision of getting drunk every night, meeting great people, pulling several thousand times and doing a bit of work somewhere in between! I was really looking forward to it – maybe too much. When you're so overly excited about something, it can never be as good as you hoped. I was convinced it would be four great years, doing what I'd wanted to do for five years, and spending a year in France despite the obvious problems of getting helpers in France and finding an accessible French uni. The problems at uni for a disabled person are obviously bigger, the problem of accommodation being the biggest, but they're used to dealing with the problems. *I'll be fine*, I thought. *My Mum and I have always negotiated the obstacles we've found up to now. We'll do it this time as well.* My Mum would be there, as would the rest of my family, whatever happened, and that's where I'm so lucky. I couldn't wish for a better family.

Uni was a problem for after the results in August. 'I might not get in yet,' I told myself, ever the realist. It was only June and there was a long summer to enjoy ahead of me. I knew I'd still see all my closest friends quite frequently until then and when I thought rationally about it, the leavers' ball wasn't quite so final. There was results night, Lucy and Charmaine's birthdays and any other nights out we didn't really plan. I'd probably end up in

Atlantis (a nightclub that had only been built that January) every Thursday, and some Wednesdays.

My memories of that long holiday seem to have merged into one long Atlantis night out. I wanted to burn the place by the time uni started!

The problem with going to the same place every week is that it begins to become boring, and I can remember so many nights when I didn't pull or even get any 'well done mates'. I'd be driving my wheelchair the mile from Atlantis to my house with Matt, Al, Dex, Rick and the other lads, discussing how boring our lives were and that there must be more to life than this endless cycle of nothingness and then Atlantis on a Thursday. When you need a 'meaning of life' discussion, Matt and Al are your men. They're up and down like yo-yos. Every time I began to feel like that, I thought, *It's only boring because I'm in between phases of my life. Uni's on its way.* Why do I think so much?

On countless occasions during those twelve or fifteen weeks, I uttered adamantly, 'I'm never going back there again.' In response to which, I'd get a knowing look from six different people that said, 'You know you'll be in there next week.' Sure enough, I was there, struttin' my stuff, well shakin' my head to the funky seventies beat. When a teenager in the nineties knows the words to every song played in a nightclub since 1971, you know he's been to the same place too often! It's embarrassing but you know why I do it. I'm too proud to go to a dating agency, that's why. I do it to continue that dubious meaning of life, yes procreation! If procreation is the only meaning of life, then why do we bother? Is it to restore the balance of nature? Do we get some strange and perverse pleasure knowing our kids will have to be bored like we are?

I love life really, and the rare nights when I do pull make it all worthwhile. It's just interesting to question what all the good, bad and indifferent things mean in the greater scheme of things. Thinking like that doesn't depress me. I think like that when I am depressed. That isn't often. I still haven't worked out why disabilities have to happen but then I'm not a genius. I'll leave that up to the scientists.

That summer I spent a lot of time with Laura, who after

managing to offload the strange and acutely psychotic Darren, soon found Craig, a lad who drank in the pub where she worked. He'd recently lost his girlfriend tragically to illness, which I was a bit concerned about. When Laura falls in love though, it's always completely and head over heels. She was convinced it would work but being detached from the situation, I was worried she'd be badly hurt. I could tell she was more in love with Craig than she had been with her previous boyfriends, and I knew that would be a problem if it didn't work out.

I only met him once and I thought he looked like a thug, with his close shaven head, but when he spoke my first impressions changed. He was a really nice lad and I thought that maybe I'd been a little quick to judge a situation I knew nothing about. Maybe it would work. He didn't sound like the sort of person who'd deliberately hurt Laura.

Just to add to the precarious nature of this whole relationship, Craig was going away to Ireland for two months to work and clear his head. When he came back, they'd be together and sod everyone else! Sounded too good to be true. This promise meant Laura taking a two-month vow of celibacy, stopping short of joining a nunnery! She didn't mind though. I think the promise of love was too strong.

The fact that her boyfriend wasn't around meant she spent more time with her mates before going to uni. She didn't have to spend all the time with her boyfriend, which was good for her mates, but maybe not so good for her. Suddenly his phone calls became fewer and fewer, until eventually she was ringing him and his phone would be switched off. Then he stopped ringing altogether. Laura became more and more upset every time I saw her and I was gutted that there was nothing I could do to make her feel better. I began to have murderous feelings towards Craig.

I didn't mind listening to Laura, or anyone for that matter, going on about lads. She'd listened to me moaning on about Michelle often enough. Laura's love life was interesting anyway. It was the craziest soap opera in history and you couldn't write a better one. Unfortunately, she had to live it and somehow the problems that Michelle and I'd had seemed insignificant compared to Laura's awkward situation.

It seemed my summer was made eventful by the love lives of my female friends. Sarah was having her problems with Noel, who apparently was taking her for granted and being insensitive, while she stressed about uni, the results, and having to leave him. That final problem soon turned out to be not so much of a problem after they went on holiday. He decided he wanted to spend time with the friends they'd met, rather than alone with Sarah. She thought it was important to spend time alone, seeing as it were the last time they'd spend a solid two weeks together for a long time. He didn't think it was so important. Such a fundamental difference of opinion proved they wanted different things from the relationship and thus the end was nigh. They don't speak any more. Another prime example of how love can ruin a perfectly good friendship. They were joined at the hip before they went out and then suddenly nothingness.

On a selfish scale, the respective love lives of Laura and Sarah worked wonders for my already flourishing friendships with them both. I was glad to lend an ear in times of crisis. In the exaggerated world of teenagers, all love problems, indeed all problems seem like crises. Everyone's in a rush to fall in love, to go to uni, to see the world, whatever it may be. They hear depressed adults saying, 'Life's short, enjoy it while you can. Do as much as you can while you're young. I missed out on so much when I were a lad,' and other such clichés, and it's true. Life *is* short, but it's not that bloody short! My Gran and Granddad have travelled around most of America since they retired. You don't have to do everything immediately. Life's constantly changing. You could end up at uni when you're forty due to redundancy or other such problems.

Obviously I can't criticise anyone for being in a rush. From being ten years old, I've wanted to be in love, to go to uni, to live happily ever after in a castle in the sky. (I don't ask for much!) I've done everything the conventional way, but who's to say that convention is the right way? I followed convention because I wanted to do things the way other kids get to do them, and later to prove that with determination, disabled people can not just survive in an able-bodied world, but can compete on the same and maybe even higher levels than everybody else. I proved for thirteen school years that with a little help the possibilities for disabled people are endless. Academically and socially I've proved that disabled people have the same feelings, the same desires, and the same value as everyone else. Hopefully people who know me or have met me agree.

And with that, it's back to the 'lost' summer. Al came out with us, in between working his big cotton socks off in the most mind-numbing and repetitive jobs possible. His love life was similar to mine, Dexter's, Rick's and Laney's (looking for a girlfriend, whilst pulling relatively infrequently with any girl desperate enough to offer). Only Matt had a girlfriend but from looking at him when they were out with us, you never would have guessed it. Charmaine tended to give him her purse and then disappear with the girls, only to return when she wanted to go home, or to ask him what was wrong. He'd sit there with his frozen frog face on. They'd then have a row, Charmaine would cry, the girls would get annoyed with Matt, the lads with Charmaine, and Matt for being a powder puff, and the night? Well the night would crash and burn. Love is definitely overrated. Why we couldn't just let them two get on with it without sticking our noses in, I don't know!

When all the ingredients for discomfort within the group come together on one night, it's a recipe for total, unmitigated disaster. The results are explosive.

Charmaine and Lucy's joint birthday do, which took place soon after the girls had returned from a girlie holiday in Torremolinos, was the only night when all the ingredients for explosion were there in the right measure. Sit back and enjoy the ride...

We decided to go for a meal to Frankie and Benny's, across the road from Atlantis, and predictably enough we were going to Atlantis afterwards. I was looking forward to hearing the same songs, in the same order, with the same 'special' guests – Dr Groove, a cheap Leo Sayer lookalike and Austin Powers, a cheap Austin Powers lookalike that we'd seen every week for the previous six months. I wasn't bothered about that because I was getting drunk with my mates, celebrating two of their eighteenth birthdays. It didn't matter where we went. There were three casualties of the meal: Baz was on holiday, Matt couldn't come for some unknown reason, and Dex 'didn't feel like' going for a meal. He would meet us in Atlantis.

Sarah looked slightly uncomfortable with all the girls, but she had Gemma and Phil to talk to.

Meanwhile, at my end of the table we were having a really good time, with Al, Alex, Pritesh (the latest lad that Lauren was just seeing but not going out with) and myself taking the mickey out of Lauren for her lack of interest in football. It was really one of those male competitions. No, not the ones that happen in the toilets! The ones where you compete to see who can make the most cutting remarks. It was a relaxed game of one-upmanship. We also had a bet, Al, Alex and I, about who could pull first, while I eyed up the waitress who I had absolutely no chance with.

While we were having a great time, there seemed to be some tense and awkward overtones emanating from the girls' end of the table. It wasn't just Sarah who looked uncomfortable. Something just didn't seem right, but I didn't know what it was.

Not surprisingly Sarah went home after the meal, which had been enjoyable, but unbeknown to us the peak of the night's enjoyment had been reached, for most of us anyway. We were at the top of 'The Big One', with a view of Blackpool below us, but we were about to hit Blackpool with a bump. First of all we sat down in our usual position and within minutes Gemma was crying. I asked the girls what was wrong and they all said, 'I don't know.' Yeah right! I sensed all had not been rosy in the gardens of Torremolinos. So Gemma and Phil's enjoyment of the night was over. Two down, ten to go.

Suddenly Lauren was crying for no apparent reason. It was turning into an excursion from a mental home! Very bizarre. Then Charmaine's 'ignore Matt operation' began, and within another few minutes Matt's face had kicked in. Things were not going well and I was beginning to think we should have gone home after the meal. Everyone was dropping like flies, so I thought I'd better dance a bit before everyone was sat in a corner with a face on. The trouble was, I hadn't been drinking because of the meal, so I felt very self-conscious about dancing. The meal had rendered me incapable of stomaching alcohol, so I was dancing sober. The paranoia that everyone was watching me set in and I could only dance for ten minutes at a time. Despite my bet, I wasn't in the mood to try my luck, basically because Michelle was there and I'd got into the 'no one measures up' mood. That's why I don't pull so often. There's so many factors that have to be perfect for me to pull that it happens very rarely.

Speaking of Michelle, where is she? I thought, and now she was out of my view my mental state plummeted to the level of the guy I'd just left sat on his own. She could be up to anything! (Not that it was any of my business.)

I went to sit with Matt and we made no secret of how we were feeling. Our faces told the story. It wasn't over yet though, for in almost the same moment our respective nights were to take a turn for the worst. First Charmaine comes over and... bang! A row explodes. Feeling a little awkward, I looked away and to my immense and heartbreaking horror, Michelle walked past holding hands with a guy who I thought was the fattest, ugliest lad in the world! Of course I would have thought that if he'd looked like Brad Pitt, but he didn't. To be honest, having seen him since he isn't really that ugly, but at that moment he was Fred Elliott!

As Charmaine started crying because of Matt, I felt like joining her. I was devastated, but surprisingly relieved. I'd needed to see that for a long time. Now I'd had visual confirmation, in all its three-dimensional, technicolour glory that she wasn't interested. Whoo–hoo!

My relief failed to prevent the inevitable upset I felt and it also failed to prevent me wanting to go home within minutes of my shocking apparition. Now I knew how Macbeth felt.

Luckily, Al had become bored of this, his four hundredth visit to Atlantis in two months and we decided to leave, swiftly followed by Gemma and Phil, who'd also decided to bail out. We were like rats leaving the sinking ship that was our night out, only we were better looking and less rabies infested. I can't even remember Dex being there and I don't know what happened to Alex, but the general consensus was that the night had died. By the way, Al won the bet, about three weeks later. Pathetic or what? That marked a change in luck for Al, who's something of a mega stud at uni, although I haven't got a clue why.

The night was useful for one thing because after a couple of days of abject misery and depression, and a very deep and meaningful conversation with Matt about the drudgery that is life, I began to feel a little better about Michelle. I remember that conversation as if it were yesterday. He succeeded in cheering me up, by taking me to watch *Austin Powers – The Spy Who Shagged Me* and then immediately depressed me with his pessimistic outlook on life! That deep and meaningful was the first time in months that we'd felt able to talk like we always had done. Our friendship was back to normal and it felt good. Up until then, we'd both been paranoid about what the other one would say to the girls but now we were past caring. We knew we could trust each other.

If that friendship was back to normal, another one was about to come to an abrupt and very final end. I'd been trying to be just mates with Michelle for a long time, without much success and I saw no reason to stop just because I'd seen her with another lad. That would have been a bit immature, seeing as it was bound to happen sometime. I would soon be at uni and so would she and by then I'd be over her anyway. I was feeling better within days of the fateful night, until the beginning of the following week that is. I'd refrained from ringing her over the weekend while I'd been feeling down, and on the Monday Matt and Al came round. Matt was a little quieter than usual. He seemed to be contemplating something, but I saw nothing strange in that. He'd had days like that before. It was just his way.

'Dave?' he said.

'Yeah.'

'There's something I need to tell you. Charmaine thought you should know…'

That sounded ominous but I thought I knew what he was going to say.

'You know that lad Michelle was with on Thursday?'

'I think I remember him,' I joked, the dull ache in my stomach growing with every syllable.

'Well she's been going out with him for the last couple of weeks.'

I was gutted. My eyes filled up but I managed to hold back the tears. I couldn't cry in front of Matt. He wouldn't know where to put his face, never mind what to say! So I just sat staring into space, as if Liverpool had lost to United in the last minute. I knew I'd be upset when the inevitable happened, but I felt upset, then empty, and then this powerful anger consumed my whole body. It wasn't a jealous anger directed at the boyfriend; it was directed at Michelle for not telling me. Everyone else knew before I did, even Matt who hadn't spoken to her in months. To hear it from Matt and not from the horse's mouth so to speak, was the bitterest of pills to swallow. It felt like a betrayal. I'd tried as hard to be friends with Michelle, in the face of unstoppable and stronger feelings than I'd ever experienced before, as I had with learning to swim, and she'd thrown it all back in my face.

'She didn't tell you because she didn't want to upset you. Well that's what Charmaine said anyway.' It was a good attempt at consolation from Matt and it could conceivably have been true. I was, however, in no mood to believe it. I was infinitely more upset than I would have been if she had told me herself. It would have been better than hearing it at the end of a Chinese whisper, which was actually half way to China by the time I got the news.

That night I wasn't the best of hosts. I said about three words all night, and they were, 'All right Al' and 'See ya!' Very articulate! This articulate phase continued when a few minutes later the phone snapped me out of my trance. 'Ring ring...' You know how it goes.

'I hope it's not Michelle,' I said to Matt.

'All right darlin',' Michelle said. Talk about bad luck! This was destined to be a bad night.

'I was all right till about five minutes ago,' I snapped, getting straight to the point.

'Why're you not all right now?'

'Heard you've got a boyfriend.' I could have waited a bit longer before I said it.

'I have,' was the reply and things went swiftly downhill from there.

'Why didn't you tell me?'

'I was going to introduce you to him on Thursday but you went home.'

'What were you going to do just shove him in front of me and say, "Dave this is my boyfriend?"'

330

'I don't know what I was gonna say. I didn't think.'

'That's your problem, you never do.'

'Yeah I'm so selfish,' she said sarcastically.

'Yeah you are. You should have told me.'

'I didn't want to upset you.'

'Well I'm more upset hearing it from Matt. You should have told me.'

'Why should I have told you before everyone else?'

'I bet Lauren knew before Thursday.'

''Course I told Lauren.'

'And Lucy?'

'Lucy guessed.'

'So Lucy knew and I know Charmaine knew.'

'Well it's up to me who I tell. Why should I have told you?'

'You know how I feel about you.'

'Yeah and that means I have to tell you everything, does it?'

'You should have told me.'

'I never had the chance to tell you, you went home on Thursday.'

'You've had two weeks to tell me. What about the last three days? You could have told me before someone else did. Were you even gonna tell me now?'

'I don't know...'

Meanwhile back in the living room, my next comment could be heard.

'F**k off. I'm f**king sick of you!' I shouted before putting the phone down, putting my wheelchair into full speed, smashing through the door and screaming, 'Stupid bitch!' in a show of extreme anger and emotional release. It was quite a moment and those were the last words she'd ever hear from me down the phone. My only regret was that I didn't think of something more witty to say. I was just too annoyed.

If she'd said, 'Sorry if I upset you by not telling you. I didn't know what to say,' I would have spoken to her when I wasn't so deeply upset but the truth was she didn't give a damn about how I felt. The fact that she was going to shove him in front of me in full view of everyone proves that. It shows a total lack of consideration of someone's feelings. The truth is she deliberately didn't tell me for long enough, so that someone else would and then she could blame them for upsetting me. She didn't speak to Charmaine for about a week after that.

And that was it. I've never spoken to her since, apart from when we've ended up on a group night out together. When I do see her I'm pleasant. I don't think there's any hard feelings any more but I've definitely been happier without her. I'm sure she's been happier without me. It was just one of those things, and maybe I was too immature to deal with the sort of feelings I had. I think she was too immature to deal with someone who felt like I did about her. I was obsessed, embarrassingly so, but I'll never forget her. She was an important part of my life for over a year.

Chapter XIII

With one part of my life over, I looked to the future, starting with the results in ten days' time. I was crying for about three of those days though.

Results day was much more nerve-racking than GCSE results day. A group of us had gone to the pub the night before, to try and forget the looming terror of the day ahead, although no one said much. It was a very subdued evening.

On the day we'd offered to give Al a lift and we both sat in the living room that we'd frequented on so many occasions, mumbling about nothing and looking very nervous. When I'm nervous I chunner and talk absolute rubbish, but I had a lot to be nervous about. Unlike everyone else, I had the one person with me who no one wants to be with them on results day. My Mum.

'You're staying in the car, Mum,' I insisted, and in I went.

I felt hypnotised when I went in, as if I was on autopilot, as I picked up my photos and approached Miss Kershaw. It was a strange situation because I just wanted to pick up the results and escape unnoticed, but no! I had to have a chat with my form tutor. I knew why they had to be there because if things went wrong they had to pick up the pieces. It didn't make the idea any more pleasant but I had to put up with it.

I smiled apprehensively as she turned the result sheet over, and I waited for my eyes to focus on the grades, which were all I'd have to show for my two years' work. French (A), German (A), English (B). I was extremely happy. I'd got the grades; I'd got into uni; and I'd also got the results I'd expected after the exams. It was a great moment, but how had everyone else done?

Al was visibly elated. He'd done as well as he'd thought possible. He was going to St Martin's at Lancaster. Lucy got two A's and an E and she was going to the same place as Al. Sarah got an A, 2 C's and a D. She was really upset about the D but managed to get into the uni she wanted to go to. Laura was crying and I thought she'd had a disaster. She was really crying with joy because she got a B in geography and didn't get into Cambridge! She was going to Bath. Dexter and Baz got a C, a D and an E. Dexter was doing nursing and Baz was avoiding uni at all costs and working at an insurance company.

Everyone was happy except Charmaine and Matt, who'd done worse than anyone expected. They were very upset and they were also better than their results suggested. Luckily, after several hours of frantic ringing and searching, they got into uni. Matt was supposed to go to Huddersfield but ended up at Preston, doing product design. Charmaine took a total change of direction, from science to business studies. She was going to Bradford.

Now the results were done, it was time to kill a few more brain cells with copious amounts of alcohol. I went home for a couple of hours to tell all the expectant relatives the news and to cheer Sarah up. She was really disappointed because she thought she'd underachieved and that people would be disappointed in her, which was never going to be the case.

The rest of the day turned into a marathon drinking session. I went to the pub at about eleven o'clock, was drunk by one and then I had to go for a haircut. I returned to the pub a couple of hours later to continue the festivities. There was only Al and me, who could handle the pace. I don't know what happened to the rest of my soft mates but I was drunk enough not to care!

Eventually I had to go home for some tea so I wouldn't collapse before the night was over. We arranged to go to town at about half eight and go round a few pubs, before going to Atlantis. We were all out and it was a great a laugh. Well it was an improvement on the last night anyway.

Most of us had about a month to go before the start of the latest stage of our education, and having got into Manchester to do English Law and French Law, I spent that month frantically preparing for my course. Al took me on a tour of Manchester city centre because sadly enough I'd never been, despite living in the close vicinity. I hadn't lived! It was huge. I was bound to get lost if I ever left the university campus which was big enough in itself!

I also had to go and visit the disabilities co-ordinator, to make final arrangements and to meet the person who would take my notes, my note-taker. I'd decided I needed one, despite a strong feeling that I didn't particularly want one. I'd need help to keep up with the lectures and to reach books in the library. I've always been reluctant to accept any help, but in this instance I knew it was necessary. She wasn't quite what I'd expected. A woman in her thirties, who could speak both French and German. I expected someone a little closer to my own age, who I could be mates with as well as have a professional relationship with. She had the right criteria as a note-taker, and some experience. *At least she'll be good at the job*, I thought.

Within a couple of days, fate cast its dice again when the note-taker decided she couldn't take up the job. She did have three kids, so I understood that she was busy. I now had to begin a further search for the perfect note-taker from a list of numbers I'd been given. It was quite a science really because most note-takers were already at uni so couldn't do all the hours I needed. After a couple of incompatible people I came across the name of Tim Birch, which surprisingly was the next name on the list. He seemed like a nice enough lad and he wasn't at uni. He already had a degree so he had the necessary experience of note taking. He also had a lot of free time because he was a freelance writer who needed some extra income. Sitting in on Law lectures seemed acceptable to him.

He gave us a definite 'yes' and I could breathe a sigh of relief. A weight had been lifted and I could now look forward to the important bit; a mad, week-long drink fest called freshers' week. There'd be several thousand good-looking females for me to chat up, well to look at anyway. I was really excited about uni. I was sure my vision would come true. It was going to be the best four years of my life and I wasn't worried at all. Freshers' week would be a bit awkward because I wouldn't have anyone to help me with the loo. Drinking a lot was off the cards so maybe 'drink fest' was an overstatement. Just 'fest' would probably be more appropriate.

There were so many things going on during freshers' week that you couldn't possibly do everything. Not that I wanted to. I was at uni for women, drinking and to get a degree. I didn't want to join any weird and wonderful clubs, such as the lesbian, gay and bisexual club. Although…

The first night of the week was the freshers' pub-crawl and Al, always one for a pub-crawl, said he'd come with me. I could drink this time! Travelling was going to be awkward, as my Mum kept reminding me. 'Don't miss the train. Make sure they've got a ramp.' Bless her! She was trying to make sure everything was perfect. Thank God my taxi arrived within minutes of the beginning of all this fuss. I'd have gone mad otherwise!

Leg one of the journey was the taxi to the station, a journey which passed without a problem. In fact I got to uni without any problems and went to the meeting place. It was one of the most intimidating experiences of my life. The place was packed to the rafters. I'd never seen so many people I didn't know before! I should have expected it really. Uni was a bigger place than secondary school and sixth form put together and I'd been nervous about meeting new people at both those places. I'd become so excited about what could be good about uni that I'd forgotten how nervy I could be. This packed pub brought me down to earth with a bump. I expected everything to be perfect straight away, even though the voice of experience was screaming at me that that wouldn't be the case. *Oh well, I was there now, I'd better get on with it*, I thought. Al said we should latch on to some other people so I went to work my magic, found out the girl was a second-year and wasn't doing the pub crawl, and then went back to Al. Things were not going according to plan so far. They were about to get worse, as we were told to get on a bus to take us two miles to the group of pubs we would be 'crawling'. Getting on a bus isn't exactly brain surgery but this was the infamous 'wheelchair accessible' bus that I talked about earlier. So Al and the driver had to lift me on to the bus, giving me whiplash in the process. Once on the bus, there was no room for me to get to the wheelchair space over in the corner, out of everyone's way. Best place for a disabled person, if you ask·me, which is exactly what another passenger on the bus thought. He struggled to squeeze past me and then said, 'You should be sat over there, out of the way.' It wasn't what he said, more how he said it, with more than a hint of annoyance. He was right but if he'd cared to look instead of shouting the odds, he'd have seen that I couldn't get out of the way.

'I can't move, dickhead,' was my less than witty reply.

Al hadn't heard him but seeing my face, he wanted to go over and explain to the man the error of his ways in a calm and rational manner. All right, he wanted to punch him.

When this journey was finally over, I just had to get off the bus. Al and two very friendly girls helped lift me to safety, up a huge, almost mountainous curb. We turned around feeling relieved and then looked around.

'Al,' I said, 'the bloody pub's on the other side of the road.'

Back down the curb we went, across the road, up an equally large curb and towards the pub entrance, where to top things off there were more steps. *I wanna go home*, I thought! Fortunately the bouncers were helpful, and with Al's help they got me inside a pub which looked like a disused church. Wooden floorboards, battered wooden seats and no room between hundreds of cramped bodies. 'Ah this is what student pubs are supposed to look like. Great,' was my first impression.

'I'll go and get us a drink Dave,' shouted Al. 'Get talking to some girls.'

I looked around and saw plenty of girls but I couldn't move to reach any of them! Just my luck. The only ones I could get to were on the opposite side of the table and I couldn't shout loud enough for them to hear me. This wasn't quite what I had in mind for freshers' week! Al and I drank up quickly, discussed how pissed off we were and made for the exit door.

'Those girls are there Dave. Should we go and join them?'

I looked over and it was the girls from the bus. They were over in the corner, beyond a group of about 300 people.

'Come on then,' I said and we went over, tapping everyone on the shoulder and moving them out of the way as we approached.

'Bloody hell!' I exclaimed. 'They're not here!' Al looked suitably fed up. 'Let's get out of here, Dave.'

My sentiments exactly. I decided this night was destined to wind us up.

Out on the street, we went to check the other pubs. Pub two? Inaccessible. Pub three? Inaccessible. Pub four? Inaccessible. Pub five? Absolutely no room at the inn. Crying was an option!

There was a way out of this nightmare; Al's sister was assistant manager of a new bar in Manchester and Al had tickets to the opening. 'Should we go to Bar 38?' he asked.

'Please. Anything to get me out of here,' I said. With that we dived into a taxi and sped off into the distance. What a relief!

Bar 38 was a really modern bar with quite a relaxed atmosphere. Al and I were soon in a better mood. Things could only get better after my first uni experience, but it had been an eye-opener.

During freshers' week I only had to go into uni on the Tuesday and the Thursday, to register and to meet the other Law students. Meeting everyone else was quite a nerve-racking hour or so. My Mum had come into uni with me, so I didn't get stuck or lost anywhere. It's a good job she did because I'm sure I would have got lost. It's a big campus. I went into the room alone however. My Mum being there would have been slightly embarrassing, especially with the stomach-churning nerves I felt. I was worried, I didn't know what to say and it showed. It was obvious who the first-years were. They were the ones who sat looking ready to throw up!

I spoke to a few second-years and third-years, who gave me the spiel about how difficult a course Law was and how I should work from the first year. That was a worry for next week though. I was still in dossing mode from the three-month break I'd just had, so the information went in through one ear and out the other. My answers to their questions ranged from yes to no and my questions from 'What's the course like?' to 'Do you enjoy it?' It was an ordeal that I didn't enjoy. Being forced to talk to people straight away wasn't my idea of fun. I preferred to do things in my own time.

My own time usually meant in about three months, so I suppose being forced to do it did help me make friends quicker. Not that I met many people who were doing my course. I only met one person doing my course and that was Damien from Gloucester. He got four A's in his A levels and seemed like a nice lad, although the only thing we had in common was the course. He wasn't a football fan, didn't watch any of the TV programmes I watched, and didn't drink much. Conversation was a struggle but I think we were both as nervous as each other, at being shoved together and told to 'make friends'. It seemed a bit false.

I was happy that I'd spoken to some people but I left the room feeling flustered and glad to be out of there. Maybe uni wouldn't be great immediately. Some of the girls were nice-looking though.

Thursday was registration day. We had a meeting with our personal tutor, Andy Bell, who gave us some forms to fill in and then sent us to the main hall for registration. Of course I couldn't get in through the same door that everyone else used, so a couple of second-years took me round to the lift. It was quite a distance from one building to the other. The whole place was massive and very intimidating, and when I got to the main hall there were large queues. Everyone looked nervous and there was an eerie silence. No one knew what to say to the next person, so they just went on with their own business of queuing and registration. I didn't like the place at that moment and I had time to dwell on that thought as I queued for three quarters of an hour.

'Don't worry about it,' I told myself. 'You'll get used to it. You always have before.' But this was much bigger than before. Until now I'd had the protection and the familiarity of sixth form but now I was thrust into the unknown, without one single person I'd known before.

'Next please!' The call of the woman at the desk caught my attention. It was my turn so I approached her. She took my picture for my library card and signed my forms. I was now an official student!

Later that day, I bumped into the sole other Turton student who'd gone to Manchester and she cut a lonely figure as well. Vanessa was good friends with Laura and so I knew her, but not very well. I had to talk to her for my own sake! She looked quite pleased to see me and we had a chat about how scary everything was. She was living there, so she'd already met a couple of people and I wondered if I should have lived there. It's the best way to meet people but, quite sensibly I thought, I'd chosen to stay at home while I settled in. There would have been too much upheaval, what with a note-taker, two twenty-four hour carers, who I'd never met before and who had no prior experience, and the actual settling down that everyone has to go through. I thought it would be too much to cope with. When someone tells you that the carers are volunteers, who could possibly be ex-convicts as Elaine (the Disabilities Co-ordinator) told me, you begin to wonder about it. I would be willing to try it in the second year when I was settled but for now the best idea was for me to be at home.

Vanessa and I discussed the freshers' ball, which was due to take place on the Saturday. I'd been a bit worried about it because I didn't want to go on my own and be wandering around aimlessly all night. Vanessa arranged to meet me with her mates at the beginning of the night. It was lucky we'd bumped into each other.

Saturday came very quickly and before I knew it, my Mum and Dad were taking me to Manchester. They were going to go out in Manchester so my Dad could come back and help me with the toilet. They also didn't want to have to drive back from Bolton to pick me up at 3 a.m. It was great of them to do that, so I could have the best night possible, and I was determined to have a good night.

They put my wheelchair back together and I arranged a time for my Dad to help me with the toilet. That was strange, drinking to a timetable, but it was the way it had to be. After all it was better than not drinking at all!

When I arrived, Vanessa wasn't there. I was now worried. *What if she doesn't come?* I thought and then, right on cue, she came in with her flatmates. They were all pleasant enough and definitely liked a drink. Most girls do, especially students.

This was one of the hugest nights out possible. There were about 4,000 freshers to be divided between about nine rooms, and every room we entered was packed. I was in awe of it, but it was so big it became impersonal. The atmosphere was similar to a nightclub but it seemed a lot more nervous. It was odd.

If you want to meet new people then that isn't the best way of doing it. I saw a couple of people from my course at the beginning of the night, and said I'd catch up with them later. No chance. I never saw them again. I also met people that night that I never saw again, ever. Come to think of it, I didn't see Vanessa for about six months after that night! That was an occurrence I'd have to get used to.

I made an effort to talk to Vanessa's mates and to a few other people I'd never met. I was determined to make friends, and that was my mistake really. I'd never forced friendships, but I'd always made friends. I was too eager to make friends at uni. I should have let friendships happen naturally.

The freshers' ball was one of the strangest events I'd ever been too but despite my discomfort at the whole night, I spoke to and danced with at least ten people I'd never met before, and who I've never met since. I chatted a couple of girls up and failed miserably in my attempts at seduction. The only phone number I did get was from a lad! *I hope he's not gay*, was my first thought, not that I've got anything against homosexuals. I just don't fancy them! When he wrote his number down with a mascara pen, I thought, *Oh dearie me!* And I never rang him up.

Vanessa went home at about one o'clock and I was left with her mates. At least I had someone to walk to the car with me when two o'clock arrived.

I'd had a good night, after getting over the shock of how many people were there but I didn't pull. Maybe uni wasn't going to be the pulling fest I'd expected. Neither my luck would change overnight nor my low confidence levels. Silly blind fool I was! Maybe students weren't as randy as I thought!

'Once I start lectures and seminars, I'll meet new people,' I told myself on the way back home. Patience was the order of the day.

My very first lesson at uni came on the following Monday, and on Sunday, I had the last, frantic organisations to carry out. Sorting my books out, putting enough notepaper in my files and ringing Tim, to tell him what time to be there, and which room to go to. He'd studied at Manchester before, so I was sure he'd know where everything was.

'Where the hell is he?' I said, under my breath, as I sat outside the lecture theatre in the science block. Five minutes later he still hadn't arrived, but I was ten minutes early. Ralph's driving had been pretty quick (that's the same Ralph from Turton. It's amazing what you talk about in a taxi for three quarters of an hour).

Another five minutes and the lecture was due to start. Constitutional and Administrative Law (the political bit) with Rodney Brazier. *Hang on a minute. He wrote the textbook.* I never expected that! So he knew his stuff then?

Tim, I'm going to kill you. That was my final thought as I entered the room. My degree started here and to say I was a little apprehensive would be an understatement! Tim's absence only served to increase my nervousness. Would I be able to write notes quickly enough? I'd soon find out, because his first words to us were, 'I think we should start straight away with the title: What is a constitution?' There were no introductions or anything. We hadn't even had time to look at his face. I can't explain what he looked like because it didn't have time to register before concentration set in. His experience of taking lectures shone through for all to see, or rather hear. Clear notes, clear headings and a very clear voice. What was a guy, who studied at Cambridge and commanded great respect from politicians and lawyers alike, doing giving lectures at Manchester University? I didn't have time to answer that question as he continued, 'The separation of powers doctrine... blah blah blah... Legislative, executive judicial.' I found I could keep up with him. Tim was redundant!

At the end of the lecture, we were given a mountainous booklet, as thick as *War and Peace*, which told us what we had to read; what we ought to read; and what we could also read. I got the shock of my life when I looked at what I had to read for the next lecture. I lost all ability for rational thought and all notion of common sense, and thought I had to read everything to do well. I was worried about how I'd get it all done, but confident that I would. A strange combination of feelings but that's my mind for you.

The next session was French speaking. French would be my salvation if Law was driving me insane, although my dull, nervous ache returned at the prospect of speaking in front of new people. I was comforted by the knowledge that everyone would feel the same.

I left the law building to travel what seemed like two miles to the languages building, wondering what had happened to Tim, and then a man caught my eye. Tim had said he'd be wearing a green bubble coat and locking up a pushbike, and this guy was doing exactly that. I didn't really think it was him, until he said in his best London accent, 'You must be David. I'm Tim.'

I didn't know whether to have a go at him for missing the first lecture, or whether to be matey with him. Technically, I was his boss but I was uncomfortable with that idea. I couldn't shout the odds for two main reasons. Firstly, in order for this arrangement to work there had to be an amount of co-operation. We were a team and if I was nice to him he'd do a better job. I also wanted to be his mate, and if I acted like a boss that couldn't happen. Anyway, he might have had a perfectly good reason for being late.

I decided on a friendly, 'What happened to you?' to which he replied, 'I'm really sorry. I got here ten minutes late and I couldn't see you in the room.'

'I'll let you off then,' I joked and we hit it off from then on. He had a quirky sense of humour and some strange stories to tell, from his studying and travelling experiences. He was away with the fairies some of the time, but he was a writer. What did I expect? He was a nice lad though, who seemed to care about me getting where I wanted to go, as much as he cared about earning some money. I soon found he was willing to stay longer in the library, without pay if necessary, and to go beyond the call of duty if I asked (nothing sexual intended). I was willing to accept him missing the odd lecture or two or three…

I told him I had a French lesson and asked him if he'd come with me, just for the first lesson. He didn't speak French so we both wondered how useful he'd be. I thought he'd be about as useful as a clock with no hands, but he could write vocab. down and put headphones on my head if necessary. I'd always managed with both those tasks at Turton, be it with the help of another student. He didn't mind just sitting in on the lessons in case I needed him, which was great.

He didn't mind taking the mickey out of my French accent either. He said I sounded like a 'drunk Manc', after only knowing me for about a week. That did wonders for my confidence. I'd show him! In the first lesson he was glad to have come along, if only to ogle at the teacher, who was admittedly attractive although Tim deluded himself that she fancied him.

'It's the body language. She's giving me signals,' he said. Yeah right! She was using body language because he couldn't understand a word she said. I don't think they're allowed to speak any English. I didn't want to burst his bubble though.

She went round the room, letting us all introduce ourselves and everyone else went before me. When it was my turn, I felt more confident than when I'd first entered the room. I didn't even go red and flustered, which surprised me, and I spoke quite clearly. My French A level oral had given me confidence, but I was also too worried about all the law work I had to do, to worry about French. Law was new to me. As for French, I knew I was good. I'd proved that.

Having escaped this introductory French lesson unscathed, my first day of lectures had come to an end. It hadn't been too bad, but when I got home, I didn't know where to start with this public law booklet. Sitting down to look at it sensibly, I thought I'd start with what I had to read from the book, and I set to making notes about it. I went for three hours a day, outside lectures, but I thought I could raise it to four if I had to. This was my first day and I was already becoming obsessed. I did three hours work that night. What's wrong with me!

By the end of the week I'd experienced all the lectures and lessons and to be honest they weren't that exciting. My other law module was legal method and the lecturer, Marie Fox, who wrote the textbook wasn't quite as easy to understand as Rodney Brazier. She obviously knew her stuff, maybe too well. She understood what she was saying but we didn't, probably because she spoke so quickly and switched from one subject to another midstream, and back to the original subject before she'd even taken a breath. I had to admit it. I needed Tim's help. Keeping up with this woman was like keeping up with my brother at Leverhulme Park. Impossible. It was the first time I had to accept help with my academic work and for once I didn't care. I was desperate to get a degree and if that meant getting over my pig-headedness, I'd do it.

As for French, I had a language lesson to go with my oral and that didn't seem like it'd cause me a problem. The teacher was Professor Annie Morton but she wasn't really how I'd expected a professor to be. I had a preconception that professors were boring intellectuals. I didn't see them as normal people, who I could get on with. This professor was a really friendly and approachable person and she didn't make an issue of the 'Professor' bit. She said we should call her Annie. She was definitely unique.

The most difficult thing was finding my way round the Law Library. It was the biggest library I'd ever seen, and I wondered how the hell I'd find the books I needed amongst the millions that were there. I knew I wouldn't be able to fit half a dozen books on my tray, or even to turn hundreds of pages over, and that's where Tim came in. We soon got a routine going, where he'd photocopy what I needed for that evening or for the weekend and then I'd either sit in the library waiting for the taxi, or go home and do it. Now if I was a sensible person, I wouldn't have needed to go near the library quite as often as I did, especially in the first year. I could have just done the work out of the books, and then done the extra work if I had time later. Even though I only had to pass this year, I worked harder than I had to. I was worried I wasn't good enough and I wanted to prove that I was.

I met some of the other people doing Law with French at a tour of the library, of all places. They all seemed down to earth and nice enough. There was Steph, Sarah, Damien who I'd already met and Julia, and a couple of others whose names escape me. After meeting them I thought I'd enjoy uni once I'd settled in.

There was only one more thing left to do that week and that was a 'get to know your fellow students' drink at the Quay Bar in Manchester. I thought I'd better go. After all, the socialising was my only reason for going to uni! I didn't know why, but one drink loosened my tongue, after I'd managed to get downstairs in the most awkward lift in the world, that is. It was a wheelchair-sized platform, no bigger, no smaller and once the door shut behind me there was no one in the lift to press and hold the button for me. That defeats the object of the lift in the first place. The sole purpose of a lift in a building with only about six steps is to help disabled people, and if they can't get downstairs it's a waste of time. I had to send one of the bar staff downstairs to call the lift down. I think they could have thought that one out a bit better. Minimalism doesn't work when it comes to lifts!

I'd expected Law students to be stuck up, and from the first couple of lectures I found that quite a few of them were. When I went for this drink I spoke to a number of people, who were down to earth, really easy to get on with, and not work-obsessed morons. No one understood some of the things I was saying, which surprised me, considering I was only twenty miles down the road from my house. People came from all over the country to go to Manchester, but I hadn't realised how few people came from up North. I also hadn't realised how broad my language was. If I said a word like 'nowt', I'd get a blank look. What? It's not as if I came from Siberia!

I had a really good laugh with a group of girls who came from London and I found out that Steph was a Liverpool fan. She suddenly looked infinitely more attractive. I don't ask for much, just a woman who likes football and me. There weren't as many gorgeous women as I thought there would be, but there were enough for me to last four years at my rate of asking one person out every six months. So there were only eight good-looking women! I didn't only go for looks though, so that meant there'd be a few others I could go for. How calculating could I be?

The first week was over, and I left the Quay Bar to return to my humble abode feeling optimistic. The people I'd met were fine but over the next few weeks the inescapable cycle of work began to get to me. I'd been used to doing a task as soon as I got it and then having a break till the next one came along. Now there was always another piece of work or note taking to be done, at the same time as doing the first one, and on top of that they'd give us essays to do or a court report. Maybe I was doing too much. I'm sure I was but I don't have it in me to give anything less than my best. I had to choose the most intense course in the world, and every time a lecturer said I had to do eight hours' work a week outside lectures for each module, I'd do it. So I was doing twelve hours lectures and twenty-four hours' work a week, plus ten hours a week travelling, and two hours a week being taught to use the software I had on my computer. That's forty-eight hours a week, nearly seven hours a day doing something uni related, and somewhere in between I had to eat and sleep. Add that to the fact that I was wandering around a freezing cold campus, getting wet and cold and then having to write, then you get a picture of how hard I was finding it. When my arms are cold I can only write very slowly and turning the pages of a book is almost impossible. That meant my first couple of hours' work was slow to say the least. Despite all this, I was reading and putting notes on all the 'must read' and 'ought to read' sections of the book, cases and periodicals, getting my essays done, and doing the court report in good time. Tim and I had a good routine going, when he turned up, and when he didn't I always had enough work to do and enough people whose notes I could borrow. That's what I get for being so popular! I even managed to get a night out once a week; only I couldn't drink more than two drinks because I couldn't go to the toilet – always a problem when you need to. I joined the Law Society, which has nothing to do with law, just getting drunk, and I went to their freshers' do at a club called Joop. They assured me they had a ramp that they could put over the steps, and I had no reason not to believe them.

On arriving at the club, having taken the wheelchair apart, getting a lift to Manchester, and putting the wheelchair back together, it turned out that they did have a ramp but the only thing that it was wide enough to support was a mountain bike! Why would anyone with even the most primitive of brains say a place was accessible when it clearly wasn't? It's just one of those mysteries. Only brute strength would get me up the six steps that faced us, and seeing as I didn't have any I had to rely on my Dad and one of his work colleagues to chuck me up there. I went inside, called an ambulance for two coronaries and got on with having a good time.

The night turned out to be as boring as hell. Most of the people on my course were there but it was awkward. We'd only just met each other, were struggling to make conversation and I felt distinctly uncomfortable with over a hundred people I hardly knew. The lack of alcohol in my body meant I was surrounded by drunks, and when they moved on to a different club I couldn't because I'd told my Mum and Dad I'd be in Joop when they came back. I was trapped with all the second and third-years, who already knew each other and I had an hour to go. *I can't sit here not talking to anyone for an hour*, I thought. I'd have looked stupid, and although I didn't like forcing myself on people, I did it. I talked a bit, danced a bit, and waited for my chariot to arrive. Luckily my Dad arrived early and I could escape the nightmare!

'How was it?' he asked.

'It were good yeah. I had a laugh.' Okay so I lied. I just wanted so much for uni to be brilliant, but it wasn't turning out that way. It was early days though.

I tried another night out with a group of girls I met in the library. It was the only time I ever saw them in the library as well! I got talking to Clare, who seemed really nice. She was very talkative and we got on really well. Even my tactless, chauvinistic jokes made her laugh. As usual, I fancied her straight away. She wasn't gorgeous, but she was attractive and very flirtatious (have I used this description before?) and we soon got bored of writing notes. We went for a coffee and had a good chat, about everything really. It felt natural and that had never happened before. It was the first time I'd met Clare and I was my usual witty and charming self. Usually I wouldn't be myself until my third or fourth meeting, but I felt like I knew her, and then I subtly switched the conversation to our love lives, at least I thought I did it subtly. She started telling me about her ex-boyfriends and I told her that I didn't have much luck with women. 'I think it's the wheelchair that does it.' Slip the sympathy vote in there. I had to do it.

When she said, 'Wheelchairs are cool,' I thought, *I'm well in here*. Then she said, 'You should be like me. Stay single till you're twenty-seven.'

Or maybe I'm not in there, then. The alarm bells had begun to ring, and there was no way I was getting involved with another girl, who wanted to be single. The 'Michelle effect' had manifested itself in a big way and I needed to escape before I fell totally for this girl. It was too soon for me to remount that particular merry-go-round!

Suddenly my knight in a shiny black taxicab caught my eye. Ralph had come to my rescue, and I now had an escape route.

'I'm afraid I'm gonna have to go. My taxi's here. Nice to meet you.'

'See you later,' she said and off I went.

I saw Clare and her mates again the next day, and I cheekily asked if I could go out with them next time they went out.

'Course you can,' they said, and that was my next night out sorted. Me and a sizeable group of girls. That'd be nice! I now knew about three lads and about fifty girls. I'd never known so many girls in my previous eighteen years sheltered life.

The pub we went to (The Footage and Firkin) was er... different to any pub I'd ever been to before; paint flaking off the roof and landing in your drink, or maybe it wasn't paint. Maybe they just had a special, limited edition, green Southern Comfort! The place was packed wall to wall with students, so once we'd all sat down that was it. Moving was not an option but at least the music was good. It was proper student music, none of your poxy boy band stuff. Rock music, now that's real music. I like a bit of aggression, but when it's blasting round your ears it doesn't help with the getting to know people process. I made the best of it though, surrounded by ten girls. That was my idea of fun!

I had a really good time. They were easy to talk to but they did prove one thing. Female students are the biggest drinkers in the world. The drinks were coming thick and fast, almost in one constant stream, all night long and eventually they were dancing on tables, which was scary but strangely enjoyable! Soon the night was over and when I'd finally negotiated the heaving crowds, my Dad was waiting outside. I went home for my five hours sleep, feeling optimistic about the friendships I could make at uni. I was beginning to feel settled. I was however disappointed that I was the only lad in the world who could go out on his own with ten girls and not pull! Poor show.

Living at home and being in a wheelchair causes problems when it comes to making friends at uni. It's like you have a completely different life to everyone else. My typical day would involve getting a taxi to uni at a set time, usually arriving earlier than everyone else. They'd come in five minutes before a lecture, so I'd at least get five minutes to talk to everyone. Then the lecture would finish and I'd go to the library with Tim, get my photocopying done and wait for the next lecture. Everyone else would go out of the lecture and straight back to their halls for a while. At dinner times, which were different for everybody, they'd go home for something to eat and I'd sit on my own in the library, unless by some fluke there was someone I knew in there. At the end of the day, I'd go back to Bolton and they'd stay in Manchester. This meant our paths would cross very rarely, if at all. So I could go a whole week or longer without seeing someone who was doing exactly the same course as me. It was hardly the best situation for making friends.

People would ask me to join them for lunch but I couldn't because I was stuck to a rigid time. The taxi would always happen to be on its way at the moment I bumped into someone I knew. Now, having to go home is a problem for students who don't live at uni but they could choose to meet up with someone, and go home an hour later. I couldn't do that. I could have got people's phone numbers, but I always thought, *I'll get it tomorrow.* Then I wouldn't see the person again for a week. My nights out became fewer and fewer, because if I didn't see anyone I couldn't organise a night out. Even when we did organise something, bad luck would conspire against me. Or maybe it was God getting revenge on me for not believing in him. Whatever it was, I was getting fed up with it.

I missed two nights out in one week because my brother, who'd just passed his driving test, decided to conduct an experiment into whether a Ford Mondeo could fit under a lorry! A feeling of intense panic came over me when I arrived home to find the car missing a large clump of its body.

'Mum!' I shouted. 'Why's the car only got one bumper?'

To my extreme shock, she said, 'Dan's had a crash.' Seeing the worry etched on my face, she added very quickly, 'But he's all right.'

That was a relief, and now I'd found out he was still alive I could go about the business of murdering him! I was supposed to be going out for a meal and a night out with my fellow Law with French students but this freak occurrence meant I couldn't get there. Lovely! So I sat at home, strangling my brother with one hand, whilst writing notes with the other. I couldn't even stop working to strangle him properly!

The car still hadn't been fixed later that week when I had

planned to go out again and frustration was beginning to set in. Why wasn't I getting a chance to make friends? If it wasn't for Tim, uni would have been a very lonely place. That arrangement was working like clockwork and, like so many times before, things had become second nature. I'd only need to spend twenty minutes a day in the library to get everything photocopied. It was very efficient.

Despite all this, something just didn't feel right, and within weeks I was bored of the endless tedium that reading cases and books about pedantic government practices and judicial precedent brought. I considered dropping French because hours of my life were taken up every night, and I needed some respite. But French was the only thing I was enjoying. I couldn't drop it now.

I decided to do my first term and my first set of exams and then consider my position, but I wrestled with the idea of leaving on many occasions before the end of term. I think I'd made a subconscious decision to quit at the end of term, but every time I thought I'd decided, something would happen to temper that idea and to make me reconsider; my first three essays for example.

I got good marks in all three of them, and I was satisfied with them, while I was still getting used to the course material and research methods. I was especially pleased, considering they told us they expected us to fail the first essay. 'Most people do,' said Marie Fox. We needed forty per cent to pass, and I got fifty-eight twice and sixty-three once, so I was doing well. I only wanted between seventy and seventy-five per cent by the end of the course! At least I now knew I was intelligent enough to do it. It was quite an ego boost, I can tell you that.

The court report created some interest for me as I watched a criminal case and a civil one. The civil cases were as interesting as a trip round a German church, something I've experienced at the hands of my sadistic Gran, but the criminal case was about a drug dealer. It kept me interested. I went to Bolton for the criminal case, having forgotten the problems caused by the building at work experience time, or hoping the problems had been solved. Obviously I didn't expect that to have happened. I'd been made cynical by the McDonald's disabled toilet incident, which by the way still hasn't been sorted out. Oh how it scarred me!

Luckily there was one room I could get into. *Hmm, which room should I choose? Room five, room five or room five!* was my first thought but I got lucky with the case. I even got to talk to one of the barristers, and my Dad told him I was going through a self-doubt phase. He's so embarrassing! I hate him!

On finding out that civil cases only happened once a month in Bolton, I decided to go to Manchester with both parents in tow because I'm a mummy's boy! My first instinct was to fall asleep, as a barrister spent what seemed like three hours, reading a statement full of long, drawn out sentences (like this one) and ridiculously long words (like 'ridiculously'). At least I was getting the information I needed.

The actual difficulty of the work wasn't a problem. It was the sheer mountainous volume of it, plus the fact that I'd grudgingly accepted that I was slower at writing notes and typing essays than everybody else. It was far too intense and I had an extra module to worry about next term. I could see no end to the tunnel, no summit to the paper mountain that was growing as I wrote, and that made me really worried. Circumstances were stopping me from spending time with my friends, and I was hardly seeing Dex and the other lads at all. I'd even work while they were in my room, doing what they do. Dex was the first to notice that I wasn't happy, apart from my Mum and Dad. I lied to everybody else. 'Yeah, it's good. I've got quite a few good friends... But it's a lot of work,' was my often repeated response to the question, 'How's uni?' My face probably showed I was lying.

October was a hectic month. I went out every Friday and two Thursdays, the Thursdays being uni nights out. One was for a girl's birthday (Sarah, who was doing my course). I was quite good friends with Sarah – when I happened to bump into her. The other night out was Halloween, and I did something I'd avoided like the plague up until then. I got dressed up as a vampire: teeth, dodgy wig and a cape, which kept getting stuck in my wheels. Wheelchairs are quite an occupational hazard but vampire capes getting stuck in the wheels wasn't one of the things I'd ever worried about, funnily enough. I looked sexy that night, with my fake blood and all the paraphernalia.

For an hour Damien, who was supposed to meet me, didn't

turn up and I was left with the second-years who admittedly made me feel welcome. They were certainly up for a good time.

When Damien and the others did arrive, I was facing the other way but I could see them through the mirror. I was a little disappointed that with a name like Damien he didn't come as the devil. He was dressed as a zombie. There was a huge crowd between me and the others, so he couldn't see me, and I had a huge cape stuck under my wheels so I couldn't move. This wasn't meant to happen.

By the time I got someone to put the cape in my bag, Damien was no longer visible! 'Great. What a disaster this night is,' I said and I set to looking for my invisible friends. Of all the things I'd ever asked someone to do for me, 'Will you put my cape in my bag?' was definitely one of the weirdest, and just as I was thinking this, I saw someone I knew. Clare and her mates were there, and I was saved! I was about to ring my Dad and go home. I was all dressed up with no necks to bite until Clare came along, although she wouldn't let me bite her neck. Well you can't have everything!

Clare and her mate Angela were a really good laugh. We had a really long chat and listened to this terrible music. I can't remember what music it was, I repressed that memory, but it was goddamn awful.

Clare was bored with the lack of good-looking men. I think we'd had the same vision of uni, only I was looking for gorgeous people of the female variety. We sat there moaning about all the work we had and how we missed our friends at home. She told me how she had a really good male friend, who she could talk to about anything, and I told her about Lucy, Sarah and Laura, and how I had the same sort of friendship with them. Mine and Clare's friendship seemed like that already. If I'd seen more of her, we could have become really close. I even told her about Michelle, who still popped into my mind every day, and who I was trying to forget. Then we suddenly got bored and she joked that she'd had enough of me. At least I think she was joking! It had been a good laugh but the guilt at not doing any work was nagging away by the end of the night. This course wasn't healthy for me!

If these nights out were enjoyable, the ones I was having in

Bolton were still the more eventful. I pulled twice in three weeks, still a record for me pathetically. One girl was too embarrassing to tell anyone other than my brother about, and the other was a really attractive blonde called Kerry. I usually let girls come to me, which is why I don't pull often enough, but this time something had given me confidence. Maybe it was a blue moon. It was one of those rare moments, when I'd actually had enough of letting nights pass me by and of walking home, saying, 'Why didn't I try my luck with that girl?'

I finished my drink as quickly as possible to get a Dutch courage boost and I trundled over. I started talking to her about some pointless things. I hate small talk because I find it the most difficult thing in the world to switch from 'What's your name?' to the more direct bit.

Suddenly I just said, 'I think you're really attractive.' That line belonged in the fifties but it was the best I could do.

'I bet you say that to all the girls,' she said.

'Only the special ones,' I replied. God how sick! I'm reaching for the nearest bucket as I think of it.

She hadn't told me where to get off yet, which was good. 'You're lovely you,' she said.

'Do you mind if I kiss you?' I asked, always the gentleman.

'Go on then.'

That was all the invitation I needed. After a couple of minutes we went dancing where one of my brother's mate's Wes Wright, cramped my style. He started talking to me and I got distracted from the main reason I was on the dance floor in the first place.

'I'm going to the toilet. I'll be back in a minute,' she said and of course in line with my track record I never saw her again! I told you, never trust a woman. I even waited for about half an hour, dancing away on my own and then I switched my attention to other women in the close vicinity. Feeling like some sort of mega stud, I chatted to a few women that night but further luck wasn't forthcoming. I was in a good mood all night but I wanted to kill Wes for ruining that moment. Only joking! I can frighten women off well enough myself, without someone else joining in.

So that was my lucky streak over, for a long while actually, but I did have another good night on Matt's nineteenth birthday. It wasn't what you'd call a massive turnout. Just me, Matt and Dexter, but we made up for it in enthusiasm. We'd fallen out with Laney over some misunderstanding and I don't know where Baz was. Once we were drunk though, and we were drunk, it didn't matter where the rest of the lads were. We'd have been too drunk to see them once we'd got into Ikon (the nightclub formerly known as Ritzy). We were having a great time taking the mickey and dancing away, and then I needed the loo. 'Whoa, hold the back page!' I hear you shout, but hear me out.

I'd obviously underestimated Dexter's drunkenness, because going to the loo this time wasn't the simple bodily function that it usually was. We got to the disabled toilet without a problem and unlocked the door with the spare key. (We'd lost the original one.) I went through the middle doorway of the three I was seeing, bouncing off the doorframe as I went, with Dex wobbling in behind me, using the wheelchair to hold himself up. Matt came in with us to help Dexter out and once inside, my worst nightmare came to fruition. As Dex pulled me forward so I could use the bottle, he didn't do so in his usual controlled way, but as if he was doing the trick where you remove a tablecloth and everything stays on the table. It wasn't a gentle hutch forward, it was a huge drunken heave forward and before I could yell 'Stop!' I was on the floor in a heap. My hands felt wet, and so did the rest of my back! *Shit. I hope that's not pee*, I thought, but what else could it have been? Liquid nitrogen?

'Dexsh, I'm shat in a pool of pish you git!' I said and I burst out laughing. Dexter was already laughing and Matt looked like he could die laughing! How the hell was I going to get up with only two drunks to help?

Dex went into stubborn mode. 'It's all right, I'll get you up.'

'Get Matt to help you.'

'No I can do it.' And as usual I couldn't stop him.

He tried to pick me up like he'd always done. The way you hold a baby. The only trouble is, I'm a big baby and there was a puddle on the floor. Sure enough, his foot slipped and he fell on his back. With my lack of bodily control, I landed on top of him and now we were both covered in someone else's urine, and we were still laughing. Matt was rolling on the floor in a carefully

355

chosen dry patch, laughing his head off.

Another example from the annals of classic night out moments. I've lived all the glorious nightmares of drunkenness. Well, maybe not all of them.

With my uni nights out nosediving into boredom, I was loving the nights out at home. Ironically, the nights out I'd wanted to escape were better than the ones I'd moved on to. I also wasn't pulling at uni but I was at home. It's strange that sometimes moving on isn't the best way to improve your life. I don't think the life I had at sixth form could be improved on and I'm probably forgetting the bad moments here. Uni was a huge anticlimax and not just for me. One or two of my mates had already left uni and Matt wasn't enjoying himself living away. We were dropping like flies but at the other end of the spectrum were the people who took to uni like ducks to water. Al was always going to fit in at uni. He loved living on his own, could drink amazing amounts of alcohol and he didn't mind working. Independent living would never be a problem for him. He dived immediately into the social scene, was pulling for fun and enjoying the course. He loved it. Sarah and Laura settled in very quickly and Dexter hadn't even started yet.

I had a reading week the week after Matt's birthday but I didn't have a break. I started to write my court report, even though I had eight weeks left to do it. I hate being a mindless obsessive! I met Tim one day that week to copy some things for me. See what I mean about him going beyond the call of duty? I just wanted to get as much done that week as possible to stay ahead of the game and I succeeded in doing that. I still had a mountain to climb but I was halfway and ahead of schedule. It wasn't too bad but when I went back the same repeating weekly cycle soon started again. I didn't have any time to myself, didn't see people for weeks on end and because of that I couldn't organise a night out. The determination to stick it out till after the first exams was still there but nothing interesting was happening to punctuate the days of constant work. My money was disappearing fast, the travelling was really beginning to irritate me and I was dog-tired. Overall uni was the definition of misery but my stubborn determination wouldn't allow me to quit. 'Never let it be said that David Withnell is a quitter!' was my thought pattern and now I really was becoming a pompous lawyer. I was referring to myself in the third person!

There was only one night out planned before Christmas and that was the Christmas do. I was looking forward to that until yet again something happened to scupper my plans. Yes, the French end of semester exam happened for one group on the day of the do, and for another group the day after. Mine predictably was the day after the do and my success obsession wouldn't allow me to go into an exam, the day after a night out. It was only a grammar exam and I only needed forty per cent, but I couldn't change my pre-exam routine. I hadn't come anywhere close to getting worse than forty per cent in a French exam in my life, and I knew I could pass, even if I was knackered. The worry it'd cause would ruin my night out so I just couldn't go, although I did keep changing my mind for about a week. Eventually, after being mithered by Steph and Sarah, I said I'd go but I didn't have a ticket. I thought that was my way out.

'We'll buy you one.'

'Okay then.' I smiled, thinking, *Bloody hell! A couple of girls try to persuade me and I'm anybody's.* I'd probably jump off a cliff if a couple of girls told me it was a good idea.

In the cold light of day, without female distractions, I agonised over whether to go out or not. Hardly a world-changing decision I know. Was I at uni to get a degree or to go out? It would have been nice if my personality would let me do both, but really I had to do the exam in the right frame of mind. I'd never have forgiven myself if I'd gone out and then failed the exam.

It was my last day of term when I went in to do the exam, my only one before Christmas and I just wanted to get it finished and have a break before starting frantic revision for my two Law exams. I also had to make sure my special arrangements had been made for the Law exams. It was going to be a fraught day of searching for people and checking my exam timetable, but that all came after the French exam.

I put all thoughts of everything else out of my mind and went into my French exam feeling surprisingly relaxed. I'd revised pretty hard for this exam and I would have been disappointed if I hadn't got full marks. I flew through the exam and checked it meticulously. If only Law was this easy!

The sacrifice of the night out had been worthwhile but sadly that was going to be my last opportunity to go out with the people from uni.

On leaving the room, I travelled half a mile to the Law building and arrived with icicles hanging from my nose and ears. I handed my court report in and then looked for Marie Fox. I couldn't find her so I made for the talking lift to go down to the third floor, to find Andy Bell. No I haven't lost it, the lift did talk. It did! 'Doors opening.' And, 'The lift is going down,' it said, which to be honest was pretty obvious. I managed to find Andy Bell and he told me that everything had been arranged. I could now relax over Christmas, knowing all I had to do was revise. The time limit had been removed for me, while I worked out how long I needed to do the exams. Relax? That's a laugh! I'd be worried about my exams all the way through the holidays.

Now it was time for me to freeze again as I set off to meet Tim for the final time that term, and unbeknown to me for the last time ever.

Four weeks off, I thought, *I need that*. And that was the first time I'd actually felt physically exhausted. Knowing I wasn't going into uni for a month should have relaxed me but I still had that intense, stressed feeling. I couldn't put the amount of work I had to learn out of my mind.

'I'm never going to remember all this information.' I'd panicked and I began to get that inadequate feeling, familiar from my first-year days. I've worked out that it's the unknown that does it to me. The first year of a new place and the anticipation of harder work worry me constantly. It happened at secondary school and to a lesser extent at sixth form, so when it came to the same experience at uni I was ready for it. That didn't stop it happening but when it did, I knew how to handle it. I told myself that things would get better once I'd done the first exams, like things always had done before. Bottling it all up had been the worst mistake I'd made as a naive first-year, who'd just gone into a wheelchair. I was scared of showing my weaknesses and feelings back then, which is why my feelings came out in floods of tears, every day. This time I wouldn't make the same mistake and that's what life is all about. The worst crime a person can commit is not learning from his mistakes and refusing to accept his weaknesses. I'm a worrier. I always have been and the way to combat worry is to accept that it's happening and to discuss it with someone who cares. For me that person is my Mum and if that makes me a mummy's boy, then that's what I am. If it's a crime to be a mummy's boy then I'm guilty as charged, "Cos I am whatever you say I am. If I wasn't then why would I say I am?' Okay, so I'm a plagiarist as well.

The amount of conversations I had before and during those Christmas holidays about whether to quit or to take the rest of the year out is huge. This was an important, possibly even life-changing decision and before I went to sleep every night until Christmas, the $64,000 question would return. I wondered if leaving would make me a wimp, a dropout in other people's eyes. Would it make me a wimp in my eyes? Would I ever forgive myself for baulking at the first sign of really hard work? I'd never quit before and I wouldn't quit without deep consideration. The possibility still remained that, after a year of settling down, I'd wonder what all the fuss was about. I didn't want to look back a year down the line and wonder if I could have done it.

I'd tell myself that I had other considerations than if I could do it. If I was knackered I could get really ill. Was a degree worth going through four years of mental and physical torture, not to mention the mind numbing boredom I felt?

There was one moment when this soul-searching almost brought me to tears. I remember it well. My brother and I had offered to take my Gran and Granddad out for a meal as a Christmas present. It was more sincere than writing, 'Thanks for everything' on a Christmas card.

They invited Ben, Andy, Ben's girlfriend Gemma and Dan's girlfriend Charlotte, who's now like one of the family. I just hoped Dan and I didn't have to pay for everyone because washing-up duty would be very likely. That would be difficult for me, considering I can't pick up a plate or even a wet sponge.

This meal was a chore for me. I didn't want to be there, mainly because my mind was filled with selfish thoughts of what to do with my life. I was pretty vacant all night.

'How's uni going Dave? Dave? *Dave!*'

'What?'

I was a bad conversationalist at the best of times but that night I was about as charismatic as the inhabitants of Albert Square. When my food arrived I didn't feel hungry. I felt that familiar ill feeling, where I was worried sick. As I choked down each mouthful, I thought, *This isn't going to happen to me again*. Uni wasn't important enough for me to become that other person, that person who was in my wheelchair in the first year and on that night in the Temple. I hated that person.

Ben and Andy wanted me to go to Atlantis and I really didn't feel like it. I wanted to hide away until I'd made my decision.

'Mum what am I gonna do? It's really getting to me,' I said pleadingly when I got home.

'I thought you were going to wait till after the exams,' was her sensible reply.

'What's the point though, if I'm just going to quit anyway. Bloody hell I don't know what to do.' It was going against my personality to quit, and I didn't like it.

We discussed the problem for a while and once I'd managed to fight the tears back, and began to think clearly again, I decided to be sensible about this decision. There was no point in leaving on a day when life was getting me down. No, I'd go back to the original plan and do the first exams. Is this annoying you? Because it's annoying me.

I did go out, by the way, but I was bored. I think what I needed was a couple of days' rest but I was too obsessed with work.

'Get all the notes you need written up,' I told myself. 'And then you can rest for a couple of days.' And that's exactly what I did. Two days later I started my revision and I looked upon things with a fresh perspective. I was now determined to do well in these exams to prove, above all to myself, that I could do it and thus from about 20 December 'Groundhog Day' began. It was repetitive déjà vu syndrome, with four hours of revision per day, twenty-minute breaks after each hour, and then I'd either go out or sleep later on. I found it easier to work when I was at home, without having to go to uni. I could work at my own pace, and didn't have to exhaust myself in the process.

Before starting uni, joining the Open University seemed like the worst idea in the world when my Mum suggested it but if I'd been able to predict this tiredness and this amount of work, I would have studied at home like a shot. I was however determined to experience the whole uni life like everyone else did but this course wouldn't allow a person in my position to do that. Never mind, I had revision to do. Hopefully things would settle down next term.

I wasn't a total recluse while I revised because I was relaxed, knowing I was getting through things and feeling that it was sinking in. I'd escaped my shackles of worry and could go out without feeling guilty. That felt good.

I didn't get too drunk when I went out because I wanted my mind to be clear for the following day's revision. Very sad I know but when I'm stressed out about work I am sad. So my nights out weren't exactly exciting. I did get a hole burnt through my brother's shirt, my pants and the back of my wheelchair at one point though which was fun.

I'd gone out in a really good mood, on one of those nights when my confidence levels were high. I had a feeling I was going to pull, which doesn't happen often, but it was a genuine feeling this time, when Matt said, 'You feeling lucky?'

I meant it when I said, "Course I am!' and amazingly enough, I wasn't disappointed.

I managed to do my disappearing act so I could go for a wander on my own, but as usual halfway through this wander one of the lads caught up with me. I wasn't bothered, I mean, that didn't ruin my animal magnetism. Sure enough, as I stopped in a strategic position, a really bonny girl, who turned out to be seventeen, started talking to me. The usual Cilla Black conversation followed.

'What's your name and where do you come from?' And being slow on the uptake, I wasn't reading the signs. She was called Gemma.

'You're really good-looking you,' she said. (I always remember people who say that.)

That sounded promising. *Play it cool*, I thought.

'You're not so bad yourself,' I understated and then we just started snogging. After a couple of minutes she said, 'Shit! I've lost my cigarette,' and I was too carried away to think anything of it. I didn't stop to wonder where it could have gone and when she'd gone to find her friends, I was in too good a mood to care. I didn't even realise what was going on, when I started to feel really hot at the bottom of my back. I just thought I was sweating a bit, until I felt a cylindrical object somewhere near my bum…

'Shit! I've lost my cigarette…' the words echoed in my ear, as suddenly it dawned on me.

'Laney, Laney?' I shouted in a moment of sheer panic.

Luckily he heard me. 'What?'

'Is there something down my back? I'm burning!'

He put his hand up my shirt and tried to find it.

'There's nowt there,' he said and suddenly it fell down my pants!

The heat was really becoming uncomfortable as I shouted, 'Lane! It's down my pants' and in a split second he cringed, shut his eyes, put his hand down the bottomless, hairy crevasse and pulled the fag out. It was a hairy moment for both of us!

You could say things were hotting up for me… I was a little hot under the collar. I was looking for some hot stuff… Enough! This was a serious incident. I could have been burnt. Knowing my luck, if I'd set on fire someone would have poured vodka on me to put it out and I'd have gone up in flames.

As for Gemma, I danced with her for a bit later on. She was very considerate, saying I should tell her if she hurt me. Usually people just grab my arms and throw them around, and I'm flopping about like a Thunderbird puppet. Baz did exactly that once and I ended up with my face resting on a girl's backside. I'm hoping he'll do that again soon!

I'm beginning to notice a pattern to my nights out in Manchester, one where every one of them is crap! A night out over these holidays was no exception.

We managed to negotiate two bars without a hiccup and then the night skied downhill through the sound barrier. First of all, Dex started to suffer from severe chest pains, after swirling two

Aftershocks around his mouth for thirty seconds before swallowing. It could only have been heartburn that struck him down because he was all right after ten minutes. He was soon raring to go again. It was time to go 'to infinity and beyond', well to a bar called Teasers anyway. We'd heard stories about the staff having to wear G-strings, so we thought we'd give it a try, purely for research reasons. When I got inside, they weren't G-strings at all. They were hot pants. No, not pants with cigarettes down them, very short shorts. They were good enough until I saw a man wearing them, a harrowing scene that still replays itself when there's a full moon out.

'Rick! What have I told you about wearing hot pants?' I said. Only joking.

Suddenly, as Dex was distracted, I needed the loo. Matt asked where the disabled toilet was.

'Upstairs,' came the reply.

Upstairs? Why would anyone in their right mind design a building where the disabled toilet is upstairs?

I thanked heavens for the small mercy that they had a disabled toilet at all and then spent ten minutes fighting the crowd to get to the lift which was at the other end of the building. It was another of those awkward platform lifts, but this time it had a shaft and we could both fit in. There was a door at the top of the shaft and one at the bottom, and the platform went up and down inside the shaft.

We reached the top and I went to the loo without a problem. It was coming down in this lift when the night turned from boring and pretty bad to disastrous. Around halfway down, the lift jerked and before Matt and I had a chance to glance in each other's direction, it stopped. Matt looked shocked and frantically pressed the alarm until someone opened the door. Fortunately the door at the top of the shaft could be opened, so we could let air in, quite an important thing really. Then Matt told me he was claustrophobic, which didn't make things easier.

'What's wrong?' came a voice from the top.

'The lift's stopped,' we cried as one.

'Pull the red lever out and turn it,' we were instructed.

'It is out,' Matt shouted, after trying to pull it out.

'Did you lean on it when you were coming down?' the voice asked.

'No.'

'You must have done,' he accused us.

'I didn't,' Matt shouted back.

This was getting us nowhere. We were stuck in a lift, and they were blaming us.

'Right. I'll shut the door. Press the button again and see what happens.'

No movement.

'Are you sure you didn't lean on it?' the repetitive and boring voice came back. He obviously didn't know what to do, because the noise of a heated yet muffled discussion filtered down to us.

We could hear the music in our cell, which lightened the mood. In fact we were just listening and singing to the music, while they argued. To add a hint of irony to the situation, 'Living on a Prayer' by Bon Jovi was played, with Matt and I singing the line 'Whoa, we're halfway there!' very loudly! The next time the button was pressed, we felt a downward jerk and then it stopped. They pressed the button over and over and we jerked slowly downwards, until it stopped again. We were three-quarters of the way down, three-quarters of the way to safety. When the lift started inching slowly upwards again, Matt and I exchanged glances and I just wanted to scream.

'Why are you goin' up again?' Matt shouted.

'It won't go down any more. We've looked underneath. It's totally knackered.'

The voice of doom had spoken and having been down there for three-quarters of an hour, we were becoming agitated. We were within three feet of the ground, only to have it taken away. This wasn't what we'd planned at the beginning of the night.

Soon the bottom door opened and we looked down through the six-inch gap between the top of the doorframe and our platform.

'Do you want a drink?' a different voice said, a deeper voice this time. Five minutes was wasted with an exchange about whether we wanted a drink or not.

'No thanks.'

'Are you sure?'

'Yes.'

'You can have a drink if you want.'

Eventually we gave in and said, 'We'll just have a Coke.' If they were that desperate to give us a drink...

The other voice interrupted with a shout of, 'Right lads. We're gonna send a ladder down...'

'Here's your drink.'

'...One of the lads is an electrician.' That sounded dangerous but he was already on his way down. We were told to move out of the way, so he could get down. Anything to get us out of there. We'd been there an hour now and there was quite a party going on. Three people in a lift!

He unscrewed the panel covering the electrics and gave me the screw to hold. Then he shouted, 'Turn the electrics off,' from which point a twenty-minute row over whether this request had been done, erupted.

'It's off.'

'No it isn't, I can see a light.'

'It's off. I promise you.'

'I'm not putting a f★★king screwdriver in while there's a light on. Turn it off.'

'It is f★★king off, you daft bastard...'

By now Matt was leaning against the wall, looking distinctly unhappy, and I was getting snappy with people asking me if I was all right. Did I have enough air and all that sort of rubbish? Did I want another drink?

'No! I didn't even want the first soddin' drink. Just get me outta here!' I felt like shouting, while I said, 'Yeah. I'll have another Coke.' It just makes life easier, and when you've been in a lift for an hour and a half, you'll do anything to make your life easier. Believe me!

'Matt, you go up the ladder and get out,' I said.

'No. I'll wait.'

Eventually someone made the first sensible suggestion of the night. 'We're gonna have to call the fire brigade.' About time! I'd had enough of these amateur lift-fixing techniques.

'We'll have to wait till everyone's out. We don't want people to think there's a fire,' the boss piped up. I thought we'd waited long enough! Thankfully it was twenty to two in the morning, and the place shut at two. I couldn't have waited much longer than that. I could see some light at the top of the lift shaft now.

Twenty agonisingly boring minutes of answering insane questions later, the screeching sirens of the fire brigade could be heard. Thank God for that.

'Send some oxygen down,' I heard.

'No. I don't need any. It's okay,' I replied. This was getting stupid. I must have protested too much methinks, because before I could say Jack Robinson (whoever he is) I had a mask pumping oxygen into my mouth. I wanted out.

Finally my saviours came tramping down the ladder. Matt was sent to safety, and I was left to explain the best way to lift me.

'Take this oxygen off first,' I said.

At least someone listened to me. I thought I'd lost my voice!

I explained the best way to do it was with one person under my arms and one under my legs, which the fireman proceeded to ignore. There wasn't enough room anyway.

'Will you be all right if I put you over my shoulder?'

'Yeah. If you're careful I should be okay.'

He lifted me up, standing on my toe and crushing my chest in the process, and soon I was sat on a chair downstairs. Now if I was a woman, I'd have enjoyed being fireman's lifted but I wasn't a woman, and I couldn't bloody breathe while he lifted me! At least after two hours in captivity, I could phone my Dad and go home.

'Dad? Sorry I haven't rang earlier but I've been stuck in a lift for two hours.'

'Ha ha ha! I'll be there in twenty minutes,' was what I heard and then I had the manager of Teasers to listen to.

He was as annoyed as I was and very apologetic. He gave me his card and said I should make a complaint, taking my phone number down as he said it. As if he was going to ring me and offer compensation! Really I should have gone mad, firstly because someone had been stupid enough to put a disabled toilet upstairs and secondly because of a shoddy lift which was obviously rarely used. It was a disgrace!

I'm a reasonable enough person most of the time and I said I just wanted the lift fixing. I didn't want any of this compensation rubbish. It was simply an occupational hazard. Teasers got lucky they got a balanced disabled person in their lift and not a bitter disabled rights activist. At the end of the day, I was safe. I was out of the lift and I had another story to look back on and laugh at. As Matt said on our reunion downstairs, 'We'd probably have had exactly the same night if we'd not been in the lift.' Uplifting thought isn't it? (Pardon the pun.)

After this ridiculously bad night, Christmas settled down to its usual pattern. Family get-togethers. Frantic last minute present buying. A night out on Christmas Eve and that was pretty much it. The long awaited and over hyped Millennium New Year's Eve passed by without so much as a whimper. We didn't even sing that song that no one knows the words to. I was just sat in the pub with a few friends and family members because taxis were so expensive that no one could afford to go out. It cost us a tenner to get into our local pub, which was full of morons. I suppose it was as good a place as any to celebrate the Millennium, apart from New York, Sydney, Rio de Janeiro…

I'd hardly seen anyone all Christmas and New Year, and it got to the seventh of January, which was Presentation Evening. I've said it before and I'll say it again. I hate things like that, but this time I was looking forward to it because most of my mates would be there. As it turned out Matt, Charmaine and Al didn't come, and Lucy had flu.

It was a typical Presentation Evening, with three different speeches. One was about how we would be missed. Another was a good luck message and the final one was an 'always stick to your dreams' type thing. Then the idea was that we all stayed for a bit, had something to eat and then went out. Everyone stayed for about half an hour, discussing whether to go to Atlantis or Ikon. Dex, Baz, Alex and I went to Ikon and everyone else went to Atlantis. That's what you get for not waiting for everyone else to make a decision before you make yours.

I had to savour that night because it turned out to be my last for a long while. The next day I felt very tired all day. I was hot and my face was aching, so presuming it was a cold I went to bed early. When I awoke the following morning, I felt horrible. I had a headache, my nose was blocked and my body seemed to be aching all over.

This must be flu, I thought. *I can't stay in bed though. I've got too much work to do.* So I got up and tried to revise and surprisingly enough, nothing went in. It was useless so I decided to have a couple of days in bed, drinking Lemsip and taking Benilyn, to try and shake it off.

'There's no point revising when you're not well,' my Mum sensibly said, in a way which made it sound like an order. She has a habit of making advice sound like an order. I was just worried about my work.

I can't miss more than a couple of days, I thought. *I'll never pass if I do.*

I'd also gone into stubborn mode, and insisted to her that I would give it a week before going to the doctor's. I didn't realise that with a condition like mine, flu could change into a chest infection within a matter of hours and that's just what happened. Silly me! Within two days of getting a cold I'd got on to the daily cycle of coughing all day long, being unable to cough up the green goo that filled my chest cavity, and also being torn between going to the doctor's and fighting a losing battle on my own. Being the person I am meant I left it as long as possible, about five days, before going to see Doctor Bunn. I'd been coughing up small amounts of phlegm every five minutes when I was overcome by a huge coughing fit and I thought I'd soon be better.

'I'm getting, *cough* some, *cough* phlegm up,' I told Dr Bunn. 'But, *cough* it doesn't seem to be, getting, *cough* better.'

Sod's law dictated that that fifth day was one of the better days, in that the phlegm was out of stethoscope range, but he gave me the usual antibiotics anyway.

'If it gets worse, come back immediately,' were his orders, so I went home and had something to eat. I managed to get the food down between coughs, despite its distinctly phlegmy taste and the stomach-churning worry about Racial Discrimination Acts whose dates I couldn't remember. This was the stuff of nightmares for me and I set to revising. My breaks between revision took a different pattern, and I knew I was absorbing absolutely nothing whatsoever, probably because it was the most disjointed revision session I'd ever taken part in. Coughing a ball of phlegm into a bowl after every sentence didn't make for an intensive four-hour revision day. I had to go back to bed.

For the next few days, things became gradually worse. The coughing happened more and more often, and my phlegm-removing success became less and less frequent. The constant coughing made me feel more and more exhausted and I was eating less and less, which in turn added to the tiredness.

When I was breathing in and the phlegm stopping me doing so, I knew things were bad. I'd take half a breath, get blocked, and breathe out again, and then when I tried to breathe in a second time, I couldn't breathe at all for about a second. The panic I felt for that second was the strongest panic a person can ever feel. You feel like you're going to die, and having felt that panic the next breath becomes almost impossible. It's a catch-22 situation. You don't want to panic because it makes your breathing harder, and yet you can't help panicking. It's torture.

As I became exhausted, weaker and thinner, to almost skeletal proportions, I found I didn't have the energy to get rid of any phlegm at all and it continued to build up. After about a week and a half of being ill, we had to call the physio out. The coughing was constant, the revision had stopped. I needed urgent help.

The physio arrived within the hour and proceeded to show me some more breathing exercises and chest draining exercises; rolling both ways; pummelling my chest in different places and directions; and I hoped this would help soon.

My chest was beginning to hurt, either because of the infection, the coughing or even the pummelling, and the antibiotics were about as useful to me as a wheelchair without wheels. I also hadn't left my bed for a week and I'd given up on making my first exam. It would be the first time I'd ever missed an exam and I was very worried. My Mum rang the university and explained the situation. They were very good about it and said I could take the exam at resit time. That made me feel slightly better.

The next night things became worse. The phlegm had been blocking my chest for a while, so my Mum started to sleep downstairs on a mattress in my room. It was lucky for me that she did, because every time I tried to breathe in after a cough, I just couldn't do it. It was up to five seconds before I forced the air in with all my might, and the panic I'd felt earlier multiplied tenfold with every second. I didn't sleep all night. I had to keep sitting up, then lying down, then rolling on my left side, over to the right and back to the centre again. In the end I was just sat up, staring into space and waiting for the next time my chest became plugged, and the already frustrating process of rolling over and pummelling began again. Why was I being made to suffer like this?

My Mum called the emergency doctor in the early hours of the morning and he looked worried. He gave us some stronger antibiotics and some vile tasting medicine and said I should call my GP if things didn't improve that day. They didn't, and by the time the following evening had crept up on me I was desperate. Even when my chest wasn't plugged, I struggled to force air in, and when it was plugged it was agony. My cheeks were aching from coughing, and tinted purple. I wasn't getting enough oxygen, energy or sleep, and I was losing the battle.

'Don't panic,' my Mum said, sounding panicky. 'If you panic, you'll make things worse. You won't be able to breathe.'

'I can't, *wheeze* breath, *wheeze* now,' I replied, and I started crying in frustration, pain and tiredness. I didn't know what to do any more. I felt like the life was being rapidly drained from my already weak body. As the tears rolled down my cheeks, I thought I was going to die, and then it stopped. Everything stopped…

'Dave? Dave? The ambulance is here. Let me get that jumper on you,' was the next thing I heard but it sounded distant.

Dr Bunn was in my room. My brother looked upset. My Dad was shouting, 'It's been bloody fifteen minutes now. He can't breathe!' down the phone. My Mum was dragging the jumper over my head and I was wondering what the hell was going on. It was a surreal moment to see all this commotion going on around me. What strange vacuum had I been in while the ambulance was called? And how long had Dr Bunn been there?

'What ambulance?' I asked after a delay of about five minutes. 'I don't need an ambulance. What are you talking about?'

'You've collapsed. Your eyes rolled back in your head and you went grey.'

That explained the vacuum away. Nee naw, nee naw... *The ambulance must be here*, I thought. That felt odd. I felt like I was outside my body, watching this happen to some other poor disabled person and I felt really insecure.

Once I realised it was me and I'd returned to my body, I was being lifted on to a stretcher, having oxygen pumped into me through a mask and leaving through the front door. Then I remembered it was Dan's mock exams that week. He looked upset and preoccupied with what was happening to me. 'Go and do your exam Dan,' I said.

As I was being loaded on to the ambulance, my Mum said, 'Tell him you're all right.'

'I'm all right Dan,' I mumbled. Obviously I wasn't all right, I was being loaded on to an ambulance, but I didn't want him to worry while he did his exam.

Once in the ambulance, I still felt very ill, but the oxygen seemed to have replenished my life force. I'd have preferred to breathe on my own. I mean it's not too much to ask, is it?

While my mind was drifting, the ambulance stopped and I'd arrived at Accident and Emergency. *Here we go then*, I thought. Surprisingly, there were no beds left. I never expected that! The paramedics, who'd been great and also very worried, told one of the doctors I was disabled and needed to be seen urgently. They were basically ignored, as the doctor said, 'Just put him on a trolley and wait out there.'

I don't care how stressed you are, or how busy you've been all day, a person should be more professional than to dismiss someone like that, especially when the patient can hardly breathe and can hear what you're saying.

My phlegm was still getting plugged quite often but I wasn't as panic-stricken as I had been at first. The constant stream of oxygen meant breathing was easier. Soon enough, I was pushed into the main treatment area to be seen 'as soon as possible'. My Mum went to get a drink for me, so my throat didn't dry up and twenty minutes later, when she returned, the doctor was just arriving to see me. It was a female doctor, who seemed quite young. When we mentioned muscular dystrophy she looked at us blankly and said, not very subtly, 'I'll be back in a minute.' Time for a sharp exit! Two minutes later, she walked past us, medical book under her arm. She'd obviously never heard of MD before, which in my condition wasn't a helpful sight.

'Should I ask if she needs any help?' my Mum said.

'No. Wait till she gets back.' Why have I got this stubbornness to delay things every time I'm ill?

On her return, my Mum said to the doctor, 'If you need to know anything, just ask. You've probably never heard of MD before.' A brave thing to say to most doctors, but this one just said, 'You're right. You probably know more than I do. I've just got to take a blood sample, David.'

'Okay then.'

She looked nervous and after the first injection, I knew why. I don't know what happened but it hurt. I cringed and blood came out of my hand on to the bedclothes instead of into the syringe. She put a plaster over the cut in my hand and stuck the needle into the other hand. This time it stung but the blood pumped into the syringe. That was lucky because I had no hands left.

The physio was called next, and when she arrived I had my head over a bowl, struggling to cough and breathe at the same time. She didn't look too shocked. She'd obviously done this before, but I on the other hand hadn't. When she brought out the chest clearing instruments I thought, *What the hell is she gonna do with them?* They looked like something out of a Freddie Kruger movie. They were dangerous instruments of torture.

'This is called a yanker,' I was told. 'And what I'm going to do is put it to the back of your throat, and it'll suck the phlegm out.'

I didn't have the energy to say, 'You're not putting any bloody plastic tubes down my throat!' and it was too late anyway.

'When I turn it on, I want you to cough as hard as you can.'

'Okaayghhh,' I said. It felt as though it was sucking my tonsils out along with the phlegm, and when I looked in the tube, there was hardly anything there. This routine repeated itself three times and it became very distressing, not to mention nauseating and exhausting. I just wanted it all to end. I wanted to sleep.

The physio went, but my ordeal wasn't over, indeed it was just beginning as the doctor came back armed with another needle.

'I'm going to take another blood sample, but it'll have to be out of your wrist.' Now that's a pretty simple thing to do to most people. Not to me. My wrists don't turn over. They've become pretty limited over the years.

'I'm gonna have to take the sample from your leg,' she said after a couple of minutes wrestling with my wrists, and I got a horrible vision of a scene from *Bottom* where Ritchie bursts an artery in his leg and a torrent of blood sprays the ceiling. Well it was possible. She'd already messed the hand sample up. As the needle entered the artery, I grimaced. That was a terrible pain!

I suddenly began to feel worse again. My breaths were short but heavy. My head was sore and I was blowing rapidly hot, then cold and then hot again. I felt feverish and wanted to get on to a ward as soon as possible.

Overall it took three hours before I was moved to a very busy ward, where I'd wait until a bed appeared on E3, the chest and lung ward, and it was on this interim ward where I met the consultant. Dr Jones arrived as I was attempting to cough my guts up for the umpteenth time. I realised why my chest was plugging so often when I managed to get rid of the tiniest amount of phlegm. It was dark green with a jelly-like consistency. I knew from my last infection that the darker the phlegm, the worse the infection. It had never been that dark before.

Dr Jones looked worried, said I should carry on with what I was doing and went away again to get a chest X-ray machine. I was hooked up to an oxygen machine on its highest possible output, and then Dexter arrived at my bedside to plunge everything into chaos!

He'd hotfooted it to the hospital as soon as he'd heard, fresh from his first attempted murder of a patient. He'd just taken his first blood pressure reading from a patient. He put the strap around her arm, turned the machine on and it started to inflate... and didn't stop. It continued to go up around her arm until it became painful and she screamed. He searched madly for the off switch before her arm went blue, but he couldn't find it. Eventually he panicked and ripped the still inflating strap from her arm, to the sound of a huge bang. Poor lad, everyone was laughing at him!

Anyway, how did he plunge things into chaos? Well, he was sat there, lifting me up every time I started to choke, and then I said I was struggling to breathe.

'Can that oxygen machine not go any higher?' he said, and proceeded to fiddle with the buttons. Naturally, the machine broke down and the oxygen stopped, at which point I feigned death. Ironic really because I nearly was dead. To my Mum's horror, I started making choking noises and shut my eyes. Then I started laughing.

'David! That's not funny!' she said. One was not amused!

Maybe it was the wrong moment to do something like that, especially when I still felt badly ill. I was still liable to choke and my Mum had seen me stop breathing once that day. The thing is though, if you don't laugh you cry and I just thought I'd lighten the moment. Maybe it was too authentic.

Dr Jones came back, took my Mum away 'for a chat' to tell her discreetly how bad I was, and I found out later that had I waited another twenty-four hours, I'd have been dead. If they didn't get me on intravenous antibiotics very quickly, I would die. So it was serious then?

He didn't tell me at that moment because he didn't want to mention death and panic me while I was so poorly. He also didn't want to mention pneumonia, in case that worried me. It wouldn't have worried me because I knew how serious it was. I was in hospital for God's sake!

Eventually, having been in hospital for about eight hours, I was moved to E3 where I'd stay for as long as it took to get better. Great. I was put into a bed in a separate room to everybody else, just to make life easier for my Mum who would stay with me for as long as it took. And so the saga continued.

I was put on to a drip, which sent antibiotics into my veins, every few hours. Another needle – marvellous! I also had nebulisers to loosen everything up, and oxygen. I was having substances pumped into me left, right and centre but I wanted to get better. It had to be done.

The next time I coughed up, it was taken away to be analysed. I'd love to be the person who looks for bugs in people's phlegm.

It sounds like fun. Dr Jones wanted to find out if I had the actual pneumonia bug, or if it was just an advanced chest infection which basically has the same effect on your chest. So while that was being done, I had to drink frequently and try and get some sleep. Easier said than done, because my chest was knackered. Breathing was such an effort that I couldn't sleep for the first couple of nights. Added to that, I'd feel immensely hot and sweaty for ten minutes and then immensely cold, but still sweaty for the next ten minutes, before getting hot again. I hoped it'd make its mind up soon. This whole illness was a nightmare!

My Mum was up and down every five minutes removing a blanket, then putting it back on, opening a window, then shutting it again, so her sleep pattern was non-existent. The phlegm wasn't blocking my chest that night though, probably because I was exhausted. My chest was too tired to move.

The following three or four days consisted of more oxygen, more antibiotics, more nebulisers, a lot of phlegm and coughing, loads of physio and one or two near-death experiences.

There was a younger physio, who I noticed was very attractive after she'd saved my life. She was carrying out the chest exercises and the rolling over procedures, when suddenly my chest plugged again. This time it was really serious. I could hear things happening around me but they didn't seem real. As I saw my life flash before my eyes, I thought I was going to find out if there was a God. I was sat up, I couldn't breathe. On to my left side, and no breath. Over to the right, still no breath and then the yanker came out. First attempt, nothing happened. Second attempt and relief! I could breathe again! While all this happened, only about ten seconds had elapsed, the longest ten seconds of my life.

'Breathe gently,' the physio said. 'You're all right now.' I was, thanks to her. Talk about staying calm under pressure!

I was panting and tears were streaming from my eyes. For the second time in two days, I'd stopped breathing. It must have been a replay, because I was unconscious for the first one.

Seriously though, she had saved me from becoming another victim of this year's flu epidemic. It was a moment I'll never forget, and it was only weeks later that I realised what that physio had done for me. 'Thanks,' was all I could say.

Another doctor who was in the room at the time looked at me and said, 'Oh my God!' What are you supposed to think, when a doctor says something like that?

That night I was close to choking to death for more sinister reasons. I had to quench my thirst, so the light bulb over my Mum's head lit up and she said, 'I know. I'll get you some fruit pastilles.' A kind gesture, you might think, but I think she was trying to kill me in a subtle way. The trouble with fruit pastilles when you've got a bad chest and your throat's tender from coughing, is that you have to chew them without coughing them out of your mouth. Then you have to swallow them, which was my problem.

I got a couple down okay, and then it came to the third.

'They're nice these... Mughhmm!' I said and it was stuck in my throat, really stuck. I guzzled down the Ribena that we'd smuggled in, and swallowed hard, trying to move this stubborn sweet and trying not to cough. Eventually it moved and yet again I could breathe that now familiar sigh of relief at prolonging my life a little further. I was shattered now and just wanted to sleep. Unfortunately my fever and overflowing phlegm wouldn't let me. Another night without sleep for both my doting mother and myself. I was beginning to get fed up with going hot then cold, and feeling ill. The antibiotics could be painful as well, fighting with the blood that was probably trying to clot around the needle inside me. When the next dose started to go into my arm, I'd get a stinging pain right down my veins until the antibiotics had mixed into the blood. I presume it was the sensation of the cold antibiotics mixing with the warm blood that did it.

Three or four days of fighting the fever later, the struggle with death appeared to be going in my favour. I didn't feel feverish, hot or cold any more and it was just the taste of the phlegm that killed my appetite. I was eating some of the food put in front of me and it was surprisingly palatable, apart from the vile, anaemic potatoes they used. It was lucky that I was eating again, albeit only a little bit because I looked like I was auditioning for a part in a *Funnybones* feature length special, bones sticking out everywhere! I even began to notice who my visitors were. Up until then I'd sensed someone trying to smuggle a video player into my room to save me from daytime TV, and I knew there was more than my Mum in the room. I was too ill to care who it was though.

The nebulisers were working well because the phlegm was loose enough to be coughed up, with the aid of Mum pushing down on my chest to propel it up my throat. I was getting rid of cups full of the stuff everyday. Sounds disgusting but I was excited that it was finally moving.

Sarah came to visit me with her boyfriend Marc. She was supposed to be coming to my house the night I went into hospital, so I had to reluctantly tell her I was there. I didn't want anyone to panic so I didn't tell anyone. Of course they all found out through my brother the grapevine, and yes they did panic.

Al came rapidly from Lancaster, Baz and Laney came nearly everyday and it goes without saying that Dexter appeared at least once every day. So did my Dad, my brother and various other members of my family. Ralph, the ungrateful dog, didn't come to see me once!

It was a great moment for Marc to meet me while I was lay in a hospital bed with my chest hairs out, but at least he could never be embarrassed around me, having seen me at that moment!

Dexter spent most of his time going on about the latest girl he was madly in love with. She was called Lesley and he had met her at uni. Having met her once, she seemed like a good choice. The question was, with his luck with women, would she be interested in him or would I have to put up with him moping while I recovered?

I obviously wouldn't have been bothered about doing that. At that moment I'd have given anything to be at home listening to him mope but I was stuck in an uncomfortable bed, coughing up phlegm into a cup. I must have been getting better because I was moaning about the bed. Bloody NHS!

The infection was gone because the phlegm was light green now and not so thick. It was now a matter of getting rid of what seemed like gallons of the stuff. It's amazing how much phlegm a chest can hold. I know, I know! I sound obsessed with phlegm but you would be too if you'd spent weeks coughing your guts up to get rid of the stuff.

The good-looking physio came back every day, which I wasn't

complaining about. She could pummel my chest whenever she wanted. A week passed by and when Dr Jones came to see me, I was desperate to go home. I was on tablet antibiotics now, so my Mum could have sorted me out just as well at home. She was doing everything for me anyway because the nurses weren't trained to move me. I didn't see the point in being there, but I didn't say that to Dr Jones.

'When do you think I can go home?' I enquired, holding the coughs in desperately.

'Well, I'll be back on Thursday, so we'll see how you're doing then. You're doing very well, son. It was touch and go for while there, in fact I'm amazed you've got so much better so quickly. It's going to take a lot of recovering till you're a hundred per cent though. See you on Thursday. Keep it up.' I think you get the picture.

I hadn't realised he was that worried about me. He'd even talked to my Mum about ventilating me if I stopped breathing again. He didn't want me to worry, but my Mum told me what he said. She thought I was well enough to handle it.

For the next three days I consciously set about getting well enough to go home on the Thursday. I got my new Law books sent in, having missed both exams, and then got into my wheelchair for the first time in what must have been weeks.

Whoa, I thought. *The room's spinning.* That was a strange sensation and not a pleasant one. Maybe I wasn't quite as well as I'd thought. My head felt light on my neck, I was wobbly and the actual ability to breathe in an upright position seemed to have deserted me. Because of that my breaths were short and I began to feel like I would collapse again. I had a quick drink and a packet of crisps and there was nothing for it. I needed to get back to bed. This was not going to be the rapid recovery I'd banked on. I wanted to get out of that hospital and straight back to uni. Hell, I was goin' to Atlantis the day I got out. How naive am I?

Gradually, over the next couple of days, I started to build up the amount of time I spent in the wheelchair. It felt like an alien position to me at first and I did feel light-headed. I was determined to get out of there on Thursday, so I forced myself to stay up longer than I wanted to. I even did some Law work so I could at least be prepared for the next term. At that moment in time I was still going back, seeing as I'd missed the exams.

So I'd be sat up for a couple of hours, feeling like I was stoned and having to take regular oxygen so I didn't keel over. I'd listen to Barry's CD player which he'd kindly donated to the David Withnell Benevolent Fund and then, when I started to cough violently, I'd get into bed to have my chest pumped. I was now totally sick of my bed, of phlegm and of the fact that I now only associated bed with phlegm and not comfort and relaxation.

The physio would come in to listen for rattles in my chest and on the Wednesday she said I'd be okay to go home if the doctor said so. That was all the encouragement I needed and I told my Mum that whatever happened I would discharge myself the next day. I probably wouldn't have done, but hey it's good to talk a good game. I was convinced I'd be going home anyway. I felt stronger and well, apart from the excess phlegm which filled my lungs. I could have lived with that.

When judgement day arrived, I waited with baited breath for Dr Jones to arrive. I wasn't happy when told he wouldn't be coming till about one o'clock, but I'd waited ten days and I could wait another three hours. I forced my last hospital meal down before meeting the parole board, and I pottered around for a bit in my wheelchair. Each minute felt like an hour and then I was distracted by the final instrument of torture – the peak flow meter. I'd been faced with this machine every time I'd visited the evil Professor, but this time I saw it as an obstacle to my freedom. When it was wheeled into my room I looked at my Mum in horror, then gave the women a disdainful look. If I could have mustered enough breath at that moment, I'd have screamed. What you have to do with this machine is take a deep breath in and then breathe out as hard as possible, for as long as possible. The machine measures how much pressure you generate. Normally when you're sat down, your readings are lower than everyone else's because you don't use certain muscles in your chest, or get as much air in as able-bodied people. I also have a weaker chest because of my disability, so my readings are lower still, and will gradually get lower as my chest weakens. That's why MD sufferers are prone to chest infections and pneumonia.

It was a little unfair to expect me to get any power into my breathing when I was just getting used to breathing normally, but nevertheless I had to do it. I breathed in as far as I could, straining with every sinew to force air in. My chest inflated by about an inch and I breathed out as hard as I could, creating the pressure of a flea landing on a dog's back. It didn't even register on the machine.

The annoyingly happy person who'd brought the machine said, 'Oh that wasn't very good. It didn't even register.'

You try doing this when you've not breathed properly for three weeks, I thought. Another equally feeble attempt meant I was becoming frustrated and feeling useless. I couldn't even breathe now and this task was an unfair one to ask of me, when I was just starting to feel better. Surely this woman could see that.

'Have another go,' she urged me.

Once again my breath made no impact and my frustration had reached fever pitch. Something had to give and when she suggested I have 'just one more go' I snapped.

'No! Just bugger off with that bloody machine!' I shouted at which point the woman looked shocked.

'David!' my Mum screeched. What did she expect? It was obvious that this wasn't working and the woman kept on and on. I simply couldn't take it any more. It was the wrong moment for me to take such a test. So what if I couldn't make much pressure? I was obviously breathing all right otherwise I'd have been dead!

'Don't worry I've got kids of my own,' the woman explained. No, it wasn't her fault, she was doing her job and I did feel guilty afterwards, despite my lack of apologies at the time. I just needed to get out of that hospital and I was worried that this machine could stop that happening.

It was strange though, that after all the needles I'd had stuck in my limbs, after all the yankers I'd had down my throat, and after all the phlegm I'd had clogging my chest, it took a machine I'd used hundreds of times before to finally make me lose my temper. The anticipation of going home after a nightmare ten days had got to me.

Finally, when the eternal morning was over, Dr Jones came in with an entourage of student doctors who were being given the chance to meet an MD sufferer, a chance which Dr Jones had never previously had. (On average a doctor meets an MD sufferer once every seventy-three years!) He told them I was an interesting lad (was it me or my disability that was interesting?) who'd arrived at the hospital with a severe case of pneumonia. He explained how debilitating that can be for a person with my condition, and that I'd had an amazing recovery from what was literally the brink of death. He also admitted that he was thrown into a panic by his first encounter with MD. I admired him for being brave enough to admit that and with that moment my thoughts of Dr Jones changed immediately. My first impression had been that he was patronising me by talking to my Mum alone. What he was really doing was panicking and wanting to guard against me doing the same. At that fragile moment, he didn't want to worry me. I now felt a great respect for the man. He really cared and his quick thinking in the face of his panic had amongst other things saved my life.

As soon as he took a breath, I cut in with, 'Can I go home then?'

'Yes you can go home, but if it gets worse again I want you straight back here. Deal?'

'Deal.'

I'd have kissed his pimply backside to get out of that hospital at that moment in time, I was that desperate. Well, maybe not, and I don't know whether it was pimply or not. I just assumed it would be. Whoopee! I was out! Not quite. I had one more panic to come. I'd been so determined and blinkered about going home that I didn't stop to think what that meant. It meant no yanker to suck out the excess phlegm, no physio on call, no oxygen, no antibiotics and totally independent breathing.

Suddenly I hit a brick wall. 'What if I stop breathing again? What if I get worse again? What if...' My head was full of worries and, right on cue, I started to cough, became flustered and felt like I couldn't breathe. It was purely psychological. I knew that and so did my Mum, but like a child I needed any form of reassurance I could get.

'Mum? I feel like I can't breathe,' I moaned.

'I'm going getting the physio then. Your Dad's on his way but you're not leaving this hospital if you don't feel right.'

'I can't feel any rattling or any problems,' the physio told me. 'You'll be fine.'

That was all I needed to hear. I made for the exit door before I could panic again, and I was out. I'd avoided the clutches of the Grim Reaper again, and I lived to fight another day.

Chapter XIV

Experiencing disability and such a terrible bout of pneumonia put many things into perspective and it provoked a lot of deep thinking on my part. This thinking, or even soul-searching was at its deepest over the following few weeks as I recovered from pneumonia, still coughing up bowls full of phlegm, and building myself up for my first night out, only to be disappointed when Thursday night arrived. I had to face the fact that I'd nearly died and come to terms with the fact that it could happen again every time I got ill in the future. That was a very sobering thought. I remember asking myself where someone with a limited life expectancy goes from a severe brush with death.

When I say it put things into perspective, in a narrower sense I mean my studying. I was halfway through the first year of my Law degree and although I really hadn't enjoyed the course for many reasons, I was determined to stick it out.

I was studying for my first set of exams when I had been struck down and pneumonia had changed everything. I still sent Tim to take my notes while I recovered at home, that is after my call it unbending determination, call it lack of common sense, or even infinite stupidity (I prefer the first one), struck its oar in again. Three days after leaving hospital, and still obviously unfit, I went back to uni. This time, this annoying character trait was misplaced.

When I woke up that morning and saw it was raining cats and dogs, I should have taken the hint and stayed at home. Getting wet could have been disastrous, but I was obsessed now. I had to go in.

Hmm, that day was a total, unadulterated disaster. I got wet on my way from the taxi to the Law building, which set my coughing off. Then I couldn't find the person I was looking for to sort my timetable clash, which gave me a serious headache. I'd arranged to meet Tim in the Student Union building, 500 yards from the Law building. Needless to say, I got wet again and my nose started running. I started coughing and had to swallow quite a lot of phlegm. Not pleasant at all. I was beginning to lose patience with this phlegm!

Tim was nowhere to be seen. He'd made another shall we say, 'Misjudgement of time.' Great note-taker, great friend. Lousy timekeeping! Well 'two out of three ain't bad' in the words of that well-known author, Meatloaf. He was only an hour late this time and by the time he arrived, I'd given in either to common sense or to phlegm. I was just waiting for my Dad to pick me up and rescue me.

That was my last day at uni and the decision I'd pondered for a long time had to be made. To leave or not to leave, that was the question and an urgent answer now had to be made. I'd missed two weeks of studying and realised that with the amount of work required, catching up would be difficult. Added to this, I'd be recovering for a while and unable to do sufficient work to keep up with the future work. Now if I was enjoying it, then maybe I could have carried on, you know I would have given it my best shot. The fact was I'd been considering leaving and doing a French and German degree anyway. I was also sensible enough to realise that overworking had been one of the reasons I became ill in the first place. If I'd stayed at uni after that first day, I'd have been back in the hospital before I could say, 'Criminal Law is...' The decision, it seemed, had already been made. By Fate or God, call it what you will, but a lawyer I definitely am not.

I realised that life's too short to do a course I didn't enjoy or which took up every waking hour. I'm fascinated by languages, and good at learning them and maybe I also needed a break from studying. Maybe pneumonia was a good thing then.

It was a sad day when I finally had to give in to my disability, or to one of its complications, and Sarah even talked about it in one of her letters. She was upset that my disability was stopping me from getting where I wanted to go, that it had stopped me achieving my goal. If I hadn't been born disabled though, would my life have taken the same path? Was my goal determined because I am disabled? Or was it something I would have wanted, even if I could walk? Mind-boggling questions indeed, but worth thinking about.

I've talked about defining moments and turning points, and this certainly was one of those, on this narrow scale and in a wider sense.

I set to thinking about everything really: the meaning of life, which people I love, and my life as a whole, and I comforted myself with the thought that so many people came to visit me in hospital and that so many people wanted me to get better. Laura's parents didn't tell her till after her exams, in case she came home from Bath which she would have done. Al came home from Lancaster, Sarah from Hull and Dexter my 'constant companion' came every day. Baz and Laney came frequently, as did all my family and Yak and Hulmey, my brother's mates, also visited me. Everyone else was extremely worried. Who was that person, who stayed with me all the time I was in hospital? Oh yeah, my Mum! She had less sleep than I did and then gave up even more sleep while I was recovering. For all of seven weeks, she looked after me selflessly. Thanks Mum, you did it again!

Lucy, Charmaine and Matt were also very worried. I tried not to tell them but they found out anyway, when I was due to leave the hospital. I've got the greatest friends in the world and they proved that in my hour of need. I love them all, and of course there's my Dad, who for all his faults is a good father but also a great mate. Last but not least there's Danny, my little bro', who's bigger than me (in some ways). He said to me he wouldn't know what to do without me. I feel the same about him. Wherever we go and whatever we do, we'll always be with each other in our hearts even if one of us ends up in heaven (if it exists).

There's so many people, who love me and that made me realise that, even if my life were to end now, it'd have been a good one. I've achieved more in the first nineteen years of my life than many people achieve in their whole life and that's something to be proud of.

I believe that it's not how long you live that matters, rather what you do while you're here and I don't think I can complain. A number of people have told me they admire me, and some people say I've been an influence on their lives. I feel that if you have a good influence or effect on the life of even one person, then you've done some good. Your life has been worthwhile and that influence is your legacy. It ensures that when you're gone, your memory lives on.

So I can now relax for a while, safe in the knowledge that I've had the desired effect. However long my life lasts, I will have done what I believe I've been put here to do. And the future? Well, I know the effects of MD and pneumonia can't be any worse than I've already experienced, so I've no fears of either life or death.

Now all I need is a girlfriend…

Printed in the United Kingdom
by Lightning Source UK Ltd.
2666